Sociological Theory and the Environment

Sociological Theory and the Environment

Classical Foundations, Contemporary Insights

Edited by
Riley E. Dunlap, Frederick H. Buttel,
Peter Dickens, and August Gijswijt

ROWMAN & LITTLEFIELD PUBLISHERS, INC.
Lanham • Boulder • New York • Toronto • Plymouth, UK

ROWMAN & LITTLEFIELD PUBLISHERS, INC.

Published in the United States of America
by Rowman & Littlefield Publishers, Inc.
A wholly owned subsidiary of The Rowman & Littlefield Publishing Group, Inc.
4501 Forbes Boulevard, Suite 200, Lanham, Maryland 20706
www.rowmanlittlefield.com

Estover Road
Plymouth PL6 7PY
United Kingdom

British Library Cataloguing in Publication Information Available

Library of Congress Cataloging-in-Publication Data

Sociological theory and the environment / edited by Riley E. Dunlap . . . [et al.].
    p. cm.
  Includes bibliographical references and index.
  ISBN 0-7425-0185-X (cloth : alk. paper)—
  ISBN 0-7425-0186-8 (pbk. : alk. paper)
    1. Human ecology—Social aspects.   2. Sociology—Philosophy.
  I. Dunlap, Riley E.
  GF21 .S66 2001
  304.2—dc21   2001044381

Printed in the United States of America

Contents

Preface

The seed for this volume was planted over two decades ago when, in the process of trying to define and codify the field of environmental sociology, Catton and Dunlap argued that this new field represented a paradigmatic challenge to mainstream sociology. First, they delineated the "human exemptionalism paradigm" that they saw as underlying mainstream sociology's theoretical perspectives and as hindering sociology's appreciation of the significance of environmental problems (and the physical environment more broadly). Then they sketched out an alternative "new ecological paradigm" that they thought would facilitate sociological recognition of the significance of these problems. Catton and Dunlap's analysis of the paradigmatic implications of environmental sociology provoked a sympathetic critique by Buttel. Buttel acknowledged the importance of the exemptionalist-ecological paradigmatic cleavage, but emphasized the continuing relevance of traditional theoretical perspectives for analyzing environmental problems. The resulting debate ended up being only the first installment in an ongoing discussion of the role of paradigms and theories in environmental sociology that has involved a growing number of scholars as the field has developed into an established sociological specialization.

Issues such as whether or not environmental sociology represents a paradigmatic challenge to the larger discipline; whether an ecological paradigm or perspective is an essential component of environmental sociology; the relevance of classical sociological theories for environmental sociology; the utility of mainstream sociological theories for guiding investigations of environmental problems; and the degree to which both classical and contemporary theories can and should be revised into "green" theories have all generated interest and debate within this relatively new field. Furthermore, the rapid internationalization of environmental sociology has brought new and often quite divergent perspectives on these issues from scholars representing diverse theoretical and methodological traditions as well as numerous nations around the world.

Consequently, in 1994, when Dunlap was elected president of the International Sociological Association's Research Committee on Environment and Society (RC

24), one of his major goals was to see these issues examined. He was particularly interested in providing a forum for exploring the rapidly emerging theoretical developments in environmental sociology. Fortunately, the secretary of RC 24, August Gijswijt, was able to find financial support for an international conference that allowed RC 24 to bring together a wide range of scholars from several nations to explore these issues.

This volume is the second to result from the conference, held at the Woudschoten Conference Center in Zeist, Netherlands, in 1997. It includes major revisions of several papers presented at the conference, as well as a few others solicited specifically for this volume. Like the first one, *Environment and Global Modernity* (2000) edited by Gert Spaargaren, Arthur P. J. Mol, and Frederick H. Buttel, it offers a good introduction to recent theoretical developments within environmental sociology. The chapters cover both classical and contemporary theoretical perspectives. Some are critical of the shortcomings of these perspectives, while others emphasize their continuing relevance for analyzing environmental problems and issues. In some cases, the authors develop "greener" versions of existing theories, and, in others, show that theories developed for other purposes nonetheless provide useful insights for understanding environmental matters. Furthermore, the theoretical perspectives presented in some chapters suggest that the authors embrace an ecological orientation (or paradigm), while the perspectives in others suggest the absence of such an orientation. This diversity is a sign of the intellectual health and vitality of environmental sociology. Taken as a whole, the chapters in this volume illustrate the vibrant and diverse nature of current theoretical work in environmental sociology.

As a result, this book should provide a valuable resource for anyone interested in exploring the increasingly salient and problematic relationship between modern industrial societies and the biophysical environments on which the survival of all human societies depends. As hopefully indicated by the various chapters, sociology in general and environmental sociology in particular have important insights for understanding the relationship between modern societies and the environments they inhabit. Environmental problems are, after all, "people problems," for humans cause the problems, are affected by these problems, and are ultimately responsible for creating solutions to them. It is for this reason that the field of environmental sociology will likely continue to grow in significance, and the editors hope that this volume will contribute to that growth.

Riley E. Dunlap
Frederick H. Buttel
Peter Dickens
August Gijswijt

Part I

INTRODUCTION AND OVERVIEW

1

Sociological Theory and the Environment: An Overview and Introduction

Frederick H. Buttel, Peter Dickens, Riley E. Dunlap and August Gijswijt

Environmental sociology, in the sense of its being a recognizable subdiscipline of the parent discipline of sociology, is essentially a quarter century old.[1] Beginning in the late 1960s and early 1970s, sociologists in a number of (mostly Western) countries began to recognize the importance of environmental issues and initiated research relating to the natural environment. Shortly thereafter, sections or research groups devoted to environmental sociology had been established in many of the major sociological associations in the Western countries. By the late 1980s, dozens of universities across the world, including a number of universities in the South, were offering courses in environmental sociology, and many of these universities had designed undergraduate or graduate curricula in environmental sociology.

But despite this impressive expansion of environmental sociology, this subdiscipline has yet to reach maturity in terms of theoretical closure or crystallization—for example, the winnowing of theoretical contenders down to two or so major traditions or schools of thought. As recently as the 1980s, it appeared that there were essentially only two major contenders for theoretical dominance in environmental sociology: the treadmill of production perspective of Schnaiberg, Gould, Weinberg, and associates (see, e.g., Schnaiberg 1980; Gould, Schnaiberg, and Weinberg 1996), and the "new ecological paradigm" view of Dunlap and Catton (Catton and Dunlap 1978; Dunlap and Catton 1994; Dunlap 1997). Each of these theoretical views remains influential today. Over the past decade or so, however, the theoretical space of environmental sociology has come to be far more complex than ever before—a

3

conclusion that one cannot help but draw after examining recent compendia such as Redclift and Woodgate (1997a) and overviews of the field such as Buttel (1996) and Dunlap (1997). This volume will provide an overview of theoretical trends and issues in environmental sociology and take stock of the growing theoretical diversity in the study of society and its biophysical environment.

This chapter and the volume as a whole are organized in terms of the three main factors that have contributed to theoretical diversity in the field. First, over the past several years there has been a productive reappraisal of the strengths and limits of the classical tradition of sociological theory for environmental sociology. This reappraisal has led to reassessments of both the contributions and shortcomings of the classical tradition as a foundation for environmental sociology in the twenty-first century. Second, environmental sociology has been enriched through the process of practitioners of some of the established midcentury-sociological theories—particularly functionalism and neofunctionalism, Critical Theory, and World-System Theory (WST)—having begun to take the biophysical environment more seriously than has been typical in these theoretical traditions. Finally, the late 1980s and early 1990s have witnessed the development of several new theoretical traditions—particularly social constructionism and cultural sociology as a whole, postmodernism, reflexive modernization, and "risk society"—that have been extended to environmental sociology and that have substantially enriched it. The remainder of this introduction will be devoted to sketching some of the new contributions that have been made possible by these three important trends in the "environment" of theory in environmental sociology.

THE CLASSICAL TRADITION AND
ENVIRONMENTAL SOCIOLOGY

As Buttel stresses in his overview of classical theory and the development of environmental sociology, it has frequently been noted that environmental sociology has by its very nature tended to be somewhat agnostic toward conventional sociological theory (see also Buttel 2000). In large part, this is because for most of the twentieth century Western sociology paid very little attention to the biophysical environment. For most of the latter half of the twentieth century, in particular, it was rare for a major sociological journal to publish a paper in which a natural-environmental phenomenon was employed as a significant independent/explanatory variable, and especially as a major dependent variable. Environmental sociology for all practical purposes did not exist until the late 1960s and early 1970s, when the environmental movement propelled environmental issues onto the public and scholarly agenda. Even then, the bulk of the sociological community, while acknowledging that "the environment" was a social concern or social problem worthy of sociological attention, was reluctant to see environmental phenomena as being of enduring sociological significance.

The pioneering environmental sociologists tended to feel that the legacy of the nineteenth- and early twentieth-century classical sociological theorists, especially their quest to distinguish sociology from the rival disciplines of psychology, biology, economics, and geography, had shifted the pendulum of scholarship too far in the direction of handcuffing sociology with the "social facts" injunction. Catton and Dunlap (1978; 1980), Murphy (1994), Martell (1994), Benton and Redclift (1994), Dickens (1992), Goldblatt (1996), and many others have insisted that nineteenth-century social thought has had the effect of steering the discipline of sociology in the direction of ignoring resources, nature, and the environment. Not only has there been sharp criticism of the classical sociologists (especially Marx, Durkheim, and Weber) within the core of environmental sociology, but Catton and Dunlap (1978; 1980) argued that the "human-exemptionalist" character of twentieth-century sociological thought—the fact that it explicitly or implicitly presumes that social-organizational, cultural, and technological innovations tend to exempt humans from the natural laws that govern other species—gives mainstream sociology an unrecognized paradigmatic character or coherence. Conversely, Catton and Dunlap argued that environmental sociology should strive for nothing less than to catalyze a fundamental reorientation of the discipline of sociology. They have suggested that the very nature of environmental sociology is that it represents a "new paradigm" (Catton and Dunlap 1978; 1980), while the apparent divisions within sociology—for example, between Marxism and functionalism—are more or less variations on the larger tendency of sociology to ignore the natural environment (see the overview in Foster 1999).

These and other influential pieces of scholarship during environmental sociology's first two decades have significant strengths and have been major contributions. Each of these scholarly traditions has been theoretically ambitious. Each has strived for a multi-institutional perspective that, for example, encompasses major literatures from such sociological specialty areas as political sociology, economic sociology, sociology of science, sociology of occupations and work, human ecology and demography, urban sociology, and so on.

This sociological aversion to the natural environment has often been attributed to the fact that the three major classical theorists, despite their many differences, tended to concur with the notion that the sociological enterprise, if it is to successfully distinguish itself from psychology, biology, economics, and geography, ought to emphasize social causes of social phenomena (what Durkheim called the "social facts" injunction). In other words, it has often been claimed that the major classical theorists strongly emphasized distinctly social concepts (such as social class, power, and culture) as independent variables and distinctly social dependent variables (such as societal development, industrialization, class formation, inequality, state-building, democracy, bureaucratization, and revolution).

While this claim—that the classical tradition failed to bequeath to sociology a clear statement about and appreciation of the relations between societies and their biophysical environments—has an element of truth, several persuasive arguments can be made about why environmental sociology ought not insulate itself from the classical tradition. As is stressed in several of the chapters in the book, the relevance of the classical tradition can be underscored by the fact that most of the influential environmental sociology scholars of the late twentieth century can be characterized fairly clearly in terms of their being influenced by one or two particular classical theorists. Dickens (1992) and Benton (1989), who are contributors to this volume, are well-known environmental-sociological neo-Marxists, and other neo-Marxists, such as Schnaiberg (1980), O'Connor (1994), Foster (1999; 2000), and Burkett (1999), have played highly visible roles in the development of environmental sociology. Another of our contributors, Murphy (1994), is widely recognized as a leading Weber scholar and neo-Weberian environmental sociologist. Catton, the author of the chapter on Durkheim, is a recognized Durkheim scholar and is among the most influential Durkheimian environmental sociologists. That so many of the world's leading environmental sociologists are as well known for their commitments to particular classical (or contemporary) traditions as they are for the specific nature of their work in environmental sociology testifies to the fact that "conventional" traditions of social theory must comprise the foundation of environmental sociology—hence the "classical foundations" component of the book's subtitle. Another argument that can be made for the continuing relevance of the classical tradition for environmental sociology is also amply represented among the authors of the chapters in part II. Dickens, Murphy, and Catton are candid in acknowledging the environmental shortcomings of the classical tradition—and of Marx, Weber, and Durkheim in particular—but each stresses that the classical theorists were far more aware of natural-environmental constraints and societal-environmental relations than is often acknowledged.

Marxism and Environmental Sociology

One of the enduring ironies of environmental sociology is that it has had a close affinity to Marxism and neo-Marxism at the same time that many environmental sociologists have been at pains to distance their work from the Marxist tradition. On one hand, Marxism and environmental sociology have had a good deal in common. Both are in some fundamental sense critical perspectives in that they tend to be critical of prevailing institutions and social arrangements. In particular, each has tended to exhibit a critical posture toward capitalist industrialization, especially of the tendency of capital toward self-expansion and of capitalism toward accumulation and growth. Neo-Marxism and environmental sociology have also had the commonality of viewing environmental degradation as a contradiction of the development of modern societies. Finally, both neo-Marxism and environmental sociology are "materialist" perspectives, albeit in somewhat different respects; nonetheless, both neo-Marxism and environmental sociology stress the notion that the realities of human life can be best revealed by uncovering the material substratum of societies.

Given these affinities between neo-Marxism and environmental sociology, it is not surprising that a good many of the influential pieces of work in modern environmental sociology have been neo-Marxist in inspiration. Schnaiberg's (1980) notions of the societal-environmental dialectic and the treadmill of production were anchored in a several neo-Marxist theories (especially in O'Connor's [1973] work on the "functions" and fiscal crisis of the state). O'Connor (1994) has developed a related but distinct neo-Marxist perspective on the "second contradiction of capital." O'Connor has posited that in addition to there being a contradiction between capital and labor (the "first contradiction,"[2] as elaborated by Marx), the expansionism of capitalism tends to cause environmental problems and create a second contradiction (which is manifested mainly as rising private costs of production). Other highly influential neo-Marxist works in environmental sociology have been Benton's (1989) *New Left Review* paper and his 1996 anthology, and Dickens's (1992; 1996) books on Marxism and critical realism. The prominence of neo-Marxism in environmental sociology can also be gauged by the fact that arguably the most prominent environmental-sociological journal article in the history of the field thus far has been that by Foster (1999) in the *American Journal of Sociology*, in which he advances Marx's notion of "metabolic rift" as a promising focal point for the development of environmental sociology (see also Foster 2000).

But while Marxism has played an exceptionally important role in the development of environmental sociology, there are also some major reasons why many environmental sociologists have sought to distance themselves from Marxism. First, as Buttel notes in his chapter in this collection, some environmental sociologists are ambivalent about Marxism on account of their disdain for the classical tradition in general. Second, many environmental sociologists sympathetic to neo-Marxism (e.g., Dickens 1992; Benton 1989) have themselves been critical of the "Prometheanism" of classical Marxism.[3] Other environmental-sociological neo-Marxists, as well as environmental sociologists who are critical of Marx and Marxism (e.g., Murphy 1994), have often pointed to the ecological problems of the Euro-Asian state-socialist countries during the 1950s through the 1980s as evidence for the fact that the overall thrust of Marxism has been the disregard of the environment and a posture of dominion over the natural world. Third, neo-Marxism has exhibited a slow but steady decline in influence within sociology, and the declining persuasiveness of neo-Marxism as a sociological theory tradition has doubtless contributed to a more agnostic view on the part of environmental sociologists toward neo-Marxism over the past decade or so. Much of the declining persuasiveness of neo-Marxism has been due to the end of the Cold War and the delegitimation of state-socialism, while another key factor has been the late twentieth-century fascination with a number of alternatives to neo-Marxism (constructionism and cultural sociology in general, postmodernism, rational choice, and various forms of the "new institutionalism"). Finally, Marxism and environmental concerns are in some sense rivals for the attention of the progressive left, and thus many environmental sociologists—particularly those with strong proenvironmental predilections—express concerns that the foci of Marxism may divert scholars and other intellectuals away from the environmental agenda.

Nonetheless, while Marxism now has its detractors among the ranks of environmental sociologists, neo-Marxism, or historical materialism, has recently found rejuvenation in a red-green form (e.g., see Benton's chapter in this volume). In many parts of Marx (early and late) and in the work of Engels, we find an emphasis on

what has been called (e.g., by O'Connor 1994) the second contradiction of capitalism. If the first contradiction is between the forces and relations of production (creating economic crisis, an increased socialization of the means of production, and an
organized labor movement), the second contradiction is between capitalism and the
biophysical resources it needs to flourish. Capital, it is argued, increasingly undermines the ecological and resource conditions necessary for its survival and growth.
And this too generates political movements. The "old" movements become combined with the "new," including those over the environment.

Dickens takes issue with these second-contradiction arguments, suggesting that
they underestimate capital's capacity for restructuring, even if environmental and
social chaos persists.[4] The second-contradiction thesis also underestimates the extent
to which environmental crises on the ground are automatically translated by social
movements into a critique of capitalism. Dickens's chapter suggests that the main
contribution of Marxism to environmental sociology may lie elsewhere. He gives
special emphasis to the technical and social divisions of labor and the politics of
knowledge. Marx emphasized the division between "mental" and "manual" work
in the workplace and the subordination of the worker within the workplace. The
process is one whereby practical knowledge (including knowledge of nature) is
actively divided from more abstract knowledge, with the latter placed in the hands
of scientists and managers. Alienation—in this case, alienation from nature—lies at
the heart of Marxian historical materialism. The social division of labor refers, inter
alia, to divisions between firms and organizations and the divisions between domestic labor in the home (including forms of self-provisioning) and that in the place of
paid work. Emphasizing the social division of labor raises the question of whether it
is always capitalism that is the guilty party as regards environmental degradation.
This reinterpretation of historical materialism suggests that environmental degradation may have as much or more to do with the impossibility of controlling *any*
advanced industrial system. An emphasis on the social division of labor also opens
up the possibility of links between Marxism and other social movements such as
feminism (see, e.g., Mellor 1997) and other areas of social theory as represented by
Beck (1992). Dickens concludes by noting that such movements and organizations
(many of which are in the "third sector") are attempting to overcome forced divisions of labor and the marginalization of popular knowledge.[5]

Weber and Environmental Sociology

Buttel notes in his chapter on classical theory and environmental sociology that
while Weber's relationship to environmental sociology is the least controversial or
problematic of the legacies of the "big three," there has been quite a rich, varied,
though relatively invisible role played by neo-Weberian scholarship in the development of environmental sociology. He suggests that there have been two different
Weberian literatures that have influenced environmental sociology. First, there has
been the work of West (1984), who has drawn from Weber's historical sociology of
religion and his empirical research on ancient society. West has emphasized what he

refers to as Weber's comparative-historical human ecology, which had two major elements. The first element was that of the role of environmental or natural resource factors playing causally important roles at times in history, and the second was the struggles by social classes and status groups over resources such as irrigation systems.

The second neo-Weberian environmental sociology has been elaborated by Murphy (1994). Murphy's neo-Weberian environmental sociology has been based largely on Weber's concept of rationalization and on the ideal-types of rationality and orientations to action drawn primarily from *Economy and Society* (Weber 1968). The essence of Murphy's (1994) analysis is that rationalization and the expansion of formal rationality have involved tendencies to an ethic of mastery over nature (or the "plasticity" of the relationship between humans and their natural environment), to the quest for technologies to realize this mastery, and to a lack of attention to human threats to the environment.

"Weber," Murphy argues in his chapter in this volume, "is the giant upon whose shoulders we stand in order to see further." Murphy's chapter is an overview of the potentials of the neo-Weberian environmental sociology he pioneered in his *Rationality and Nature* (1994), although he is also critical of certain components of Weber's work. Murphy's chapter is especially significant for emphasizing themes of human agency, social structure, and unanticipated consequences; the reality of nature; the implications of rationalization; concepts of technology, social divisions, and their reunification; alienation from nature; and the role of meaning in social action. Murphy's arguments are also provocative in showing how the recent work of Beck (1992) can be seen as an example of how Weberian ideas remain relevant to contemporary environmental sociology.

Murphy makes several persuasive arguments about the relevance of Weber to environmental sociology. He notes, for example, that intrinsic to the study of environment and society is the structure-agency dilemma. Murphy endorses Weber's subjectivist posture on the structure-agency issue and Weber's emphasis on social action and how peoples' actions generate structural change, often in highly unpredictable ways. People, according to Weber, become prisoners of the "cage" of their own making. The implications for environmental questions are obvious. Humans are in danger of making a world that controls them, rather than vice versa.

A second strength of Weber's sociology for the study of environment and society is his having recognized the material reality of nature. Although Weber's work is well known for its subjectivism—with its emphasis on how people interpret their circumstances—and for showing that such interpretations could have real, material effects, this did not lead Weber to underestimate the objective reality of the natural world. His emphasis on linking subjective meaning to social action can also be readily extended to include the meanings and actions of future generations. A third contribution of Weber to environmental sociology is his sociology of rationalization, including but not limited to the (attempted) rationalization of the processes of nature. Nevertheless, such rationalization only leads to further ethical problems and decisions, all of which create a heightened need for human decision making. In the end, these ethical dilemmas create huge question marks over the rationalization project itself.

Weber's early understanding of alienation from nature is also, Murphy argues, useful for environmental sociology. In a society based on agriculture, nature tended to be seen as being composed of unusual and largely unknown natural forces. The "urban tradesman," by contrast, is much less affected by natural events. He or she is separated from the realities of nature and, in theory at least, can see a rational and causal connection between means and ends. With the growth of rationalization, however, urban dwellers are increasingly exposed to nature as a "problem."[6]

While recognizing the many strengths of Weber's work for the study of environment and society, Murphy takes issue with Weber on several points. First, Murphy departs from Weber on matters related to technology. "An inanimate machine," Weber argued, "is mind objectified." Murphy argues that this posture is inadequate (as does Catton in this volume). Machines are not just a product of mind, but are a result of the interaction between the human mind and nature. It is becoming increasingly clear that technology is the means by which ecological equilibria are upset and unanticipated consequences of technology are generated. Murphy is also critical of Weber regarding the effects of rationalization and knowledge. Weber contended that the tendency is toward the creation of self-contained separate spheres, as each sphere (religious, economic, political, scientific, and so on) generates its own sets of priorities, values, and so on. But Murphy, borrowing from Beck (1992), argues that there is an important countertendency—that of the reintegration of formerly separate spheres. A particularly critical instance of the countertendency is when "the scientific" becomes political, one of the master processes involved in the risk society.

Durkheim and Environmental Sociology

Many environmental sociologists' views of Durkheim are shaped by the view, expressed first and most forcefully by Catton and Dunlap (1978), that Durkheim's "social facts" injunction represents the antithesis of environmental sociology (but see Prades 1999). Durkheim, by defining sociology's subject matter as the study of "social facts," which are to be explained by other "social facts," can be interpreted as ruling out biophysical phenomena as either independent or dependent variables. Thus, as necessary as it might have been at the time for Durkheim to insist on the social facts injunction in order to legitimate sociology as a discipline, Dunlap and Catton view this injunction to have become something of a fetish of mid-twentieth-century sociology and to have led to a tendency toward sociocultural determinism.

Both Buttel and Catton (in this volume), however, suggest that there are several reasons that sociologists ought not to rule out Durkheim's work as being relevant to environmental sociology. Buttel, for example, stresses that Durkheim's *Division of Labor in Society*, which historically served as the source of the basic ideas of demographic human ecology, contains many of the building blocks for macrosociological analysis of the relationships between societies and their resource bases. Catton's chapter calls particular attention to how a reassessment of Durkheim's sociology can open up productive new lines of inquiry in environmental sociology. Unlike most commentators, Catton suggests that Durkheim was sympathetic to explanations other than the purely social. He notes that Durkheim is well known for two major theoretical arguments: his resistance to biologically based explanations and the fact that his overarching model of social change involves mechanical solidarity giving way to organic solidarity. Durkheim may have been striving to carve out a new science of sociology anchored in these two main arguments, but that does not mean he was unaware of what disciplines such as biology and psychology had to offer.

Catton makes the provocative argument that Durkheim's reasoning in his model of the transition from mechanical to organic solidarity was highly influenced by Darwin but that, at the same time, he got Darwin's theory wrong. While Durkheim's faulty interpretation of Darwin now seems even more wrong in the light of contemporary biological and evolutionary thought, Catton suggests that Durkheim's reasons for misinterpreting Darwin did not include any aversion to biology per se. Durkheim believed that the shift toward a society made up of a high division of labor was, and would continue to be, bound together by high levels of mutualism between unrelated individuals. This, he suggested, was an echo of what happens generally in nature. But Darwin did not make such an argument himself; Darwin, and modern biologists, did not present a picture of generally greater interdependence emerging from increasing complementarity among species. Part of the confusion lies in Durkheim assuming that all competition occurs in the same region, whereas evolution is mainly "allopatric" (species developing relatively separately) as distinct from "sympatric" (species evolving in the same region). The outcome is complex, with competitive and mutualistic relations coexisting alongside each other. Mutualism emerges, but not as a result of separate species combining with each other in the struggle to survive. Rather, it emerges in some instances as a result of competitive relations (e.g., between predator-prey species) becoming in due course mutualistic. This places the emphasis back on ecological systems, an emphasis largely neglected by Durkheim. Catton makes the important and often neglected point that Durkheim's theory was developed in response to his society (France)—a point that could be made with regard to many of the other classical theorists in this volume. Wishful thinking that socially divided French society would become mutualistic led Durkheim, Catton argues, to a selective reading of Darwin.

Finally, Catton argues for a model of social change that draws on evolutionary thought, but in a different way from that proposed by Durkheim. Such an evolutionary model would envisage human society as made up of culturally evolved subspecies, each with its own environmental demands. Whether mutualism overtakes predatory instincts is a matter for debate—it is certainly not predetermined (see also Freese 1997). Note also in this regard that Catton's chapter is distinctive in this collection in that his is the only one to introduce ecological theory as such. The exceptional character of Catton's chapter raises some important general questions. Can ecology and ecological theory form the main basis for an environmental sociology? If so, how? If not, how can they be combined? Or is such a combination too difficult to even attempt?

ENVIRONMENTAL SOCIOLOGY AND TWENTIETH-CENTURY SOCIOLOGICAL THEORY

There is not nearly as much literature on environmental sociology's relationship to twentieth-century sociological theory as there is on the classical tradition, but if anything the environmental-sociological verdict on twentieth-century theory has been nearly as uncomplimentary. Buttel suggests in his chapter in this volume that many of the ostensible shortcomings of the classical tradition for environmental sociology have been due more to their treatments by twentieth-century theorists than to intrinsic defects. The often-cited Catton and Dunlap (1978) criticism of the legacy of the classical tradition is actually directed at midcentury sociological theories or paradigms, rather than at the classical theorists' writings themselves (as is emphasized in Dunlap's chapter in this volume).

The contributors to this volume concern themselves with three of the most important (mid) twentieth-century sociological theories: Parsonian/social systems theories, "critical"/Frankfurt School theories, and World-System theories. Each of these midcentury sociological theories could in some sense be viewed as being even more innocent of environmental phenomena than were the major classical theories—not surprisingly so, because twentieth-century industrial society seemed especially removed from its ecological base (Catton and Dunlap 1980: 16–18). Parsons, for example, almost never referred to nature or the natural world, and when he did so it was usually to make the observation that such phenomena lie largely outside the arena of sociological analysis. Essentially, the same observation could be made about the major Frankfurt School figures such as Horkheimer, Benjamin, Adorno, and Marcuse (who were the founders of "Critical Theory") and about Wallerstein (the sociologist most closely associated with WST).

Parsons, Social-System Theory, and Neofunctionalism

Papadakis is not hesitant to acknowledge that Parsonian/social-systems theories have largely ignored the biophysical environment. Papadakis, however, notes that Luhmann, one of the most influential Parsonian theorists in the 1980s, made significant contributions to the study of environmental movements and environmental politics. Papadakis takes as his starting point Luhmann's neofunctionalism. Systems theory typically envisages social systems as characterized by interacting individuals and institutions. For Luhmann, the main form of such interaction is communication between the interacting subsystems (social and political organizations) that constitute society. Communication, he argues, "is what makes society a reality."

According to Luhmann, the central problem of modern society is that subsystems largely fail to communicate. They are "self-referential," too tied up in their own discourses and understandings to be able to "appreciate" other subsystems. Economic subsystems, for example, have a different modus operandi than political subsystems, with a resulting failure of communication. The picture here is therefore one of self-reproducing subsystems, with politics no longer being in charge. "This has," according to Papadakis, "powerful ramifications for discussions about the capacity of political systems to manage demands for environmental protection, economic development, and social justice."

Papadakis, however, mounts a sustained criticism of Luhmann. Luhmann, Papadakis believes, is overly pessimistic about the capacity for organizations involved in environmental questions to communicate. Communication is far more possible than Luhmann suggests. Coordination, or at least "coordinated dissent," is likewise far more feasible. Furthermore, new social movements (NSMs) are able to shake the "self-referentiality" of subsystems, ensuring that social systems do not just simply reproduce themselves. More generally, Papadakis's chapter raises important questions regarding the functionalist tradition and its "upgrading" by Luhmann via an emphasis on communication. Papadakis's chapter also makes observations from a neofunctionalist perspective that exhibit linkages with Dickens (in this volume) on the disabling effect of the social division of labor and with Critical Theory's views on communication and communicative action.

Critical Theories and the Environment

The starting point for Wehling is the work of the critical theorists based at the Institute of Social Research in Frankfurt. Key authors include Adorno, Benjamin, Horkheimer, Marcuse, and Habermas. What contribution can these critical theories, and this sociological tradition, make toward environmental sociology? Wehling argues that aspects of some of these writers' works (particularly those of Benjamin and Adorno) can be seen as making important potential contributions. In general, however, Critical Theory has not been extensively engaged with environmental questions. While Habermas and others have been centrally concerned with rationality, communication, and the impossibility of imposing rational solutions to pressing issues, these issues have not tended to include environmental questions. Rather, the referents of rationality and irrationality have largely been questions of social order and the impossibility of a politics aimed at rational solutions. Habermas's "linguistic turn" arguably has, if anything, diverted attention away from the Frankfurt School's potential engagement in the relations among societies, individuals, and nature. Nevertheless, the emphasis of Habermas and other critical theorists on communication and meaning can still be important.

Wehling believes that the early work of Benjamin and other critical theorists can be rescued to create a new kind of sociology, a sociology with environmental questions (or what Wehling would prefer to call "society-nature relations") at its heart. Benjamin's work, for example, referred not only to the mastery of nature by human society, but also particularly to the *kinds* of mastery over human beings that are entailed in such mastery. Benjamin was also centrally concerned with interpretations and social constructions. Although Benjamin is best known for his "urban" sociology (through his "Arcades Project"), his work contains the seeds for a new kind of environmental sociology, one that is simultaneously "environmental" as well as social.

Wehling's chapter concludes by sketching out what such a sociology of society-nature relations might look like. It would include the social relations formed in particular societies that are constructed in the interaction with nature. This new sociology of society-nature relations would also include a major focus on the symbolizing processes by which people communicate over nature. Wehling feels that the emphasis on cognition and communications central to Critical Theory can make a significant contribution to the debate between realists and social constructionists. This is one of the most significant contributions of this chapter. Critical analysis of how the sciences (including the social sciences) are constructed or defined (by the media, politics, and so on) does not necessarily mean that environmental problems are immaterial. Wehling's environmental version of the critical school calls for analysis of the complex interactions between real material processes on the one hand and their interpretation on the other.

World-System Theory

Roberts and Grimes begin by noting that WST evolved out of efforts over the past thirty years to explain how and why some countries in the world economy have been able to grow in power and wealth while others remain trapped in apparent stagnation. They note that World-System analysis has been "omnivorous" in its theoretical scope at the same time that it has drawn primarily on the Marxist and political economy traditions.[7] Its particular analytical features are the notions that there is a single global-scale division of labor, that there is a cyclical nature of capitalist production, and that there exists unequal exchange between peripheral (and semi-peripheral) and core economies. Roberts and Grimes argue that early WST managed to "miss the 'green boat' of environmental sociology." Nevertheless, the last few years have seen "an explosive boom" in WST proponents addressing environmental questions.

They proceed to sketch out what WST may have to contribute to a new, environmentally oriented, social theory. "We believe," they argue, "World-System Theory has a potential contribution to make on *most* pressing environmental issues, such as global warming, deforestation, resource depletion, water struggles, ozone, food crops, the increasing frequency of major storms and human recovery from them, biodiversity, compensation of locals for management of neighboring endangered species, enactment and enforcement of international treaties, coordination of NGOs, and so on." Their chapter offers a number of specific and useful suggestions regarding links between the tenets of WST and specific environmental questions. For example, global economic forces and the dependency of poor societies help explain why "peripheral" countries devastate their soils and contaminate their rivers. Second, societies and regions with high levels of environmental consciousness and governments that attempt to regulate industrial pollution may be forced to lower their demands to compete for globally mobile capital investment. Third, WST's emphasis on economic cycles and history is able to illustrate the connection between economic decline and ecological degradation. Fourth, WST holds that societies tend to remain fixed at certain economic and social levels and this, they argue, implies that economic growth per se will not overcome environmental degradation.

The chapter explores further possible connections between environmental problems and economic cycles, commodification, proletarianization, bureaucratization, globalization, and interstate conflict. At the same time, Roberts and Grimes acknowledge that WST may overemphasize economic explanation, "while remaining virtually mum on culture" and having little to say regarding gender. WST also involves tendencies toward teleology and overgeneralization. But the chapter remains optimistic. Each of the weaknesses in WST is seen as repairable given suitable attention, and none is fatal to the central insights of the WST paradigm.

Exemptionalism and the New Environmental Paradigm

Dunlap's chapter on "Paradigms, Theories, and Environmental Sociology" is in some sense a bridge between the concerns of the section on classical theory, the concerns of the present section on twentieth-century theory, and concerns relating to late twentieth-century environmental sociological theory. As noted earlier, Dunlap, along with Catton, was among the first of the scholars to have raised issues concerning the shortcomings of mainstream sociological theorizing for understanding societal-environmental relations. Their writings posited that the Western cultural tradition had led to a collection of classical and twentieth-century theories that together tended to downplay the role of biophysical factors as causal and dependent variables and that was reluctant to deal with environmental phenomena. Dunlap and Catton thereby became known for the proposition that a more ecological social theory must necessarily be one built around premises different than those of sociology's nineteenth- and twentieth-century theoretical heritage, which they have referred to collectively as the exemptionalist (or human exemptionalist) paradigm (the HEP). Dunlap and Catton's writings on theories and paradigms became highly influential, but occasionally controversial, within environmental sociology. Much of the history of environmental sociology in the West has turned on Dunlap-Catton's writings and has involved debate on issues such as whether their new ecological paradigm (NEP) is adequate for guiding empirical research, whether the classical tradition is of use in environmental sociology, and whether the NEP or more conventional theoretical divisions within environmental sociology will have the greatest "primacy" in the subdiscipline.

Dunlap's chapter reflects on several of these nearly twenty-five-year-old controversies by focusing on debates between Catton-Dunlap and Buttel on paradigms and theories in environmental sociology. In addition to pointing to areas of agreement between them and Buttel, Dunlap notes how some of the debates that have occurred have involved miscommunication and misunderstanding. He stresses, for example, that the referent for their category of exemptionalism was not mainly classical sociology, but rather the uptake of the classical tradition by *mid-twentieth-century* sociologists and sociological theories. He also argues that neither he nor Catton ever intended a blanket denunciation of the classical tradition in sociology, nor did they intend for the NEP to provide specific theoretical guidance for research. Drawing on Sayer's work on paradigms and methods in contemporary sociology, Dunlap suggests that paradigmatic discourse can be useful but that we need to recognize the limits of paradigmatic analysis.

Dunlap notes that the literature that has evolved from his and Catton's work on paradigms tends to fall within one of three categories, which he labels "strong," "moderate," and "weak" interpretations of their conceptualization of paradigms. He admits that some ambiguities in their writings have led to erroneous "strong" interpretations of their analysis—particularly to the notion that he and Catton were suggesting that the NEP was being advanced as a new, or superior, sociological theory of environment. Dunlap is more sympathetic with the moderate interpretation—that HEP-NEP cleavages should be seen as contenders for primacy in environmental sociology along with more conventional classical or contemporary theoretical groups (such as neo-Marxism). He is most comfortable, though, with the weak interpretation—that the major purpose of the HEP-NEP distinction was for it to serve as the centerpiece of a plea for sociology to remove its "ecological blinders" and a call for there to be new, green versions of a range of sociological theories and methodological traditions. Dunlap concludes by suggesting that while green social theory has not become dominant in sociology, there are a number of indicators that a sensitivity to ecological conditions is gaining ground in sociology as a whole, and that environmental sociology and greener versions of sociological theory are directly or indirectly influencing theory, research, and discourse within the larger discipline. He suggests that this outcome is consistent with their original intentions and that this should be the yardstick according to which their arguments and analyses should be judged.

SOCIOLOGICAL THEORY AND ENVIRONMENTAL SOCIOLOGY AT THE TURN OF THE MILLENNIUM: MODERNITY, CULTURE, AND THE NATURAL WORLD

It is widely recognized that sociological theory at large has exhibited some dramatic changes over the past decade and a half. Four of the major shifts in Western sociology over the past fifteen or so years have been particularly influential in the development of environmental sociology. These four shifts, which overlap to a significant degree, are as follows. First, there have been new theories of modernity. Of particular importance has been the work of Giddens (1991; 1998) on modernity and reflexive modernization, and Beck's (1992) work on reflexive modernization and the "risk society." An integral component of this trend for environmental sociology has been a particular derivative type of reflexive modernization theory known as ecological modernization (see especially Mol 1995; 1997; Spaargaren 1996). Second, there has been an outpouring of literature on postmodernity and postmodernization. Third, there has been a proliferation of perspectives from cultural sociology, including not only postmodernity perspectives, but also discourse-analytical, social-framing, and NSMs' perspectives. Fourth, social-constructionist perspectives from the sociology of science have been extended to the realms of political and social movements in general, and to the arenas of environment, resources, and environmental knowledges and movements in particular.

The simultaneous rise to prominence of these four perspectives in both mainstream as well as environmental sociology has some interesting implications for the latter subdiscipline. On the one hand, among the reasons that modernity-related, postmodernist, cultural-sociological, and social-constructionist perspectives have become more central to social theory since the 1980s has had to do with the growing prominence and sociological recognition of the importance of environmentally related phenomena. Thus, many otherwise mainstream sociological theorists such as Giddens came to view the growing role of environmental movements and of NSMs in general, the growing importance of natural symbols in social identities, and the rise of environmental symbols and claims in politics as being of prime importance in the modern world. And for many theorists, there was a felt need to shift toward one or another of the four types of novel, innovative theories in order to account adequately for emerging phenomena such as these. In the process, environmental sociology has become more "mainstreamed" within sociology as a whole. It was, however, "nonenvironmental" sociologists, rather than primarily self-identified environmental sociologists, who were responsible for having done so (e.g., Macnaghten and Urry 1998; Eder 1996).

On the other hand, while environmental sociology has become a more mainstream or accepted subdiscipline within sociology, this has occurred in ways that challenge—quite creatively, we believe—some of the premises and assumptions of the first generation of environmental sociologists. These new, more sociologically central or mainstream views tend to involve one or both of two premises: (1) that "modernization" (the advance of scientific knowledge, the division of labor, "globalization," and new patterns of technological change in industry and in consumption), rather than being the key "driver" of environmental degradation, may be among the more potent solutions to environmental problems; and (2) that "the environment" is as or more socially salient with respect to beliefs, ideologies, discourses, and "social constructions" as it is with respect to material-physical constraints and limits.

The authors in part IV of this volume show that the new trends in social-environmental theory at the end of the century have opened up provocative and useful debates about the future course that environmental sociology should take. Three of the chapters in part IV (by Seippel, Shove and Warde, and Benton), while acknowledging the utility of one or more of the four trends in modern sociological theory, tend to come down more so on the side of the traditional materialist environmental sociological position, albeit in quite different ways. The other three chapters (by

Yearley, McKechnie and Welsh, and Hannigan) make strong cases that environmental sociology can benefit by embracing these new trends in sociological theory.

Environmental Movements and the Greening of Capitalism

Seippel's chapter, while focusing on environmental politics, raises some important questions for environmental sociology as a whole regarding the level (macro, meso, micro) at which environmental sociology is constructed. His chapter is also important in its implication that no *one* theory may be capable of being *the* basis for an environmental sociology.

Taking as his starting point Merton's 1960s critique of sociology, Seippel makes a plea for more middle-level theory. Thus, environmental sociology tends to operate at a very abstract level, and it would benefit, Seippel believes, from a switch toward meso- or microlevel analysis. The chapter starts by examining the processes of social differentiation—arguably the most general or overarching processes characteristic of modernity, and a cluster of processes recognized and explored by a diversity of theorists. A focus on social differentiation processes inevitably leads to a focus on the political system and to the links between the political system and other systems and organizations. This further leads to what a range of authors have to say about the political system and its relation to environmental politics. This includes work on the "new middle class," their changing values, and the (linked) rise of NSMs. For Seippel, coming to grips with middle-level analysis (with its focus on social structure, culture, and organization) allows a sounder understanding of the complexity of environmental politics and of the many mediating factors and processes involved in environmental politics. What emerges is a complex picture of the political intermediation process in late modern society—a complexity that, in his view, is not captured too well by fashionable perspectives such as risk society, NSMs, or ecological modernization.

He goes on to outline and evaluate three other areas of "middle-range" theory on environmental movements: "political opportunity structure" perspectives (where the focus is on the role of distinct social classes in political mobilization), "cultural framing" perspectives (which center on the meaning or significance of social movement actions), and "mobilizing structures" perspectives (which are oriented toward the repertoires and organizational forms of social movements). Finally, the chapter returns to grand theorizing in environmental sociology, asking what these middle-range theories may have to offer. Beck's (1992) notion and theory of "risk society" and Deep Ecology (see Taylor 1995) are the two types of theory addressed. Both perspectives have useful things to say about environmental politics, the creation of environmental values, and so on. But the middle-range theories outlined earlier raise serious questions regarding their generalizations. It is not at all clear, for example, that the political system is always and everywhere so enfeebled in modern society as Beck suggests.

Benton's chapter on reflexive modernization and green socialism has obvious connections to our earlier discussions about neo-Marxism and environmental sociology. Benton's chapter is in one sense a neo-Marxist analysis, though equally fundamentally it is a critical reflection on several closely related trends in environmental sociology and sociology at large—namely, the explosion of interest in "modernity" and reflexive modernity—of concern in part IV of this volume. Benton comments on the overarching enterprise of reflexive modernity, particularly the versions by Giddens (1991) on the four institutional dimensions of modernity and that by Beck (1992) on the ideal-types of industrial society and risk society. Benton also comments briefly on the closely related perspective of ecological modernization (see Mol 1995).

Benton begins, and is harshest with respect to, Giddens's work on modernity. He is particularly critical of Giddens's use of ideal-types and the tendency toward an ahistorical linear-evolutionary view of social change. But Benton is most critical of Giddens's claims that class has ceased to be a major structural principle of late capitalism, that the welfare state and political struggles over social insurance are now obsolete, and that class identity is in sharp and irrevocable decline.

Benton is more receptive to several of the views of Beck (1992), particularly the important role that environmental and technological risks, and pervasiveness of the social perceptions of these risks, plays in contemporary capitalist societies. He also finds Beck's analysis of new types of social movements intriguing, though Benton is insistent that radical "generative," "life," and "subpolitics" have by no means supplanted class politics. Benton's argument, however, is not a straightforward assertion of the standard doctrines of neo-Marxism. While his analysis is in a definite sense a neo-Marxist one, he takes issue with one of the central postulates of late twentieth-century neo-Marxism: that the self-expansion of capital and the material requirements of capitalist expansion must inevitably undermine the survival base of capitalist societies. Essentially, then, Benton takes issue with "second-contradiction-type" arguments (e.g., of O'Connor 1994).

Benton, while cautious about many of the received explanations for the greening of advanced capitalist societies, agrees with the ecological-modernizationist claim that capitalism is quite "flexible" and under certain conditions can be redirected to make possible economic growth with tolerable or declining levels of environmental degradation. He is doubtful that this greening of capitalism will be made possible through an evolutionary move toward reflexive modernity. Instead, his argument, based on his perspective of green socialism, is that the green restructuring can only come about through red-green coalition movements. He concludes by arguing for the centrality of class—or, in other words, socialist—politics as a foundation for these coalitions.

Consumption and Environment

The idea that levels of consumption are linked to environmental degradation has traditionally been one of the cornerstones of late twentieth-century environmental thought. The central role of consumption has likewise been a key component of the environmental-sociological tradition influenced by neo-Malthusian notions (e.g., Catton 1976; 1980). Thus, while the authors of many of the most influential works in environmental sociology that have striven to distance themselves from neo-Malthusianism, they have nonetheless stressed the critical role that consumption institutions play in leading to environmental degradation (e.g., Murphy 1994; Redclift 1996). Shove and Warde note, however, that despite the long-standing emphasis of environmental sociology on consumption-driven explanations of environmental degradation and the growing fascination with consumption on the part of cultural sociologists and adherents of postmodernity and ecological modernization views, there have been only modest advances in harnessing the sociology of consumption to environmental analysis. Shove and Warde are as interested in how environmental questions raise new challenges for the sociology of consumption as in how the sociology of consumption can contribute to environmental sociology.

Mainstream social science has long tended to regard consumption as being relatively epiphenomenal compared to the role played by the master social institutions of the economy and production, states and politics, family, education, and culture. Explanatory arguments in which consumption plays a prominent role have often tended to be dismissed by referring to them as "circulationist," "Malthusian," and the like. And most social scientists who do look at consumption phenomena usually tend to consider consumption practices and behaviors as being derivative of (rather than causal forces that shape) the core institutions of class and status, political power and the state, and values and culture.

A good example of the status of arguments about the centrality or importance of consumption in the social sciences is that scholars who stress consumption more often than not feel the need to justify such an emphasis. For example, Spaargaren, the influential Dutch proponent of ecological modernization, devotes nearly ten pages of his 1996 book *Ecological Modernization of Production and Consumption* to emphasizing why it is legitimate to study the sphere of consumption. Similarly, Redclift, in his 1996 book *Wasted*, devotes nearly as many pages explaining why a study of the significance of consumption should not be regarded as an archaic Malthusian exercise. Perhaps the best indication of the marginality of consumption in mainstream social science is that Edgell, Hetherington, and Warde (1997) felt compelled to title their widely cited anthology *Consumption Matters*.

To be sure, there are now several fields in which study of the sphere of consumption tends to be seen as legitimate and in which consumption practices are seen as constituting an institutional complex with some amount of autonomy. For example, the notion that meaning and identity are increasingly shaped through the practices of consumption rather than through one's role in the division of labor and production is a core postulate of postmodernism. Second, the study of consumption has been given increased impetus through the growing influence of Bourdieu (1977) and his notions of "distinction" and cultural capital. Third, theorization of the role of consumption has been one of the staple concerns of environmental sociology (see, e.g., Redclift 1996)—so much so that agnosticism toward the emphasis on consumption (e.g., by Schnaiberg 1980) has often been perceived by many scholars in the field as reflecting an extreme or idiosyncratic position. The rise of cultural sociology and social constructionism in the late 1980s and 1990s has also led to growing attention to consumption practices (see especially Eder 1996; Warde 1997). Nonetheless, it is only recently that the work of Bourdieu (on the analysis of distinction), Castells (1980, on the state and collective consumption), and cultural studies scholars has been devoted to establishing a viable non-Malthusian perspective on consumption, and little of this work has been applied to environmental questions.

Shove and Warde aim to explore possible contributions of the sociology of consumption to environmental sociology by outlining six mechanisms that might be contributing to escalating levels of consumption. The first is the process of social comparison, whereby people's consumption styles are an expression of class taste, that is, an attempt by (middle-class) groups of people to distinguish themselves from one another (following Bourdieu). Second is the creation of self-identity, whereby people in modern societies are constantly projecting messages to one another via their acquisition of goods and lifestyle practices (following Beck 1992; Giddens 1991; 1998; Bauman 1993). Third is mental stimulation, whereby people consume things and learn new tastes as ways of overcoming boredom (what the authors refer to as the "eulogization of variety"). Fourth is the "Diderot effect," whereby the acquisition of a new item renders the owner's old items unacceptable. The result is a "rolling effect," with replacement of old articles quickly spreading to the owner's other possessions. The fifth is specialization, whereby the separation of leisure activities into a variety of specialized fields leads to increasing consumption (e.g., running, training, squash, and tennis—each requiring a special type of shoe). The final mechanism involves sociotechnical systems, whereby the acquisition of new, supposedly "time-saving" devices leads to new forms of consumption or heightened expectations (e.g., washing machines leading to new expectations as to how often items are washed).

Shove and Warde argue, however, that existing sociology of consumption still offers rather little in terms that are of interest to environmental sociology or to the creation of more environmentally sustainable practices. This is partly because understanding the simple acquisition of an object gives little understanding about how the object is *used* and the implications for energy and other resources (e.g., water). What, for example, are the social conventions underlying the ways in which central heating systems are used or the frequency with which washing machines whir? Understanding consumption will entail extending the scope of the sociology of consumption away from the individual consumer. What are the factors (e.g., the levels of public infrastructure or the spatial arrangement of gasoline stations) that shape the levels and types of consumption? What are the broader trends in electricity supply that create new forms of consumption? This chapter therefore raises important questions as to whether the sociology of consumption, and of "environmental consumption" in particular, can be adequately understood without reference to the social organization of supply, including state intervention. Similarly, Shove and Warde raise important questions as to whether the sociology of consumption can afford to remain so focused on the choices made by individuals in the market.

Social Constructionism and Environmental Sociology

During the first fifteen or so years of North American environmental sociology, until roughly 1990, there was an almost universal commitment of the environmental sociology community to a realist epistemology and materialist ontology.[8] In fact, prior to the late 1980s a sizable share of the North American environmental sociology community saw its mission as being to bring the ecological sciences and their insights to the attention of the larger sociological community. Some environmental sociologists had such strong commitments to the ecological sciences that they felt it was appropriate to evaluate environmental-sociological literature in terms of whether it supported or undermined the persuasiveness of ecological-scientific positions on global environmental change and related issues.

Since the mid-1980s, however, there have been two social changes—one in sociology and the other in society at large—that have had contradictory implications for environmental sociology and that have led to some protracted controversies in the field. The first change—the growing interest in environmental matters within mainstream sociology—occurred primarily as a reflection of the cultural turn of the discipline in the Anglo-American world and because of growing discipline-wide interest in ecology as an ideational phenomenon and as a focal point of modern social movements. The second change was the growing national, and especially international, attention to global environmental change in general and atmospheric warming in particular.

Though both of these social changes could be seen as being positive for the "mainstreaming" of environmental sociology in the sociological discipline and in policymaking circles, each led to debate and controversy. The cultural turn of sociology, for example, had contradictory implications for the core of environmental sociology; while the attention to environmental matters in the larger discipline was welcome, the grounds of this attention—their having been rooted to some degree in idealism and in nonrealist or nonobjectivist ontologies—were resisted by many in the subdiscipline. Likewise, while environmental sociologists found that the rise of concern with global environmental change gave the field new impetus (Dunlap and Catton 1994; Rosa and Dietz 1998), controversies over global change in national and international politics (Yearley 1996) would ultimately spill over into environmental sociology itself.

The principal pivot of controversy over the cultural sociology of environment and the environmental sociology of global change was the emergence of a social-constructionist literature on global environmental change. Prior to the 1990s, social constructionism had been largely confined to the social problems and sociology of science literatures. Beginning around 1990, however, social constructionism was increasingly employed to understand "framing" processes within social movements. Also, sociologists of science were increasingly extending the tools of constructionism to the environmental and ecological sciences (e.g., Yearley 1991; 1996; Wynne 1996). A number of environmental sociologists (Taylor and Buttel 1992; Hannigan 1995) proceeded to apply constructionist insights to the processes according to which global environmental and climate change knowledge claims were being "framed."

The thrusts of the social-constructionist literature on global environmental change were several-fold. It was argued that global change served simultaneously as a scientific concept and social movement ideology and that social movement claims and items of scientific knowledge were mutually constitutive. A number of analyses suggested that the way that environmental movement organizations appropriated knowledge from climate scientists was partial and selective (e.g., placing great stress on Third World sources of global warming and biodiversity destruction, while saying little about the likelihood that living standards in the affluent countries might need to be constrained in order to substantially reduce greenhouse gas emissions). The selective appropriation of global change knowledge was suggested to be, at least partly, a conscious strategy by environmental organizations to make the most attractive possible case to the public and to political elites about why there needed to be a strong policy response to global change issues. Social constructionists also argued that the movement claim that the most significant environmental problems facing human societies are global ones was as much a sociocultural construct as a demonstrated scientific fact.

A number of social constructionists also observed that there was a small but influential minority of climate scientists who were not in agreement with much or all of the stylized knowledge about the anthropogenic causes of global climate change. At a minimum, these scientific disagreements were predicted to provide the basis for many corporations, state officials, and interest groups whose interests were not well served by an agenda of reducing greenhouse gas emissions to make a persuasive case that there is "uncertainty" with regard to the validity of global circulation models of global warming that predict substantial atmospheric warming into the twenty-first century. "Uncertainty arguments" (see Hannigan 1995) would indeed prove to be crucial to anticlimate change interest groups (such as the corporate-sponsored Climate Coalition in the United States) in making the case that the evidence about global climate change is not sturdy enough to justify major, privately costly policy changes. In addition, the existence of differences of scientific perspective about global warming might imply that there was premature closure—by climate scientists, environmentalists, and environmental sociologists—on the consensus surrounding global environmental and climate change.

Of particular significance in the mid-1990s' debates over social constructionism was the fact that several observers (Taylor and Buttel 1992; Yearley 1996) had noted that there has been a long history of global environmental claims being seen by Third World state officials and many citizens of developing countries as being inconsistent with their interests. Third World critics of prevailing constructions of global warming, for example, argued that environmental groups and officials tended to exaggerate the role played by tropical deforestation, while accordingly minimizing the Organization for Economic Cooperation and Development countries' contributions to global warming. Third World critics also suggested that if the world is a commons and each world citizen were entitled to an equal share of the biosphere's pollution absorption capacity, the bulk of this capacity ought to go to the Third World citizens who represent about three-quarters of the world's population. Thus, Third World groups tended to resist calls by environmental groups and international organizations to play major roles in reducing global greenhouse gas emissions. Yearley (1996) has also noted the discursive significance of the fact that global environmental change had been "constructed" through use of the imagery conveyed in the Brundtland report's (World Commission on Environment and Development 1987) notion of "our common future"—that all the world's citizens have a common stake in preventing global environmental calamity. Yearley (1996) has suggested that this notion of collective interest in responding to global warming serves to conceal the fact that the costs of global warming and of *responding to* global warming will be highly differentiated across world nations and the social groups within them.

The social-constructionist literature generated an immediate and animated response from a number of environmental sociologists (e.g., Martell 1994; Murphy 1994; 1997; Dunlap and Catton 1994; Redclift and Woodgate 1997b). The critics of constructionism, while conceding that there are social processes involved in translating climate science findings into a policy program, have nonetheless suggested that constructionism has served to distort the realities of how the climate science community perceives global warming issues. It was suggested that portraying global warming predictions as a mere "knowledge claim" underestimates the degree to which there is scientific consensus around global warming. Relativizing knowledge about global warming can only serve to diminish its credibility within sociology and society at large. The critics of social-constructionist accounts of global warming were not only concerned with how these accounts might lead to distorted views about climate and environmental sciences; there was also the broader concern that social constructionism deflects attention from the material dimension of science and technology in general (Murphy 1997). Social constructionism's critics have also suggested that this approach serves to reinforce the "exemptionalism" of mainstream sociology and to legitimate sociology's lack of attention to the biophysical environment. Finally, the critics have suggested that because social constructionism is contradictory to the core postulate of environmental sociology—that the biophysical and social worlds are connected by webs of cause and effect—the growth of constructionism could serve to undermine the stature of environmental sociology.

As central as the debate over social constructionism has been to the pulse of the field during the early and mid-1990s, our prediction is that a decade or so hence this debate will have been seen as not particularly meaningful. The social constructionists and their critics have tended to talk past each other to a considerable degree. On the one hand, the critics of social constructionism seem to have misperceived the degree to which constructionists are motivated by the goal of relativizing or challenging the facticity of global warming and related knowledges. While there are indeed some constructionists in the sociology of science and cultural studies who are so motivated, the constructionists in environmental sociology are primarily interested in how scientific knowledges are "represented," how environmental movements and environmental researchers interact in the representation of environmental knowledges, and how environmental issues are "framed" in the public sphere (see, e.g., Capek 1993; Hannigan 1995). On the other hand, social constructionists have a tendency to exaggerate the degree to which this perspective is a coherent theory. In effect, social constructionism and related approaches (e.g., discourse analysis; Hajer 1995) are more a set of concepts and methodological conventions than they are a full-blown theory. As an example, the geographers Braun and Castree (1998) have published a highly influential anthology based on the notion that constructionism needs to be joined to more fully formed theories such as neo-Marxism in order to provide clear analytical leverage in understanding social processes that shape environmental issues.

Hannigan, in his contribution to this volume, argues that "recently the concept of culture has begun to move into the forefront in environmental theory, alongside the more established human ecology and political economy approaches." Although the concept of "culture" is treated differently by different authors, there is a common unifying theme emerging—that of a separation between "rational" technical-scientific discourse on the one hand, and "a more experiential and holistic grassroots culture of the environment on the other."[9] Hannigan is keen, however, not to remain concentrated on "broad brush" theories of culture. Hannigan, much like Seippel, wants to develop mesotheoretical levels of analysis using recent work on environmental social movements and the sociology of religion.

Hannigan's emphasis is on "fluid" movements. Unlike "linear movements," which focus on a particular issue such as ozone depletion or global warming, fluid movements form "communities of discourse" that define and redefine new areas of popular discourse. He gives examples of "the sublime," which informed environmental consciousness in eighteenth- and nineteenth-century America and Britain, and "the frontier," which informed attitudes toward nineteenth-century American landscape and contemporary Australian environmental culture.

Hannigan's chapter is structured around three topics, drawing very usefully on specific examples. The first is the cultural roots of social movements—that is, the links between "environmental" culture and the culture of the wider society. Thus, environmental culture draws on existing metaphors (e.g., managing the environment as "stewards" for "future generations") that resonate more widely. The second is the creation of an environmental culture. This concerns the means by which movements create their own internal culture—the creation of general values, holding of certain people in high esteem, telling of everyday stories, key occasions/gatherings, and so on. The third is that of environmental rhetorics and residues. The interest here is in how the cultures/discourses of the new movements in turn feed back on and shape wider social and political discourses. We all "know," for example, that the McDonald's hamburger chain is responsible for massive deforestation and methane emissions in South America. But none of us has the slightest idea about where we got this information.

Hannigan concludes by making another appeal for more meso-/middle-range theoretical work, a point consistent with Seippel's article in this volume. Hannigan looks to "grounded middle-range theory," rather than permitting cultural work on the environment "to drift into a wasteland of undirected linguistic and discourse analysis where little effort is made to relate cultural meanings and practices to the overlapping domains of economics and politics." Nevertheless, he does not explore how such "overlapping" between culture and economics should be conceptualized. This seems a very significant gap and opportunity in the literature on cultural sociology and the environment. A promising starting point in this regard might be Williams's *The Country and the City* (1973), in which he shows that changing concepts of the countryside (and the city) are closely related to social and economic crisis.

As noted earlier, Yearley (1991; 1996) has played a major role in the development of a constructionist perspective in environmental sociology. The importance of Yearley's contribution to this volume is that it clarifies the value of social constructionism to environmental sociology in three critical respects. First is the construction of particular environmental problems. Taking the Brent Spar episode as a key example, Yearley shows that certain kinds of "environmental problems" surface at the expense of others. This process can be explained with reference to, for example, the particular expertise possessed by nongovernment organizations such as Greenpeace and the Worldwide Fund for Nature and the role of the media. The media (apparently) prefers stories that are "soluble." Continued bad practice or intractable problems are not "news."

The second contribution of constructionism to environmental sociology concerns the matter of what is or is not counted as "the environment." "Nodal institutions" (e.g., government agencies or the media) are responsible for creating "environmental problems." Notable, for example, are different attitudes toward population. Many in "the North" (particularly right-leaning ideologues in the North) see population as a pressing problem for the environment. Meanwhile, development campaigners in "the South" point to excessive consumption in the United States and elsewhere. Yearley points to the ways in which "surrogates" (especially wildlife and human health) are used in environmental campaign strategies.

The third area of contribution of constructionism to environmental sociology is in demonstrating that science is itself "socially constructed." Yearley uses "biodiversity" to advance this argument, suggesting that it has been consistently used by biological scientists and ecologists as a scientific measure. But Yearley stresses that biodiversity does not comprise a measure that can be used in all circumstances (since, e.g., some "natural areas" such as boglands have naturally little biodiversity). Some areas, such as gardens, have high biodiversity but this does not necessarily make them biologically valuable. Finally, the claimed equation between protected areas and high levels of biodiversity is often based on just a few examples. In summary, "an apparently systematic term has displaced previous more qualitative approaches. However, the term bears signs of its own construction."

Yearley concludes by commenting on the increasingly influential theory of "ecological modernization." As advanced by writers such as Mol (1995; 1997) and Spaargaren (1996), ecological modernization implies a direction to development whereby "technological development, industrial policy, and environmental improvement can pull in the same direction." But Yearley argues that making this assertion as a statement of what is currently happening (as distinct from what could happen) is unjustified. Addressing a problem from an increasingly "scientific" angle "does not necessarily yield the best or most correct construal of the problems facing society." Yearley concludes by supporting those saying "ecological modernization" is an ideology, one easily latched on to by policymakers, politicians, and so on (a point somewhat similar to that made by Hajer [1995]).

McKechnie and Welsh's chapter is yet another contribution to this volume in which the authors have felt obliged to address the increasingly prominent ecological modernization tradition of Mol (1995; 1997), Spaargaren (1996), and associates. McKechnie and Welsh, however, are more concerned about addressing the applicability of several closely related modernist perspectives, such as the reflexive modernization theories of Beck (1992), Giddens (1991), and Lash (e.g., Beck, Giddens, and Lash 1994), and the related European NSMs tradition. Their reflections on reflexive modernization and reflexivity show that these terms do not necessarily reflect a coherent vocabulary and ontology among their adherents. Beck, Giddens, and Lash are shown to define reflexive modernization and reflexivity in quite different ways. While McKechnie and Welsh have a number of problems with these concepts, they are most troubled by Giddens's use of the reflexive modernization concept.

McKechnie and Welsh have two interrelated objections to the increasingly widespread and casual use of the notions of reflexive modernization, reflexivity, and NSMs. First, they use a number of empirical examples of contested environmental struggles in the United Kingdom (e.g., direct action against road projects, the nuclear controversy involving nuclear fallout from Chernobyl, and sheep farming) to show that these structurally derived overarching categories tend to obscure rather than illuminate the content of environmental struggles. Second, they make a particularly strong case that while reflexive modernization, reflexivity, and NSMs may reflect relatively well the nature of political action organizations and the discursive practices of well-placed activists, they are not useful in reflecting the concerns, discourses, and strategies of subordinate groups (and "silent social spaces"). McKechnie and Welsh argue for the need for "a new language of discovery" that will help to uncover the realities of deep cultural conflict over symbolic and material resources. If reflexivity and NSMs capture reasonably well the structural locations, concerns, and discourses of articulate environmental activists who contest policy and mainstream science at centralized levels of decision making, "civil sociations," "proxemics" (situated local practices), and prophecy are more useful in depicting the "inarticulate speech of the heart" that comes to the fore during the symbolic and cultural contestations of concern within their chapter. Reflexivity, reflexive modernization, and NSMs, in the view of McKechnie and Welsh, are essentially modernist categories and presume the dominion of science and instrumental rationality within social relations. They argue particularly strongly for the utility of their notion "civil sociation," which they define as "specifically local/proximate/proxemic sources of reflection with a particularly strong aesthetic component." While these civil sociations lie outside of dominant modernist institutions and discourses, they are sites of passion and vitality and are perhaps the best hope for "transcendent visions," without which, McKechnie and Welsh note, all there is is "better rationality and more capitalism"—a prospect that is less than inspiring.

SOME FINAL WORDS

This volume demonstrates that theory in environmental sociology has exhibited several major trends over the past decade. First, the theoretical repertoire of environmental sociology is significantly larger, and the scope of theoretical work is significantly more complex, than during the first two decades of the subdiscipline. Second, environmental sociologists are more actively engaging the major theoretical issues of discipline-wide relevance. Third, environmental sociology is tending to maintain its character or integrity in the sense of placing a high priority on conceptualizing the human relationship to the natural world as both antecedent and consequence.

No doubt, there can come a point at which a subdiscipline has become too eclectic and so unfocused so that it is has become a subdiscipline in only the loosest sense. Has environmental sociology come to be characterized by excessive pluralism or by theoretical disarray? We think not, for one basic reason: While the environmental-sociological theoretical repertoire is clearly more diverse and substantial than it was in the 1980s, there has been a surprising degree of continuity in the empirical issues of concern to environmental-sociological theorists and researchers over this period of time. The empirical issues of interest are to a significant degree the same ones that commanded attention in the late 1980s and early 1990s: the nature of environmental social movements; states, politics, and environmental policy formation; environmental attitudes, beliefs, and values; the relationships between consumption and production institutions; the reciprocal impacts of societies and environments; the role of technology in social and environmental change; and the significance of "the global" in terms of "environmental scale" and social institutions. Thus, the new directions of theory represented in this volume mostly contribute to rather than undermine continuity and cumulation in environmental sociology.

Finally, it is worth noting that *Sociological Theory and the Environment* is a product of a very special type of collaboration among a group of several dozen scholars that has been made possible through the auspices of the Environment and Society Research Committee (RC 24) of the International Sociological Association. With a few exceptions, the chapters in this volume were prepared for an RC 24-sponsored conference on sociological theory and the natural environment held at the Woudschoten Conference Center near Geist, Netherlands. The chapters have been revised in light of the commentary at the Woudschoten conference and through subsequent interactions at and following the International Sociological Association World Congress for Sociology held at Montreal in August 1998. We believe this book represents far more than the mere fact that international scholarly collaboration can occur and bear fruit. We also suggest that global intellectual cross-fertilization has been extremely healthy for environmental sociology in several additional ways; these chapters point the way to an exciting future of cross-cultural analysis, cross-national comparison, world-systemic insight, and global-scale socioecological analysis.

NOTES

1. This is not to deny that there was a substantial community of sociologists (mostly rural sociologists) who had been actively engaged in sociological research on natural resource issues for more than a decade (Field and Burch 1988).

2. The first contradiction is the tendency toward realization crisis or overaccumulation of capital, which is induced by the private appropriation of surplus and the tendency under capitalist competition for wages to be insufficient to purchase commodities.

3. Some neo-Marxists not only have agreed with the notion that Marx had Promethean views (e.g., Grundmann 1991), but also have defended Marx on this account and have argued that contemporary forms of environmentalism and environmental mobilization are inconsistent with the Marxist tradition.

4. The Roberts and Grimes chapter in this volume on the World-System approach to environmental sociology is also germane to the neo-Marxist tradition in the field.

5. Also note that Dickens's chapter includes a brief account of "critical realism," a notion that he pioneered in his first book in environmental sociology (Dickens 1992). While a good share of environmental sociology during its first-quarter century has been self-consciously "realist" (or "objectivist"), some more recent works in environmental sociology have been critical of realism (e.g., Yearley's chapter in this volume). Realism is the doctrine that there are structures and forces independent of our direct experience of objects and is typically put forward in opposition to idealism—the notion that there is no reality apart from that which is perceived. Dickens notes that as persuasive as realism might seem, and as persuasive as it was to Marx, it has two key limitations. First, adherence to realism tends to lead to reductionism, and second, a realist epistemology tends to ignore mediating and contingent factors in explanations and fails to appreciate the contestedness of science. Dickens has advanced the notion of critical realism as a means of simultaneously avoiding the idealist alternative and the shortcomings of realism. By critical realism, Dickens means a posture that takes a historically specific view of causation and maintains a distinction between underlying mechanisms and "contingent conditions" (which may include environmental phenomena).

6. Note the connection to the alienation theme in Marxism (in Benton's chapter in this volume).

7. Note that Roberts and Grimes's and related "environmentalized" forms of World-System analysis (see also Ciccantell and Bunker 1998) are yet another dimension of the often-unrecognized linkages of neo-Marxism to natural resources and the natural world.

8. But as will be noted later, Macnaghten and Urry (1998) have noted that while materialist and idealist ontologies are normally thought of as being mutually exclusive, North American environmental sociology has maintained a materialist ontology in its theoretical work on explaining environmental destruction, while exhibiting an idealist ontology in its treatment of environmental attitudes and movements.

9. Note that this is a theme addressed by a number of authors in this collection, not just those on the "cultural" side of environmental sociology.

REFERENCES

Bauman, Z. 1993. *Postmodern Ethics.* Oxford: Basil Blackwell.

Beck, U. 1992. *Risk Society.* Beverly Hills, Calif.: Sage.

Beck, U., A. Giddens, and S. Lash. 1994. *Reflexive Moderisation.* Cambridge: Polity.

Benton, T. 1989. "Marxism and Natural Limits." *New Left Review* 178:51–86.

———. ed. 1996. *The Greening of Marxism.* New York: Guilford.

Benton, T., and M. Redclift, eds. 1994. *Social Theory and the Global Environment.* London: Routledge.

Bourdieu, P. 1977. *Outline of a Theory of Practice.* Cambridge: Cambridge University Press.

Braun, B., and N. Castree, eds. 1998. *Remaking Reality.* London: Routledge.

Burkett, P. 1999. *Marx and Nature: A Red and Green Perspective.* New York: St. Martin's.

Buttel, F. H. 1996. "Environmental and Resource Sociology: Theoretical Issues and Opportunities for Synthesis." *Rural Sociology* 61:56–76.

———. 2000. "Classical Theory and Contemporary Environmental Sociology: Some Reflections on the Antecedents and Prospects for Reflexive Modernization Theories in the Study of Environment and Society." In *Environment and Global Modernity,* ed. G. Spaargaren et al., 17–39. London: Sage.

Capek, S. 1993. "The 'Environmental Justice' Frame: A Conceptual Discussion and an Application." *Social Problems* 40:5–24.

Castells, M. 1980. *The Economic Crisis and American Society.* Ed. A. P. J. Mol and F. H. Buttel. Princeton, N.J.: Princeton University Press.

Catton, W. R., Jr. 1976. "Why the Future Isn't What It Used to Be (and How It Could Be Made Worse Than It Has to Be)." *Social Science Quarterly* 57:276–291.

———. 1980. *Overshoot.* Urbana: University of Illinois Press.

Catton, W. R., Jr., and R. E. Dunlap. 1978. "Environmental Sociology: A New Paradigm." *The American Sociologist* 13:41–49.

———. 1980. "A New Ecological Paradigm for Post-exuberant Sociology." *American Behavioral Scientist* 24:15–47.

Ciccantell, P., and S. G. Bunker, eds. 1998. *Space and Transport in the World-System.* Westport, Conn.: Greenwood.

Dickens, P. 1992. *Society and Nature.* Philadelphia: Temple University Press.

———. 1996. *Reconstructing Nature.* London: Routledge.

Dunlap, R. E. 1997. "The Evolution of Environmental Sociology: A Brief History and Assessment of the American Experience." In *The International Handbook of Environmental Sociology,* ed. M. Redclift and G. Woodgate, 21–39. Cheltenham, UK: Edward Elgar.

Dunlap, R. E., and W. R. Catton Jr. 1994. "Struggling with Human Exemptionalism: The Rise, Decline and Revitalization of Environmental Sociology." *The American Sociologist* 25:5–30.

Eder, K. 1996. *The Social Construction of Nature.* London: Sage.

Edgell, S., K. Hetherington, and A. Warde, eds. 1997. *Consumption Matters.* Oxford: Basil Blackwell.

Field, D. R., and W. R. Burch Jr. 1988. *Rural Sociology and the Environment.* Westport, Conn.: Greenwood.

Foster, J. B. 1999. "Marx's Theory of Metabolic Rift: Classical Foundations for Environmental Sociology." *American Journal of Sociology* 105:366–405.

———. 2000. *Marx's Ecology: Materialism and Nature.* New York: Monthly Review.

Freese, L. 1997. *Environmental Connections: Advances in Human Ecology.* Supp. 1. Pt. B. Greenwich, Conn.: JAI Press.

Giddens, A. 1991. *The Consequences of Modernity.* Cambridge: Polity.

———. 1998. *The Third Way.* Cambridge: Polity.

Goldblatt, D. 1996. *Social Theory and the Environment.* Boulder, Colo.: Westview.

Gould, K. A., A. Schnaiberg, and A. S. Weinberg. 1996. *Environmental Struggles.* New York: Cambridge University Press.

Grundmann, R. 1991. *Marxism and Ecology.* New York: Oxford University Press.

Hajer, M. 1995. *The Politics of Environmental Discourse.* New York: Oxford University Press.

Hannigan, J. 1995. *Environmental Sociology.* London: Routledge.

Macnaghten, P., and J. Urry. 1998. *Contested Natures.* London: Sage.

Martell, L. 1994. *Ecology and Society.* Amherst: University of Massachusetts Press.

Mellor, M. 1997. "Gender and the Environment." In *The International Handbook of Environmental Sociology,* ed. M. Redclift and G. Woodgate, 195–203. Cheltenham, UK: Edward Elgar.

Mol, A. P. J. 1995. *The Refinement of Production.* Utrecht: Van Arkel.

———. 1997. "Ecological Modernization: Industrial Transformations and Environmental Reform." In *The International Handbook of Environmental Sociology,* ed. M. Redclift and G. Woodgate, 138–149. London: Edward Elgar.

Murphy, R. 1994. *Rationality and Nature.* Boulder, Colo.: Westview.

———. 1997. *Sociology and Nature.* Boulder, Colo.: Westview.

O'Connor, J. 1973. *The Fiscal Crisis of the State.* New York: St. Martin's.

———. 1994. "Is Sustainable Capitalism Possible?" In *Is Capitalism Sustainable?* ed. M. O'Connor. New York: Guilford.

Prades, J. A. 1999. "Global Environmental Change and Contemporary Society: Classical Sociological Analysis Revisited." *International Sociology* 14:7–32.

Redclift, M. 1996. *Wasted.* London: Earthscan.

Redclift, M., and G. Woodgate, eds. 1997a. *The International Handbook of Environmental Sociology.* London: Edward Elgar.

———. 1997b. "Sustainability and Social Construction." In *The International Handbook of Environmental Sociology,* M. Redclift and G. Woodgate, 55–70. London: Edward Elgar.

Rosa, E. A., and T. Dietz. 1998. "Climate Change and Society: Speculation, Construction, and Scientific Investigation." *International Sociology* 13:421–455.

Schnaiberg, A. 1980. *The Environment.* New York: Oxford University Press.

Spaargaren, G. 1996. "The Ecological Modernization of Production and Consumption." Ph.D. diss., Wageningen University.

Taylor, B. R., ed. 1995. *Ecological Resistance Movements.* Albany: SUNY Press.

Taylor, P. J., and F. H. Buttel. 1992. "How Do We Know We Have Global Environmental Problems? Science and the Globalization of Environmental Discourse." *Geoforum* 23:405–416.

Warde, A. 1997. *Consumption, Food, and Taste.* London: Sage.

Weber, M. 1968. *Economy and Society.* Ed. G. Roth and C. Wittich. 1922. Reprint, Berkeley: University of California Press.

West, P. C. 1984. "Max Weber's Human Ecology of Historical Societies." In *Theory of Liberty, Legitimacy and Power,* ed. V. Murvar, 216–234. Boston: Routledge and Kegan Paul.

Williams, R. 1973. *The Country and the City.* New York: Oxford University Press.

World Commission on Environment and Development. 1987. *Our Common Future.* New York: Oxford University Press.

Wynne, B. 1996. "May the Sheep Safely Graze? A Reflexive View of the Expert-Lay Knowledge Divide." In *Risk, Environment, and Modernity*, ed. S. Lash, B. Szerszynski, and B. Wynne. London: Sage.

Yearley, S. 1991. *The Green Case*. London: HarperCollins.

———. 1996. *Sociology, Environmentalism, Globalization*. London: Sage.

Zimmerer, K. 1994. "Human Geography and the New Ecology." *Annals of the Association of American Geographers* 84:108–125.

Part II

THE CLASSICAL TRADITION AND ENVIRONMENTAL SOCIOLOGY

2

Environmental Sociology and the Classical Sociological Tradition: Some Observations on Current Controversies

Frederick H. Buttel

Sociology is often pointed to as the social science discipline with the strongest linkages to the classical tradition. For example, most sociology Ph.D.s have a basic familiarity with the sociologies of Marx, Weber, Durkheim, and so on, and it is essentially universal that sociologists who consider themselves to be "theorists" have close familiarity with the primary works of the major classical theorists.[1] Classical theory remains a core requirement in most graduate sociology programs throughout the Western world. Virtually every sociological theory text on sociological theory makes the claim that classical sociology has strongly influenced the development of the sociological discipline and that classical theory is still highly relevant to the sociological enterprise (e.g., Morrison 1995). One frequently encounters claims that virtually all important sociological notions—even the ideas of contemporary postmodern theorists—were "anticipated" by the classical theorists (Hughes, Martin, and Sharrock 1995).

But despite the clear role that the classics continue to play in contemporary sociology, the typical sociologist in the world today would be very unlikely to consult, much less devote serious study to, the *Grundrisse, Capital, Suicide, Division of Labor in Society, Economy and Society,* or *The Protestant Ethic and the Spirit of Capitalism* during a typical workday (or a typical work-year, for that matter). Pieces of classical sociological scholarship are rarely cited in the contemporary sociological research literature. Many influential sociological theorists such as Giddens (1987: chapter 2) and Wallerstein (1991) have claimed that the contexts and assumptions of nineteenth-century classical theory are no longer relevant to the late twentieth century and that progress in social theory will require jettisoning the classical sociological tradition. Some sociologists now go so far as to say that by the 1940s the "classical project"—the development of sociological abstraction aimed at addressing moral and political problems—had undergone "dissolution" (Wardell and Turner 1986).

The less-than-complete fidelity of modern sociology to its classical heritage arguably has been the case more so in environmental sociology than in any other late twentieth-century specialty area. During most of environmental sociology's first-quarter century, it was conventional wisdom that "mainstream" or conventional sociology had gone astray (by having ignored the biophysical environment) and had only limited relevance to environmental sociology (because of the many decades of innocence about the role of biophysical factors in social life). Most overviews of the field (e.g., Dunlap and Catton 1979; Buttel 1986; 1996; Goldblatt 1996; Martell 1994) began, almost by ritual or reflex, with a critical commentary on the past century or so of sociology and how it had gone wrong in dispatching the biophysical environmental as a set of phenomena worthy of sociological interest. Many environmental sociologists (e.g., Catton 1980) began to chart courses of inquiry in which the works of mainstream sociology—both classical and contemporary—played little role. Indeed, a certain component of the momentum behind environmental sociology in the late 1970s and 1980s had to do with its iconoclastic stance toward conventional sociology. The preoccupation of early environmental sociology with accounting for why Western sociology was incapable of accounting for environmental crises and problems provided much of the focus of environmental sociology during its early years.

In this chapter, I provide a brief overview of and commentary on environmental sociology's ambivalence toward the classical tradition during its first-quarter century. I note that environmental sociology in its earliest days (particularly the early 1970s) was not particularly dismissive or rebellious toward classical sociology—or toward midcentury sociology for that matter. I then turn my attention to the period, from approximately the late 1970s through the late 1990s, when the received view in environmental sociology was that the classical tradition was substantially flawed in terms of setting forth promising perspectives for understanding environmental problems and issues. Finally, I note the renaissance of attention of environmental sociologists to classical sociology and identify some ways in which environmental sociology's incipient rapprochement with the classical tradition will benefit not only environmental sociology, but also the larger sociological community through a more comprehensive perspective on the classics.

A BRIEF HISTORY OF THE ENVIRONMENTAL SOCIOLOGICAL REACTION TO THE CLASSICAL TRADITION

It is useful to begin with two observations about American sociology in the 1960s and 1970s, the decade immediately preceding the rise of environmental sociology.

First, standard accounts of the classical tradition at the time made virtually no reference to notions such as the environment, ecology, or nature. As a representative example, take Coser's *Masters of Sociological Thought* (1971), which was clearly one of the most influential secondary treatments of the classical theorists of its era. To my knowledge, the only references made about the environment, ecology, or nature in Coser's book were (1) oblique references to Chicago-style human ecology in connection with Cooley and Park, and (2) a very strong claim by Coser on the first page of the chapter on Simmel (177), in which Coser stresses that Simmel categorically rejected "organicist" theories. Thus, Coser, like virtually all theorists of his era, had almost completely sanitized secondary accounts of the classics of any mention of their treatments of nature, natural resources, the environment, and the biophysical world.

Second, it is also the case that the works of the "pre-exemplars" of environmental sociology (those who in some sense did environmental sociology before the subdiscipline was recognized) were largely anchored in midcentury sociology, for example, the neo-Ogburnianism of Cottrell (1955) and the functionalism of Firey (1960). For example, the first major work of contemporary (post–Earth Day) environmental sociology, Burch's *Daydreams and Nightmares* (1971), reflects an eclectic (or agnosically respectful) posture toward the classics. Early environmental sociological research on the environmental movement (Burch, Cheek, and Taylor 1972) was quite similar to ordinary public opinion and attitude research of the day. In most every respect, protoenvironmental sociology from the 1950s through the early 1970s was indistinguishable from "mainstream" sociology of the time. Even the most central works of the first stage (from Earth Day until approximately 1975) of modern environmental sociology in North America (e.g., Burch 1971; Burch, Cheek, and Taylor 1972; Klausner 1971) were not particularly rebellious about either mainstream sociology or the classical tradition. In these early days of environmental social science, the principal voices of theoretical defiance on behalf of the environment were *not* those of environmental sociologists. Instead, nonsociologists such as Webb (1952), Wilkinson (1973), and Bookchin (1971) were the most visible or influential social science scholars who criticized mainstream inquiry for its lack of attention to the environment.

This second stage of the development of (North American) environmental sociology consisted of the elaboration of what I have earlier (Buttel 1986) referred to as the "new human ecology," and what Dunlap and Catton have referred to as the "new ecological paradigm." Integral to the new human ecology was a certain hostility toward mainstream sociology, as well as the desire to build a new sociological theory in which biophysical variables would play a definite and central role. The most central figures in the new human ecology were, of course, Dunlap and Catton. In their late 1970s and early 1980s writings, Dunlap and Catton articulated the notion of "paradigm" as part of an ecological critique of mainstream sociological theory (e.g., Catton 1976; Catton and Dunlap 1978; Dunlap and Catton 1979; 1983). There is scarcely a significant text in environmental sociology today that fails to cite one or more of these early works by Dunlap and Catton as having provided the template for modern environmental sociology.

The Catton and Dunlap (1978) article and its sequel (Dunlap and Catton 1979) would ultimately become two of the most widely cited pieces in support of the interpretation that environmental sociology came of age through a rejection of classical theory.[2] In retrospect, we can see that it is somewhat arguable whether this is the correct interpretation of their papers. In essence, the early Catton-Dunlap papers made the claim that conventional twentieth-century sociology, despite persistent debate among functionalists, neo-Marxists, symbolic interactionists, and so on, exhibited a shared exemptionalism—a presumption that humans and societies are essentially exempt from the laws of the biosphere. To be sure, Catton and Dunlap discussed some of the historical roots of exemptionalism, claiming that Durkheim's social facts injunction typified and legitimated the exemptionalist posture. The interpretation of Catton and Dunlap as having categorically rejected the classical tradition arguably rests as much on my own interpretation of their work (e.g., Buttel 1978) as on their own writings. Nonetheless, the tenor of the times was that many environmental sociologists were receptive to the notion that mainstream sociology had serious shortcomings on account of the influence of the classical theorists. The assertion that the classical tradition was irrelevant to environmental sociology remained an article of faith within North American (and to a considerable, but lesser, extent in European) environmental-sociological circles (Dickens 1992; Martell 1994), and the late 1970s papers by Catton and Dunlap were almost always cited in support of this proposition. Essentially, then, the core of North American environmental sociology—or, in other words, the new human ecology—has tended to be formed in *opposition or in response* to mainstream sociology and/or the classical tradition.

CLASSICAL SOCIOLOGY AND
THE ENVIRONMENT

Even if we accept that a successful environmental sociology had to be formed in opposition to so-called mainstream sociology—and I grant that not all observers would agree on this score—is it also the case that environmental sociology has had to distance itself from the classical tradition?[3] This question, in my view, does not lend itself to a convenient response. It can be argued, for example, that each of the three major classical theorists can be seen to have developed or elaborated one or more theoretical premises or methodological injunctions that can be regarded as "exemptionalist" or as unconducive to considering biophysical factors as independent or dependent variables. Again, Durkheim is well known for his "social facts" injunction—the notion that the role of sociology is to explain or account for "social facts," while employing (exclusively) other social facts as explanatory factors. Durkheim's social facts injunction was propounded to distinguish sociology from psychology and biology and to distance it from utilitarianism. Marx's relentless critiques of Malthus were intended to distinguish historical materialism from the oversimplifications of Malthusian population/food arithmetic. Weber could not have been more emphatic about the fact that sociology is a discipline in which evolutionary reasoning, and any other styles of reasoning from biology and the natural sciences, must be rejected because societies and natural systems have qualitatively different dynamics.

In evaluating the ostensible "exemptionalism" of the classical theorists, we ought not ignore that some very constructive purposes were served in the classical theorists' having distanced themselves from "organicism" and having established the legitimacy of a social science distinct from both the natural sciences and humanities or "moral sciences." Durkheim, Weber, and Simmel, for example, helped to establish sociology as we know it through their critiques of evolutionism, idealism, utilitarianism, and historicism. Their work along with that of Marx helped to establish sociology as an overarching social science discipline committed to science and objectivity and to a comprehensive and historically informed account of social structure and change.

Humphrey and I (Buttel and Humphrey 2002) have argued elsewhere, however, that there is, in a certain important sense, *a classical environmental sociology.* Elements of environmental sociology have roots deep in nineteenth-century social thought. Not only did Marx, Durkheim, and Weber incorporate what we might regard as ecological components in their works, they did so from a variety of standpoints. Among the multiple ecologically relevant components of their works are materialist ontologies (in the case of Marx and Engels), biological analogies (Durkheim), use of Darwinian/evolutionary arguments or schemas (Marx, Durkheim, and Weber), the notion of nature-society "metabolism" (Marx), and concrete empirical analyses of natural-resource or "environmental" issues (Marx and Weber).

Marx and Engels worked from a materialist ontology, which should be understood to mean not only a structural/nonidealist posture and an emphasis on the conditions of production and labor, but also an understanding that, in principle, the predominance of the sphere of production and social labor cannot be understood apart from nature. This is particularly clear if one reads the early "philosophical" works by Marx (those published in 1844 or earlier), in which the notions of "nature" and the material world are employed frequently, and in a nondeterministic or dialectical manner (Parsons 1977). It is thus no accident that contemporary works in environmental sociology that are explicitly neo-Marxist (e.g., Dickens 1992) often draw their main inspiration from the works of the early Marx. But while the work of the young Marx was quite ecological in some respects, this does not imply that the later work of Marx (and Engels) was devoid of references to nature and the natural world.[4] Marx and Engels, for example, frequently referred to the penetration of capitalism as a cause of massive air pollution and other threats to the health and welfare of workers and to the need for political economy to treat relations between society and nature (Dickens 1992; Parsons 1977). Parsons (1977) and Burkett (1996) have noted how Marx was fascinated by agronomy and the biology of agricultural production, and in *Capital* Marx often used agronomic examples to demonstrate the role of nature in social production (for more recent and detailed analyses of this point, see Foster [1999; 2000]). Burkett (1996), in his elegant defense of Marx against claims that his methodology is unecological, makes particular note of the fact that Marx's analysis of modes of production includes not only class (or people-people) relations, but also the relations of material appropriation (people-nature relations). Marx and Engels's schema positing the contradictory development of class societies and the revolutionary transformation from one mode of production to another contains an evolutionary component based on Darwin's work (Lopreato 1984). As I note later on, environmental social-science theories have tended to incorporate one (and sometimes both) of two constitutive elements: a materialist outlook and an emancipatory orientation. Thus, among the reasons for the particular relevance of the young Marx to environmental sociology is that Marx's work prior to 1845 or so tended to reflect both materialist and emancipatory postures. Furthermore, I suggest that Marx's use of the notion of metabolism ("*Stoffwechsel*," typically translated into English as "material exchange" between "man and nature") has led to a very interesting and provocative renaissance of Marxist theory in environmental sociology.

Like Marx, Durkheim also set forth a modified evolutionary schema and relied heavily on metaphors from Darwinian evolution and organismic biology. While Durkheim questioned Spencer's argument that evolutionary change led to continuous progress, his theory was based on an evolutionary view of social change (Turner 1994). The master direction of change was from primitive societies with a low division of labor to modern societies with a complex division of labor (at least according to *The Division of Labor in Society* [1893]). Durkheim, however, differed from Spencer in emphasizing the disruptive qualities of change. The transition from primitive to modern societies was accompanied by anomie and a breakdown of social solidarity and regulation. While Durkheim anticipated that modernizing societies would ultimately exhibit new, more effective organic solidarity, he regarded the establishment of adequate integration and solidarity to be problematic.

Durkheim freely used biological concepts in presenting his theories of social evolution and solidarity, as is evident in the concept of organic solidarity. *The Rules of Sociological Method* (1895) referred to various types of societies along the continuum from traditional to modern as "species" or "societal species." Moreover, his most famous work *The Division of Labor in Society* (1893) set forth the major elements of a theoretical perspective that has come to be known as (classical) human ecology. The *Division*'s famous schema for explaining the transition from mechanical to organic solidarity was rich in imagery about population density, resource scarcity, and competition for survival that bears a strong resemblance to more modern notions of human ecology.

A final classical theorist widely considered to be among the most influential in Western sociology is Weber. While Marx and Durkheim largely assumed that there was some knowable a priori direction of social change, Weber firmly rejected the theoretical viewpoint that there was a unilinear course of societal development. Social change was determined by shifting constellations of subjective, structural, and technological forces that were ultimately rooted in human motivations and history. Moreover, Weber (1968) was an outspoken opponent of social Darwinism, and he frequently stressed how social science differed from biological sciences and that the methods and concepts of the former must be different than those of the latter. As such, Weber's work has been taken to be the first decisive break from nineteenth-century evolutionism anchored in biological analogies (for comprehensive overviews of "social evolutionism," see Sanderson [1990], Burns and Dietz [1992], and Dietz and Burns [1992]). Interestingly, Weber's works that most clearly reflect the break with biological analyses are those such as *The Agrarian Sociology of Ancient Civilizations* and his *General Economic History*, in which material on the impacts of social structures on natural resources or the impact of natural resources on social organization is most prominent. However, these are two of Weber's works that are least often read by sociologists during their first courses in social theory and that are least often discussed in major secondary treatments.

The multiple respects in which Weber's work can be seen to accommodate an environmental or human-ecological dimension can be most dramatically illustrated by contrasting the neo-Weberian environmental sociologies of West (1984) and Murphy (1994). These two scholars draw on what might be regarded as entirely different "corners" of Weber's work. According to West (1984), from Weber's historical sociology of religion and his empirical research on ancient society one can distill a human ecology that is rich and provocative for contemporary environmental sociology. Weber's historical and comparative method rested on environmental factors playing casually important roles at times in history. Weber treated environmental factors as interacting in complex casual models, and they "frequently affect complex societies through favoring the 'selective survival' of certain strata over others" (232). It is arguably the case that Weber's (probably unintended) use of Darwinian imagery was truer to Darwin's theory than was that of Spencer and others. Thus, for West the relevance of Weber's work to environmental sociology is not only that Weber analyzed concrete instances of struggles over resources (e.g., control of irrigation systems), but also that Weber's causal logic was essentially a Darwinian one that still has the potential to help build bridges between sociology and the ecological sciences.

While West's (1984) account of Weber's sociology of environment and natural resources is anchored in Weber's comparative macrohistorical sociology, Murphy (1994) has developed a Weberian environmental sociology based largely on a completely different literature: Weber's concept of rationalization and his ideal-types of rationality and orientations to action drawn primarily from *Economy and Society* (1968). Murphy (1994) argues that rationalization and the expansion of formal rationality have involved the tendency to an ethic of mastery over nature (or the "plasticity" of the relationship between humans and their natural environment), to the quest for technologies to realize this mastery, and to a lack of attention to human threats to the environment. Similar to Weber's notion of charismatic authority, Murphy suggests that the ecological irrationalities caused by rationalization will stimulate social movements that aim at "derationalization" or "rerationalization" of modern institutions.

It is useful to conclude this discussion of classical sociology and the environment with a few observations that depart in some respects from the conventional wisdom within environmental sociology during the late 1970s to the late 1990s. One must indeed recognize that there is something to the notion that the major classical theorists tended to take radically sociological (and thus "exemptionalist") positions. Indeed, as will be noted later, one of the characteristics of the sociological project as it emerged from the key figures of nineteenth-century thought was that a sociological explanation is more elegant to the degree that its underlying concepts are thoroughly social, and that as such they abstract beyond the natural world. But while classical theory did tend toward a radically sociological outlook, the classical theorists by no means completely neglected the biophysical world. We thus need to recognize that the "exemptionalism" of the classical tradition can be exaggerated and that the neglect of the biophysical environment in twentieth-century sociology cannot be accounted for only by the "exemptionalism" of the classical tradition. Also, as will be stressed later, we need to bear in mind that a large share of the contemporary environmental sociological theory literature has been explicitly anchored in the works of one or more classical theorists.

The lack of attention to the environment in sociological inquiry has arguably had as much or more to do with the historical conditions of the establishment of sociology in the nineteenth and early twentieth centuries. First, there was an imperative to distinguish sociology from other natural and social science disciplines (especially psychology, biology, economics, philosophy, and religious studies). Second, we also need to take into account the historical role of the strong reaction against social Darwinism and geographical-environmental determinism. Finally, the lack of attention to the environment was as much a reflection of Western culture—of its Enlightenment influences, its consumerism, its having been mesmerized by the five-hundred-year boom, its colonial and postcolonial expansionism, its celebration after the defeat of fascism, and so on—as it was a prescription from the classical theorists. In fact, classical theory is much more "ecological," or much more likely to recognize the materiality (Buttel 1996) of social life, than was mainstream post–World War II sociology. The dominant forms of sociology at midcentury—Parsonian functionalism, postindustrial society theory, logic of industrialization theory, modernization theory, and pluralism—were arguably far less anchored in the natural world than were the sociologies of Marx, Durkheim, Weber, Simmel, Tönnies, and so on.

The classical tradition, of course, should not be seen as being above criticism. There are clearly some definite limitations of classical theory for understanding the environment. Interestingly, among the limitations of the classical tradition for understanding the environment are several shortcomings—its Eurocentricity, its assumption of the national-state as the self-evident unit of analysis, and its innocence about "globalization"—that it shares with most of contemporary environmental sociology.

THE THEORETICAL DEVELOPMENT OF NORTH AMERICAN ENVIRONMENTAL SOCIOLOGY

To the extent that the classical tradition can be regarded as "exemptionalist" or unecological, I consider the exemptionalism of the classical theorists to have been more a necessary step in the development of a nondeterministic sociological tradition and a creative synthesis of extant sociologies than a fatal flaw. This is to say, the classical tradition represented the liberation of social science from a series of reductionisms and chauvinisms—of biological analogies, utilitarianism, the German (neoclassical economics) analytical school, psychology, clericalism, nationalism, and so on. Overcoming these reductionisms and prejudices enabled the development of an overarching or encompassing social science discipline that would be able to accommodate a variety of explanatory schemes and methods, to explore a variety of empirical problems, and to do so while observing an ethic of objectivity.

Likewise, we need to be respectfully critical of 1970s and 1980s North American environmental sociology as having been a necessary, but incomplete, step in the development of thought about societal-environmental relations. I believe that North American environmental sociology should be seen as a point of departure, rather than as an end-point for a period of "normal science," primarily on account of the fact that this literature was developed as much in reaction to mainstream sociology and in metatheoretical terms as it was developed as a source of specific hypotheses to explain societal-environmental relations.

Though the underlying strategy for promulgating a "new ecological paradigm" in sociology was not often clearly articulated, the pioneers of North American environmental sociology can be seen to have reacted to, and to have striven to influence, mainstream sociology by employing three major arguments: First, the authors of the major works in environmental sociology tended to stress documenting the seriousness of the environmental crisis (e.g., Catton 1980; Catton and Dunlap 1978; Schnaiberg 1980), mainly by citation to popularized treatments of ecology by persons such as Ehrlich and Commoner. The tendency for environmental sociology to be situated in ecological literatures that call attention to environmental crisis remains strong today (e.g., Murphy 1997; Dunlap 1997). Second, these major works tended to theorize about how and why the regular or customary institutional dynamics of modern industrial societies—market processes, capitalist relations, industrial relations, urbanization, political democracy and corporatist structures, social norms and cultural values, and science and technological innovation—have tended to involve *intrinsic or necessary trends to environmental degradation and crisis.*[5] Third, while the overall stress of these theories was to explain degradation, and thus was essentially pessimistic, at the same time these theories all held out hope that these dynamics can and would be negated or overridden through public value change and/or environmental movement mobilization. Thus, public value change and the environmental movement were portrayed as being rational and necessary responses to environmental crisis, and social policy change resulting from movement mobilization and pressure was seen to be the principal mechanism of environmental improvement (e.g., Milbrath 1984; see the discussion in Yearley 1996).

Catton and Dunlap have articulated each of these three rationales for a specialized field of environmental sociology and for why these premises should be reflected in mainstream sociology in a particularly clear way. During the early years of North American environmental sociology, Catton (1976; 1980) documented in particularly comprehensive fashion the ominous implications for the human species of ongoing trends toward environmental destruction. In so doing, he showed that the core institutions of contemporary industrial societies had been developed during a long period of (apparent) abundance—the "500-year boom" dating from the heyday of mercantilism and the beginnings of capitalism—though Catton has hastened to stress that much of this abundance was ephemeral because it was based on past or future "ghost acreage." Catton suggested further that these institutions have persisted up to this day and have had remarkable momentum and inertia. Dunlap and Catton (1994) have also stressed the continuing force of the "dominant Western worldview" among publics in terms of how this worldview props up the institutional practices portrayed in Catton's earlier work (e.g., Catton 1976). Finally, Dunlap and Catton (1994) have developed strong arguments about why environmentalism is a progressive force that should be supported by the social science community.

Schnaiberg's environmental sociology (Schnaiberg 1980; Schnaiberg and Gould 1993; Gould, Schnaiberg, and Weinberg 1996), probably second only to Dunlap and Catton's (1994) in its influence throughout North America, has likewise been anchored in a conceptualization of the powerful momentum behind environmental destruction. Schnaiberg has argued that the environmental crisis is due primarily to there being a strong tendency to an environmentally destructive "treadmill of production." By "treadmill of production," Schnaiberg means that the competitive character of capitalism and the imperative for states to underwrite private accumulation while dealing with the social dislocations of private accumulation combine to virtually compel private and public policies and practices that lead to exponential, capital-intensive, environment-degrading economic growth. Thus, the actions of private firms and state managers, as well as consumer-citizens and labor groups, all combine to reinforce the treadmill character of industrial accumulation. Schnaiberg and colleagues have also portrayed the environmental movement as the principal countervailing social mechanism for societies to improve their environmental performance (Gould, Schnaiberg, and Weinberg 1996).[6]

There are certain shortcomings of the predominant conceptualizations of environment-society relations in North American environmental sociology literature; however, though these shortcomings have little to do with their orientation to the classical tradition. One limitation of the traditional North American environmental sociology literature is that it has devoted far more attention to theorizing environmental degradation than to theorizing environmental improvement (see Buttel 1996). As obvious as this limitation may seem, it needs to be recognized that shifting to a stress on environmental improvement is by no means unproblematic. Since environmental sociology's justification within the larger discipline is that it is better able than mainstream sociology to recognize why environmental problems are serious, getting worse, and could imperil human survival, the subdiscipline has historically had something of a self-interest in emphasizing degradation and crisis over improvement. Accordingly, North American environmental sociology literature has not devoted a great deal of attention to improvement processes—and to the degree that environmental reform is discussed it is presumed that environmental movement mobilization resulting in state policy change is the master process. A related shortcoming of North American environmental sociology literature is that it has arguably overestimated the coherence of environmental movements and exaggerated the degree to which environmental improvement will ultimately derive from environmental movement mobilization.

RETHINKING ENVIRONMENTAL SOCIOLOGY
IN CLASSICAL CONTEXT

With this background, we can examine the first-quarter century of North American environmental sociology by reflecting on its historical tendencies from a classical sociological perspective. Four sets of observations deserve mention here. First, environmental sociology has tended to have several contradictory affinities. On the one hand, environmental sociology has tended to be materialist (in its stress on the natural world and the material substratum of human life) and objectivist (in its stress on the negative consequences of science and technology and its strong endorsement of the project of the ecological and environmental sciences). On the other hand, environmental sociology has been sympathetic with the emancipatory or liberatory impulse as articulated by ecology movements of various stripes. Environmental sociology has thus also tended toward idealism (in terms of its often utopian posture toward environmental movements and its sui generis posture toward environmental orientations and values).[7] Most of the highly visible works in the field have aimed to incorporate both materialism-objectivism and emancipation-idealism. Much of the progress made in synthesizing these two outlooks has come from reexamining the classics (e.g., Murphy 1994; 1997). One should not, however, exaggerate the degree to which progress toward synthesis has been made. Macnaghten and Urry (1998: chapter 1), for example, claim that the coexistence of objectivism and idealism in environmental sociology, and the lack of critical reflection on this contradiction, has rendered the subdiscipline largely irrelevant to understanding the embeddedness of the natural world in social practices and behaviors. They note that objectivism and idealism coexist as well with "environmental instrumentalism," the doctrine that environmental behavior must be approached from the vantage point of identifying incentives or constraints rooted in policy that can steer rational social conduct in an environmentally friendly direction. Their analysis of the internal contradictions of late twentieth-century environmental sociology is provocative, but it is also somewhat overargued in the sense that it basically reflects the view that any perspective other than a semiotic or ethnomethodological one is incapable of fully comprehending human behavior.

A second observation is that environmental sociology has some strong affinities with the classical tradition that are often unrecognized. Swingewood (1991) has stressed that the nineteenth-century classical tradition was essentially pessimistic in that it stressed the negative social implications—anomie, alienation, the "iron cage," and disenchantment—of industrialization. Giddens (1987) has likewise stressed the fact that the classical tradition was preoccupied with changes in the economy and in the structure of production as the prime movers in shaping social change in modern societies. It is significant that most of the field of environmental sociology has tended to be a relatively pessimistic sociology (because of its being anchored in arguments about the intrinsic tendencies to environmental degradation) and has stressed the importance of the economy, capitalism, and the structure of production in creating environmental problems. It is thus no accident that as much as environmental sociologists have been critical of the shortcomings of classical theory, their work has tended to fall back on many of the concepts and methodological principles of the classical tradition. It is worth noting along this line that perhaps the most visible publication in the history of North American environmental sociology has been Foster's (1999) article on Marx's concept of "metabolic rift" in the *American Journal of Sociology*. In this article, Foster makes the claim that Marx's fascination with agronomy and his use of the concept of "metabolic rift" are not only of potentially great relevance to environmental sociology, but also critical to understanding the corpus of Marx's work (for an elaboration of both arguments, see also Foster [2000]).[8]

Third, it could be argued that classical sociology's chief limitation—and one that has yet to be grappled with effectively in environmental sociology—is the presumption of "society" as the basic unit of analysis. As much as environmental sociologists might claim that global environmental threats justify the existence of our subdiscipline (Dunlap and Catton 1994) and that international environmental regime formation represents a new principle of social organization and change (Frank, Hironka, and Shofer 2000), most environmental sociology has been limited by its having remained rooted in the classical view of social analysis that derived from the epoch of state- and nation-building in Europe.

Fourth, Gross (1999) has set forth a fascinating historical argument about cycles of sociological fashion regarding the society and nature dualism in American sociology. He has observed that in the early days of American sociology the influence of the European classics was relatively minimal, and that the "classics" that most affected the establishment of American sociology were those of the homegrown theorists such as Ward, Thomas, Sumner, Giddings, Odum, Bernard, Ross, and Ogburn. Gross notes that the exemptionalism of early twentieth-century American sociology can be exaggerated. In particular, he notes the striking preoccupation of prominent American sociologists with the natural environment during the first decade of the century and then again during the 1930s. In essence, then, the post–World War II sociological embrace of economic development and the expansion of consumption was a decisive break with earlier homegrown traditions, rather than a progressive elaboration of exemptionalism or of classical sociology.

CONCLUSION: FURTHER
THEORETICAL EXHORTATIONS

I have strived to advance a perspective on theory in environmental sociology that is appreciative of the continued relevance of the classics but not preoccupied by either the strengths or shortcomings of the classical tradition. The classical theorists' works can always be read in several different ways. These works may be regarded as grand syntheses or major leaps forward in social thought, or alternatively as insightful and comprehensive grapplings with extant rival schools or traditions of thought (e.g., Weber's relationship to the German analytical school, the German historical school, neo-Kantian methodology, and Marxism). One can also see the classics as hopelessly dated works that do not have much to say about an epoch that departs so much from that of the nineteenth century and as a continuing source of insights and methodological approaches that are applicable to most of the empirical problems we might develop. My guess is that environmental sociology will always essentially consist of a set of perspectives that have definite lineages to the classical theorists while also having an ecological-materialist ontology of some sort (e.g., notions such as "ghost acreage," treadmill of production, risk society, and ecological modernization) superimposed on them. Another aspect of classical theory that is very positive for environmental sociology is that which Wardell and Turner (1986) have referred to as the "classical project." The future of environmental sociology may well be determined by whether it is able to restore the "classical project" of uniting sociological abstraction with a meaningful role in addressing moral and political issues.

It is in my view clearly the case that environmental sociology has increasingly strayed from the new human ecology or materialist core that predominated in the late 1970s and 1980s. A number of theoretical views that may be regarded in one respect or another as "exemptionalist"—social constructivism, risk society, Critical Theory, and ecological modernization—have become established within the field. On the whole, this has been a positive development. Environmental sociology has been more than capable of assimilating these divergent views. Environmental sociology is strong and well established enough that it can tolerate, and even thrive within, theoretical pluralism. The diversification of the field is opening up avenues of theoretical innovation and synthesis that were not present a decade ago (Buttel 1996). Furthermore, this more diversified theoretical base is increasing the opportunities for environmental-sociological theory to be integrated more closely into concrete empirical research. The overall trends thus strike me as being very positive.

NOTES

1. By contrast, few economics graduate students today, including those aiming at scholarly careers in economic theory, spend as much as a semester studying the primary works of

Smith, Marshall, Ricardo, Keynes, and so on, and in fact most contemporary graduate students never take a course in classical economics. Only a tiny minority of Ph.D. economists today read extensively from the primary works of all four of these classical economics figures.

2. Likewise, observers who are critical of the notion that the classical sociological tradition has little to offer environmental sociology (e.g., Foster 1999) usually attribute this latter position to one of the early Catton and Dunlap papers.

3. This section of the chapter draws heavily on Buttel (2000).

4. Note, in particular, that many of the influential neo-Marxist statements in environmental sociology in recent years (Burkett 1996; Foster 1999; Benton 1996; O'Connor 1994; O'Connor 1998) have rested heavily on the work of the late Marx, such as *Grundrisse* and the three volumes of *Capital*.

5. The emphasis on the inherent or intrinsic tendency to environmental destruction or degradation should also be seen as one of the principal ways in which environmental sociologists distinguished their work from that of the neo-Durkheimian "human ecologists." Among human ecology's central concepts were those of adaptation and equilibrium, which implied a tendency for social institutions over time to come into symmetry or stability with respect to environmental resources. Mainstream North American environmental sociology practitioners thus tended to regard human ecology as having a benign or unrealistic view of the stresses humans were placing on the natural environment and an overly optimistic assessment of the capacity of institutional processes for responding to environmental problems (Buttel and Humphrey 2002).

6. It is worth stressing, though, that during the more than twenty-five years of Schnaiberg's work in environmental sociology it has been seldom that he has been preoccupied with exemptionalist tendencies within conventional sociology, with ostensible shortcomings of the classical tradition, or with establishing environmental sociology as a paradigm. Schnaiberg's environmental sociology appears to have been anchored mainly in O'Connor's (1973) political sociology, which stresses the functions played by states, the contradictions of state intervention, and the tendency toward fiscal crisis. While O'Connor is now regarded as an important figure in environmental sociology (see, e.g., O'Connor 1998), his *Fiscal Crisis of the State* (1973) had little to say about environmental issues.

7. Note that I am not disagreeing about the fundamental importance of "environmental movements." My concern is that one cannot theorize the role of environmental movements in dealing with ecological issues apart from the contradictory roles of states in this process. That is, while environmental conservation and protection are directly or indirectly state-regulatory practices and the role of states in a societal division of labor is to "rationalize," states face conflicting imperatives (accumulation [or the responsibility for satisfactory aggregate economic performance] and legitimation) and formidable pressures from various groups in civil society (especially capital) that cause them to be internally conflicted over or reluctant to invoke environmental protection policies and practices.

8. As Smith (1998: 71–75) has noted, however, some of the most trenchant ecological criticisms of Marx have come from neo-Marxists (e.g., Benton 1989). Furthermore, other neo-Marxists such as Grundmann (1991) have characterized Marx's core position as a Promethean model of the domination of nature and have defended this position vigorously.

REFERENCES

Benton, T. 1989. "Marxism and Natural Limits." *New Left Review* 178:51–86.
———, ed. 1996. *The Greening of Marxism.* New York: Guilford.

Bookchin, M. 1971. *Post-scarcity Anarchism*. Berkeley: Ramparts.

Burch, W. R., Jr. 1971. *Daydreams and Nightmares*. New York: Harper and Row.

Burch, W. R., Jr., N. H. Cheek, and L. Taylor, eds. 1972. *Social Behavior, Natural Resources, and the Environment*. New York: Harper and Row.

Burkett, P. 1996. "Some Common Misconceptions about Nature and Marx's Critique of Political Economy." *Capitalism-Nature-Socialism* 7:57–80.

Burns, T. R., and T. Dietz. 1992. "Cultural Evolution: Social Rule Systems, Selection, and Human Agency." *International Sociology* 7:259–283.

Buttel, F. H. 1978. "Environmental Sociology: A New Paradigm?" *The American Sociologist* 13:252–256.

———. 1986. "Sociology and the Environment: The Winding Road toward Human Ecology." *International Social Science Journal* 109:337–356.

———. 1996. "Environmental and Resource Sociology: Theoretical Issues and Opportunities for Synthesis." *Rural Sociology* 61:56–76.

———. 2000. "Classical Theory and Contemporary Environmental Sociology: Some Reflections on the Antecedents and Prospects for Reflexive Modernization Theories in the Study of Environment and Society." In *Environment and Global Modernity*, ed. G. Spaargaren et al., 17–39. London: Sage.

Buttel, F. H., and C. R. Humphrey. 2002. "Sociological Theory and the Natural Environment." In *Handbook of Environmental Sociology*, ed. R. E. Dunlap and W. Michelson. Westport, Conn.: Greenwood.

Catton, W. R., Jr. 1976. "Why the Future Isn't What It Used to Be (and How It Could Be Made Worse Than It Has to Be)." *Social Science Quarterly* 57:276–291.

———. 1980. *Overshoot*. Urbana: University of Illinois Press.

Catton, W. R., Jr., and R. E. Dunlap. 1978. "Environmental Sociology: A New Paradigm." *The American Sociologist* 13:41–49.

Coser, L. A. 1971. *Masters of Sociological Thought*. New York: Harcourt, Brace, Jovanovich.

Cottrell, F. 1955. *Energy and Society*. New York: McGraw-Hill.

Dickens, P. 1992. *Society and Nature*. Philadelphia: Temple University Press.

Dietz, T., and T. R. Burns. 1992. "Human Agency and the Evolutionary Dynamic." *Acta Sociologica* 35:187–200.

Dunlap, R. E. 1997. "The Evolution of Environmental Sociology: A Brief History and Assessment of the American Experience." In *The International Handbook of Environmental Sociology*, ed. M. Redclift and G. Woodgate, 21–39. Northhamton, Mass.: Edward Elgar.

Dunlap, R. E., and W. R. Catton Jr. 1979. "Environmental Sociology." *Annual Review of Sociology* 5:243–273.

———. 1983. "What Environmental Sociologists Have in Common (Whether Concerned with 'Built' or 'Natural' Environments)." *Sociological Inquiry* 53:113–135.

———. 1994. "Struggling with Human Exemptionalism: The Rise, Decline and Revitalization of Environmental Sociology." *The American Sociologist* 25:5–30.

Durkheim, É. 1893. *The Division of Labor in Society*. Paris: Alcan.

———. 1895. *The Rules of Sociological Method*. Paris: Alcan.

Firey, W. 1960. *Man, Mind, and Land*. New York: The Free Press.

Foster, J. B. 1999. "Marx's Theory of Metabolic Rift: Classical Foundations for Environmental Sociology." *American Journal of Sociology* 104:366–405.

———. 2000. *Marx's Ecology*. New York: Monthly Review.

Frank, D. J., A. Hironka, and E. Shofer. 2000. "The Nation-State and the Natural Environment over the Twentieth Century." *American Sociological Review* 65:96–116.

Giddens, A. 1987. *Social Theory and Modern Sociology.* Oxford: Polity.

Goldblatt, D. 1996. *Social Theory and the Environment.* Boulder, Colo.: Westview.

Gould, K. A., A. Schnaiberg, and A. S. Weinberg. 1996. *Environmental Struggles.* New York: Cambridge University Press.

Gross, M. 1999. "Early Environmental Sociology: American Classics and Their Reflections on Nature." *Humboldt Journal of Social Relations* 25:1–29.

Grundmann, R. 1991. *Marxism and Ecology.* New York: Oxford University Press.

Hughes, J. A., P. J. Martin, and W. W. Sharrock. 1995. *Understanding Classical Sociology.* London: Sage.

Klausner, S. A. 1971. *On Man in His Environment.* San Francisco: Jossey-Bass.

Lopreato, J. 1984. *Human Nature and Biocultural Evolution.* Boston: Allen and Unwin.

Macnaghten, P., and J. Urry. 1998. *Contested Natures.* London: Sage.

Martell, L. 1994. *Ecology and Society.* Amherst: University of Massachusetts Press.

Milbrath, L. 1984. *Environmentalists: Vanguard for a New Society.* Albany: SUNY Press.

Morrison, K. 1995. *Marx, Durkheim, Weber.* London: Sage.

Murphy, R. 1994. *Rationality and Nature.* Boulder, Colo.: Westview.

———. 1997. *Sociology and Nature.* Boulder, Colo.: Westview.

O'Connor, J. 1973. *The Fiscal Crisis of the State.* New York: St. Martin's.

———. 1998. *Natural Causes.* New York: Guilford.

O'Connor, M., ed. 1994. *Is Capitalism Sustainable?* New York: Guilford.

Parsons, H. L., ed. 1977. *Marx and Engels on Ecology.* Westport, Conn.: Greenwood.

Sanderson, S. K. 1990. *Social Evolutionism.* Oxford: Basil Blackwell.

Schnaiberg, A. 1980. *The Environment.* New York: Oxford University Press.

Schnaiberg, A., and K. A. Gould. 1993. *Environment and Society.* New York: St. Martin's.

Smith, M. J. 1998. *Ecologism.* Minneapolis: University of Minnesota Press.

Swingewood, A. 1991. *A Short History of Sociological Thought.* 2nd ed. New York: St. Martin's.

Turner, J. H. 1994. "The Ecology of Macrostructure." In *Advances in Human Ecology*, vol. 3, ed. L. Freese, 113–138. Greenwich, Conn.: JAI Press.

Wallerstein, I. 1991. *Unthinking Social Science.* Oxford: Basil Blackwell.

Wardell, M. L., and S. P. Turner. 1986. "Introduction: Dissolution of the Classical Project." In *Sociological Theory in Transition*, ed. M. L. Wardell and S. P. Turner, 11–18. Boston: Allen Unwin.

Webb, W. P. 1952. *The Great Frontier.* Boston: Houghton Mifflin.

Weber, M. 1968. *Economy and Society*, ed. G. Roth and C. Wittich. 1922. Reprint, Berkeley: University of California Press.

West, P. C. 1984. "Max Weber's *Human Ecology of Historical Societies.*" In *Theory of Liberty, Legitimacy and Power*, ed. V. Murvar, 216–234. Boston: Routledge and Kegan Paul.

Wilkinson, R. G. 1973. *Poverty and Progress.* New York: Praeger.

Yearley, S. 1996. *Sociology, Environmentalism, Globalization.* London: Sage.

3

A Green Marxism? Labor Processes, Alienation, and the Division of Labor

Peter Dickens

What are the implications of Marxist social theory for our understanding of environment-society relations? What are the implications of contemporary environmental consciousness for Marxism? These are the main questions this chapter will address.

For many people, Marxism would not be the obvious place to start an environmental analysis. Its commitment to the social relations and processes surrounding industrial production, its emphasis on material growth, its Promethean commitment to modernity, and its tacit endorsement of anthropocentric thinking are all some way from much contemporary mainstream ecological thought and politics (Eckersley 1992; Soper 1995). Furthermore, the environmental results of actually existing socialism also seem to leave Marxism as a "nonstarter." Despite the important work of Schmidt (1971), Smith (1991), Grundmann (1991), and others to be referred to in this chapter, "the armoury of Marxism-socialism to counter the rhetoric and politics of a rising tide of ecological movements has not been well stocked" (Harvey 1996: 194).

Much of this literature suggests, however, that Marxism still has a great deal to offer. But, as this chapter suggests, there remain some elements of the Marxist tradition (or what I prefer to call radical political economy) that are likely to prove more productive than others in understanding and confronting environmental concerns. Furthermore, these are largely neglected even by contemporary green Marxists.

This chapter critically assesses one influential link between Marxism and environmental concerns. It then identifies those areas of Marxism that seem to offer the greater promise for the sociology of the environment. In the conclusion of this chapter, there is an emphasis that the labor process is the key yet neglected way in which Marxism can contribute to an ecological sociology. But this chapter also suggests that the social division of labor is a key way in which knowledge is fragmented. It leads to the alienation of people from themselves and their environment. One result is people in modern societies alienating themselves through fetishizing a notion of "nature" that is pure, untouched, and unworked on by human beings. An emphasis on the social division of labor also indicates how Marxism can combine with feminism and other types of politics and social theory.

There are some uncomfortable messages for Marxists here, since the New Right has long emphasized the social division of labor, while Marxists have been concentrating much more on the technical division within the workplace. However, neoliberals overestimate the role of the market as a coordinating device for regulating the division of labor. The difficulties of a society regulating itself in relation to society-environment problems will be a key theme in this chapter. There remain, in other words, extremely difficult problems of coordination within the social division of labor, whether by the market, the state, or other forms of management.

CAPITALISM AS ITS OWN GRAVEDIGGER?

A good place to start our exploration is with the influential arguments of O'Connor (see, e.g., 1996). Over recent years, his work has generated a good deal of discussion and debate within the pages of *Capitalism, Nature and Socialism.* Essentially, his argument is that capitalism is (almost literally) its own gravedigger. It is creating environmental conditions that threaten to undermine capital accumulation itself. Crisis is of course a central feature of much of Marx's work. And the central contradiction with which Marx is usually associated is that between the forces and relations of production. He argued, as is well known, that technologies introduced to deskill the factory worker and to decrease wages constantly generate crises of overproduction. But such changes in the forces of production are held to be in contradiction with the social relations of production. Overproduction leads to large-scale layoffs and declining profit levels. This was assumed by Marx to lead to the socialization of the means of production in the interests of planning and, at the same time, the creation of an organized labor movement. And all this was of course seen by Marx as presaging a transition to communism.

In a parallel way, Marx briefly argued that there was a contradiction between capitalist growth on the one hand and the environment and labor power on the other. Thus, in *Capital* he wrote: "In modern agriculture, as in urban industry, the increase in the productivity and mobility of labour power is purchased at the cost of laying waste and debilitating labour power itself. Moreover, all progress in capitalist agriculture is a progress towards ruining the more long-lasting sources of that fertility" (quoted in Perelman 1996).

This is, therefore, what O'Connor calls the "Second Contradiction of Capitalism." It is the tendency for capitalism to create further barriers to capital accumulation, in effect ruining the very conditions it needs in order to expand. And this contradiction, combined with that between the forces and relations of production, is seen as another route to socialism. Fusions between "red" and green politics would constitute an alliance against capitalism and against capitalism's degradation of the environment. Again, this would be part of a transition to socialism; this time, however, toward a socialism that is "green" as well as "red" (Benton 1996a).

The question therefore arises whether such prominence should be attached to this second contradiction. And indeed O'Connor's assertion has led to considerable debate within the pages of *Capitalism, Nature and Socialism*. Does collectively or communally organized production necessarily overcome the second contradiction? Some collectively organized forms of production (such as participatory forms of production associated with some contemporary aid programs) do indeed seem to be environmentally successful (Chambers 1988; Wade 1988). At the same time, however, communism in its state-dominated form was very often an unmitigated disaster as regards to both environmental degradation and the health of the industrial worker. So we must be careful in equating socialism or communism with environmental degradation. But these examples suggest there is no guarantee that a transition to socialism actually would necessarily herald an improvement in the use of resources or in improvement of labor power. This is a point I take up later in this chapter. But, staying for now with O'Connor's assertions, the high level of abstraction at which the second contradiction is spelled out leaves it peculiarly difficult when it comes to the actual, concrete relations between society and environment. As Toledo puts it:

> The so-called ecological crisis includes a myriad of different phenomena. There are at least ten different processes provoking global environmental conflicts: deforestation, soil pollution, loss of biodiversity, toxic wastes, urban contamination, destruction of marine resources, the greenhouse effect, energetic misspending, the destruction of the ozone layer. Thus how is it possible to attribute to capitalism the responsibility for every environmental problem? (1996: 223)

Toledo could, incidentally, have made a similar point about a socialist society's relations with nature. The range of processes involved would be just as great and it would be just as difficult to argue that "socialism" is generally important for "the ecological crisis."

It would also be unwise to ignore the relations between concrete effects "on the ground" and forms of politics. Politics (and arguably environmental politics in particular) responds to everyday concrete outcomes and events. It responds to, for example, pollution in the streets affecting children's health. It responds to denial of access to the countryside or to insufficient space for public association. There is no necessary reason why, for example, the presence of dirty streets leads to a wider political consciousness of capitalism and its second contradiction. Recognition of such a contradiction is always mediated by the actualities of everyday life. As Benton puts it: "[I]t is often these more indirect and attenuated effects of the second contradiction on peoples' quality of life that form the 'raw materials' of environmental issues and struggles" (1996a: 190). Furthermore, there is of course no guarantee that the experience of such day-to-day social-cum-environmental difficulties automatically transfer themselves into some kind of socialism. It seems just as likely that they will lead to reactionary forms of politics or at the very least some form of "not-in-my-backyardism."

All this is not to argue that the sphere of production should be relegated in importance when it comes to an understanding of contemporary society's relations with nature. Nor is it to suggest that consumption practices and politics outside the workplace should be given prominence over the sphere of production. Indeed, as I will argue very shortly, processes and relations within the sphere of production should indeed be retained as central to our understanding of society-environment relations. This definitely means that we need to return to the labor process, the sphere of analysis with which more conventional Marxism is located. But the argument here is that environmental politics are always mediated by concrete realities. And, even more importantly, it is that the precise way in which the dominance of production is specified by O'Connor is wrong.

O'Connor has therefore identified and emphasized a broad but important tendency as capitalism uses the raw materials it needs for the making of commodities. It is also important in attributing special significance to the sphere of production. Nevertheless, he severely underestimates the capacity of capitalism to restructure its way out of crisis. In much the same way that the "first contradiction" between the social forces and social relations actually led to slow reformist shifts in power relations between the classes (including, e.g., the socialization of the means of production in the form of funds held for workers' pensions), there seems every likelihood that capitalism will again reorganize itself in such a way as to deal with environmental crises. Or to put this another way, it is unlikely to continue indefinitely contributing to its own decline and eventual apocalyptic downfall. This is not of course to argue that capitalism will completely and unproblematically "resolve" the second contradiction. The imposition of environmental costs on the politically weakest peoples will continue, with demands for environmental justice becoming if anything increasingly strident (Harvey 1996). Rather, it is to say that capitalism will, jellylike, adapt to and recover from environmental threats to its profitability, while resisting the more strident demands for a decent environment.

Thus, typically such "ecological modernization" is likely to entail not a retraction from society's already complex relations with nature, but rather a restructuring of that relation. There are signs that this is already happening. First, many of the newest technologies (e.g., lasers, computer-based applications, and biotechnology) often entail industry needing fewer raw materials than in the past. Fiber-optic cables and satellite communications, for example, have dramatically reduced dependence on copper by using materials in plentiful supply. The raw material for computer chips is, for example, sand. And this is available in an unlimited supply. It might be unwise, however, to overcelebrate such switches in demand to other sources of materials. It might well be, for example, that such industries might be doing what seems a "right" thing for the wrong reasons. They might, for example, be switching to sand simply because it is cheap and easy to obtain. Meanwhile, however, such exploitation may be undermining social and ecological systems. Similarly, a company using cheap resources in some parts of its labor processes could be degrading the environment in others.

A characteristic and perhaps more important feature of capitalist industry's new relationship with nature is not just that of turning to plentiful and cheaper resources. Rather, it consists of commodifying resources that in the past were free. Thus, the typical response by capitalism to a second contradiction is to envisage capitalism and private-property relations as the solution rather than the problem (Saunders 1995). The examples are numerous. They include the purchase of rain forests by pharmaceutical companies, the genetic engineering of animals and plants, and, through the new reproductive technologies, the manipulation and reconstruction of life itself.

This chapter will pursue some of these developments shortly. But to summarize here, the notion of the second contradiction severely underemphasizes the capacity of capitalism to restructure in crisis conditions. Marxian thinking would continue to give a premium to dialectical ways of analysis here (Harvey 1996). The relationships between society and nature are constantly in flux and subject to restructuring and renegotiation. What constitutes that relationship is always renegotiable and indeed what constitutes "nature" and "society" is continually subject to change. This is partly a product of capital foreseeing and adapting to changed circumstances, but it is also a product of changing forms of politics and consciousness. There is a strong argument for saying we are now witnessing the slow emergence of a form of "ecological capitalism," albeit one that is at the moment extended mainly to leading-edge industries and to the more affluent societies. But all this again implies that socialists would be wrong to wait for capitalism to self-destruct due to its own rapaciousness. It (and more particularly its share and pension holders) will simply not allow that to happen.

NATURE AND THE LABOR PROCESS

So what would be the key contribution by Marxism to contemporary environmental sociology? It would again be at the heart of Marxist theory, in an area where almost all environmental analysis consistently fails to look. This is the labor process; the process by which the natural world becomes transformed into what human beings need and the process by which peoples' *own* nature becomes transformed. To quote Marx himself:

> Labour is, first of all, a process between man and nature, a process by which man, through his own actions, mediates, regulates and controls the metabolism between himself and nature. He sets in motion the natural forces which belong to his own body, his arms, legs, head and hands, in order to appropriate the materials of nature in a form adapted to his own needs. Through this movement he acts upon external nature and changes it, and in this way, he simultaneously changes his own nature. He develops the potentialities slumbering within nature, and subjects the play of its forces to his own sovereign power. (1976: 283)

The labor process is, then, the two-way interaction between the creative working human being and the natural world. There are three principle elements involved. First, there is work itself, a purposive activity. Second, there are the instruments and technologies that facilitate the labor process. Most obviously, of course, these are the tools that enable people to conduct labor. Less obviously there are the forms of infrastructure (roads, computers, and so on) that indirectly contribute to the labor process. In both cases, these elements, "the means of production," can be envisaged as a worked-on "second nature" and as such are the results of earlier labor processes. Third, there are the elements with which we are most concerned here, the objects within the natural world on which the labor is being exerted.

They also include preexisting processes within nature. As Benton (1996b) points out, Marx's exposition of the relations between "man" and nature seems to assume a handicraft model. That is, objects are made by elements taken from nature. But of course human societies interact with the world in more complex ways than this. They are often using or deploying the powers of nature. These powers are both enabling and constraining. They have long been the basis of agriculture. Thus, such capacities, or genetically inbuilt tendencies, are not thoroughly transformed by the industrial labor process. Rather, they are used and exploited to the ends of human societies. And, while they are empowering to people in human society, they can also be constraining. It is now perhaps becoming increasingly clear that there are limits to which the powers of nature can be worked on before nature starts to take some form of "revenge" on the human societies using them. This is one of the main messages of Lovelock's "Gaia Hypothesis" (1979). He has long argued that the earth is a self-balancing mechanism that is "actively made fit and comfortable by the presence of life itself" (quoted in Dobson 1991: 264). Lovelock's analysis, and in particular the way it has been taken up by the green movement, can be criticized for an inadequate attention to the social and political mechanisms causing environmental degradation. Indeed, it is an example of what this chapter calls "fetishized" thinking about the environment. But Lovelock deserves credit for publicizing and popularizing the retributions likely to stem from physical and biological limits being reached as a result of human activity.

The labor process on the forces of the natural world remains a common feature of all forms of society and a central condition of human existence. It is the means by which human beings produce what they need. It presupposes on the one hand people with their labor and on the other hand the natural world. The next stage is to specify the kinds of society with which we are dealing. Only in this way can we begin to specify the implications both for human beings and the natural world. What is distinctive about the labor process on nature under capitalism? It entails the increasing humanization of many features of nature. It now includes, for example, work on the genetic structure of animals that regulates the capacities of animals and plants to grow. And, in the case of the new reproductive technologies, such humanization includes manipulation of the capacity of animals and human beings to reproduce their own kind. Again, none of this means that nature has "ended" as suggested by, for example, McKibben (1990) and Giddens (1991). Its powers of development and change remain intact, while modern labor processes and technology, harnessed to the natural and physical sciences, are influencing the *ways* in which nature is shaping up.

It is unnecessary and inappropriate here to explore in great detail the implication of the labor process for human beings. While it is still not a central feature of contemporary Marxism, the labor process now has a reputable and scholarly tradition of analysis and political activism (see, e.g., Braverman 1974; Thompson 1989). Briefly, capitalism labor power, or peoples' capacity to work, is purchased on the labor market by capital. So too are the means of production and those elements of the natural world that are judged necessary for the creation of commodities. These elements are then combined into a labor process that is performed under supervision and control of managers. The labor process becomes simply a means by which the elements capital has purchased (labor power, the means of production, and the raw materials and processes of nature) are combined. The products belong not to those who made them, but to the owners of the means of production. They have now become commodities, the value of which exceeds the sum of the values of the labor power and the means of production consumed in the production process.

Many implications flow from this process. One reason for reminding ourselves of the above well-worn and apparently anthropocentric analysis is the implication for *human* nature. One implication of Marxism for environmental sociology is to include humans as part of "nature." Large parts of Marx (certainly the early Marx) see human beings as themselves part of "the environment." And my particular emphasis here shows what happens to *human* nature under specifically capitalist forms of the labor process. Here, we find the subordination of human labor to capital and, more particularly, the creative abilities of human beings being systematically denied. Thus, a central feature of Marx (and especially the young Marx) is the notion of a "species being," a set of creative and purposive capacities that become denied through deskilling and mass production. Furthermore, human beings are a species that is uniquely sensitive to aesthetic and spiritual qualities. But capitalism has managed to triumph over even this feature of humans' distinctive, possibly unique, "species being." Nature becomes a means to an end. It becomes valued primarily for its cash value rather than its inherent aesthetic or spiritual appeal. The dealer in minerals sees only the commercial value, not the beauty and peculiar nature of the materials (Marx 1975: 353).

It may well be asked whether the ways in which precapitalist societies labored on nature to produce the things they needed were any less alienating than those under capitalism. In *Grundrisse* (1973), Marx provides an extended but largely neglected answer to this question. In precapitalist societies such as in Rome and Greece, the Middle Ages, and "the Asiatic mode of production," people as a natural species retained a close association with nature. There remained, in short, a close identity between people and nature. People could see and experience how they related to the natural world. Furthermore, as a member of some kind of small community, they retained an understanding unalienated relationship with their own species. Yet this relatively unalienated relation with land and community was clearly of no enormous advantage to many people, particularly to slaves and serfs. Indeed, as Marx bluntly suggests, slaves in antiquity or serfs in the Middle Ages were treated *as* animals or parts of nature. Thus, Marx knew full well that all was not sweetness and light before capitalism and that, furthermore, capitalism and what he called "human mastery over the forces of nature" resulted, for all its sins, in the further realization of human powers and potentials. Alienation, in short, is the price of modernity. The mastery of nature and its regulation is the price human beings pay for freedom.

For many writers in the environmental field, much of the previous analysis will confirm the principle problem with an environmental Marxism. This is the essentially anthropocentric vision of such a politics (Eckersley 1992). But this is not, or does not need to be, the central problem with a green Marxism. As Hayward has spelled out, a concern with environment and "learning to live within natural limits, rather than to overcome or continually push them back," can be just as much a humanist as an ecocentric objective (1994: 75). In other words, we could become better *humans* as a result of learning to live within limits and respect the needs of other species. Furthermore, the word "mastery" can have a number of meanings. It can indeed mean the uncontrolled destruction of species and physical resources. But it can also mean simply human beings' steadily improving *understanding* of nature. Marx, it must be said, is contradictory and by no means clear about these distinctions. Writing in the mid-nineteenth century, there was no particular reason why he should have been. This means that his work needs clarifying and fleshing out in relation to our concerns a century and a half later.

POWER, KNOWLEDGE, AND THE
TECHNICAL DIVISION OF LABOR

One central element of the labor process is the *technical* division of labor in the place of paid work. This division of labor has been referred to by Sayer and Walker as "an irreducible technical foundation in the nature of the work to be done to produce a desired result from materials provided by nature and by history" (1992: 16). No one worker can master more than a small number of tasks. The materials, tools, and products involved in a modern industry must result in widely varying types of work. Furthermore, some kind of overarching control and coordination needs to be exercised over this technical division of labor. That is, the very complex processes by which nature is converted into the things people need and buy all require some degree of management or a supervisory process.

As I will outline later on, such a division is almost certainly a necessary feature of a modern society, capitalist or otherwise. There remains the difficult issue, however, of how and whether the technical division of labor necessitates power relations that remove skills, knowledge, and power. But the point of raising the issue here is to emphasize the extent to which the division of labor removes peoples' understanding of themselves and their relationships with their products, with nature, and with other species. Again, it results in alienation, the failure of people to understand the very world they are making.

At this point, however, we need to recognize that there are a number of dimensions to alienation as outlined by Marx. Perhaps the most important one in terms of general application is the sense of loss or absence of something that is essential to humans' well being. Paradoxically, this understanding forms a relatively small part of Marx's own work and has had little development since. Bhaskar describes this more general meaning as "estranged, split, torn or estranged from oneself" (1994: 114). This implies being estranged from something that is essential or intrinsic to a human being's nature. The result is again our profound failure to understand the world around us, a world that we as a society are actively making.

This more general understanding of alienation again links back to the labor process. (Although, as I will discuss later on, it would be unwise to link it entirely to the labor process at the point of employment). As is well known, the central feature of Marx's analysis is that labor becomes subordinated to capital in the industrial labor process. With the coming of machinery and machinofacture, he argues, the labor process is continuously transformed and revolutionized in pursuit of increased productivity. Machinery becomes the active factor in the labor process. It imposes continuous, standardized, and repetitive tasks on the laborers. In short, a strict factory discipline is imposed. And, most importantly from our viewpoint, the rise of modern society is characterized by scientific knowledge of the properties of the physical, chemical, and biological world being imposed on supposedly less "rational" forms of understanding. The process, as Braverman puts it, "assumes an increasingly scientific character as knowledge of natural laws grows and displaces the scrappy knowledge and fixed tradition of craftsmanship" (1974: 155). In this way, new hierarchies of mental and manual labor are created. Manual labor starts to have its basis in science rather than in skill. The apprenticeship of craftsmen in the nineteenth century included training in algebra, geometry, and trigonometry and in the properties of materials used in the craft. "Craft," Braverman says, "provided a daily link between science and work, since the craftsman was constantly called upon to use rudimentary scientific knowledge, mathematics, drawing, etc., in his practice" (133). The mid-nineteenth-century Mechanics Institutes, which can still be seen in many British cities that date back to nineteenth century, are a monument to this link between science and work for many craftsmen. Similarly, Thompson described how the weavers maintained a knowledge of abstract ideas in addition to their own crafts.

> Every weaving district had its weaver-poets, biologists, mathematicians, musicians, geologists, botanists. . . . There are northern museums and natural history societies which still possess records or collections of lepidoptera built up by weavers; while there are accounts of weavers in isolated villages who taught themselves geometry by chalking on their flagstones, and who were eager to discuss the differential calculus. In some kinds of plain work a book could actually be propped on the loom and read at work. (1975: 322)

Deskilling and the supplanting of crafts with scientific knowledge is a fairly familiar result of the "Taylorization" of work. As I will mention later on, however, this process may now be undergoing change with the advent of the new information technologies. The point of introducing here the deskilling of the nineteenth-century craft work is simply to emphasize that modernity, and the modern labor process in particular, brings with it not only an increasing alienation of *human* nature, but also, with the rise of science, an alienation between the worker and external nature. Furthermore, it means that abstract scientific knowledge starts to dominate over what Marx called "manual labor." As Braverman again puts it: "The more science is incorporated into the labour process, the less the worker understands of the process; the more sophisticated an intellectual product the machine becomes, the less control and comprehension of the machine the worker has. In other words, the more the worker needs to know in order to remain a human being at work, the less does he or she know" (1974: 425).

It would be better, however, to generalize from the skill of manual workers to refer to the separation and removal of all forms of knowledge that are tacit (i.e., difficult to quantify, describe, and express), local, lay, and concrete. When it comes to knowledge of how human beings interact with the environment, this can become disastrous. Tacit, local, lay, and concrete forms of knowledge may of course be parochial and highly inaccurate. But to separate them from more abstract types of understanding and to subordinate them as "emotional," "irrational," and therefore unimportant is a first step toward the relegation of certain groups of people such as children and, as will be seen later on, women. The division of labor may be an essential feature of modern society, but forms of subordination are essentially political in nature.

Contemporary ecologists and environmentalists often complain of the fragmentation of understanding in a world where humans and ecological systems are all highly interrelated. What they do not do, however, is adequately spell out the *reasons* for such fragmentations. And it is the labor process, the social relations stemming from the labor process, and the difficulties of a society steering itself as a result of the technical and social divisions of labor where they would do well to start. Similarly, those concerned with the industrialization of farming are rightly ashamed of the controls and cruelties imposed by humans on nonhuman species. But as Noske (1989) points out, the regulation of farm animals and their separation from their own offspring and from the natural world can all be seen as the result of a labor process similar to that originally analyzed by Marx. Their powers, much like those of industrial workers, have been increasingly subjected to mechanization, rationalization, and automation. Furthermore, and again there are strong parallels with the treatment meted out to human beings, divisions of labor are created even between animals of the same species. Some cattle, for example, are bred for beef and others for milk.

Returning to divisions within the human world, there is a range of other ways in which knowledge is divided in modern society. First, this applies to disciplinary divisions resulting from the separation between the physical, natural, and social sciences

(Dickens 1996). And these again all lead to a form of alienation of which Marx briefly spoke. These are again the results of complex divisions of labor, this time between different types of specialists and "mental laborers." To some degree, it is understandable that such divisions have become a central feature of intellectual and academic life. They are, after all, oriented toward discovering real causal processes and laws within each of these different areas of scientific endeavor. And yet, in a world where nature is being increasingly socialized by human beings, it is doubtful if such watertight compartments can continue to be insisted on.

Again, such disciplines as physics, biology, and sociology have made immense strides on their own and this must always be remembered. But they also lead to various forms of reductionism (such as those attempted by sociology, as well as those offered by subjects such as sociobiology and physics with its fashionable "theories of everything") and they again lead to the kinds of alienation alluded to earlier. The socialization of nature has taken an extraordinarily detailed and fragmented form and this has again led to human beings in modern society simply failing to *understand* the world in which they live and are themselves helping to make. The processes involved are beyond their understanding. All this is a result of power relations in the form of professionalized knowledge combining with the subordination of the lay, tacit, local, and concrete understandings (Dickens 1996). Once more, however, the political question is whether, and to what extent, such centralizations and concentrations of knowledge can be overcome in a modern society. Are they simply an unfortunate but necessary feature of the modern human condition? Or can the division of labor that is a necessary feature of modernity be recast in more emancipatory forms?

There is a second important way in which human beings in modern society are alienated from their environment. And it was Kropotkin, the anarchist writer, who drew particular attention to this problem. Writing about one hundred years ago, he noted the extent to which countries and regions were becoming specialized as part of a globally organized *spatial* division of labor (Kropotkin 1985; Dickens 1997). Thus, to an increasing extent people were surrounded by, and working on, a particular *kind* of nature. The labor process was therefore of a particular kind in each region. Russia was growing corn, Britain was manufacturing cotton and iron goods, Belgium was making woolen clothes, and so on. Interestingly, Kropotkin implied that there might even be a natural spatial division of labor, one based primarily on locally available resources. It was precisely this local division that capitalism was threatening to obliterate.

All the divisions outlined by Kropotkin have now been subject to great change, but his point is retained, if anything in strengthened form. This again implies that it is increasingly difficult for people to gain an adequate understanding of their relationship with the physical environment as a whole simply through direct experience. They are, to use Marxist concepts I will develop later on, "alienated" or "estranged." They rely on, for example, markets and sources of information beyond their control and to which they have made little contribution. The importance of this is considerable. Markets typically deal with *general* information. To put it bluntly, highly specific and local knowledge does not sell well. It is in this way that abstract and global knowledge comes to dominate over more concrete and local understandings (Sohn-Rethel 1978). Again, markets cannot be assumed to operate as simply coordinating producers and consumers since certain types of knowledge are programmatically omitted from the production process if they cannot be sold on the market.

THE SOCIAL DIVISION OF LABOR

This chapter has so far argued that the labor process and the division of labor are key contributions that Marxism can make to environmental sociology. So far, however, it has concentrated on the division of labor between workers *within* the place of paid work, each performing a partial operation, with management relegating certain kinds of knowledge. But we should consider too the *social* division of labor, that is, the division *between* enterprises. Here, in the formal economy at least, people relate to one another as producers of different products. They relate to each other "as producers of different products, working for separate capitalists" (Sayer 1995: 44).

At this point, Marxism begins to combine with some of the concerns of other types of social theory considered in this volume. On the one hand, this broader and more general notion of the division of labor between enterprises was of course a leitmotif of post-Marxian sociologists such as Durkheim and Tönnies. On the other hand, Marxism has either largely ignored this aspect of the division of labor or assumed that the technical division of labor is the only source of anarchy in a capitalist society (Sayer 1995). To the extent that the social division of labor is considered by Marxism, it remains cautious about assumptions made by the early social theorists regarding the possibilities for coordinating and regulating the divisions of labor. In addition to the market, custom, authority, and state planning have been made the main ways in which regulation resulting from environmental destructiveness of the social division of labor have been attempted. But, as Sayer argues, there are real reasons for remaining doubtful about the potential of these devices. They all require trust, consensus, and acceptance of a form of moral order. Furthermore (and again the neoliberals are better at pointing this out than socialists), state planning has been remarkably unsuccessful in its coordinating role of linking producers and consumers. Regarding the environment, we again need only to remind ourselves of the disasters of state socialism.

An emphasis on the *social* division of labor makes alliances with those "critical voices" *within* Marxism who argue that it overstates the importance of relations and processes within the workplace of the formal economy. Other relations and divisions clearly need to be considered and to be part of the environmental debate. They include relations between men and women, between adults and children, and between races. Perhaps best represented are the critical voices from feminism. As an ecofeminist, Mellor argues, for example, that:

In *The German Ideology*, in Marx's discussion of the social relations of production, he talked first of "the procreation of life, both of one's own labour and of fresh life by procreation." Why should the means of survival (a biological imperative) be allowed into historical materialism but not the means of reproducing life itself? Furthermore, if the means of survival produced definite social relations and particular forms of consciousness, why not the means of procreation? (1996: 256)

Referring to the work women do, Mellor argues that: "this is the most fundamental division in society, that women are primarily (but not all and not always) responsible for meeting the immediate needs of others while men (again, not all and not always) are not" (259).

Thus, it can well be argued that Marxian political economy is weakest in taking on board the social division of labor. This means that the cultural and biological reproduction of our own species as a result of predominantly female labor are left out of the picture. And, when we turn to scientific knowledge and forms of lay, concrete, and local understandings, we find a similar process of alienation occurring outside the technical division of labor. In the late eighteenth century, for example, women's role in the raising of families was often combined with access to, and use of, scientific Enlightenment knowledge. As Shteir puts it, "women botanized in the fields and at home, within families, and among friends. They used botanical interests and skill within print culture and featured botany in their poems, books, and essays" (1996: 57). By the 1860s, however, abstract science was being actively promoted and professionalized by bodies such as the British Association for the Advancement of Science. Science became monopolized by a mainly male profession. The result was that women's continuing role as homemakers became separated from botanical science. "After the 1860s," Shteir writes, "the locus of learning shifted from home-based and mother-centred education to laboratory-based school science" (235). In short, women had become deskilled in a way similar to craftsmen.

In turning to the sphere of social life outside the place of paid work, there is much, as indeed Sayer (1995) has argued, that Marxism can learn from the New Right. It is the promoters of this latter philosophy who are much more sensitive to the *social*, as distinct from the technical, division of labor (see also Dickens 1996). Hayek (1988) is especially important in regard to the social division of labor. He uses the word "catallaxy" to refer to the millions of widely dispersed, varied, connected, and exchanged knowledge between small institutions and households. "Catallaxy" is roughly equivalent to the social division of labor. It has evolved spontaneously into very complex and variable forms. Furthermore, as Hayek (1988) persuasively argues, such a system is impossible to understand, still less to control.

But more important than simply "adding on" elements of the social division of labor and, as part of this, giving greater strength to relations such as those of gender and race, it is important to explore how such divisions combine. And in regard to the social division of labor, there are some important issues arising in regard to the environment. For by including the social division of labor, or the divisions between firms and enterprises, we start to encounter one of the main reasons why a modern society is anarchic, uncontrollable, and largely unable to confront environmental change.

First, it is worth noting that the relations between the technical and social divisions of labor are in constant flux. In the environmental field, for example, it is notable how practices such as growing one's own food have been largely penetrated by capital and turned into large-scale industries. All this is in line with Marx's predictions 140 years ago that capitalism and the market will constantly extend themselves into spheres of social life outside of capitalist production. As Marx put it: "Capital conquers the whole of production and therefore the home and petty form of industry—in short, industry intended for self-consumption, not producing commodities, disappears" (Marx 1969: 159).

Local exchange and trading schemes (LETS), however, are an attempt to recover the situation, to bring the practice of provisioning into an enterprise outside of the technical division of labor and within enterprises subject to community control.

More broadly, there is a central tension between the technical and social division of labor that is of special significance in regard to society and the environment. In *Capital* (1976), Marx referred to the contrast between the two different types of division of labor in a modern capitalist society. The division of labor in production is planned, regulated, and supervised to the "nth" degree by the powers of capital. But there is nothing like as much coordination within the *social* division of labor, that is, between the capitalist and other enterprises. As Marx put it: "In the society where the capitalist mode of production prevails, anarchy in the social division of labour and despotism in the manufacturing division of labour mutually condition one another" (477). So while each firm is, to use Sayer's word, "despotically" managed to produce use-value and profits, within the broader social division of labor the picture is one of anarchy. Furthermore, the notion that the relationships between different capitalist interests should be planned (by, e.g., a government operating in some wider good) tends to be treated with suspicion and cries of "unwarranted interference" in their private affairs.

Hayek and neoliberal thought celebrates diversity within catallaxy or the social division of labor. But the downside of such diversity is surely that of no one having a clear knowledge of his or her circumstances and of the relations between society and environment in particular. Some of the environmental implications have become clear with the recent deregulation and privatization of public transport in Britain. A deregulated rail or bus transport system is extraordinarily well organized at the level of the individual firm, but extremely disorganized in terms of interfirm connections (this even extends to companies hiding timetables from one another). The implications for the passengers and for the possibilities of a reduction in car use are self-evident. At the same time, it is easy to forget that previous centralized bureaucratic attempts at regulating a state-owned system itself often produced unsatisfactorily coordinated systems.

It is also argued by many on the political right that a "green capitalism" will overcome these fragmentations through the market itself (see, e.g., Saunders 1995). By making the producer pay for environmental despoilations or allowing capital to further "conquer the world" by privatizing the environment itself (and thereby enabling the owners of the spoiled environment to recover their costs through, if necessary, the courts), a more holistic system based on the market will be remade in which companies respond to consumer demands.

The privatization and marketization of the environment is indeed a logical outcome of neoliberal thought, but it will leave intact the central tension observed by Marx long ago. Such privatization will lead to individuals, companies, and organizations becoming responsible for their *own* property and self-interest. But it is unclear why this should lead to strategies that are both socially and environmentally benign.

REIFICATION, COMMODITY FETISHISM, AND ALIENATION

The combined effect of the technical and social division of labor therefore fragments knowledge and understanding. One result for human beings is a form of alienation, one in which they do not understand themselves and their relationship with their society and environment. But attention should also be given to Marx's key ideas as to how human beings come to alienate themselves. As I hope to show, these again have some direct implications for the sociology of the environment.

God, Feuerbach had argued, is a self-alienated man. He is "man's essence." People alienate themselves by elevating to the status of a god or higher being something that they have themselves made. And the dealienation of human beings is found through the abolition of man that has been made God. Marx of course agreed with Feuerbach's criticism of religious alienation, but he argued throughout his work that such religiosity was only one form of self-alienation in a modern society. Philosophy, common sense, art, morals, and even the state are all forms of alienation, the latter being "an alienated community." To put this another way, there are many ways in which people alienate themselves from the products of their own work and construct them, or fetishize them, as apparently independent beings toward which they must bow and scrape. Alienation is thus complete. Not only have people fashioned objects to which they are no longer attached, they end up worshipping as things the very objects they have made.

Perhaps the best-known form of such fetishism in Marxism is that of the commodity. The complex relationships that we have with other human beings is primarily through the market. It is made via combinations of things and commodities rather than through social relations. This kind of relationship obscures real, underlying, social relations and processes, especially those within the sphere of employment. Furthermore, and central to our concerns, it obscures the ways in which modern society works on raw materials and the powers of nature to produce the things it needs. The fetishism of commodities is the process by which the products of human work start to seem as though they are independent realities, independent of how they came to be made. Therefore, much of life in modern societies concentrates not only on things rather than relationships, but it also concentrates on things that are bought and sold.

What has all this to do with social theory and the environment? As I have argued in detail elsewhere, much of the environmental movement (and indeed some types of theory associated with this movement) fetishizes the notion of "nature" as a wholly independent reality to be worshipped (Dickens 1992; 1997). An example is the so-called Gaia hypothesis mentioned earlier. Little or no attention is given by this analysis to social relations and the dialectical interplay between human society and the powers of the natural world. In short, it ignores the ways in which the powers of nature are worked on. Fetishism of a primordial "nature" is also a feature of the so-called deep greens. They maintain what Martell (1994) describes as "an awed and humble respect" for nature and even suggest that it offers lessons for the ways in which humans should themselves organize. Such "awe" and "respect" is another example of fetishization. "Nature" is something that human societies have long been involved in shaping and using, even though the underlying causal powers of the nonhuman role remain intact.

A supposedly "independent nature" that is not in any way touched by human beings and their conversion of nature into commodities is, therefore, a fiction. And it becomes even more dangerous when it is attributed independent powers that threaten, God-like, to wipe out a sinning race of humans. This is unfortunately the case with the kind of millenarian "end-of-the-worldism" again all too present in much environmental thinking. If it is not the ozone layer that will get us, it is global warming. And if it is not global warming, it is chemicals in the water resulting in declining sperm counts, and so on. A better way is to consider such threats as broad tendencies. These threats may not be inconsiderable. But we do not know how they combine with one another and, perhaps even more important, we are left innocent of the power relations and forms of knowledge that have gone into their making.

In line with Marx's original thinking about fetishism, the separation of items within nature (e.g., genes, organs, and even babies) in contemporary society is combined with *commodity* fetishism. In other words, monetary values are attached to these items and they are bought and sold not only in isolation from underlying and often invisible social relations and production, but also from ecological and environmental systems as a whole. Such processes are of course part of the steady (almost literal) penetration and fragmentation by the market of living things. And, as environmentalists are indeed right to argue, the implications may be startling or even disastrous. Bovine Spongiform Encephalopathy (BSE) is a case in point of one small element of the food chain being isolated, manipulated, and sold without reference to the system as a whole and by a particularly powerful set of commercial interests. Other similar negative impacts on human beings may take place as a result of the genetic manipulation of food and the powerful vested interests. Furthermore, the complex relationships are not understood by sciences, which are again isolated, reductionist, and not programmed to see beyond their own noses. All this supports the critique of the market as a simple way of coordinating producers and consumers. Producers are often at a considerable advantage relative to consumers. This particularly applies to knowledge and information. As Sayer puts it: "Markets are fields of power-struggle in their own right, and prices themselves reflect the relative power of the participants in the market" (1995: 91). Fetishism is therefore a result of nondialectical thinking. By ignoring relationships, processes, flows, whole organisms, and change, fetishism asserts a "nature" that humans have created but of which they are not apparently part. Commodity fetishism (including so-called green consumerism) is the latest and most modern way in which humans overemphasize what Harvey calls "the self-evident world of things" (1996: 50).

RADICAL POLITICAL ECONOMY AND THE ENVIRONMENT: VISIONS OF THE FUTURE

"Red-green" politics are now becoming a focus of action and more theoretical and political debate. At a practical level, there is a vast range of projects and undertakings within localities. Many of these are attempting to overcome the technical, social, and spatial divisions of labor by, for example, communally organized labor processes, horizontal networking between organizations, and a special emphasis on concrete experience of the kind achieved in localities. Examples are LETS, organic farming groups, and credit unions. Further initiatives have stemmed from the 1992 Rio de Janeiro conference on the environment and development. These include unlikely alliances across the social division of labor between, say, local residents' associations and local industries.

These developments are in some degree reflected in more theoretical and political debate. Britain's Red-Green Study Group (1995), for example, has recently offered three central themes for a reorganized society that is both socially just and environmentally sustainable. Their stress on "building from below" (53) argues for forms of politics rooted in everyday struggles, action and experience, with a strong emphasis on locality and community. "Enabling from above" (55) argues for a large-scale change in definitions of common sense. It would open up new public spaces for public debate and emphasizes the need for networks between communities. Finally, the group's red-green vision again argues for diversity and against top-down blueprints. It also insists on a stronger moral purpose and on the democratization of modern science and technology, rather than the kind of outright rejection proposed by many green activists.

But the problem of the division of labor remains. Communism, Marx famously argued, would bring about the end of the division of labor. The division between mental and manual labor and between society and environment would be complete. And in an often lampooned section of *The German Ideology*, he and Engels offered a vision of society in which the division of labor had been overcome. But it is a remarkable passage since it illustrates what a collectively organized society might mean for the individual.

In communist society, where nobody has one exclusive sphere of activity but each can become accomplished in any branch he wishes, society regulates the general production and thus makes it possible for me to do one thing today and another tomorrow, to hunt in the morning, fish in the afternoon, rear cattle in the evening, criticize after dinner, just as I have a mind without ever becoming hunter, fisherman, herdsman or critic. (1969: 295)

Marx's point is that mental labor would be put on a par with manual work. Criticizing after dinner would, for example, have a status equal with rearing cattle. Furthermore, the same person would do both the criticizing and the rearing, and the society that people are helping to make would not enforce particular types of work on particular people.

Nevertheless, how realistic is such a vision of an unalienated person in a socialist, communist, or communally organized society? Can one person in a modern society seriously be expected to engage in such a wide range of activities? As a number of authors have pointed out (see, e.g., Nove 1983; Sayer 1995), the division of labor was a distinctive, even dominant, feature of state socialist society. And it is indeed difficult to imagine a future, modern society, in which people and their knowledge are not in some degree specialized. But there will remain intractable difficulties surrounding the technical division of labor *within* the place of employed work and the social division of labor *between* organizations.

Unless, therefore, significant social and political shifts are made to occur, the alienating divisions of labor between and within organizations is likely to remain a continuing problem and obstacle to a less alienated relation between a modern society and nature. And again, the paradox is that such division is in many respects highly desirable since it brings about efficient production, developments in science and technology, and increased material well being. Harvey puts the central tension as follows:

[The] never-ending estrangement of consciousness permits reflexivity and the construction of emancipatory forms of knowledge (such as science); but it also poses the problem of how to return to that which consciousness alienates us from. How to recuperate an unalienated relation to nature (as well as unalienated forms of social relations) in the face of contemporary divisions of labour and technological-social organization, then becomes part of a common project that binds Marxists and ecologists ineluctably together. (1996: 198)

So the key theoretical and political question for a radical political economy (one that draws from Marx but continues to build on what he said) is whether it is possible to have a society composed of necessarily high technical and social divisions of labor but that does not dissolve into divisions between abstract and other forms of knowledge. Such divisions are, as we have seen, a result of the systematic denigration of not only subordinate classes, but also of working-class children, women, and ethnic minorities. Certain forms of knowledge (tacit, local, lay, and concrete) are being consistently subjugated as part of such marginalization, while other forms (explicit, global, expert, and abstract) usually dominate. At issue here is, of course, not just knowledge but *power*. But how are these power relations to be reversed and how are marginalized forms of knowledge to be reasserted?

Many of the classic interventions from the left have addressed technical divisions of labor and power relations within the place of paid work. But difficulties remain. First, divisions within the social division of labor were either not confronted or found peculiarly intractable. For example, the Lucas Aerospace initiatives and the Greater London Council's attempt to encourage worker democracy within organizations made significant gains in regard to workers having some degree of control over the technical division of labor and the products of their work (Wainwright and Eliot 1982; Rustin 1986). And these included, in the case of Lucas, the conversion of the manufacturing process away from the manufacture of weapons and toward more environmentally acceptable products such as public transport. But despite their attempted links with "the community," they still largely failed to seriously confront the fragmented relations *between* organizations and the tenuous and often problematic links between technical divisions of labor on the one hand and social divisions of labor on the other. Second, it is arguable that even technical divisions of labor were not adequately addressed by these social innovations. The Lucas Aerospace workers were still primarily male and were perhaps overemphasizing their supposed skills in an elitist and eventually workerist way.

So how might we proceed? It is difficult to see a straightforward overcoming of these obstacles in a modern society. A possible way forward in terms of reversing the obstacles to understanding posed by the technical and social divisions of labor might be via new forms of electronic communication such as the Internet. These technologies at least open the *prospect* of people (based in households as well in a range of companies and other organizations) being able make themselves more aware of links between local and specialized knowledge on the one hand and more abstract ideas on the other. As Ainley (1993) has argued, Braverman's deskilling thesis perhaps came too soon to recognize that parallel reskilling can take place with the advent of computers and information technology. "As the information generated by the technology became more widely accessible," Ainley writes, "some reskilling and even enskilling occurred among the core of remaining employees and the managers—positions rendered increasingly similar and overlapping" (23).[1]

The new communications technologies therefore offer a possible means by which the kinds of alienation described here can start to be overcome. Perhaps, too, they open up the possibility of giving lay people access to abstract science, allowing them to interrogate general ideas on the basis of their own concrete and local knowledge. As a result of the dialectical interplay of these different levels and forms of knowledge, the outcome could be a far more complex but in the end more emancipatory *combination* of understandings. The new technologies suggest the possibility of not only "reskilling and enskilling" within capitalist enterprises, but also the eventual fusion of different types of knowledge previously monopolized within different parts of the *social* division of labor.

Three considerable difficulties remain, however. First, there is the now well-rehearsed problem of "the information rich" and "the information poor" with information not only being determined by who has access to the hardware, but also by the eventual ownership of information and its regulation via charging mechanisms. A second, perhaps even more important problem, is the distinction between information and understanding. The vast amount of data available via such technologies is not the same thing as providing an understanding of complex relations between society and nature. Ways need to be found of making a "public space" for such technologies, using them to enable previously unrecognized understandings to be asserted, and linking lay knowledge to more official "science" and abstraction.

But will vested interests start moving in on these technologies, again marginalizing more specific and threatening forms of understanding? This links to a third emergent problem with the new information technologies. The ways they are *actually* being used suggests that existing power relations, divisions of labor, and divisions of knowledge in contemporary society may be simply reproduced and made even more fragmented by the new technologies. Within the technical division of labor, it seems clear that the new communications technologies are not being widely used to link industrial workers' understandings of their impacts on the environment to the kinds of understanding advanced by scientists and managers within their firms. Certainly, within the social division of labor the information exchanged is of a highly arcane kind. The connections between specialized knowledge and the wider picture are still not being made. And the possible openness of the new technologies may be still further undermined if certain kinds of knowledge (such as those on the Internet) become owned by vested commercial interests and made available only to those who pay. This again threatens to fragment knowledge and to ensure that divisions between the technical and social division of labor are not only retained but even exacerbated.

Nevertheless, the emergent new media, and the empowering possibilities they open up, currently offer perhaps the best possibilities for overcoming the alienation and incoherence resulting from the technical and social divisions of labor. If they are not used as an unthinking technical fix, but as a means by which people can relate their own lay and local knowledge to the abstractions of official science, they may yet herald the emergence of a society that better understands its relations with nature. Multiple but coordinated knowledges are the trademark of the unalienated individual. The new communications technologies could start to overcome the alienation of people from the natural and social worlds by recognizing the knowledge of the relatively powerless and systematically linking it to abstract science.

The new communications technologies therefore represent a possible public space for the acquisition and transfer of knowledge, skill, and power. They open up the possibility of overcoming the kinds of chaos that this chapter has identified, especially that within the social division of labor. The new communications technologies could therefore be the twenty-first-century equivalents of the nineteenth-century Mechanics Institutes. They provide one way of overcoming the forms of alienation identified by Marx 150 years ago.[2]

NOTES

1. Interestingly, Marx foresaw a time when high levels of unemployment would lead to the industrial worker becoming what would now be called "multiskilled." Such a workforce, he believed, would be: "That monstrosity, the disposable working population held in reserve, in misery, for the changing requirements of capitalist exploitation, must be replaced by the individual man who is absolutely available for the different kinds of labour required of him; the partially developed individual, who is merely the bearer of one specialized social function, must be replaced by the totally developed individual for whom the different social functions are different modes of activity he takes up in turn" (1976: 618).

2. A substantial research project on ways in which the new communications technologies can overcome the marginalization of certain people and their knowledge has been carried out by John Parry and myself. The work focuses particularly on children. Details can be obtained from John Parry, Institute of Education, University of Sussex, Brighton, United Kingdom.

REFERENCES

Ainley, P. 1993. *Class and Skill: Changing Divisions of Knowledge and Labour.* London: Cassell.

Benton, T. 1996a. "Introduction to Part III." In *The Greening of Marxism*, ed. T. Benton. New York: Guilford.

———. 1996b. "Marxism and Natural Limits: An Ecological Critique and Reconstruction." In *The Greening of Marxism*, ed. T. Benton. New York: Guilford.

Bhaskar, R. 1994. *Dialectic: The Pulse of Freedom.* London: Verso.

Braverman, H. 1974. *Labor and Monopoly Capital: The Degradation of Work in the Twentieth Century.* London: Monthly Review.

Chambers, R. 1988. "Sustainable Rural Livelihoods: A Key Strategy for People, Environment and Development." In *The Greening of Aid: Sustainable Livelihoods in Practice*, ed. C. Conroy and M. Litvinoff. London: Earthscan.

Dickens, P. 1992. *Society and Nature: Towards a Green Social Theory.* London: Harvester.

———. 1996. *Reconstructing Nature: Alienation, Emancipation and the Division of Labour.* London: Routledge.

———. 1997. "Local Environments, Alienation and the Division of Labour." *Local Environment* 2:83–87.

Dobson, A. 1991. *The Green Reader.* London: Deutsch.

Eckersley, D. 1992. *Environmentalism and Political Theory: Toward an Ecocentric Approach.* London: University College.

Giddens, A. 1991. *Modernity and Self-Identity: Self and Society in the Late Modern Age.* Oxford: Polity.

Grundmann, R. 1991. *Marxism and Ecology.* Oxford: Oxford University Press.

Harvey, D. 1996. *Justice, Nature and the Geography of Difference.* London: Blackwell.

Hayek, F. 1988. *The Fatal Conceit: The Errors of Socialism.* London: Routledge.

Hayward, T. 1994. *Ecological Thought: An Introduction.* Oxford: Polity.

Kropotkin, P. 1985. *Fields, Factories and Workshops Tomorrow.* London: Freedom.

Lovelock, J. 1979. *Gaia: A New Look at Life on Earth.* Oxford: Oxford University Press.

Martell, L. 1994. *Ecology and Society: An Introduction.* Oxford: Polity.

Marx, K. 1969. *Theories of Surplus Value.* London: Lawrence and Wishart.

———. 1973. *Grundrisse.* Harmondsworth, UK: Penguin.

———. 1975. *Early Writings.* Ed. L. Colletti. Harmondsworth, UK: Penguin.

———. 1976. *Capital.* Vol. 1. Harmondsworth, UK: Penguin.

Marx, K., and F. Engels. 1969. *The German Ideology.* London: Lawrence and Wishart.

McKibben, B. 1990. *The End of Nature.* Harmondsworth, UK: Viking.

Mellor, R. 1996. "Ecofeminism and Ecosocialism: Dilemmas of Essentialism and Materialism." In *The Greening of Marxism,* ed. T. Benton. New York: Guilford.

Noske, B. 1989. *Humans and Other Animals: Beyond the Boundaries of Anthropology.* London: Pluto.

Nove, A. 1983. *The Economics of Feasible Socialism.* London: Allen and Unwin.

O'Connor, J. 1996. "The Second Contradiction of Capitalism." In *The Greening of Marxism,* ed. T. Benton. New York: Guilford.

Perelman, M. 1996. "Marx and Resource Scarcity." In *The Greening of Marxism,* ed. T. Benton. New York: Guilford.

Red-Green Study Group. 1995. *What on Earth Is to Be Done? A Red-Green Dialogue.* Manchester: Red-Green Study Group.

Rustin, M. 1986. "Lessons of the London Industrial Strategy." *New Left Review* 155:75–84.

Saunders, P. 1995. *Capitalism: A Social Audit.* Buckingham: Open University Press.

Sayer, A. 1995. *Radical Political Economy: A Critique.* London: Blackwell.

Sayer, A., and R. Walker. 1992. *The New Social Economy: Reworking the Division of Labour.* Oxford: Blackwell.

Schmidt, A. 1971. *The Concept of Nature in Marx.* London: New Left Books.

Shteir, A. 1996. *Cultivating Women, Cultivating Science.* Baltimore, Md.: Johns Hopkins University Press.

Smith, N. 1991. *Uneven Development: Nature, Capital and the Production of Space.* 2nd ed. Oxford: Blackwell.

Sohn-Rethel, A. 1978. *Intellectual and Manual Labour.* London: Macmillan.

Soper, Kate. 1995. *What Is Nature?* Oxford: Blackwell.

Thompson, E. P. 1975. *The Making of the English Working Class.* Harmondsworth, UK: Pelican.

Thompson, P. 1989. *The Nature of Work: An Introduction to Debates on the Labour Process.* London: Macmillan.

Toledo, V. 1996. "The Ecological Crisis: A Second Contradiction of Capitalism?" In *The Greening of Marxism,* ed. T. Benton. New York: Guilford.

Wade, R. 1988. *Village Republics: Economic Conditions for Collective Action in South India.* San Francisco: International Centre for Self-Governance.

Wainwright, H., and D. Elliot. 1982. *The Lucas Plan: A New Trade Unionism in the Making?* London: Alison and Busby.

4

Ecological Materialism and the Sociology of Max Weber

Raymond Murphy

Weber is the giant upon whose shoulders we stand in order to see further. Inspecting his work is justified to extend our sight and grasp. Weber's work is particularly promising as a cornerstone for research because it perceives the complexity of life and is open to diverse elements. It is not reductionist, resisting the opposing temptations of reducing the material to the cultural or the cultural to the material. Weber emphasized the importance of bureaucratic organization without losing sight of the relevance of the capitalist market, of status groups without forgetting social classes, of intentions without neglecting causes, of culture without underestimating interests, and of the social without foreclosing the significance of the nonsocial for social action: "Weber had no reluctance to admit the causal significance of non-social factors for social processes" (Albrow 1990: 146).

Feuer (1959) once wrote that every age has its own Marx. By that he meant that every age has a different reading of Marx: the age of Lukacs had a different Marx than the age of Althusser, and that was later replaced by the Marx of Thompson. The same is true of Weber. The age of Parsons produced a different Weber than the age of Collins and Parkin. With environmental problems looming, perhaps we need a different Weber still.

It is well understood that Weber gave an important place to human agency and hence to creative voluntary action in determining outcomes. Intentions result in actions that have effects, even if the effects are not those that were intended. The importance Weber placed on a systemic or structural dynamic is not, however, so well understood. Some readers, even neo-Weberian ones, have looked at Weber's work in a way that they fail to perceive any such dynamic.[1] "Weber presents us with a set of static comparisons rather than a self-propelling system. . . . The comparisons

. . . take Protestantism, Confucianism, Hinduism, and so forth as so many givens
. . . each of the necessary conditions happened to be added one after another until
the right 'mix' was reached for the capitalist takeoff" (Hanneman and Collins 1987:
91–92).

This reading of Weber's work has come under increasing criticism. At one level
of analysis, religions and institutional arrangements can indeed be taken as "givens"
and the mix of these givens either promoted or hindered the takeoff of capitalism.
Weber did not, however, limit himself to that side. He also investigated the social
construction of capitalism that then took on a dynamic of its own. "The Puritan
wanted to work in a calling; we are forced to do so . . . victorious capitalism, since
it rests on mechanical foundations, needs its support [of religious asceticism] no
longer" (Weber 1930: 181–182). Thus, Weber argued that rational structures were
"not only stronger in the sense of providing technically better solutions to enduring
problems, but that they evoked, and enlisted, the motivation which contributed to
their further development. Western rationalism on this account contained an inherent dynamic" (Albrow 1990: 196). Albrow has succeeded in his attempt "to dispel
the impression, largely cultivated by Parsons, that Weber was uninterested in structure. The case is made here that, on the contrary, he was, explicitly and consistently,
directly concerned with the problems of identifying structure in social action" (9).

Weber's work provides an excellent basis for developing a synthesis of what Dawe
(1978) refers to as human-agency sociology and social-system sociology because it
takes both into account: creative human agents who unleash systemic, structural
processes that take on a dynamic of their own, hence humans risk becoming prisoners of their social constructions that turn out to be an "iron cage." Environmental
problems created by humans constitute a poignant illustration of spontaneous
human actors unintentionally unleashing dynamic processes that trap them, namely,
the systemic processes of nature. The pursuit of the means to manipulate nature and
the means to dominate humans, which constitutes a central part of what Weber
referred to as formal rationalization, has both a logic and contradictions of its own.
One of the principal contradictions that comes back to haunt humans involves precisely those processes of nature let loose by the disruption of the self-regulating
mechanisms nature has created.

Weber ended his book *The Protestant Ethic and the Spirit of Capitalism* with the
following words: "[I]t is, of course, not my aim to substitute for a one-sided materialistic an equally one-sided spiritualistic causal interpretation of culture and of history. Each is equally possible, but each, . . . accomplishes equally little in the interest
of historical truth" (1930: 183). It is necessary to see beyond the received stereotype
of Weber: that of a cultural historian opposed to the materialism of Marx. As the
previous quotation states, Weber never intended that his work be given a one-sided
antimaterialistic interpretation. For an approach to merit the adjective "Weberian,"
systemic materialism, including ecological materialism, must be incorporated into
it. "Weber's ecological analysis emphasized the interactive role of geography, climate, natural resources, and the material aspects of technology in the structure and
change in historical social structures" (West 1985: 216). Albrow even concludes that

"Weber's hostility to idealist interpretations of social life was more intense than his rejection of materialism" (1990: 257).

Recently, Weberian scholars have shown that Weber "retreated to the two 'interpretive' projects that made him world famous: *Economy and Society* and *The Economic Ethics of the World Religions*" (Roth 1996: 465) after failing in his bid to include naturalist sociology in the German Sociological Society. Weber argued in favor of analysis on the biological as well as institutional level. He even immersed himself in physiology and naturalist psychology in an article entitled "On the Psychophysics of Industrial Labour" (465).

Sociological theory that deflects attention away from the dynamic processes of nature, which cannot be reduced to a social construction but which interact with social constructions, takes sociology in a misleading direction. Weber was well aware of this, and hence, despite his emphasis on values and agency, he did not propose a reductionism to the social. He held that "culture was grounded in, even if not determined by, nature and to take the social out of the realm of natural causality altogether was to confuse the ideal and dogmatic formulations of jurists [and we might add, many sociologists] with empirical reality" (Albrow 1990: 257). Understanding the distinctive element of intentions among humans does not require the neglect of nature and the effect of its ecosystems on social action. Sociology must have as its foundation a synthesis of both the social and natural construction of reality, that is, it must examine the relationship between social action and the processes of nature.

BEYOND THE SOCIAL
CONSTRUCTION OF NATURE

The difference between the Weberian conceptions of the natural and social worlds is summed up by Albrow as follows:

> the thunderstorm is not changed, nor its prevalence affected in the slightest by our classifying it with atmospheric electrical phenomena. The philosophical point that our concepts for the natural world are all products of the mind remains just that, a philosophical point. The ideal nature of our concepts for ordering the natural world does not change the reality of the world. Cultural reality was different. The aims and purposes of human beings constituted that world. A view of the world could shape that world. (Albrow 1990: 153)

Although Albrow correctly understands that the natural world cannot be reduced to human conceptions of it, he fails to emphasize that those conceptions can change the natural world. The conception that the natural environment is plastic and malleable has led to the use of rivers, lakes, and oceans as waste sinks and the atmosphere as a huge toxic emission chamber, with the resulting pollution, greenhouse effect, ozone layer depletion, acid rain, and so on. Even thunderstorms might have changed as a result of actions associated with this plasticity-of-nature premise. Certainly, earthquakes have been documented to have occurred as a result of human action (Perrow 1984) based on the plasticity misconception. The concepts constructed in nuclear physics, which correspond to specific processes of nature, enabled humans to develop nuclear weapons. Intercontinental ballistic missiles with nuclear warheads developed using these concepts would, if used in a war to achieve human purposes, dramatically change the reality of the natural environment. The concepts of chemistry describing other processes of nature led to the development of the chlorofluorocarbon (CFC) based air conditioner, and it is modifying the ozone layer. Human conceptions and purposes, particularly scientific and technological ones, are making a major difference in the natural world on our planet.

Albrow is none the less correct in depicting nature as a force with its own dynamics. It is necessary to see beyond restricted theories of the social construction of nature. Perrow (1984) has documented that human attempts to remake the natural world through high technology have led to the unleashing of catastrophic forces of nature in the form of what he calls "normal accidents." Humans do shape their natural environment, perhaps more powerfully by the unintended and often perverse consequences of their actions than by their intended consequences, and they are in turn shaped by natural forces, for example, by the unforeseen effects of pollution. Cultural (and social) reality is different from the reality of nature, but they are intimately related.

The tension between the social and the natural is an implicit underpinning of Weber's work. "It is the fate of the human being to be the bridge between these dichotomies. . . . The person is both animal nature and spiritual essence. Human history is precisely the story of the struggle between those two sides" (Albrow 1990: 186). West recalls for a forgetful sociological audience the importance of the interaction of ecological and social factors in Weber's explanation of historical societies and social change. He concludes that environmental constraints "impinge increasingly as central causal factors in emerging societal transformations in both the developed and developing world. A reorientation to a broader ecological sociology as Weber envisioned it will be crucial for understanding these societal changes and grappling with their consequences" (1985: 233).

For example, the history of Ireland is the chronicle of conquest and struggle, exclusion and usurpation, the Protestant ethic and the resistance of Roman Catholics, the rise of capitalism and the destruction of local crafts, status groups and social classes, traditional domination and modern rationalization. This social side is not diminished by stating that it is also the history of a potato parasite—phytophtora infectans—that was imported into a peculiarly humid climate from America via Belgium, resulting in famine that killed a million people and forced a million and a half more to emigrate (Woodham-Smith 1962; Lyons 1971; 1979). It is this interaction between social action and the processes of nature that left its mark on Irish society and culture, on the Irish Diaspora, and reduced the Irish language to a plot in the cemetery of dead languages.

Social action and social structure are closely related to natural processes. This includes the dynamics of the human body. People in wheel chairs are acutely aware of how they have been excluded from institutions by stairs and narrow toilets built by and for able-bodied persons. Sociological theories of cultural reproduction have failed to draw out the implications of an elemental phenomenon: you cannot study

Hegel at the university if you cannot use its toilet. Structures of closure have had and continue to have a physical basis.

A SYSTEMIC DYNAMIC PROMOTING
HUMAN AGENCY

Paradoxically, for those who believe in the mutual exclusiveness of sociology based on structural or systemic dynamics and sociology based on human agency and projects, the structural transformation of systems has given added importance to decisions. In particular, rationalization in terms of the cumulative development of the means to manipulate the processes of nature has resulted in choices where no choice was possible before. In Weberian terms, the expanding mechanical foundations of modern life do not just force people into specialized callings, they also open up new areas of decision. Indeed, they force decisions on humans. Beck expresses this strongly, in fact too strongly: "[S]tructures change structures, by which action is made possible, indeed compelled" (1994: 175). *A* decision and *an* action are compelled, but the content of the decision and the action is open. The role of agency is enlarged by this structural change, not diminished. The consequences of bad decisions have, however, to be suffered. Hence, there often exists an ambivalent attitude toward such modern rationalization, warranting neither optimism nor pessimism.

People no longer just die. The development of medical technology has forced families or doctors to decide whether or not to give cardiopulmonary resuscitation, remove the respirator, withdraw intravenous feeding, and so on. The development of artificial respirators has affected the taken-for-granted conception of when death occurs: with help, one can be breathing but brain-dead. The decision to "pull the plug" and let a person die (the most widely accepted form of euthanasia) becomes a decision only when applied science develops a plug to pull. Decisions then have to be made concerning what pulling the plug means, in particular, which plug it is legitimate to pull. Is pulling an intravenous needle equivalent to pulling the plug on an artificial respirator or is it equivalent to starving a person to death? Some elderly people now live with tubes in their throat, intravenous needles in their veins to inject nourishment and blood-pressure adjusting medication, and are badly bruised from repeated attempts to hit shriveled veins for those needles and for blood tests. At what point does caregiving become artificially keeping someone alive and at what point does it turn into prolonged torture? Is consent the crucial issue for pulling the plug or is it pain for those who cannot give informed consent? Scientific development and its application have forced new decisions on humanity.

Should nature's process of aging be the (sole, main, or secondary) criterion determining who may or may not receive transplants of organs in short supply? If so, at what age should people be excluded: ninety, eighty, seventy, or sixty? Should a nonalcoholic have priority over an alcoholic for a liver transplant if livers are in short supply? Should nonsmokers get priority over smokers for lung transplants? Should a child of normal intelligence have priority over a severely retarded child for a transplant of an organ difficult to acquire? How will the various criteria—age, self-abuse, and "normal"—be weighed? Will money or fame be allowed to overwhelm all the other criteria for reception of rare donor organs or use of expensive technology? The development of science and technology inflicts new questions on humans, but does not impose the answers. It opens up new areas of choice and decision. The elaboration of techniques to see the fetus has similarly influenced taken-for-granted conceptions of when human life begins: at birth, at conception, or somewhere in between? Tests are being developed to detect defects of the fetus, thereby providing information for choices where no choice was possible before. Previously, parents learned after birth that their child had Down's syndrome. Applied science has now developed means to detect it fairly early in pregnancy. The cross can for the first time in history be lifted before birth, but should it? Is it a cross or is it diversity? Hereditary conditions like hemophilia, mucoviscidosis, muscular atrophy, Huntingdon's syndrome, and schizophrenia can be diagnosed in the fetus. If the test is positive,[2] the decision can be made to abort the fetus and, if everyone does the same, eliminate the condition. Parents are now winning lawsuits against physicians for "wrongful birth" if the doctors did not predict a debilitating disease inherited by their children, such as Duchenne muscular dystrophy (*Ottawa Citizen*, 15 May 1996: Al–A2; 12 June 1996: Al–A2). If abortion is permitted anyway, the decision has to be made whether to donate the organs and tissue of the aborted fetus to other humans or fetuses in need instead of wasting them. The Human Genome Project holds the prospect of a menu for designer children giving parents and society the power to decide what characteristics to choose for their children or on the contrary to decide not to use the menu and instead let nature continue rolling the dice.

Death and birth now involve a maze of decisions. The development of the capacity to manipulate nature, far from diminishing decisions, compels humans to decide in areas where no decision was previously possible.

Just like manipulating nature inside the human body, manipulating it outside has the unintended consequence of opening up new areas of decisions. This can been seen in the ecological domain. Today, the "much-vaunted global integration of the world economy depends on fossil fuel-driven transport systems composed of planes, ships, and trucks" (Hawken 1993: 211). This dependency on environmentally degrading technical processes leads to the question: Is global integration worth the pollution? Newly discovered means of manipulating nature enable humans to achieve specific goals, but bring along unintended consequences as well. This raises questions concerning the value of the goals themselves.

The potentially destructive consequences of greenhouse gas emissions (carbon dioxide, methane, and nitrous oxide) resulting from technological development led to the decision in Rio de Janeiro in 1992 to return to 1990 emission levels by the year 2000. This in turn required a series of lower-level decisions by the signatories concerning production and use of fossil fuels, taxation of such fuels, methods of manufacture, and so on. Britain, Germany, and Switzerland chose to honor the agreement they had signed and made the necessary, but difficult, lower-level decisions. The other industrialized countries decided to take the path of least political resistance and renege, to run the risk of increased emissions, and to foist that threat on the other nations of the world. The worse offenders have been the United States and Canada. Structural developments bring new issues into the realm of conscious decision, but do not determine the content of those decisions. The choice can always be made to run the risk of ruin.

In the past, people fished for codfish off the Grand Banks of Newfoundland and took for granted that the supply would remain abundant. The development of radar-equipped, motorized, refrigerator boats with huge fine-meshed nets that vacuum fish from the ocean resulted in the depletion of fish and the collective decision by the Canadian government to close the fishery so that stocks could recover. This in turn led to a quarrel between government scientists exposed to short-term-interest pressures to reopen it and independent scientists holding a longer-range perspective on the well being of those fishing grounds. Whereas the self-regulating mechanisms of nature ensured the abundance of fish in this area prior to technological development, conscious human decisions now determine the future of those fishing grounds.

In Weberian terms, formal rationalization on the institutional level—the development of calculable, efficient means and procedures such as science, technology, the market economy, formal organization, and the legal system—raises new questions of substantive rationality, which refers to the value of the ends pursued by those means. Similarly, on the cultural and individual levels, instrumental rationalization—action viewed as a means to achieve anticipated consequences—results in new issues of value rationality. New *questions* and new *issues* do not necessarily mean substantively rational *answers* in terms of specific values, such as ecological values. Formal, instrumental rationalization can be closely associated with ecological irrationality, as the examples in the previous three paragraphs show.[3]

There is another sense in which structural developments have fostered agency. Reconstructing institutions and technology to restore the self-regulating mechanisms of nature beneficial to humanity requires human imagination. Far from being mutually exclusive, structural developments of systemic processes including ecosystemic ones have created new possibilities and needs for human projects.

The Enlightenment and the increase of knowledge—in particular, a scientific understanding of nature—can be referred to as reflective modernization. Over the long run, the resulting structural dynamic of technological development has led to reflexive modernization, defined as the "unintentional self-dissolution or self-endangerment" (Beck 1994: 176) of modern society. Manipulations of nature turn back to imperil the human manipulators. They challenge individuals and collectivities to redefine structures and reinvent society and its politics. This lays the conditions for a possible new ecological enlightenment and a more extensive reflective rationalization. Reinventing structures does not mean individuals becoming ever more free of structures. Instead, there exists a dialectical relationship between structural dynamics and human agency.

TECHNOLOGY AS NATURE MANIPULATED

Marxists have all too often been prone to adore at the alter of Marx instead of perceiving his errors and correcting them. That must not be allowed to happen to
Weber. Despite the richness of his contribution, a certain critical distance from
Weber is necessary. There is much in Weber's work that requires either improvement or modification to take into account developments since his time.

Although Weber's programmatic affirmations demonstrate a willingness to incorporate the processes of nature into sociological theory, some of his substantive characterizations have missed the mark on this score. For example, in one of his many
memorable expressions Weber contended that "an inanimate machine is mind
objectified" (1978: 1402). This one-sided, oversimplified view has been characteristic of sociology, leading it to neglect the role of nature. Correcting Weber on this
important point will hopefully contribute to a correction of contemporary sociology.[4]

Machines involve not just the mind, but also nature and its dynamics. Machines
are more accurately portrayed as "nature manipulated" than as "mind objectified."[5]
Both Weber and contemporary sociology have deflected attention away from an
important point: machines consist of the redeployment of the forces and materials
of nature and hence embody those forces and materials.

For example, the construction of the automobile makes use of some of the materials of nature. Its functioning utilizes nature's process of combustion and its force of
propulsion. The materials are reassembled and the processes redeployed, in a manner
not found in nature, with the purpose of achieving efficient transportation.

Machines also consist of the redeployment of the dynamics of nature in another,
more negative way. To continue with the same illustration, the humanly produced
artifact, the automobile engine, produces waste in the form of air pollution. This in
turn threatens to let loose forces of nature that could have unintended and incalculable consequences, such as the greenhouse effect and other manifestations of global
environmental change. In one sense, all waste that is produced by the human transformation of raw materials into commodities, as well as those commodities themselves when disposed of as waste, are objects resulting from human mental processes
and as such are a variety of forms of "mind objectified." If machines constitute
"mind objectified," so does the pollution resulting from them. Humans, not nature,
produced, used, and discarded tires, wine bottles, polychlorinated biphenyls (PCBs),
CFCs, and dioxins. The human mind has transformed nature's raw materials and
returned them to nature altered in ways that, as they accumulate, threaten in the
long run to unleash forces of nature that will be detrimental to all living species,
including humans.

Examples abound of technology, not just as "mind objectified," but more accurately as the interaction between the human mind and the processes of nature. The
air conditioner consists of a series of chemical and physical processes reassembled in
a new way to pump heat out of hot spaces where humans live, work, and play,
thereby attaining human comfort. The CFCs that are let loose, however, rise to the

upper atmosphere where they react chemically in a manner that depletes the ozone layer hitherto protecting humans and other species from dangerous radiation from the sun. Genetic technology today involves the discovery of the genes that produce specific effects, then reassembling them—as indicated by the terms recombinant DNA, gene splicing, and so on—in combinations not found in nature. This results in the possibility of producing new forms of living species, including new varieties of humans since we, like other species, are a genetically based form of life. It also results in unprecedented dangers.

Machines, and technology in general, are the means by which humans manipulate the processes of nature in the course of their purposive action, often disrupting the self-regulating mechanisms nature has constructed, thereby unleashing unexpected processes of nature. Machines do not imply nature mastered. Their development can, if it disrupts the ecological equilibrium constructed by nature, lead to the iron cage of a degraded ecosystem incapable of sustaining human society. Machines and technology shape the way humans interact with the processes of nature, creating new possibilities and dangers. The first industrial revolution consisted in the discovery of ways to release and use the energy stored by nature in the form of coal to power steam engines in order to produce textiles and other goods previously crafted by human hands.

The second industrial revolution, roughly from 1860 to World War II, harnessed the dynamics of electricity and released the energy stored by nature in oil and gasoline to provide light and transportation, to run motors, and to develop means of instantaneous communication. The internal combustion engine became the workhorse of agriculture, and the living workhorse either disappeared or was changed to pet status. Breeders manipulated the processes of reproduction to develop types of cows that yielded more milk and strains of high-growing cotton that could be machine picked.

The third industrial revolution occurred after World War II when humans developed the means to piggyback on the processes of the electron and steer those electronic processes in order to produce "thinking machines" capable of performing conceptual functions and coordinating production (Rifkin 1995: 59–60). The semiconducting capacities of silicon were used to store and retrieve information. Laser-generated light waves were employed to transmit large volumes of data, images, and voices over long distances using the dynamics of refraction and the properties of flexible, threadlike fibers of glass and plastic, a development we all know as fiber optics. Means were developed to employ gravitational forces to maintain satellites in orbit and to use light rays and other forms of radiation to transmit information between points on Earth using satellites. Methods were elaborated to release the energy of the atom and its nucleus in nuclear reactors and bombs.

Now, in perhaps a fourth industrial revolution that will have the most extensive consequences of all, genetic processes have been discovered and genetic components are being recombined in amalgamations not found in nature in order to create new forms of life to satisfy human need and caprice: "[M]olecular biologists are able to add, delete, recombine, insert, stitch, and edit together genetic materials across biological boundaries, creating novel new microorganisms, plant strains, and animal breeds that have never before existed in nature" (Rifkin 1995: 118).

For example, researchers—financed by DuPont—at the University of British Columbia in Canada have isolated and identified seven genes that enable spiders to make different varieties of silk. Some of these silks are as elastic as rubber and others as strong as steel and have many uses in biomedicine and the automobile industry. The researchers are attempting to capitalize on these capacities with which nature has endowed spiders by genetically engineering their genes into microbes, which would then become silk factories. Genetic engineering also has the potential to revolutionize agricultural, economic, and environmental practices.

There are several points to be made here. First, many of the momentous changes in society have resulted from the human manipulation of nature. Technology and machines that recombine the processes of the material world furnish the means for new social constructions. "Corporations and nation-states are, after all, creatures of the industrial era" (Rifkin 1995: 238). Steam technologies in the first phase of the industrial revolution enabled a reduction in the work week from eighty to sixty hours, and their replacement by electrical and oil technologies permitted a further reduction to forty hours (Rifkin 1995: 222). This decrease in work time provided the basis for many of the social changes that occurred during these periods. These industrial revolutions have had an enormous impact on our way of life, on social structure, and on previously taken-for-granted ways of thinking. The manipulation of nature's processes is an indirect, unauthorized, and often unintended way of revolutionizing society.

The second point is that machines and technology consist of human constructions using, not inert building blocks, but rather the dynamics of nature. These dynamics are often communicated by variants of the word "action": Newton showed that to every *action* there is an equal and opposite re*action*, there are chemical re*actions*, radio*activity* and nuclear re*actors*, the *action* of electrons, geothermal *activity*, and so on. To these can be added the actions of nonhuman species, from cows to oil-slick-eating bacteria, that are manipulated (genetically or otherwise) to attain human goals.

Nature's *actions* do not involve purposes, meanings, or intentions. This must not, however, lead to the erroneous conclusion that nature is static, uncreative, and the like. Nature and the technology and machines constructed from nature consist of processes, dynamics, forces, and emergent properties. It is incorrect to conceive of machines and technology as human constructions *rather than* as the dynamics of nature. The two are not mutually exclusive. Machines and technology consist instead of the recombination and redirection of the processes and materials of nature. They involve learning from what is found in nature, taking materials from it, and redeploying its dynamics in order to construct tools not found in nature to satisfy human need, pleasure, and whim.

The third point follows from the second. Enriching humans by rearranging the dynamics of nature also endangers humans. It involves hazards as well as prospects, perils in addition to possibilities. The risk is that these humanly produced recombinations of nature's processes have the potential of interacting with one another and with nature's constructions in a way destructive to humans and other forms of life. Unlike nature's constructions, they have not been slowly verified over a long period of time through the evolutionary process of natural selection so as to ensure they fit together harmoniously. Whatever advantages they may have, they also contain an equilibrium-disrupting potential, some more than others. The technological manipulation of nature now occurs on such a massive scale that these hazards are no longer just local dangers, but are instead threats to the life-supporting infrastructure of the planet as a whole. Machines—so-called mind objectified—carry the risk, at its most extreme, of reducing the mind to fossilized remains because of the forces of nature they embody and unleash.

REUNITING AUTONOMOUS
SPHERES OF VALUES

Weber argued that rationalization, and in particular the accumulation of knowledge, has "pressed towards making conscious the *internal and lawful autonomy* of the individual spheres [of values]; thereby letting them drift into those tensions which remain hidden to the originally naive relation with the external world" (1958: 328).

He used the expression "spheres of values" to refer to a variety of phenomena, one of which was the development of autonomous spheres of ethics, religion, aesthetics, economics, politics, law, science, and so on. These are spheres of activity with their own distinct requirements and values. The religious sphere emphasizes brotherliness, the political sphere demands a willingness to use violence, the economic sphere requires that people be treated as means to attaining economic goals, and so on (Brubaker 1984). The process of rationalization, and in particular specialization, increased the latent tension between these spheres by intensifying their autonomy.

Weber was correct up to a point. He seemed, however, to perceive the growing autonomy of these spheres of values as a universal consequence of rationalization. He may have been wrong in this respect. Their increasing autonomy may well have been characteristic only of the semimodern period of primary modernization.[6]

Modern rationalization, with its growing capacity to manipulate nature, affects the relationships between these manifestly autonomous spheres of values. Although tensions between them remain high, there are indications of their movement toward reintegration as rationalization becomes reflexive. Beck contends that, as the economy produces ecological risks, "public awareness of the dangers, with the participation of many institutions and groups—in research and television, law and policy—undermines the economy's autonomy, drawing the economic system into social disputes, down to the details of its production" (1995: 141–142). Rifkin argues that the replacement of human labor by computerized machines—as a result of the exploitation of the semiconducting dynamics of the silicon chip—frees up humans and allows us to develop a social economy "centered on human relationships, on feelings of intimacy, on companionship, fraternal bonds, and stewardship" (1995: 292).

Costly developments in medical technology force ethical questions concerning medical practices on humanity on a daily basis, with economic pressures bearing down. For example, in one city there were seven applicants for each space on the kidney dialysis machines, so a hospital committee was struck to decide who received treatment and who was excluded. The group that had to make these decisions about the quality of life and even about life or death was nicknamed the "God Committee." Spheres that had diverged autonomously as specialized disciplines in semimodern industrial society—spheres such as medical science, economics, politics, ethics, and law—are being recoupled by the implications of the new-found manipulations of nature.[7]

New genetic technologies can now combine traits that had been unique to particular species, thereby genetically producing new forms of life. Because humans, like other species, have been created genetically by nature, this new technology opens the possibility of combining human traits with those of other species. Human DNA has already been implanted into a mouse (the humanized mouse was patented by DuPont in 1988) in order to test carcinogens. The development of the means of genetic manipulation can be turned back on the very species—humans—that developed it. This reflexive quality of genetic manipulation then creates the need for reflective rationalization to steer such formal rationalization in terms of substantive values.[8] The discoveries of the processes of nature in genetics, like those of nuclear physics, have led to ethical reflection concerning phenomena that were previously taken for granted. Conditions have similarly been created promoting political struggle to orient such research and its applications.

The destruction of habitats of nonhuman species by industrial development also forces new questions on humans. These questions concern the biological repercussions on humans ourselves, the morality of the unwanted but probable extinction of species by humans, the economics of preventing such extinction, legislative issues of constructing laws and enforcement procedures to prevent extinction, and political strategies to mobilize support for it. The consequences of the human manipulation of nature throw down the ethical challenge of deciding how to achieve self-mastery in order to avoid triggering socially and ecologically catastrophic results.

Reflexive rationalization has set the conditions for the reintegration of these autonomous spheres in the attempt to develop a more reflective rationalization and a symbiotic relationship with the processes of nature (Murphy 1994: 249–254). The fact that nature is an interdependent whole invites humans to unite independent value spheres so as to deal with the consequences of the manipulation of nature. Bosserman concludes that "specialization is diminishing in the face of this new evidence" of the global nature of systems (1995: 55).

Serres (1992: 136) argues that for the first time in three hundred years science is now addressing itself to law and reason is addressing itself to judgment. Reason is now beginning to balance off reason as it becomes the arbitrator that has the potential to reduce our exposure to risk (143–144). Hawken contends that our "personal values, which have become so distant and removed from the juggernauts of commerce, must become increasingly important and, finally, integral to the healthy functioning of our economy" (1993: 136).

FROM PRIMARY TO REFLEXIVE
ALIENATION FROM NATURE

Weber also broached the subject of rationalization as alienation from nature. This took two related forms.

First, he contrasted "agricultural work that is exposed to unusual and unknown natural forces . . . [with the work of urban tradesmen that] makes the connection between means and ends, success and failure relatively transparent. . . . [The latter work] is much less affected by unpredictable natural events. . . . The resulting rationalization and intellectualization parallel the loss of the immediate relationship to the palpable and vital realities of nature" (1978: 1178). Albrow contends that "Weber uses the term *Entfremdung*, 'alienation,' to designate the position of those urban groups to mean precisely the separation of daily life from a unity with nature" (1990: 73). Weber argued that "the forces of nature become an intellectual problem as soon as they are no longer part of the immediate environment" (1978: 1178).

Second, alienating rationality meant that intellectualization promoted a belief by individuals in the mastery of a world that was in principle totally explicable, yet at the same time those individuals had no control over it (Albrow 1990: 122).

Weber presented a valuable characterization of alienation from nature under primary modernization. Urban groups seem detached from nature in their climate-controlled, concrete-and-glass buildings connected by paved highways. They see only meat on their plate, not the factory farms that produced these animal body parts. Science appears to be leading to the mastery of nature that is in principle wholly explicable even though no one individual has control over it.

Separation from nature leading to nature as an intellectual problem is at the heart of important paradoxes. Peasants had no qualms about slitting the throat of animals, as Benton (1993) points out. Many urban dwellers find such an action intellectually problematic, even if their usual response is simply to let slaughterhouses do the dirty work for them. The struggle over the fur industry finds North American Indians enthusiastically supporting the yeas and Bardot leading the nays. The environmental movement has not been a rural movement; on the contrary, it finds most of its support among educated urban dwellers.

Weber's ideas about alienation from nature none the less need to be updated. Both aspects at the root of alienation—separation from nature and belief in mastery over it—are being undermined by environmental problems. As these unintended consequences of rationalization turn back against humans, urban dwellers are becoming aware that they too are threatened by unusual, unknown, and unpredictable natural forces.

Some of these risks are immediate and palpable. As they pump out the aquifers and pollute the air, the inhabitants of Mexico City perceive in their sinking cathedrals and experience with each breath that they are undermining the immediate environment necessary to sustain their lives. The residents of other urban areas with air-quality and water-quality problems worry that Mexico City, because of its peculiar location in the mountains, may be experiencing early what we will all experience later. The citizens of Venice see their buildings and statues corrode. Tourists flee their cities only to find that an oil slick has contaminated the beach at their favorite resort.

Other dangers can be known only through intellectualization, such as the incidence of melanoma because of the depletion of the ozone layer, the greenhouse effect on climate, the development of antibiotic-resistant bacteria because of the overuse of antibiotics, the hazards of aging nuclear reactors on the outskirts of metropolitan areas, and so on. Science informs the urbanites of England that modern tall factory chimneys, which improved the quality of their air, did so at the cost of acid rain in Sweden. Sociology informs those who listen that high-technology accidents are normal (Perrow 1984).

Humanity has been moving along two related growth curves. The first consists of the dynamic of formal rationalization, and in particular, the cumulative growth of scientific and technological knowledge. The second involves the accretion of pollution. At low points on these curves under primary rationalization, urban groups could manipulate nature with apparent impunity and live the double illusion of separation from nature and mastery of it. At later points—the period of reflexive rationalization—even urban groups begin to realize that they too are exposed to "unusual and unknown natural forces" and "unpredictable natural events." The globalization of pollution has unintended local consequences, for example, unusual and unknown climate fluctuations. Hence, changes in the global environment become changes in the immediate environment. Urban dwellers experience and learn the infinite and emergent qualities of nature and begin to doubt that it is totally explicable even "in principle."[9] The taken-for-granted beliefs of primary rationalization—separation from nature and mastery of nature—become increasingly problematic. Yet business as usual keeps people acting as if they were separated from nature and as if they mastered it. Alienation from nature takes on a new form under reflexive rationalization.

Nature was a material problem for peasants in the preindustrial period. Under primary rationalization, it became an intellectual problem for urban workers who discovered means to control it and make it vanish from their immediate environment, as Weber stated. Under reflexive rationalization, unusual and unknown forces of nature and unpredictable natural events unleashed by the human manipulation of nature become palpable and/or conceptualized. Nature is thereby becoming both a material and an intellectual problem.

ENLARGING CONSIDERATION

Weber's theory of social action provides elements that can be used to analyze cultural change to deal with environmental problems. "Action is 'social' insofar as its subjective meaning takes account of the behaviour of others and is thereby oriented in its course" (Weber 1978: 4). Social action "may be oriented to the past, present, or expected future behaviour of others. . . . The 'others' may be individual persons, and may be known to the actor as such, or may constitute an indefinite plurality and may be entirely unknown as individuals" (22). The example Weber gives is of actors who accept money in payment because they expect other actors, including those they do not know, to accept it in exchange for goods and services in the future. "Concretely it [economic activity] is social, for instance, if in relation to the actor's own consumption the future wants of others are taken into account and this becomes one consideration affecting the actor's own saving. Or, in another connexion, production may be oriented to the future wants of other people" (22). Weber is probably thinking here in terms of the predominant form of future orientation in the market, namely, a short-term, instrumental orientation to satisfy one's own wants. His conception none the less opens up other possibilities.

Social action in Weber's sense goes far beyond face-to-face interaction of individuals. It includes action that is oriented in its course to previous generations of humans by way of oral traditions, family stories, history and art books, museums, television and movie documentaries, and so on. It encompasses action oriented to unseen other members of the present generation through media that Weber never knew, such as television, fax machines, the Internet, and so on. And there is no reason why social action could not be oriented to the needs of future generations by taking into account their requirements.

In practice, however, the needs of future generations have not been taken into account in this generation's own consumption. Those needs have not promoted saving, in particular of the environment, by the present generation. Up to now, humans have been oriented only to present and past humans. They have not been oriented toward descendants in terms of bequeathing an environment propitious to meeting their needs. Hence, the present generation runs the risk that successors will be oriented toward it in terms of bitterness and resentment.

Future generations of humans constitute an indefinite plurality and are entirely unknown as individuals to the present generation. This does not prevent social action from being oriented to them. Environmental problems are challenging the present generation of humans to be less obsessed with its own wants and less indifferent to the needs of future generations of humans. The present generation as a social actor can take into account to a greater extent future generations and their needs and thereby reorient the course of its own action. Environmental problems carry with them the potential to broaden the human focus beyond caring only for *this* generation of humans.

For some, probably most in the present generation, the motivation to become good stewards of the environment in order to meet the needs of future humans comes from direct family bonding: the thought of the environmental legacy left to children and grandchildren. For others, the motivation is a matter of principle: caring for all humans, not just the present generation, and treating them with justice. Whether the motivation derives from family ties or from extending the principles of justice, equality, and caring to future generations, the goal-oriented social action is the same: preventing the degradation of the life-supporting ecosystem so that future generations of humans can meet their needs.

Social action does not have to be oriented only to immediate others in space or in time. It can also be oriented to future others, that is, future generations and their needs for a healthy environment. A major cultural change promoted by the threatening character of environmental problems consists of future generations becoming significant others for the present generation, with present social action becoming oriented in its course to them.

NOTES

1. Giddens specifies such a dynamic as follows: Agency "has to be related conceptually to a theory of institutions, and to the large areas of social life [and we can add, material life] that not only escape human intent but in some sense condition it" (1980: 886–887).

2. In the preliminary tests, "positive" results are probabilistic rather than definitive. For example, a "positive" result for Down's syndrome in the enhanced maternal serum alpha-fetoprotein test indicates that the probability is greater than the 1 in 375 cut-off value chosen by physicians. Although this probability is much higher than an average pregnancy, 374 of 375 babies would be born without Down's syndrome. The more conclusive test, amniocentesis, can itself induce miscarriage by introducing a needle into the womb, and the probability of this occurring is not much lower than the probability of a Down's syndrome birth.

3. This argument is elaborated by Murphy (1994: chapter 2), who provides a detailed description of the Weberian conception of rationalization and its relevance for environmental issues.

4. See Murphy (1997: chapter 5) for a treatment of these issues from a different angle.

5. Weber's expression is also an oversimplification in another sense: It ignores that machines involve an element of "mind replaced." Braverman (1974) and Rifkin (1995) show how automated machines have supplanted the mind of the craftsman and more recently that of the worker and even the middle manager: "All of the skills, knowledge, and expertise that were heretofore embedded in the minds of the workers were effectively transferred onto a tape" (Rifkin 1995: 67–68) by numerical control. Machines are the medium by which the minds of craftsmen and workers have been displaced by those of engineers and computer programers.

6. The distinction between primary and reflexive modernization is taken from Beck (1992).

7. This recoupling is not necessarily a positive development. It contains its own set of risks, particularly the risk of the economic dominating the ethical (see Murphy 1997: chapter 9).

8. Albrow (1987) has used the Weberian perspective of the intensification of rationalization to study the regulation of the scientific manipulation of human genetic material.

9. See Murphy (1994: 15–16) for an analysis of the assumptions of primary modernization that nature is finite and that knowledge leads to mastery of nature. These assumptions may have to be replaced under reflexive rationalization by the postulates that nature is infinite and emerging, hence knowledge increases without a decrease in ignorance and without an increase in control over nature.

REFERENCES

Albrow, M. 1987. "The Application of the Weberian Concept of Rationalization to Contemporary Conditions." In *Max Weber, Rationality and Modernity*, ed. S. Whimster and S. Lash, 164–182. London: Allen and Unwin.

———. 1990. *Max Weber's Construction of Social Theory*. London: Macmillan.

Beck, U. 1992. *Risk Society: Towards a New Modernity*. London: Sage.

———. 1994. "Self-Dissolution and Self-Endangerment of Industrial Society." In *Reflexive Modernization*, ed. U. Beck, A. Giddens, and S. Lash, 174–183. Stanford, Calif.: Stanford University Press.

———. 1995. *Ecological Politics in an Age of Risk*. Cambridge: Polity.

Benton, T. 1993. *Natural Relations*. London: Verso.

Bosserman, P. H. 1995. "The Twentieth Century's Saint-Simon: Georges Gurvitch's Dialectical Sociology and the New Physics." *Sociological Theory* 13:48–57.

Braverman, H. 1974. "Labor and Monopoly Capital: The Degradation of Work in the Twentieth Century." New York: Monthly Review.

Brubaker, R. 1984. *The Limits of Rationality: An Essay on the Social and Moral Thought of Max Weber*. London: Allen and Unwin.

Dawe, A. 1978. "Theories of Social Action." In *A History of Sociological Analysis*, ed. T. Bottomore and R. Nisbet, 362–417. New York: Basic.

Feuer, L., ed. 1959. *Introduction to Basic Writings on Politics and Philosophy: Karl Marx and Friedrich Engels*. New York: Anchor.

Giddens, A. 1980. "Classes, Capitalism, and the State." *Theory and Society* 9:877–890.

Hanneman, R., and R. Collins. 1987. "A Dynamic Simulation of Marx's Model of Capitalism." In *The Marx/Weber Debate*, ed. N. Wiley, 91–120. Newbury Park, Calif.: Sage.

Hawken, P. 1993. "The Ecology of Commerce." New York: HarperCollins.

Lyons, F. S. L. 1971. *Ireland since the Famine*. London: Weidenfeld and Nicholson.

———. 1979. *Culture and Anarchy in Ireland, 1890–1939*. Oxford: Oxford University Press.

Murphy, R. 1994. *Rationality and Nature*. Boulder, Colo.: Westview.

———. 1997. *Sociology and Nature: Social Action in Context*. Boulder, Colo.: Westview.

Perrow, C. 1984. *Normal Accidents*. New York: Basic.

Rifkin, J. 1995. *The End of Work*. New York: Putnam's.

Roth, G. 1996. "The Complete Edition of Max Weber's Works: An Update." *Contemporary Sociology* 25:464–467.

Serres, M. 1992. *Le contrat naturel*. Paris: Flammarion.

Weber, M. 1930. *The Protestant Ethic and the Spirit of Capitalism*. Trans. T. Parsons. 1904–1905. Reprint, London: Unwin.

———. 1958. *From Max Weber*. Ed. H. H. Gerth and C. Wright Mills. 1946. Reprint, New York: Oxford.

———. 1978. *Economy and Society*. Ed. Guenther Roth and Claus Wittich. 1922. Reprint, Berkeley: University of California Press.

West, Patrick C. 1985. "Max Weber's Human Ecology of Historical Societies." In *Theory of Liberty, Legitimacy and Power: New Directions in the Intellectual and Scientific Legacy of Max Weber*, ed. V. Murvar. London: Routledge, Kegan Paul.

Woodham-Smith, C. 1962. *The Great Hunger: Ireland 1845–49*. London: Hamilton.

5

Has the Durkheim Legacy Misled Sociology?

William R. Catton Jr.

Foundations for environmental sociology might have been provided by Durkheim's theory of organic solidarity arising in human society through division of labor. He tried to draw on what seemed to be known in biology, a realm he implicitly saw as more comprehensive than the domain of the not-yet-institutionalized science called sociology. But ecological knowledge that makes it easy now to express the problem addressed by Durkheim as the transformation of antagonistic interactions into mutualistic interactions was not then available. His definition of that problem's resolution (specialization enabling organic solidarity to develop by lessening *competition*) was off target. However, subsequent theory development and findings in evolutionary ecology can now turn sociological attention toward a subtly yet fundamentally different transformation: conversion of *predatory* interactions into mutualistic interactions by outcome-changing factors. Issues urgently needing sociological consideration include threats to societies' future from biosphere-damaging industrialism and whether industrial-level division of labor actually tends to foster anomie more than organic solidarity.

Ever since Durkheim, sociologists have believed that two quite different binding forces may hold a human society together—"mechanical solidarity" and "organic solidarity." One is cultural, based on *identification* of a society's members with each other in view of shared traits or a common heritage. The other is fundamentally ecological, based on the *interdependence* of a society's members resulting from the diversity of various members' roles in achieving collective adaptation to the circumstances in which life is lived.

Despite this ecological nature of what Durkheim called "organic solidarity," two things have impeded recognition of him as a precursor of environmental sociology.

First, most of his intellectual heirs have overemphasized his admonition to avoid linking social facts to "facts of a lower order" (psychological, biological, and so on). Sociologists have continued seeking always to explain social facts by linking them only to other strictly social facts. If such a rule for sociological method was useful in establishing sociology as an autonomous discipline, it became too constrictive in the following century when vast increments of both population and industrial technology had drastically altered the ecological situation of humankind in the biosphere. Second, as this chapter will show, potentially ecological contributions of Durkheim's study of the effects of occupational specialization were thwarted by his having misunderstood some biological insights on which he did draw.

Writing when industrialization was bringing enormous change, the first major sociological question raised by Durkheim (1984: xxx) was, as we shall see, a special human case of a broader ecological-evolutionary problem: the rise of mutualistic symbiosis among diverse species. He asked, "How does it come about that the individual . . . can become at the same time more of an individual and yet more linked to society?" The joint occurrence of these two trends seemed contradictory, but he explained it by saying the increasing division of labor was transforming one kind of social solidarity into another.

SOCIOLOGISTS' AMBIVALENCE

Durkheim's work already reflected more than a century ago what Buttel has called sociology's "ambivalent relationship with biology and other disciplines pertaining to the natural environment" (1986: 337). Although "shaped by reaction against biological reductionisms of various sorts (especially social Darwinism and environmental determinism)," says Buttel, theorists in sociology have been "powerfully influenced by images of organismic development, evolution, and adaptation" (337).

Division of labor, Durkheim insisted, was "a general biological phenomenon" and the conditions fostering it were "the essential properties of organised matter" (1984: 2–3). Durkheim (1984) was writing before there was a biological discipline of ecology from which to borrow concepts, but his ideas about the replacement of one kind of social cohesion by another rested on some ideas he had drawn from Darwin's *Origin of Species*. Sociologists ought to wonder whether biological evolution, *as it is now understood*, really does provide the essential premise for Durkheim's argument. His reading of Darwin was selective, as we shall see, and this selectivity misled him.

Several generations of sociologists have been trained to believe human differences are now so thoroughly culture-based that biological evolution can be set aside as no longer humanly relevant, but their professional vocabulary continues to include Durkheim's concept of "organic solidarity." To sociologists using the phrase, the adjective "organic" has apparently ceased to seem biological. Among *socioculturally* differentiated humans, Durkheim's term has come to be regarded as a properly *sociological* designation for interdependence.

Sociology had a distinctive subject matter, Durkheim (1982) insisted, since social phenomena are not explainable by reference to individual biological (or psychological) characteristics. But it was against the social evolutionary views of Spencer and others that Durkheim (1984) argued. Since these arguments purported to draw support from Darwin, Durkheim could not afford to discard evolutionary notions entirely. So his *Division of Labour in Society* used "an evolutionary framework."

In that framework, under certain conditions largely undifferentiated societies (characterized by mechanical solidarity) evolve into modern societies with a complex division of labor (characterized by organic solidarity). What were these conditions under which societies would so evolve? Durkheim emphasized (1) increased population density, (2) the resulting intensification of the struggle over scarce resources, and (3) other social morphological factors.[1] These were the antecedents of industrialization and increasingly complex division of labor. His focus on them actually laid some foundations useful for an environmental sociology, but its development would not occur until many decades later. He tried to show how—by mitigating direct competition over resources and by causing cultural changes that would redefine and expand resources—the social division of labor helped adapt denser and more populous societies to their environments (Buttel 1986: 339–340).

Interdependence was a core concept. It seemed to Durkheim an essential aspect not only of the occupational world, but also of primary group relations, for he wrote that "we seek in our friends those qualities we lack, because in uniting with them we share in some way in their nature, feeling ourselves then less incomplete. In this way," he said, "a veritable exchange of services occurs . . . and it is this . . . *division of labour*, that *determines these relations of friendship*" (1984: 17, emphasis added).

This view of interpersonal relations led Durkheim "to consider the division of labour in a new light" (1984: 17). It caused him to argue that the economic services rendered by division of labor "are insignificant compared with the moral effect that it produces, and its true function is to create between two or more people a feeling of solidarity" (17).

He came to see division of labor as a mechanism that allowed persistence of social relations between a society's otherwise competing members. By specializing, people not only limited their range of competition, they also became interdependent.

According to Durkheim's theory, this "organic" solidarity could not arise among unbonded individuals. The existence of a prior bond ("mechanical" solidarity) among a society's members was necessary for the emergence of the new, interdependence-based, solidarity, but as the organic kind of solidarity developed he hoped it would function as the replacement bond between people among whom mechanical solidarity was disintegrating.

Does the elaborate division of labor in today's world (entailing interdependence among differentiated roles) really produce the organic solidarity Durkheim believed was an expectable result of increasing occupational specialization? Will such organic solidarity protect today's industrial societies from collapse under present and now foreseeable disintegrative pressures, including those arising from what the requirements of industrial civilization inexorably do to the biosphere?[2]

AN ECOLOGICAL WORLDVIEW AND
DURKHEIM'S CONCERN

For all its merits, Durkheim's theorizing about organic solidarity was hobbled by the unavailability a century ago of today's knowledge of ecology and evolution. This chapter explains how a crucial misconception occurred and suggests some implications of a different approach that was not really possible when Durkheim wrote. Essentially, as some acquaintance with concepts of modern ecology enables us to see, Durkheim was trying to explain how competition could be abated as a supposed prerequisite to the rise of what ecologists now call mutualism. But perhaps competition abatement was not the real problem. Instead, the real challenge, which no one in Durkheim's time was conceptually prepared to recognize, may have been to account for emergence of mutualism from a different kind of antagonistic relation.

There is more than a rough correspondence between a "role" in sociology and a "niche" in ecology.[3] Reappraisal of the theory of organic solidarity must therefore consider the ecological worldview and the kinds of issues it prompts one to address. For Durkheim, the members of a human society must depend on limited resources, and when faced with increasing population density they would have been destructively competing with each other had they not learned to specialize. Human occupational specialization was, for Durkheim, a special case of niche differentiation (to put it in modern ecological language).

The ecologist's concept of a community, defined as "an assemblage of organisms living together," shows that some of Durkheim's major concerns when he wrote about division of labor were indeed ecological. The ecological community derives structure from interactions of various sorts in which energy flows from plants to animals and microbes, matter cycles among these various organisms, and "services" are provided by the various constituent populations to each other (e.g., bees pollinating flowers, plants releasing oxygen for animals to breathe, and so on). Some interactions benefit both member populations (mutualism). Some benefit one while doing no apparent harm to the other (commensalism). And some are detrimental to one or both species (predation, parasitism, and competition) and the problem these pose for the ecologist is this: How can such "antagonistic pairs of species" persist together without one driving the other to extinction? Thus, the ecologist asks essentially the question that challenged Durkheim: "What mechanisms stabilize these negative interactions, allowing persistence?" (Connell 1980: 132).

It is evident today that there is *throughout the living world* mutual dependence of populations of differentiated organisms living in symbiosis with each other. With modern knowledge, we can explore parallel cases at various levels from microscopic to global. Even more clearly than in the time of Durkheim, we can indeed see division of labor in human society as a special instance of that widespread pattern, symbiotic mutual dependence among diverse organisms (Hawley 1950: 29–31; Duncan 1964; Love 1977). Members of a single species, *Homo sapiens*, are able as a result of sociocultural differentiation, to function as if they were an assortment of different species. In view of what he did say about division of labor, can anyone doubt that a

Durkheim further informed by late twentieth-century ecological literature would see each occupational category as having its own specialized resource requirements, patterns of association, and effects on the whole community?

For ecologists, differentiated organisms living interdependently are each other's *symbionts.* Sociologists must recognize an important extension of the meaning of the ecological term "symbiont." Humans do have symbionts that are nonhuman (e.g., crop plants, livestock, seeing-eye dogs, and brewer's yeast), but in the ecology of human beings, it is common for many of our symbionts to be differently specialized members of our own species. Using different skills and paraphernalia, and thus functioning as if they were different species, many symbionts of humans can be other humans. In the resources they require and the ways they impact the shared environment, occupationally specialized humans differ from other humans in other occupational specialties.

This broadened ecological perspective about symbiotic relations highlights the plausibility of Durkheim's comparison of human occupational specialization to speciation (cf. Cain 1960; Stephan 1970).

DURKHEIM'S SUPPOSITIONS

Durkheim regarded biological facts as supportive of his sociological analysis. But when evolutionary theory was so new and nascent, a social theorist of even Durkheim's ability and zeal could not discern unerringly its true implications for sociology. Durkheim supposed Darwin's theory of the origin of diversity between species provided a basis for understanding division of labor within a human population.

"Darwin very aptly remarked," said Durkheim "that two organisms vie with each other more keenly the more alike they are. Having the same needs and pursuing the same purposes, they are everywhere to be found in a state of rivalry. So long as they possess more resources than each needs," said Durkheim, paraphrasing Darwin, "they can still live cheek by jowl. But if each happens to increase in number in such proportions that all appetites can no longer be sufficiently assuaged, war breaks out and it is the more violent the more striking the shortfall, that is, the numbers vying with one another are greater" (1984: 208–209).

Still relying on his reading of Darwin, Durkheim went on to say, "The situation is totally different if the individuals coexisting together are of different species or varieties. As they do not feed in the same way or lead the same kind of life, they do not impede one another. What causes some to flourish lacks value for others. The occasions for conflict are therefore less" (1984: 209).

But Darwin's actual theory of speciation does not support (in the way Durkheim supposed) the fundamental idea deeply embedded in modern sociology by our Durkheimian heritage—that organic solidarity is the direct (and normal) result of division of labor, a potentially positive basis for societal well being. Only in Book III did Durkheim consider adverse consequences, calling them "abnormal forms," and Book III comprises less than 15 percent of the entire dissertation, a mere 50 pages out of 341 total pages of text.

As Durkheim wrote about specialization of functions, the type of biological thought on which he drew had to do primarily with the structure and physiology of organisms, *not their ecology,* a difference not sufficiently clear in his time. There is less excuse today for the fact that very few sociologists even yet adequately consider the involvement of human societies in ecosystems. Ecosystems were defined by Tansley as the whole interactive complex of organisms and physical circumstances constituting "the basic units of nature on the face of the earth" (1935: 299). The very existence of these natural units involves a circular "exchange of materials between the living and nonliving parts" (Odum 1953: 9) and between different living components, as well as "noncircular flows of . . . energy and information" (Duncan 1964: 37).

Writing early in the final decade of the nineteenth century, when the word "ecosystem" was not yet coined and the concept not yet crystalized, Durkheim may be forgiven for not having adequately perceived human societies as subsystems within ecosystems (see, in contrast, McDonnell and Pickett 1993; Bennett 1993; Dunlap and Catton 1994). It is no wonder his study of division of labor was unable to make best use of some of the nonhuman examples of task specialization and interdependence he invoked. As other early sociologists had done, Durkheim made use of an analogy between a society and an organism. Had he been in a position to consider human division of labor as a special instance of the more general biological phenomenon of *interspecific* division of ecological functions, this would have had some implications Durkheim never suspected.

He began Book III by saying that thus far he had studied division of labor "only as a normal phenomenon. Yet, like all social facts, and *more generally,*" he added, "*like all biological ones,* it manifests pathological forms that we must analyse" (1984: 291, emphasis added). Additional knowledge about speciation processes and their consequences that have accumulated through advances in evolutionary science since Darwin's time requires challenging Durkheim's relegation of anomie to the side-effect category—as an "abnormal expression" of division of labor.

DURKHEIM'S RELIANCE ON DARWIN

How much did Durkheim rely on Darwin and biology? Today's sociologists are taught to think that Durkheim (1982: 134, 141) adamantly insisted on sociology's separation from other sciences.[4] They overlook the way Durkheim deplored the fact that "the jurist, the psychologist, the anthropologist, the economist, the statistician, the linguist, the historian . . . go about their investigations as if the various orders of facts that they are studying formed so many independent worlds" (1984: 304). Instead, he said, "these facts interlock with one another at every point. Consequently the same should occur for the corresponding sciences." Remembering Durkheim for his idea that "the causes of social phenomena are internal to the society," which led to his "rule" that "[t]he determining cause of a social fact must be sought among antecedent social facts," sociologists are too unmindful of the fact that he explicitly denied "society is outside nature" (322). He cited several physiologists who had shown "that the law of division of labour applies to organisms as well as to societies," and he said division of labor was accordingly not merely a "social institution whose roots lie in the intelligence and the will of men, but a *general biological phenomenon*, the conditions for which must seemingly be sought in the essential properties of organised matter. The division of labour in society appears *no more than a special form of this general development*" (3, emphasis added).

He believed complex organisms result when "in certain conditions, the simpler ones remain grouped together in such a way as to form entities of greater size" (Durkheim 1984: 277).[5] He was hardly insisting on separation of the sciences when he went on to say: "The growth of organic substance is therefore the fact dominating all zoological development. It is not surprising that *social development* is subject to the same law" (277, emphasis added).

A continuum of symbiosis exists all the way from this microlevel to the entire biosphere.[6] At all levels, differentiated entities relate to each other interdependently. There is a *web* of life. Durkheim clearly understood Darwin on this point, much better than did other social commentators in the last decades of the nineteenth century. The hindsight advantage afforded by some acquaintance with modern evolutionary studies reveals more fully than ever Durkheim's avoidance of an egregious misconception of Darwinism that was all too common among Durkheim's contemporaries. Darwin's acceptance of Spencer's phrase "survival of the fittest" as a supposed synonym for natural selection misled many so-called social Darwinists who too easily misunderstood fitness in moralistic or chauvinistic terms. To Durkheim's credit, his focus was quite different. He concentrated on Darwin's idea of speciation as niche diversification and on resource partitioning as its result.

For Durkheim (1984: 213–217), the importance of this niche-differentiation process seemed to be its effectiveness in alleviating the competition that otherwise seemed inevitable when increasing population pressed on limited resources. The language was different a century ago, but essentially what Durkheim believed was that competing species coevolve so that their niches become differentiated enough for many species to coexist harmoniously. Darwin-like (1859: 110–119), he wrote that organisms differing from each other in resource requirements compete less intensely with each other than organisms whose demands on their surroundings are identical or nearly so. Durkheim specifically cited Darwin (1859: 121) as a source for the idea: "For it should be remembered that the competition will generally be most severe between those forms which are most nearly related to each other in habits, constitution, and structure" (Durkheim 1984: 208).

This is the basis, then, for Durkheim's contention that, among humans, occupational differentiation served the same function as speciation served among nonhumans. The musician no more competes with the carpenter than the moose with the beaver. To each his own niche. In modern ecological terms, Durkheim's theory was about "niche widths" being narrowed as niches became more numerous. When niches don't overlap, their occupants don't compete.

Were Durkheim living today, however, it seems doubtful he could observe our fractious world (Birnbaum 1969; Dionne 1991; Harris 1989; Kaplan 1994) with such equanimity as to presume that organic solidarity was still the ascendant effect of advanced industrial division of labor, while anomie was merely an avoidable side effect. A two-part question about Durkheim's reliance on Darwin needs therefore to be considered: (1) Did Darwin really see minimization of competition as "the function" of speciation? (2) Had Durkheim misunderstood Darwin after all, even though not in the same way others of his time were misconstruing "survival of the fittest"? Sociologically, as we shall see, a further question remains: If division of labor allows coexisting specialists to compete less with each other, does that bind them together? Does cohesion enhancement follow from competition mitigation? These questions call for careful study not only of Durkheim's *Division of Labour in Society*, but also of Darwin's *On the Origin of Species by Means of Natural Selection*.

Actually, Durkheim had unwittingly reversed the real meaning of what Darwin was saying, as can be seen by looking at the sentence in *context*—between two adjacent sentences of Darwin's that show he was writing about a process of competition enhancement, not competition abatement.

> *As in each fully stocked country natural selection necessarily acts by the selected form having some advantage in the struggle for life over other forms, there will be a constant tendency for the improved descendants of any one species to supplant and exterminate in each stage of descent their predecessors and their original parent.* For it should be remembered that the competition will generally be most severe between those forms which are most nearly related to each other in habits, constitution, and structure. *Hence all the intermediate forms between the earlier and later stages, that is between the less and more improved state of the species, as well as the original parent-species itself, will generally tend to become extinct.* (1859: 121, emphasis added)

Sociologists also need to know about some important advances in evolutionary science in recent decades that appear to contradict Durkheim.

STREAM SPLITTING: NEW OPPORTUNITIES OR DEAD-END STREET?

To depict life and evolution in vivid terms for the nonbiologist, Dawkins (1995) described a species metaphorically as "a river of DNA" flowing through time rather than space. When this river divides and becomes two or more rivers, speciation has occurred; one species has split into two or more species. Biologists mean by "speciation" the *differentiation* of a population into distinct types that do not interbreed and whose genetically produced traits are adapted to different environmental conditions, so Dawkins's image of splitting streams can be helpful in reassessing Durkheim's theory about division of labor.

Speciation is said to be *allopatric* when it results from two or more subpopulations becoming separated when some geographic barrier intervenes, thereby splitting streams of descent from the original population of organisms. Each separated subpopulation must adapt to its particular habitat. When an existing species thus divides into two, for some environmental reason, organisms descended from a common ancestor have gone their separate ways, so they, in turn, will be ancestral to *separate* streams of descendants.

Separate species have separate niches. That is, each species has its special resource requirements, differs from other species in its interactions with other organisms, and has different impacts on its surroundings. In any ecosystem, these differing species are in various ways interdependent (because of their differences). Between human occupational specialties, likewise, resource requirements, interactions with others, and environmental impacts also differ, just as they do between species.

Among *socially* differentiated humans, it is streams of *cultural* "descent" that are divided—by *specialized socialization* (with or without any concomitant division of genetic inheritance). The dividing stream image (from Dawkins) suggests it was quite reasonable for Durkheim (1984: 222, 224) to regard human interdependence arising from *social* differentiation into occupational specialties as a sociological counterpart of the interdependence among other species attributable to their differences from each other. The term "quasi speciation," introduced by Hutchinson (1965), has been used[7] to refer to nongenetic differentiation of a human population into differently specialized subgroups by use of alternative tools, customs, or symbols.

Sociologists who happen to renew acquaintance with biological literature today may learn that the diversity on which interdependence depends is not necessarily a condition protecting former competitors from each other. Modern ecological knowledge is not supportive of Durkheim's (1984: 205–217) leap from the facilitation of greater total number of inhabitants accommodated by an area to greater interdependence and solidarity among them. Much more has been learned since Darwin about the forces and conditions that bring about the stream splitting called speciation. Mayr has written that each species is "a biological experiment. . . . The probability is very high that the new niche into which it shifts is an evolutionary dead-end street. There is no way to predict, as far as the incipient species is concerned, whether the new niche it enters is a dead-end or the entrance into a large new adaptive zone" (1963: 601). This cautionary insight from Mayr should probably be applied to the cultural quasi species that arise within one biological species, *Homo sapiens*. A cultural breakthrough that moves a portion of humankind ecologically into a new niche (or new complex of niches), may likewise be either a dead-end or an "entrance into a large new adaptive zone." Perhaps at the time of entry—and even, perhaps, for many generations afterward—it may be impossible to discern whether the destiny toward which it is going to lead is desirable or disastrous.

Consider the horticultural revolution. In Neolithic times, humans began learning how to function as managers, rather than mere members, of ecosystems. Was this a great leap forward or a commitment to eventual disaster?[8]

What about the industrial revolution? We began earnestly harnessing fossil energy to human tasks—and this led to exponentially advancing technology, vast urban complexes, enormously ramified occupational specialization, intricate and increasingly global webs of exchange, interdependence, and mutual exploitation. The further ramified division of labor involved in all this has increased human commitment to managing (rather than just participating in) ecosystems. Did this open the gates into an earthly paradise or were we stepping incautiously onto a steepening slippery slope?

SYMPATRIC OR ALLOPATRIC SPECIATION?

An ecologist's stipulation that "[t]he likelihood of coevolution between two competing species depends [not only] upon how similar their resource requirements are [but also] how often they meet" initially seems to echo Durkheim's (1984: 203) use of the concept of "moral density" (meaning, essentially, frequency of interactions—which might depend somewhat but not entirely on sheer population density) as a causal variable to account for niche divergence (i.e., occupational differentiation). Here, though, ecological research findings are hardly supportive of Durkheim, for coevolution between actual competitors is unlikely. It is more likely to happen "in pairs of species on different trophic levels than in pairs competing on the same trophic level" (Connell 1980: 137). Species are more likely to have diverged as they evolved in separate places. If they later come together, they are able to coexist *because they have already become adapted to different resources or to different parts of the habitat.*

This new understanding of speciation undermines Durkheim's thesis that competition-reduction was division of labor's "function." How so? Although divergence may facilitate later coexistence, if speciation occurs "allopatrically," then we must recognize that among the geographically separated populations it was not any *need to coexist* that operated as a selection pressure shaping the evolution of differences between these species. Darwin sensed this, so it calls into question the accuracy (as well as the validity) of Durkheim's reliance on Darwin.

As evolutionary biologists understand speciation, it is usually a branching process resulting when a population spreads into a number of areas, and some areas become isolated from others through geological or climatological change. The separate subpopulations, subjected to different selection pressures, evolve differently. Eventually, they may become sufficiently unlike to be separate species. Thus, among animals, and especially vertebrates, most speciation has for some time now been considered allopatric, not sympatric (Jordan 1905; Wright 1943; Lack 1947; 1949; Ford 1949; Mayr 1954; 1959; 1963; 1982; White 1968; Shorrocks 1978; Vrba 1985; Loomis 1988; Lynch 1989; Dawkins 1995).

How then can whatever species diversity is found within a particular community have arisen? After further geologic or climatic change has removed former barriers, a number of allopatrically originated species perhaps eventually find niches on common ground (as each disperses from its place of origin). Some niches are more and some less complementary to each other and this does influence which in-migrating species will succeed in coexisting on common ground. But the complementarity was not "selected for" by the evolutionary constraints to which the formerly allopatric species were subjected *as they evolved in their scattered environments.*

When various species happen to come together, if they have changed enough in their formerly separated environments, they do not interbreed. Reproductive isolation is the defining feature of biological species (Mayr 1957) and Darwin's achievements included recognizing the importance of this (Sulloway 1979: 28–30). But geographic isolation precedes and facilitates reproductive isolation (Wright 1943; Lack 1949).

That sequence is important for our reappraisal of the Durkheimian foundation of sociology. The question of sympatric versus allopatric speciation had not become an issue at the time Durkheim wrote, but he would apparently have been predisposed toward seeing speciation as sympatric. Spencer had attributed different occupational aptitudes to the fact that people had lived in different surroundings. Although Spencer did not use today's evolutionary vocabulary, he thus appeared to be seeing division of labor as having allopatric roots. In Book II, chapter 2, of *The Division of Labour in Society*, Durkheim had dissented. In flat disagreement with Spencer, Durkheim wrote, "If labour becomes increasingly divided as societies become more voluminous and concentrated, it is not because the external circumstances are more varied, it is because the struggle for existence becomes more strenuous" (1984: 208–209).

According to the assumption Durkheim was incorrectly imputing to Darwin, intensification of the struggle for existence would suffice to cause an ancestral species population to divide into differently specialized daughter species even while *sharing the same environment*, and would thereby allocate that environment's resources in a less competitive manner than organisms that remained undifferentiated would have done.

To use modern ecological vocabulary (not yet devised by the time of Darwin, or even Durkheim, but increasingly familiar now to environmental sociologists), Durkheim was taking Darwin's idea of speciation to be a means of enlarging, by resource partitioning, an environment's total carrying capacity. Diversifying a *particular* environment's inhabitants would enlarge the number of inhabitants it could support. And although Durkheim was implicitly supposing that the process occurred sympatrically, Darwin's explanation of speciation, on which Durkheim supposed he was leaning, actually envisioned allopatry. New species and their parent species might be prevented from competing with each other, Darwin had suggested, if "the modified offspring of a species get into some distant country . . . *in which child and parent do not come into competition*" (1859: 121–122, et passim, emphasis added). Departure rather than difference might be the means of escaping extinction! Emigrate or perish.

Wilson says "the niche differences that guarantee [diverse species'] coexistence are simply accidental outcomes of their divergent evolution in the period prior to contact" (1975: 276). And Mayr says that "polytypic species with striking variation are invariably secondarily fused mosaics of former founder populations" (1989: 155)— meaning descendants of formerly dispersed small clusters of ancestors.

Paragraphs in which Durkheim invoked Darwin clearly indicate that Durkheim did not suppose Darwin was writing about "accidental outcomes" or "secondarily fused mosaics," that is, terms that acknowledge the allopatric aspect of speciation. Species diversity viewed that way hardly serves as a model for expecting "organic solidarity" to be the main effect of division of labor in society. Nor, so viewed, would the species diversity found in communities "reassembled" by migration support the functionalist notion that minimization of competition is the advantage of specialization that enables specialization to evolve.

SELECTIVELY MISREADING DARWIN

So, although Durkheim thought the essential premise for his argument was supported by Darwin, he was seriously misreading Darwin. Of course, it is natural to pay more attention to some of the material we read than to other portions. Each of us resonates more with certain ideas than with others. Everyone reads selectively. To say that Durkheim did so is not to denigrate his scholarship. But it does add to our understanding of the influences that shaped his metasociological legacy and the sociological ideas of his modern legatees.

Durkheim's selectivity in reading Darwin was shaped by convictions much like today's lingering tendency to regard evolution as "sensible and predictable progress, continuously moving toward desired ends by working for the good of groups and communities" (Gould 1995: 8). Durkheim was motivated to read Darwin in that way so he could suppose the more extensive division of labor developing in his time would result in organic solidarity. He ardently wanted to believe the past troubles his native France had survived were prelude to a progressive future (see, e.g., Coser 1977: 149–163).

By having selectively read *On the Origin of Species*, it was possible for Durkheim to suppose he had support from Darwin for his implicit assumption that species diversity evolves because competing species need relief from competition. Durkheim's assumption was tantamount to supposing that speciation occurs sympatrically and results from a quest for minimal competition and maximal biomass support. But Durkheim could only have supposed that was Darwin's view by persistently missing a point Darwin (1859: 200–201, 205, 243) had repeatedly cautioned his readers about—that natural selection does not alter one species just for the benefit of other species. Character displacement between two species A and B, which increases the difference between them, does not occur by selection pressures altering species A *for the advantage* of species B. Changes in A occur because they are *advantageous for A*. If the increased difference somehow benefits B as well, that is incidental. Darwin (1859: 200–201) was quite explicit about this.

Besides, coevolution does not always increase *differentiation*. It can sometimes increase the *resemblance* between two species. Mimicry and protective coloration are cases in point (see Rothschild 1967; Wickler 1968; 1976; Owen 1980; Marden 1992). Mimicry occurs when a prey species achieves reduced vulnerability by evolving visual resemblance to another species that escapes predation by being unpalatable to their common predator. Durkheim appears to have remained unacquainted with the fact that interspecific similarities (not just differences) could result from natural selection.

Durkheim's innocently selective reliance on Darwin also overlooked something else Darwin had explicitly recognized—that products of speciation could be very much embroiled in *interspecific* competition, sometimes to the point of one species bringing another to extinction. Clearly, Darwin was not writing about differentiation as a *mitigator* of competition when he wrote that the "modified descendants of any one species will succeed by so much the better as they become more diversified in structure, and are thus enabled to *encroach* on places occupied by other beings" (1859: 116, emphasis added).

Supposing the passages quoted from Darwin supported his argument, Durkheim resorted to a questionable organismic analogy—"within an organism what lessens the rivalry between the different tissues is the fact that they feed on different substances" (1984: 209).[9] With the brief declaratory sentence, "Men are subject to the same law," Durkheim moved from species diversity (and tissue differentiation) to occupational diversity—from physiological and ecological division of function to societal division of labor. Different occupations, he said, "can coexist without being forced into a position where they harm one another, for they are pursuing different objectives" (209).

Plausible as it seemed for Durkheim (1984: 209) to suggest that the soldier could pursue military glory, the priest moral authority, the industrialist wealth, and the scientist professional fame, all freed from mutual interference by the diversity of their respective goals, his presuming a Darwinian basis for that plausibility was possible only because of his neglect of some essential details of Darwin's argument.

Darwin's view of diversity was not what Durkheim construed it to be— principally a means of minimizing competition. For Darwin, diversity involved enhanced specialization, and specializing was a means of gaining competitive advantage rather than avoiding competition. When Durkheim was reading Darwin, the science of ecology was too unformed for the issue to be clear. Durkheim appreciated the apparently harmonious symbiosis prevailing among diverse associated species and was unlikely to see the association as a matrix of interspecific competition *and species displacement* going on and on.[10] His apparent image of such an advanced seral stage in a biotic community was the image expressed millennia earlier in the Bible by Isaiah: "The wolf shall dwell with the lamb, and the leopard shall lie down with the kid; and the calf and the young lion and the fatling together" (11:6). Today, with ecologically informed hindsight, environmental sociologists can recognize that Durkheim thought Darwin had described a drive toward universal mutualism (i.e., toward unequivocally and mutually beneficial interdependence of all species associated in a given community). But it is not true that all interspecific relations tend toward mutualism. Predatory and parasitic relations continue to exist (and additional ones continue to evolve).

HOW MUTUALISMS EVOLVE

Could sociological theorists legitimately argue that Durkheim's misreading of Darwin doesn't matter—that even if diversity among species evolves allopatrically rather than sympatrically, what really matters is the fact that diversity enables some formerly allopatric species to coexist without competing when they happen to get together? And even if Darwin saw specialization raising rather than lowering the perils of competition, didn't Durkheim endow sociology with a valid insight about division of labor when, by considering its equivalence to speciation, he saw how vital it is to recognize that *organic solidarity may break down if no sufficient vestige of mechanical solidarity remains?*[11]

The vocabulary of modern ecology makes it clear that Durkheim's concept of organic solidarity represented a human instance of the type of bond among assorted specialists that ecologists would call *mutualism.*[12] Because neither in Darwin's time nor in Durkheim's was there yet a developed science of ecology; there was also no adequate ecological vocabulary for either man to use in formulating questions about interdependence between species populations, such as: How might antagonistic relations become mutualistic relations? As we can now recognize, that was the question Durkheim was trying to answer (for the special case: human society). What Durkheim's *Division of Labour in Society* purported to offer was a theory as to how mutualistic relations arise and replace the competitive relations otherwise prevalent in a society too populous for mechanical solidarity. When sociologists cease insisting that there can never be meaningful parallels between human relations and relations among nonhuman organisms, we can meaningfully compare Durkheim's theory with what evolutionists and ecologists have learned about the way mutualisms develop.[13]

The fact that mutualism "is not as common in the natural world as predation and parasitism" (Rickleffs 1979: 226) turns out to be important for reappraising Durkheim's idea of the way organic solidarity develops. Although the concept of organic solidarity does signify mutualism between human symbionts, the question remains: Does such human mutualism result from a process comparable to the model Durkheim supposed he was deriving from Darwin—speciation leading to interdependence between *sibling* species?[14]

Plants and animals, "most remote in the scale of nature, are bound together by a web of complex relations," said Darwin (1859: 73), who understood well that only some of these relations were mutually beneficial to the interacting organisms. Such "complex co-adaptations" could be observed "everywhere throughout nature" (Darwin 1859: 132).

Perhaps Durkheim had not fully grasped the "large and metaphorical sense" in which Darwin used the phrase "struggle for existence." To illustrate it, Darwin had described an example of the kind of interaction modern ecologists call mutualism. On an apple tree, he wrote "several seedling missletoes [sic], growing close together on the same branch, may . . . be said to struggle with each other. As the missletoe is disseminated by birds, its existence depends on birds; and it may metaphorically be said to struggle with other fruit-bearing plants, in order to tempt birds to devour and thus disseminate its seeds rather than those of other plants" (1958b: 63). The mutualism here was between bird and plant, not between one plant and another.[15] And even Durkheim would presumably never have imagined that sibling subspecies might be evolving on that apple tree and *using their differences to become noncompetitively interdependent* with each other, that is, to interact mutualistically. Some significant flaws in what Durkheim *had* tried to read into Darwin, however, are revealed by this mistletoe example.

First, there is the extreme remoteness of the time when plant and animal kingdoms diverged. This makes it extremely far-fetched to imagine that any competition-reducing differentiation occurring among a population of some organic species ancestral to both a plant and a seed-consuming bird could account for bird-mistletoe differences and thereby buttress Durkheim's belief that competition-abatement was the antecedent to organic solidarity. Second, human division of labor can hardly be analogous to the differentiation occurring *within* the mistletoe population. Mistletoe forms that were less able to attract seed-consuming (and thus seed-dispersing) birds were outcompeted by forms more attractive to birds. Darwin's example provided no reason to imagine that competition between forms had *abated* through specialization, nor evolved into a "division of labor" among mistletoe varieties.

Did organic solidarity have to follow a diminution of competition, as Durkheim assumed? Ecological and evolutionary studies since his time show the real issue had been muddled by that assumption. He would have been astonished by later biologists' discovery that the absence of antagonistic relations was not a prerequisite for the evolution of mutualistic relations. Mutualistic relations evolve among former predator-prey pairs of species, not just between former competitors or commensals.

So what *are* the ecological bases for the evolution of mutualism? Durkheim was missing an important point that Darwin seemed to sense. Eventual mutualists do not need first to attain a neutral commensalism resembling the circumstances that underlie Durkheim's "mechanical solidarity." Mutualisms actually often *depend* on "pre-existing antagonistic interactions" (Thompson 1982: 69) between the species that are going to become mutualists.

Durkheim would have been astonished to learn that most mutualistic relationships have probably evolved from host-parasite, predator-prey, or plant-herbivore interactions (Rickleffs 1979: 226), rather than among formerly competing conspecifics. There are initially *antagonistic* interactions (e.g., predator-prey pairs) in which selection pressures, over time, convert them directly into mutualisms (Thompson 1982: 61–69; Catton 1998a: 113–116) without the conversion passing first through a neutral phase. Examples include insect pollination of flowering plants[16] and the evolution of fleshy fruits that attract vertebrates to serve as seed-dispersal agents. In each case, the plant species has evolved a "substitute bait" (nectar in flowers to attract insects that formerly *consumed* pollen and fruits encasing seeds to be discarded or passed by fruit-eating animals[17] that formerly would have digested the seeds).

There are also examples of mutualism between two vertebrate species, possibly evolved from former predator-prey interactions: "cleaner fish" feed on ectoparasites and other materials harmful to the host fish on whose body surface or within whose oral and gill cavities the "cleaners" feed (Thompson 1982: 67–68).

IMPLICATIONS FOR SOCIOLOGY

A modern Durkheim could draw the following conclusion: Not only is there "close evolutionary dependence of many kinds of mutualism on pre-existing antagonistic interactions," but it is precisely those antagonistic interactions *from which the parties cannot escape* that may evolve toward mutualism through a change of outcome (Thompson 1982: 69). Traits arise in prey and/or predator that *change the outcome.* In the evolution of each of these mutualisms from antagonistic interactions, if the interaction were avoidable by predator choosing alternative prey or by prey emigrating, the selection pressure favoring a modified outcome would be missing.[18]

Suppose Durkheim had been somehow prepared to work out the implications of these statements as they might apply to human occupational categories (as quasi species). Sociologists may legitimately imagine he might then have been led, three-fourths of a century before Schnaiberg (1975; 1980), to some notion of a "societal-environmental dialectic." Remember, Durkheim sought to account for the simultaneous but "contradictory" increase of individuality and interdependence.

Between the interacting *species populations*, a preexisting "bond" did exist, but an inescapable predator-prey relationship was not a bond based on similarity between the species, so it was hardly analogous to mechanical solidarity as described by Durkheim. Yet, it was from this preexisting bond (this antagonistic interaction from which the parties could not escape) that a mutualistic relation evolved—as one party evolved some new trait(s) to change the outcome of the interaction. To Durkheim, it seemed abatement of competition by means of differentiation was an essential development that removed an otherwise insurmountable barrier to mutualistic interdependence. That was why division of labor was supposed to result in organic solidarity.

He expected it to work that way in human society "because," he supposed, it works that way among nonhuman species interacting in nature. But the pattern conceived by Durkheim is not the way it works in nature. Were he reading Darwin today (with ecological-evolutionary hindsight), Durkheim would not be so likely to suppose that Darwin saw it that way. Mutualism can evolve from antagonism without the intervening "neutral" (competition abated) stage. Evolutionary ecologists now know that mutualism evolves by some adaptation of structure or behavior that *changes* the outcome of an interaction from which the parties cannot withdraw.[19]

MUTUALISM LOST?

Durkheim aside, we now know that mutualism can arise from such forms of conflict as parasitism or predation. But is that direction of change invariable? Evolution may also in some circumstances go in the reverse direction (Vandermeer 1984: 224). Mutualistic interactions among humans, not just among nonhumans, can perhaps, under conditions we need to be studying, revert to parasitic or predatory relations.

Rethinking Durkheim in light of modern evolutionary biology can thus lead to questioning the strength of social cohesion possible in a modern, high-energy, pluralistic, industrial society. Modern conditions require sociologists to focus more than Durkheim did on anomic division of labor. Does anything ensure that the effects of *industrial-level* social differentiation must be forever benign? Apprehensions expressed early in the twentieth century by Ross (1907), that division of labor could put us asunder in a life of mutual predation, may fit current societal conditions and events more closely than does Durkheim's prematurely hopeful anticipation of new cohesiveness.

Was organic solidarity the main effect of industrial-level division of labor, as Durkheim contended so hopefully in 1893? Or were humans becoming entrapped in a system that would not only undermine the ecosystem foundations for human societies, but would also nurture whatever antisocial tendencies people might have? Ross saw industrial-level interdependence as a condition that puts people "at one another's mercy" and thereby makes possible "a multitude of new forms of wrong doing" (1907: 4). Ross's view was reiterated three generations later as the explanation for America having become a "litigious society"—because "new kinds of harms" have been created by new conditions (Lieberman 1981: 19). It was when some sociologists began serious consideration of some of these new kinds of harms that environmental sociology started to emerge.

Is there some optimal level of division of labor? If so, should we suppose today's "developed" societies are advancing toward it, or have they already surpassed such an optimum? According to Ross (1918), who believed "the bonds uniting successive generations" might fail, there was already in his time "less care for posterity." For Durkheim's hope to be fulfilled, the kind of mutually predatory "interdependence" that so appalled his American contemporary would have to be a rare or at least incidental consequence of division of labor at the modern industrial level. Because Ross was using a vocabulary different from Durkheim's, the issue was less than explicitly joined. However, Ross can be seen in retrospect to have regarded anomie, rather than organic solidarity, as the *essential* (most often expectable) effect of the advanced division of labor so characteristic of an industrial society.

Today, disunity and cynicism about major institutions are evidently increasing (Collier 1991; Schlesinger 1992; Cannon 1994; Raasch 1995). Have we in fact become a society of predators on each other, as vividly described by Blumberg (1989)? Do television advertisers and business management theorists today consistently assault traditional values of loyalty, respect, and decorum, as argued by Frank (1995), who says the ethos of modern commerce "is the root cause of the unease" felt by people today toward the culture surrounding them?[20]

Another expression of deep anxiety by Ross (1918: 621) is perhaps today more timely than ever if a former U.S. secretary of the interior was right when he declared *Homo sapiens* a "threatened species" due to the "twin specters" of "overpopulation and unbridled technology" (Udall 1967). Half a century earlier, Ross cited deforestation, erosion, and silt-clogged waterways that he personally had observed while touring in China, and alluded to others' writings about Italy, Greece, and Africa, especially Egypt, and concluded that "quite in a day's work, a people can so dissipate or use up its natural resources as to leave the land scarcely habitable" (1918: 621). A considerable literature has explicated and amplified that concern, ranging from Carson (1962) and Mines (1971) to McKibben (1989) and Ward (1994).

Now, if sociologists begin taking into account the ecosystem context of human societal life, we can at last put into perspective a political clash of worldviews that has polarized human affairs in recent decades. If the Marxist labor theory of value oversimplified the economic process, so has what one writer (Dionne 1991: 347) calls the "capital theory of value" espoused by many on the political right (who romanticize "the brave, risk-taking souls who provide investment capital" while they overlook "the much larger group that ultimately makes a company successful: the people who work for it"). Environmental sociologists can see that *both* of these opposing "theories of value" oversimplify. Both tend to neglect the fact that human "value-adding" processes depend on the availability of natural resources and on the "services" provided by other symbiont types (such as various other organic populations and our ecosystem partners). Durkheim established groundwork for transcending these mutually myopic views, at least when he granted sociological relevance to Darwin's understanding of the struggle for existence as Malthusian[21] competition for resources, in scarcity intensified by population growth.

Stressing the ultimate global interdependence of our time, Brown and Flavin (1999) note the impossibility of any country acting alone being able to stabilize its climate, protect the diversity of life on Earth, or protect oceanic fisheries. "These goals can be achieved only through global cooperation that recognizes the interdependence of countries." Furthermore, "[e]fforts to restore a stable relationship between the economy and its environmental support systems depends on social cohesion within societies as well" (20).

Insofar as the within-species symbioses among humans are based on sociocultural differentiation (which may be volatile), they are probably much more fragile than mutualism based on the more durable genetic differentiation for symbionts of different species. As small antagonisms add up, a society's organic solidarity may fracture. How much social distance between its components can a society afford? Durkheim (1984: 316–322) did express concern that when inequality was excessive or perceived as unfair it could prevent division of labor from fulfilling what he took to be its "normal" function, that is, producing organic solidarity. And like Durkheim a century ago, Brown and Flavin (1999: 20) see both international and within-nations cohesion jeopardized by serious maldistribution of wealth.

Industrial societies entering the twenty-first century with an extremely ramified division of labor are burdened with the divisive effects of other significant forces: resurgent nationalisms, smoldering ethnic hostilities, proliferating technology, and festering religious strife (Birnbaum 1969; Harris 1989: 494–498; Collier 1991; Schlesinger 1992; Kaplan 1994; Yinger 1982; 1994). Sociologists today should question whether division of labor can, in these circumstances, still foster the organic solidarity postulated by Durkheim. Under present and future aggravation of those circumstances (by further demographic increase, resource depletion, and global climate change), can it remain a sufficient binding force to protect us from a seriously threatening array of disintegrative pressures?

NOTES

1. Among other relevant aspects of societal structure, excessive inequality could endanger society, according to Durkheim (1984: 316–317), and the services exchanged between differentiated persons or groups must be reasonably equivalent in social value (embodied labor). In short, he seemed to regard restraints on predatory or parasitic human relations as prerequisites for organic solidarity. Although his work on "social morphology" has been seen as relevant to, and a forerunner of, human ecology, Durkheim has not been regarded as a human ecologist (Schnore 1958).

2. Merton (1934), in one of his earliest papers, expressed concern that "unilinear evolution" in the direction posited by Durkheim's view of division of labor might continue until it would become self-defeating, with ever more frequent occurrences of anomie rather than any further increase of organic solidarity. Doubt has also been cast (see Schwartz and Miller 1964) on the validity of Durkheim's hypothesis that penal law (indicative of mechanical solidarity) prevailed in societies with a simple division of labor whereas restitutive law (supposedly indicative of organic solidarity) only became prevalent with more of an elaborate division of labor.

3. In fact, sociology can be considered an ecological science. Although sociologists study the behavior of creatures who are all one biological species, they are studied as socially and culturally differentiated, interacting, and interdependent entities (Catton 1993b). Probably most sociologists would agree with Cain's remark to the Ecological Society of America, when he sought to narrow the gulf between social and biological science by saying "a study of ecology without consideration of the roles played by man" would be partial and misleading (1960: 160). But Cain also insisted in the same presidential address that "a study of man without due consideration of his biotic and abiotic co-members of the ecosystem" was wrong.

4. By the 1970s, Durkheim's antireductionism rule had become so ingrained in our discipline that a colleague and I pointed to its unquestioned acceptance by most sociologists as a major impediment to recognition of the sociological significance of ecological problems (Catton and Dunlap 1978). Actually, Durkheim did not allow this dictum—which served him so well in his analysis of suicide—to limit his work altogether. Evolutionary theorizing was implicit in the reason Durkheim had given for needing to study functions as well as causes in explaining a social fact. A social fact, he said, "must generally be useful to continue to survive. If it lacks utility, that very reason suffices to make it harmful, since in that case it requires effort but brings in no return" (1982: 124). In short, Durkheim had shown awareness of selection pressures. His concern with functions thus represented an implicitly evolutionary approach. But when British social anthropologists (who also claimed him as an intellectual forebear) used concepts involved in Radcliffe-Brown's definition of "function," this led toward the "dehistoricizing" of anthropology (Stocking 1988: 136). They paid increasing attention to synchronic rather than diachronic sociological problems. How an institution might have developed through the ages seemed less important than how it functioned in its

relations to other components of an existing society and culture. Going even further, Malinowski (1926; 1939) emphatically shifted anthropology's focus to the consequences of a "part" for some "whole" (i.e., for a more inclusive structure). Functional explanations (of these "parts") were not to be concerned with their origins, distribution, or diffusion, but were mainly concerned with showing how universal forms of social organization contribute to social cohesion, effectiveness, and continuity. But even though Malinowski (1962: 86–87) believed this way of considering the part's usefulness for the whole enabled functional analysis to reduce the danger of distorting facts and posing insoluble issues, it no longer spotlighted adaptation to the nonsocial environment. "Functional analysis" thereby came to be regarded not as an aspect of evolutionary theory but as an alternative to it. Insistence that we must consider social phenomena so sui generis that interactions with the biophysical environment seem sociologically irrelevant thus come to be taken as what Coser calls the "main thrust of Durkheim's overall doctrine" (1977: 129).

5. Durkheim would surely have seen as corroboration of this idea a subsequent discovery about the very nature of eukaryotic cells. (They are the kind of cells of which we consist, as do all other multicellular animals and the plants on which we and they depend). The organelles (plastids and mitochondria) within eukaryotic cells are now known to be derived from symbiotic microorganisms that were long since internalized by these cells' remote ancestors (Margulis 1970; 1993; Douglas 1994).

6. For an elaboration of this point and a discussion of its implications for sociological human ecology, see Catton (1995).

7. See Catton (1980: 279).

8. I was told by Mulloy in 1973 that humanity had been, in his view, "doomed since the Neolithic." Mulloy believed the horticultural revolution had put humankind on track toward the ultimate disaster of overshooting global carrying capacity. Mulloy's own archaeological research on Easter Island had convinced him (1974: 29) that its Polynesian inhabitants in precontact times had been "technologically successful" and "must have rejoiced in the solid assurance that their success was permanent," even though they were, in fact, facing catastrophic collapse from the damage their success had cumulatively done to their finite environment. For further insights in this regard, see Bahn and Flenley (1992) and Catton (1993a).

9. Had there existed an already advanced science of ecology in Durkheim's time, and had it achieved by then what would later become its most fundamental concept, the ecosystem, so that Durkheim could have been more familiar with interspecific competition and other symbioses, he might have been dissuaded from resorting to the misleading physiological image of "rivalry between different tissues." Durkheim obviously supposed that the specializing of different tissues within an organism to perform particular physiological functions supported his view of human occupational specialization. But when Darwin mentioned tissue specialization, he was referring not to competition between tissues within one organism, but to the different adaptations of herbivores versus carnivores, for he wrote, "No physiologist doubts that a stomach by being adapted to digest vegetable matter alone, or flesh alone, draws most nutriment from these substances" (1958b: 116).

10. Environmental sociology has developed partly in response to the disharmonies that became so evident in the latter part of the twentieth century and shocked sociologists of the once-prevalent functionalist persuasion. For further elucidation of Darwin's un-Durkheimian view of specialization, see Catton (1998a).

11. Calling attention to the kind of problem Ogburn (1957) later termed "cultural lag," Durkheim wrote that "the structure of our societies" had undergone profound changes with unprecedented rapidity, and the morality associated with mechanical solidarity had been

eroded "without its successor developing quickly enough to occupy the space left vacant in our consciousness" (1984: 339). The problematic future of human societies today results from similar cultural lag that is at least as serious. Brown and Flavin sound much like Durkheim when they say, "The trends of recent years suggest that we need a new moral compass to guide us into the twenty-first century—a compass that is grounded in the principles of meeting human needs sustainably. Such an ethic of sustainability would be based on a concept of respect for future generations" (1999: 21).

12. For ecologists, mutualism (a strong and reciprocal interdependence between different but associated life forms) is one type of symbiosis. "Symbiosis" is often used outside scientific ecology literature to mean mutualism, as if there were no other types of "living together." But there are others, such as parasitism—a "one way" interdependence where the parasite benefits at the host's expense. Many mutualisms arise between allopatrically (rather than sympatrically) evolved species (Vandermeer 1984: 223).

13. It is important to keep in mind that Durkheim had clearly forsaken the "no biological parallels" stance by citing Darwin in ostensible support of his theory.

14. When a given population's gene pool undergoes the "stream splitting" called speciation, the various "daughter species" descended from the single ancestral species are "sibling species" to each other.

15. Ecologically informed environmental sociologists must recognize that the expression "struggle for existence" did not in Darwin's writing mean strife. It meant striving (in competition with other strivers). The competition could be direct or indirect. Before Darwin, people aware of competition in nature thought of different species competing with each other. Inspired by Malthus, Darwin focused instead on the struggle of different individual members of a species, competing within an ecological niche for resources (including "services" provided by other species). Between the numerous mistletoe on the same branch, there was direct competition for space and nutrients. Between the mistletoe and "other fruit-bearing plants," there was indirect competition for the service of seed-disseminating birds. Natural selection of improved means of attracting the birds led to mistletoe-bird mutualism, better seed dispersal for the mistletoe, and better nutrition for the birds.

16. It is a tempting speculation to imagine Durkheim relying more on Darwin's (1877) research monograph about insect fertilization of orchids instead of misconstruing *On the Origin of Species* as he did; how different would have been the ideas about social cohesion in the minds of subsequent sociologists? Perhaps, too, sociologists' aversion to biological considerations (supposedly in compliance with the discipline's taboo against "reductionism") might not have loomed so large in our view of the Durkheim legacy.

17. Might sociology have been set on a different course if Durkheim had read Darwin's *On the Origin of Species* less selectively and given more thought to the following passage: "In the course of two months, I picked up in my garden 12 kinds of seeds, out of the excrement of small birds, and these seemed perfect, and some of them, which I tried, germinated" (1859: 361)? Readers may also think about squirrels and acorns or see themselves in the symbiotic role of seed-dispersal agents if they think of eating watermelon or cherries on a picnic.

18. This differs fundamentally from what Durkheim presumably would have expected (at least when he wrote *Division of Labour in Society*). He assumed the prior interaction pattern would have been a kind of coexistence characterized by mechanical solidarity (and collective conscience). As population pressure (material density) and the resulting aggravation of life's complexity (moral density) increased, that mechanically solidary coexistence was put in jeopardy by intensified "struggle" (competition).

19. It is an ironic fact that Durkheim did work out a similar principle (in later writing

about human exogamy) when he said, "Once the practice was constituted, it would be maintained by changing its character" (1963: 86, 109–110). But he did not apply that idea to division of labor nor use it to refine his theory of organic solidarity.

20. Durkheim is cited in later sociological literature far more often than Ross, but this greater prevalence of Durkheim's prospecialization view and comparative neglect of Ross's "at one another's mercy" view in sociology really does not settle the question of which view is more valid. Perhaps a majority of sociologists have been committed by tradition of the discipline to a mistaken impression of the way things work, an impression that precludes serious sociological attention to escalating impediments to mutualism.

21. In his autobiography, Darwin (1958: 120) made a point of the fact that from reading Malthus's essay, which expounded the theory of exponentially growing populations pressing on less than adequate resources, he "had at last got a theory by which to work" in his effort to explain the process of evolution. It was because of his own "long-continued observation of the habits of animals and plants" that Darwin was well prepared to appreciate the ubiquitous struggle for existence. That struggle was the circumstance under which a process of natural selection could be expected to operate. For an indication of the modern relevance of such concepts, see Catton (1998b).

REFERENCES

Bahn, Paul G., and John Flenley. 1992. *Easter Island, Earth Island*. New York: Thames and Hudson.

Bennett, John W. 1993. *Human Ecology As Human Behavior: Essays in Environmental and Development Anthropology*. New Brunswick, N.J.: Transaction.

Birnbaum, Norman. 1969. *The Crisis of Industrial Society*. New York: Oxford University Press.

Blumberg, Paul. 1989. *The Predatory Society: Deception in the American Marketplace*. New York: Oxford University Press.

Brown, Lester R., and Christopher Flavin. 1999. "A New Economy for a New Century." In *State of the World 1999*, ed. Lester R. Brown, Christopher Flavin, and Hilary French, 3–21. New York: Norton.

Buttel, Frederick H. 1986. "Sociology and the Environment: The Winding Road toward Human Ecology." *International Social Science Journal* 109:337–356.

Cain, Stanley A. 1960. "Some Principles of General Ecology and Human Society." *American Biology Teacher* 22 (March): 160–164.

Cannon, Angie. 1994. "Fed Up: A Less Kind, Less Gentle America Emerges in Poll of Nation's Mood." *Tacoma News Tribune*, 21 September, A3.

Carson, Rachel. 1962. *Silent Spring*. Greenwich, Conn.: Fawcett.

Catton, William R., Jr. 1980. *Overshoot: The Ecological Basis of Revolutionary Change*. Urbana: University of Illinois Press.

———. 1993a. "Carrying Capacity and the Death of a Culture: A Tale of Two Autopsies." *Sociological Inquiry* 63 (May): 202–223.

———. 1993b. "Sociology As an Ecological Science." In *Human Ecology: Crossing Boundaries* (Selected Papers from the Sixth Conference of the Society for Human Ecology, Snowbird, Utah, October 2–4, 1992), ed. Scott D. Wright, Thomas Dietz, Richard Borden, Gerald Young, and Gregory Guagnano, 74–86. Fort Collins, Colo.: Society for Human Ecology.

———. 1995. "From Eukaryotic Cells to Gaia: The Range of Symbiosis and Its Relevance for Human Ecology." In *Advances in Human Ecology*, vol. 4., ed. Lee Freese, 1–34. Greenwich, Conn.: JAI Press.

———. 1998a. "Darwin, Durkheim, and Mutualism." In *Advances in Human Ecology*, vol. 7, ed. Lee Freese, 89–138. Greenwich, Conn.: JAI Press.

———. 1998b. "What if Malthus Were Writing Today?" *Organization and Environment* 11 (December): 434–437.

Catton, William R., Jr., and Riley E. Dunlap. 1978. "Environmental Sociology: A New Paradigm." *The American Sociologist* 13 (February): 41–49.

Collier, James Lincoln. 1991. *The Rise of Selfishness in America*. New York: Oxford University Press.

Connell, Joseph H. 1980. "Diversity and the Coevolution of Competitors, or the Ghost of Competition Past." *Oikos* 35:131–138.

Coser, Lewis A. 1977. *Masters of Sociological Thought: Ideas in Historical and Social Context*. 2nd ed. New York: Harcourt, Brace, Jovanovich.

Darwin, Charles. 1877. *The Various Contrivances by Which Orchids Are Fertilised by Insects*. London: John Murray.

———. 1958. *The Autobiography of Charles Darwin 1809–1882*, ed. Nora Barlow. New York: Norton.

———. 1859. *On the Origin of Species by Means of Natural Selection*. London: John Murray.

Dawkins, Richard. 1995. *River out of Eden: A Darwinian View of Life*. New York: Basic.

Dionne, E. J., Jr. 1991. *Why Americans Hate Politics*. New York: Simon and Schuster.

Douglas, Angela E. 1994. *Symbiotic Interactions*. New York: Oxford University Press.

Duncan, Otis Dudley. 1964. "Social Organization and the Ecosystem." In *Handbook of Modern Sociology*, ed. Robert E. L. Faris, 36–82. Chicago: Rand McNally.

Dunlap, Riley E., and William R. Catton Jr. 1994. "Toward an Ecological Sociology: The Development, Current Status, and Probable Future of Environmental Sociology." In *Ecology, Society and the Quality of Social Life*, ed. William V. D'Antonio, Masamichi Sasaki, and Yoshio Yonebayashi, 11–31. New Brunswick, N.J.: Transaction.

Durkheim, Émile. 1963. *Incest: The Nature and Origin of the Taboo*. Trans. Edward Sagarin. 1897. Reprint, New York: Lyle Stuart.

———. 1982. *The Rules of the Sociological Method*. Ed. Steven Lukes. Trans. W. D. Halls. 1895. Reprint, New York: The Free Press.

———. 1984. *The Division of Labour in Society*. Trans. W. D. Halls. 1893. New York: The Free Press.

Ford, E. B. 1949. "Early Stages in Allopatric Speciation." In *Genetics, Paleontology, and Evolution*, ed. Glenn Lowell Jepsen, Ernst Mayr, and George Gaylord Simpson, 309–314. Princeton, N.J.: Princeton University Press.

Frank, Thomas. 1995. "The Profit Value of Bad Family Values: Corporate America Has Found that Cultural Decay Is Very Good Business." *Washington Post National Weekly Edition*, 19–25 June, 25.

Gould, Stephen Jay. 1995. "Spin Doctoring Darwin." *Natural History* 104 (July): 6–9, 70–71.

Harris, Marvin. 1989. *Our Kind: Who We Are, Where We Came from, Where We Are Going*. New York: Harper and Row.

Hawley, Amos H. 1950. *Human Ecology: A Theory of Community Structure*. New York: Ronald.

Hutchinson, G. Evelyn. 1965. *The Ecological Theater and the Evolutionary Play*. New Haven, Conn.: Yale University Press.

Jordan, David Starr. 1905. "The Origin of Species through Isolation." *Science* 22 (November 3): 545–562.

Kaplan, Robert D. 1994. "The Coming Anarchy." *Atlantic Monthly* 273 (February): 44–76.

Lack, David. 1947. *Darwin's Finches: An Essay on the General Biological Theory of Evolution*. Cambridge: Cambridge University Press.

———. 1949. "The Significance of Ecological Isolation." In *Genetics, Paleontology, and Evolution*, ed. Glenn Lowell Jepsen, Ernst Mayr, and George Gaylord Simpson, 299–308. Princeton, N.J.: Princeton University Press.

Lieberman, Jethro K. 1981. *The Litigious Society*. New York: Basic.

Loomis, William F. 1988. *Four Billion Years: An Essay on the Evolution of Genes and Organisms*. Sunderland, Mass.: Sinauer Associates.

Love, Thomas F. 1977. "Ecological Niche Theory in Sociocultural Anthropology: A Conceptual Framework and an Application." *American Ethnologist* 4 (February): 27–41.

Lynch, John D. 1989. "The Gauge of Speciation: On the Frequencies of Modes of Speciation." In *Speciation and Its Consequences*, ed. Daniel Otte and John A. Endler, 527–553. Sunderland, Mass.: Sinauer Associates.

Malinowski, Bronislaw. 1926. "Anthropology." *Encyclopedia Britannica*. 13th ed. London: Encyclopedia Britannica.

———. 1939. "The Group and the Individual in Functional Analysis." *American Journal of Sociology* 44 (May): 938–964.

———. 1962. *Sex, Culture, and Myth*. New York: Harcourt, Brace.

Marden, James H. 1992. "Newton's Second Law of Butterflies." *Natural History* 101 (January): 54–61.

Margulis, Lynn. 1970. *Origin of Eukaryotic Cells*. New Haven, Conn.: Yale University Press.

———. 1993. *Symbiosis in Cell Evolution*. 2nd ed. San Francisco: Freeman.

Mayr, Ernst. 1954. "Geographic Speciation in Tropical Echinoids." *Evolution* 8 (March): 1–18.

———. 1957. "Species Concepts and Definitions." In *The Species Problem*, ed. Ernst Mayr, 1–22. Washington, D.C.: American Association for the Advancement of Science, Publication No. 50.

———. 1959. "Isolation As an Evolutionary Factor." *Proceedings of the American Philosophical Society* 103 (April): 221–230.

———. 1963. *Animal Species and Evolution*. Cambridge, Mass.: Harvard University Press.

———. 1982. "Speciation and Macroevolution." *Evolution* 36 (November): 1119–1132.

———. 1989. "Speciational Evolution or Punctuated Equilibria." *Journal of Social and Biological Structures* 12 (April–July): 137–158.

McDonnell, Mark J., and Steward T. A. Pickett, ed. 1993. *Humans As Components of Ecosystems*. New York: Springer-Verlag.

McKibben, Bill. 1989. *The End of Nature*. New York: Random House.

Merton, Robert K. 1934. "Durkheim's Division of Labor in Society." *American Journal of Sociology* 40 (November): 316–328.

Mines, Samuel. 1971. *The Last Days of Mankind: Ecological Survival or Extinction*. New York: Simon and Schuster.

Mulloy, William. 1974. "Contemplate the Navel of the World." *Americas* 26 (April): 25–33.

Odum, Eugene P. 1953. *Fundamentals of Ecology*. Philadelphia: Saunders.

Ogburn, William F. 1957. "Cultural Lag As Theory." *Sociology and Social Research* 41 (January–February): 167–174.

Owen, Denis. 1980. *Camouflage and Mimicry.* Chicago: University of Chicago Press.

Raasch, Chuck. 1995. "Who's Sour Now? Public Tops Press in Cynicism, Poll Finds." *Tacoma News Tribune,* 22 May, B6.

Rickleffs, Robert E. 1979. *Ecology.* 2nd ed. New York: Chiron.

Ross, Edward Alsworth. 1907. *Sin and Society: An Analysis of Latter-Day Iniquity.* Boston: Houghton Mifflin.

———. 1918. "Social Decadence." *American Journal of Sociology* 23 (March): 620–632.

Rothschild, Miriam. 1967. "Mimicry: The Deceptive Way of Life." *Natural History* 76 (February): 44–51.

Schlesinger, Arthur M., Jr. 1992. *The Disuniting of America: Reflections on a Multicultural Society.* New York: Norton.

Schnaiberg, Allan. 1975. "Social Syntheses of the Societal-Environmental Dialectic: The Role of Distributional Impacts." *Social Science Quarterly* 56 (June): 5–20.

———. 1980. *The Environment: From Surplus to Scarcity.* New York: Oxford University Press.

Schnore, Leo F. 1958. "Social Morphology and Human Ecology." *American Journal of Sociology* 63 (May): 620–634.

Schwartz, Richard D., and James C. Miller. 1964. "Legal Evolution and Societal Complexity." *American Journal of Sociology* 70 (September): 159–169.

Shorrocks, Bryan. 1978. *The Genesis of Diversity.* London: Hodder and Stoughton.

Stephan, Edward G. 1970. "The Concept of Community in Human Ecology." *Pacific Sociological Review* 13 (Fall): 218–228.

Stocking, George W., Jr. 1988. "Radcliffe-Brown and British Social Anthropology." In *Functionalism Historicized: Essays on British Social Anthropology,* ed. George W. Stocking Jr., 131–191. Madison: University of Wisconsin Press.

Sulloway, Frank J. 1979. "Geographic Isolation in Darwin's Thinking: The Vicissitudes of a Crucial Idea." *Studies in the History of Biology* 3:23–65.

Tansley, Arthur G.1935. "The Use and Abuse of Vegetational Concepts and Terms." *Ecology* 16 (July): 284–307.

Thompson, John N. 1982. *Interaction and Coevolution.* New York: Wiley.

Udall, Stewart L. 1967. "Foreword." In *Man . . . An Endangered Species?* Department of the Interior Conservation Yearbook No. 4. Washington, D.C.: U.S. Government Printing Office.

Vandermeer, John. 1984. "The Evolution of Mutualism." In *Evolutionary Ecology,* ed. Bryan Shorrocks, 221–232. Oxford: Blackwell Scientific Publications.

Vrba, Elisabeth S. 1985. "Introductory Comments on Species and Speciation." In *Species and Speciation,* Transvaal Museum Monograph No. 4, ed. Elisabeth S. Vrba, ix–xviii. Pretoria, South Africa: Transvaal Museum.

Ward, Peter. 1994. *The End of Evolution: On Mass Extinctions and the Preservation of Biodiversity.* New York: Bantam.

White, M. J. D. 1968. "Models of Speciation." *Science* 159 (March 8): 1065–1070.

Wickler, Wolfgang. 1968. *Mimicry in Plants and Animals.* Trans. R. D. Martin. London: Weidenfeld and Nicholson.

———. 1976. "Mimicry and Camouflage." In *Encyclopedia of Ecology,* ed. Bernard Grzimek, Joachim Illies, and Wolfgang Klausewitz, 134–154. New York: Van Nostrand Reinhold.

Wilson, Edward O. 1975. *Sociobiology: The New Synthesis.* Cambridge, Mass.: Belknap.
Wright, Sewell. 1943. "Isolation by Distance." *Genetics* 28 (March): 114–138.
Yinger, J. Milton. 1982. *Countercultures: The Promise and Peril of a World Turned Upside Down.* New York: The Free Press.
———. 1994. *Ethnicity: Source of Strength? Source of Conflict?* Albany: SUNY Press.

Part III

ENVIRONMENTAL SOCIOLOGY AND TWENTIETH-CENTURY SOCIOLOGICAL THEORY

6

Social Theory and the Environment: A Systems-Theoretical Perspective

Elim Papadakis

One way of considering the utility of sociological theory for understanding environmental problems is to raise the question of the effectiveness of measures to deal with them. By effectiveness, I mean the capacity of political institutions and organizations to attract support for, and then implement, policies over which there is broad consensus. Can contemporary political institutions and organizations respond effectively to challenges like disquiet about the environment? Can they defuse conflict between environment and development and implement ideas like sustainable development? One way of shedding light on these possibilities is to consider recent developments in systems theory.

SYSTEMS THEORY: AN OVERVIEW

The question of effectiveness in dealing with environmental problems leads one to a further question: Effective from whose point of view? From the point of view of the "social system"? In other words, does this presuppose an "objectivist" analysis of "interests"? Or does it mean effective from the point of view of particular players in the game of politics? In other words, does this assume a "subjectivist" analysis of "interests"?

The focus in this chapter is primarily on accounts of social change that refer to social systems. These accounts are most notably associated with Parsons (1951). In developing a theory of social action (or social interaction), Parsons argued that social systems tend toward equilibrium. Society or a social system is viewed as comprising different (and interrelated) parts. A social system is therefore characterized as a system in which social actors interact with one another in ways aimed at maintaining the system. Social actors comprise not only individuals but groups and institutions.

Parsons, whose point of departure is a preoccupation with the emergence and maintenance of social order, argues that social interaction is underpinned by tendencies toward achievement of a consensus in values across society. In other words, social systems (comprising different but interrelated parts) tend toward a state of equilibrium. The equilibrium is maintained through socialization of individuals (i.e., assimilation of values). This helps to shape and regulate their behavior. Among the pivotal institutions in ensuring that this takes place are families and schools. Another important function of social institutions is to ensure social control by discouraging deviation from social norms.

Social systems like society have, according to Parsons, four "functional prerequisites." The first is "adaptation" and refers to the relationship between a social system and (how it adapts to) its "environment." The term "environment" is here used to refer to the distinction drawn by Parsons between a social system and its surrounding environment (and not to the issue of environmental protection). Take, for example, the capacity of the economy to adapt to its environment. The second is "goal attainment" and concerns the requirement for all societies to establish and achieve certain objectives. The role of government is crucial in this regard. The third prerequisite is "integration" or the "adjustment of conflict," that is, the capacity to regulate potentially conflictual relationships (e.g., by legal means). The fourth is "pattern maintenance" and relates to upholding patterns of values and thereby maintaining stability of a social system and functions played by families and religion.

Apart from this focus on the stability of the social system, Parsons posits an important link between social action and the social system through "pattern variables" (or cultural values). Parsons argues that there are tensions between cultural values, some of which are commonly associated with simple or preindustrial societies and others associated with complex or advanced industrial societies. For instance, conflict may emerge between values linked to a focus on achievement (like performance in the workplace measured by diligence and the application of certain skills) or on ascription (in other words, your status at work or in society may be decided by ethnicity or the standing or rank of your family). Similarly, your position or role in society may be determined by "universal" criteria or principles (as in the goal of a legal system to treat everyone equally) or by particularist considerations (like where you come from, the standing of your parents, or your religion). Parsons has also drawn distinctions between social relationships that are shaped primarily by emotional or affective responses to particular situations and instrumental approaches that are determined more by an apparent focus on long-term considerations (including calculations of costs and benefits to be derived from different courses of action).

Systems theory has been promoted as a way of understanding the shift from a preindustrial to an industrial society. The latter is said to adopt values that are instrumental and universal, while the former is characterized by affective and particularist values. Above all, advanced industrial societies are apparently characterized both by high levels of social differentiation (i.e., people take on different roles and are rewarded in different ways) and by social integration (i.e., dissemination of universal values that condition our responses serve to ensure the maintenance of social cohesion and social order).

The approach by Parsons has been highly influential among writers who are interested in understanding the shift from preindustrial to industrial societies. In particular, the focus on the complex interrelationships between the different parts of society, the impact of social institutions on individual behavior, and the critique of utilitarian economic approaches remain lasting legacies of this approach (Robertson and Turner 1992). As Robertson and Turner point out, among the influences on Parsons (who anticipated contemporary interest in multidisciplinary approaches that synthesize a variety of fields of knowledge and action) were the work of Weber and most notably of Durkheim. After a period of immense influence, particularly on American sociology in the 1950s and 1960s, Parsons's work, especially his systems theory, was strongly criticized and rejected by sociologists in Europe and the United States. However, by the 1980s there was a significant reappraisal of his work and an appreciation that, despite its flaws, provided an important stimulus to sociological thinking (see Sciulli and Gerstein 1992 and their reference to work by Münch 1981; 1982; Alexander 1983; Habermas 1981; Bershady 1973).

The most frequent criticisms have been that many of Parsons's claims were not backed by empirical evidence, for instance, the presumed consensus in values. The claims about the effect of consensus on social equilibrium are also open to question. Systems theory, as developed by Parsons, tends, according to many critics, to underestimate the degree of conflict that drives social change (Dahrendorf 1959; Coser 1956). This tied in with highly influential criticisms by left-wing writers that Parsons was too closely aligned to mainstream American democratic politics and modern capitalism (Mills 1959; Hacker 1961; Gouldner 1970). The context for these kinds of criticisms was the growing dissatisfaction in the 1950s and 1960s among young people and intellectuals with established authority, which manifested itself through antiwar and peace movements as well as student uprisings. Another criticism is that systems theory adopts teleological explanations (Black 1961). In other words, social institutions are said to have their own rationality independent of the objectives of individuals. This relates to a final point: The focus on the impact of social institutions on individual behavior may lead to a neglect of the influence of individuals in shaping social institutions (Wrong 1961; see also Bershady 1973).

Despite these objections to specific aspects of Parsons's work, writers like Robertson and Turner (1992) and Sciulli and Gerstein (1992) have noted its enduring legacy, particularly in prompting others to take up the challenge of developing radically different versions of systems theory. One of the most methodical attempts to do this has been the adaptation and reconstruction of Parsons's approach by Luhmann, the German social theorist.

Most of this chapter focuses on the efforts by Luhmann to provide a radically different response from Parsons to the question of maintaining social order (see Murphy 1992) and to consider the value of these efforts for understanding the challenges of environmental protection. In tackling the question of the utility or effectiveness of different approaches to environmental questions, I am seeking neither to defend Luhmann nor become involved in debates between the critics of either subjectivism or objectivism.

THEORIES OF INSTITUTIONAL CHANGE

Before attempting to identify how systems theory can be utilized for understanding environmental problems, I want to focus on how systems theory has been developed by Luhmann and on how this relates to the renaissance of studies of institutions and institutional change influenced by writers like March and Olsen (1984; 1989) and many others (Evans, Rueschemeyer, and Skocpol 1985; Brennan and Buchanan 1985; Hall 1986; Shepsle 1989; North 1990; Ostrom 1990). As in systems theory, this literature views institutions as having the potential to shape individual behavior. The new literature on institutions is more precise than Parsons's systems theory to the extent that it regards institutions as structures, comprising rules and standardized procedures, for shaping both individual and collective behavior. This includes political behavior and other forms of social behavior and communication between individuals. The focus is not simply on the legislature, the legal system, or the state and formal organizations—although they can all be described as institutions. Rather, it is on how rules and organizational forms associated with these structures organize political life and "transcend individuals and buffer or transform social forces": "When individuals enter an institution, they try to discover, and are taught the rules. When they encounter a new situation, they try to associate it with a situation for which rules already exist" (March and Olsen 1989: 160).

The "new institutionalism" draws attention to the "autonomous role for political institutions" and how bureaucracies, legislatures, and courts are "collections of standard operating procedures that define and defend interests" and are "political actors in their own right" (March and Olsen 1984: 738). Although sociologists make other distinctions between types of institutions, like the "new institutionalists" they have drawn attention to how rules, social practices, and continuous repetition of patterns of behavior are among the distinguishing features of institutions (Abercrombie, Hill, and Turner 1988: 124). In some respects, this is familiar. The novelty of recent debates simply lies in emphasizing the influence of political institutions. The significance of this work, particularly the contribution by writers like Putnam (1993) and Jänicke (1990) are discussed in Papadakis (1996).

The relevance of Luhmann to these debates lies in the following questions on potential roles for political institutions and organizations in environmental protection:

- What if political institutions and organizations cannot always become *the* central agencies for social change?
- What are the obstacles that prevent political institutions and organizations

from rendering policy more effective and what are the options for overcoming these hurdles?

This issue of the centrality of political institutions and organizations has been raised by poststructuralist and postmodernist writers and by systems theorists like Luhmann. Although he has little in common with the postmodernist writers, Luhmann shares their reservations about notions of social structures with a central, guiding principle (Neckel and Wolf 1994: 70). According to Luhmann (1990b), political theorists have struggled to visualize modern society as a system without a central agency. Drawing on the classics, they have attempted "to conceive the state or politics as the guiding centre for everything that occurs in and with it" (1990b: 32). If, as Luhmann argues, this is not the case, we are faced with a difficulty. To focus on the responsiveness of political institutions and organizations may raise unrealistic expectations about their capacity to address problems.

LUHMANN AND THE LIMITS OF POLITICS

The following account of the work by Luhmann represents a paradox. It suggests that out of his pessimism we can still derive an optimistic account of the influence of politics on environmental protection. His ideas are interesting because they provide insights into the difficulties of implementing policies and a stimulus for thinking in a constructive way about environmental problems. In other words, it may emerge that one can adapt Luhmann's work as a heuristic device even if it is found wanting as a complete theory.

Using similar concepts to the ones developed by Parsons, Luhmann (1990b) is not so much interested in political institutions or organizations as central agencies for the whole of society, but in how the political system functions as simply another "subsystem" of society. He therefore makes the distinction, apparently following Parsons, between a social system and its "environment."

There are, however, some fundamental differences between the approaches by Luhmann and Parsons. Luhmann learned a great deal from Parsons (and was a visitor at Harvard in 1960–1961), and shared with him an interest in bringing to bear a wide range of disciplines in trying to understand how social order is maintained. In addressing this issue, Parsons relied heavily on Hobbes and advocated shared values as the solution to profound conflicts; by contrast, Luhmann places interpersonal trust at the center of his project (Murphy 1992), thereby providing an important stimulus to a new set of approaches (Sciulli and Gerstein 1992: 305).

By focusing on interpersonal trust, Luhmann emphasizes the notion of communication rather than action. Hence, one of his works is entitled *Ecological Communication* (1989). The notion of a social system is used to refer to the communication that occurs within different areas of society. For Luhmann, a social system arises from a degree of unity based on communication. Luhmann (1980) argues that "self-reference and complexity were precisely the concepts which Parsons' design was unable to incorporate" (Rossbach 1993: 109). Luhmann (1980) finds Parsons's functional method wanting. Rather than accepting Parsons's emphasis on causal explanations, Luhmann's functional approach posits the possibility of several or no solutions to a problem (see Rossbach 1993: 87).

In reformulating Parsons's method, Luhmann develops systems theory "not as a theory of specific objects but rather as a theory that observes reality using a specific distinction, namely the system/environment distinction" (Luhmann quoted in Sciulli 1994: 38). This represents a crucial conceptual distinction for Luhmann (1982). Its significance is summed up by Turner: "[A]ll social systems exist in multidimensional environments, which pose potentially endless complexity with which a system must deal. To exist in a complex environment, therefore, a social system must develop mechanisms for reducing complexity. Such selection creates a boundary between a system and its environment, thereby allowing it to sustain patterns of interrelated actions" (1986: 103). Although the distinction between a system and its environment appears to be similar to the one drawn by Parsons, Luhmann posits a dynamic relationship that focuses on how a system reproduces itself rather than on the objective existence of a particular system. In addition, Luhmann's theory of social systems posits the existence of multiple subsystems (political, educational, economic, scientific, environmental, and other subsystems) that operate through "communication" rather than "action."

His notion of a social system has several implications, and the following points are relevant to how we conceptualize the significance of politics and society and the capacity of politics to address environmental protection:

1. One of Luhmann's principal aims is to draw us away from dichotomies and concepts like the distinction between state and society. Luhmann proposes the following alternative: "Society is the all-encompassing social system that orders all possible communications among human beings. The political system is one of its sub-systems alongside other sub-systems for religion, science, economy, education, family life, medical care etc." (1990b: 30).

2. The reformulation of the distinction between state and society by Luhmann reflects the unease felt by many social scientists in using the term "society." For instance, many sociologists are dissatisfied with the "common-sense" usage of "society," which refers to the boundaries of nation-states.[1] They have therefore moved away from the notion of society in so far as it implies a unitary concept linked to a particular territory or an attempt to divide "society" into different parts or levels (Mann 1986).[2] Similarly, Luhmann places little value on territorial distinctions between societies. Instead, the notion of independent entities within an "all-encompassing social system" lies at the core of his conceptualization of society. As noted earlier, the political subsystem is simply another entity alongside the educational, economic, scientific, and other subsystems.

3. For Luhmann, society is not simply made up of human beings but of the communication between them. Communication between human beings is what

makes society a reality. Furthermore, each subsystem (e.g., the political system) realizes in action society from a specific point of view. However, this view is made up of two perspectives—one that is particular to the subsystem and the other that reflects environmental factors. For instance, "the economic and education systems belong to the environment of education and the economy" (Luhmann 1990b: 30).

4. The "systems" approach serves to highlight the challenges facing the political system and the possibilities for meeting them. Rather than promote politics as a central force in society, Luhmann identifies the dilemmas confronting the political system (see Luhmann 1975). However, by contrast to Jänicke and other political scientists, he does not appear overly concerned about the subservient role of politics. For Luhmann, the government is there to protect and legitimate the bureaucracy so that the administration can "concentrate on the actual task of running the country" (Jänicke 1990: 25).

5. Although it responds to new challenges, the modern state is burdened by past practices and customs (tradition), which present serious obstacles to addressing problems arising from complex modern societies in an innovative way (see Luhmann 1990b: 27–28).

Several aspects of this critique by Luhmann are pertinent to the focus in the chapter on the capacity of politics to tackle environmental problems. With the growing complexity of social systems, "the past cannot serve as a guide to the present or future because there are too many potentially new contingencies and options" (Turner 1986: 116). Luhmann challenges and reassesses old ideas and develops new concepts. Rather than present the standard Marxist critique of the state, which focuses on the power of the economy (rather than politics), and of capitalists and on the ownership of the means of production (Luhmann 1990b: 28–29), he questions the nineteenth-century European assumption of a separation between state and society and suggests that the state is "nothing" outside society. The implications of this challenge are far-reaching. The state, rather than assuming a central position in influencing society, is part of society. The notion that political institutions shape social forces therefore becomes less tenable. This has serious implications for any plans to tackle environmental protection primarily by means of political action.

Like Weber before him, Luhmann may seem pessimistic. Yet, in challenging prevailing perceptions about the central role of politics, he may create new possibilities for rendering politics more effective. His work can stimulate innovative approaches. Though he highlights some of the obstacles that prevent effective political responses, I will concentrate on how groups and organizations with divergent interests and driven by different logics (e.g., economic growth, environmentalism, or political power) can engage in some form of constructive dialogue or, in the words of Habermas (1981), "rational communication." This is not to suggest that the process of dialogue will be easy. One of the aims of this chapter is to focus both on impediments to and possibilities for successful implementation of policy. The focus will be on Luhmann's critique of these possibilities and on adaptation by political institutions to the challenges posed by environmentalists.

LUHMANN'S SYSTEMS THEORY AND THE PROBLEM OF COMMUNICATION

The focus by Luhmann on communication between subsystems that realize action in society from a specific point of view is pivotal.

* How, when new challenges emerge or there are shifts in values, do established political organizations react?
* How can empathetic understanding of divergent viewpoints or goals be achieved?
* What are the possibilities for adaptation, conciliation, and compromise? How are apparently conflicting principles resolved in a pragmatic manner?

According to Luhmann, established political organizations have great difficulty in responding to new challenges and it is very hard to attain empathetic understanding between divergent viewpoints.

However, there are some gaps in his account that invite further comment. For instance, his account does not or cannot identify the mechanisms whereby systems respond to "environmental factors" or how these factors change systems.[3] Luhmann suggests that subsystems are sensitive to what takes place in their environment. Yet, he argues that this openness is severely restricted; in other words, subsystems are only open to what goes on in their environment so long as they translate what occurs in the external environment into their own language. There appears little scope for what goes on in the environment of a subsystem to change the subsystem. Luhmann, in other words, is pessimistic about the likelihood of actors (operating within the framework of a subsystem as politicians, lawyers, industrialists, environmentalists, and so on) suspending their own view of reality in order to comprehend fully that of actors operating in the context of another subsystem. Later on, I argue that Luhmann ignores aspects of his own argument about how political and other systems *are* sensitive to what occurs in their environment. He also overlooks the fora that do sanction social actors from different subsystems to sustain a dialogue.

On a more positive note, he highlights the key issue of action by human beings and its relationship to structural or systemic factors. He conceptualizes in novel ways the problems facing contemporary institutions. For instance, he uses the concepts of "autopoiesis" and of "self-referential systems." The term "autopoiesis" is derived from the work of two Chilean biologists, Maturana and Valera (see Rossbach 1993: 99), and reflects widespread interest in self-organizing systems. Luhmann traces the origins of the concept to around 1600 but is mainly interested in work carried out in the 1960s (Luhmann 1995: 8). These ideas influenced Luhmann in trying to move out of the restrictive frames of reference of most sociological writing (Luhmann 1995: 11).[4]

Autopoietic systems are defined as "systems that reproduce all the elementary components out of which they arise by means of a network of these elements themselves and in this way distinguish themselves from an environment—whether this takes the form of life, or consciousness or (in the case of social systems) communication" (Luhmann 1989: 143). Autopoiesis is "the mode of reproduction of these systems." Self-reference is used to describe "every operation that refers to something beyond itself and this back to itself" (145).

On this issue, Luhmann draws a sharp distinction between his own work and that of Parsons, who had no interest in self-referential systems: "Parsons, after all, found no place for himself in any of the more tiny boxes of his system. Because it excludes its author (and its reader?), his theory can claim to be general but not universal" (Luhmann quoted in Sciulli 1994: 39).

Luhmann goes beyond Parsons by trying to understand how systems reproduce themselves through their own internal dynamics. He addresses some of the shortcomings of the Parsonian approach through a more persuasive account of how systems reproduce themselves: "For example in Parsons's functional differentiation of society into four subsystems and each of these into four sub-subsystems, etc., the substantive analytical categorizing always is theoretically motivated by an observer who remains external to the system being analysed. Parsons's functionalism is unable to appreciate how a system could constitute itself through its own autopoietic processes" (Krippendorff 1991: 139).

Even if we reject Luhmann's overall theory of functional evolution for its lack of specificity, his interest in autopoietic processes highlights a fundamental problem in all forms of communication between human beings, namely, to what degree we can view the world from the standpoint of another person. Again, one should stress that this focus on human beings is based on the notion of social actors operating within the framework of a subsystem (i.e., as politicians, environmentalists, lawyers, educators, the clergy, and so on). Luhmann, by contrast to Habermas, is pessimistic about the possibilities for empathetic understanding of different points of view arising from another subsystem.[5] How far can we suspend our own view of reality in order to comprehend fully that of another person? The answer to this question is crucial to understanding the possibilities for implementing effective reforms, for instance in environmental policy.

Luhmann does not conceive society in terms of "central agencies" or an "apex" or "center." By focusing on processes of communication among human beings, he arrives at the "radical" conclusion that: "Modern society is a system without a spokesman and without internal representation" (1990b: 32).

Luhmann therefore addresses directly the question of whether or not political systems can cope with demands to solve problems like environmental degradation. He also draws on the example of the (in)capacity of the welfare state to deal with a burgeoning number of problems and responsibilities. The political system can no longer hope to represent the whole of society (1990b: 14). Ever since the eighteenth century, the old structures of authority, founded on a highly stratified system, have been replaced by a system based mainly on "functional differentiation." This creates a "legitimation crisis" in the sense that every system is faced by "the imperative to legitimate itself" (19). Politics, like all other systems, thereby becomes "self-referential":

> Whatever can become politically relevant results from a connection with whatever already possesses political relevance. Whatever counts politically reproduces itself. And this occurs by encompassing and absorbing interests from the social environment of the political system. Politics conditions its own possibilities—and apparently becomes sensible thereby to what its environment offers or requires. It is not understood adequately as a closed or an open system. It is both at the same time.
>
> The difficulties that theory-formation and on-going scientific research encounter here are rooted in their object. We will subsume them under the concept of self-referential system.
>
> A system is called self-referential that produces and reproduces the elements—in this case political decisions—out of which it is composed itself. (39–40)

This has powerful ramifications for discussions about the capacity of political systems to manage demands for environmental protection, economic development, and social justice.

One could dismiss the notion of self-referential systems as "logically circular and therefore empty" (Luhmann 1990b: 41). Yet, the concept of self-reference can improve our understanding of environmental and other problems. First, as Teubner has proposed in his analysis of the legal system, the notion of a system that is both "open" and "closed" enables us to transcend the limitations of theories that view (legal) change as "either purely internal and independent or exclusively the result of external events": "Legal and social changes are, for the neo-evolutionist, related yet distinct processes. Legal change reflects an internal dynamic, which, nevertheless, is affected by external stimuli and, in turn, influences the external environment" (1983: 249).[6]

Second, Luhmann submits that criticisms about the circularity of his arguments overlook the origins and "inevitability" of self-referential systems and the problems raised by these developments.[7] Openness to the environment is crucial to the survival of the political system. However, the "real condition of operation" lies in self-reference, "in the continual reference of politics to politics" (Luhmann 1990b: 42). For modern states, traditional bases (of law and constitutional order) are no longer sufficient. Deficiencies in awareness by the political system of its environment cannot be adequately addressed by using traditional legal and constitutional mechanisms. Here, Luhmann steers us away from reliance on tradition and, intentionally or not, impels us to concentrate on innovation.

Efforts by political theorists to grasp new situations by adopting traditional ways of conceptualizing social systems and traditional forms of logic (notably the use of adversarial logic and of rigid dichotomies and categories) create several difficulties. Some of these difficulties are identified in the analysis of self-referential systems:

Luhmann refers to how symbols like "money," "love," "power," and "truth" are organized into "binary codes" in order to achieve simplification in a complex environment. These symbols are used, respectively, in the systems of the economy, family, politics, and science.

Along with the advantage of simplification come many disadvantages. Binary coding, by definition, makes it hard to conceive of alternative ways of perceiving situations and processing information. The deployment of dichotomies in political debate may impact on attempts to create more effective policies. Luhmann perceives this problem in all areas of communication. Following Luhmann, "environmental protection versus development" represents a new dichotomy, with all the ensuing problems of communication.

Binary codes do not allow for exploration of a wide spectrum of alternatives. They restrict choices and impose constraints on tackling new situations and on communication between existing subsystems. Hence, the economy as a self-referential system may only respond to concern about environmental protection by "translating" it into the language of "payments and prices":

> These codes are totalizing in the sense that they exclude other possibilities of ordering information. A system can react to the environment only in terms of its code. For example, the binary code of the economy, payment/nonpayment, forces communications to be expressed in the language of prices and profits. This means that the economy can react to the environment, but as an autopoietically closed system it can do so only if it translates the language of nature into that of payments and prices. Whatever cannot be expressed in this language cannot be processed by the economy qua autonomous system. (Fuchs 1990: 748)

The outcome of this "structural blindness" of the economy to problems that cannot be translated into the language of payments and prices is illustrated by Luhmann: "Even if, for example, fossil fuels deplete rapidly it may 'still not yet' be profitable to switch to other forms of energy" (1989: 57, quoted in Fuchs 1990: 748).

- Under these conditions, how can political institutions and organizations respond to challenges posed by environmentalism?
- Can they only respond according to their own self-referential logic or can they be reshaped in order to meet some of the more fundamental demands of environmentalists?
- What fora exist to facilitate translation of the different logics (e.g., environmental protection and development) of the subsystems?

Luhmann argues that political systems are a long way from resolving these problems under conditions of rapid social change (1990b: 44). Apart from making hasty decisions, self-referential political systems prevent change by not taking decisions: "This means doing nothing as long as this does not put one in a position of 'blame' " (44).[8]

Luhmann acknowledges that in books like *Ecological Communication* he is more pessimistic than optimistic about modern society (though he adds that in comparing modern society with any of its predecessors "there seem to be more reasons to be optimistic and to be pessimistic at the same time" [Luhmann quoted in Sciulli 1994: 44]).

There are certainly plenty of reasons for being pessimistic and focusing on difficulties faced by governments to enact changes in environmental policies despite the obviousness of the problem. For instance, as early as 1922 the International Council for Bird Preservation was concerned about oil pollution of the oceans.[9] On the face of it, the British government responded quickly by enacting legislation on oil pollution in the same year. In the early 1950s, people discovered that oil poured out of tankers into the ocean was the main cause of pollution at sea. At a meeting organized by the British government in 1954, thirty-two countries promoted an International Convention for the Prevention of Pollution of the Sea by Oil. It took four more years for the agreement to be ratified by only some of the countries. Enforcement was limited and resisted by shipping interests, especially in the United States. The problem became more acute in the 1960s, and some catastrophes received worldwide publicity (like the spillage of 117,000 tons of crude oil off the southwest coast of England from the tanker *Torrey Canyon* in 1967 and the blast from an oil platform off the coast of Santa Barbara, California, in 1969). However, the problem was even greater. It was estimated that in the late 1960s, there were an average 10,000 spillages of oil and other hazardous substances per annum in navigable waters of the United States.

Despite efforts to regulate the industry, the disasters continue. On March 24, 1989, more than ten million gallons of crude oil spilled into Prince William Sound, Alaska, from the *Exxon Valdez* oil tanker. The political response to this calamity seemed appropriate. The U.S. Congress obtained assurances from oil companies that they would only use double-hulled ships in Prince William Sound. However, the measure was not enforced by governments that were reluctant to challenge a powerful economic interest group. There is a history of similar behavior by governments:

> Note the similarities between the *Valdez* oil spill and the circumstances surrounding the passage and implementation of the Oil Pollution Act of 1924. It is interesting that in both cases the federal effort grew out of public response to a perceived crisis (waste and pollution from oil and an earlier major ocean oil spill respectively) and resulted in congressional action with poor enforcement. Thus federal policy makers were able to satisfy their constituents without alienating an important and influential economic interest group. (Smith 1992: 157)

It comes as no surprise that for over two decades scientists, environmentalists, and local citizens had been warning of the dangers of an accident in Prince William Sound (Buchholz, Marcus, and Post 1992: 47–48).

The reluctance by governments to confront large corporations and the denial by established organizations of a problem is confirmed by the case of the chemical plant at Minamata, Japan, which released mercury into the ocean. Though severe neurological disorders and illnesses were detected among the local population as early as the mid-1950s, the company at first disavowed any connection. In the 1960s, it paid victims some compensation but rejected any connection between its practices and the health of the local population. Only in 1973, following a protracted protest campaign and evidence of serious damage to the health of people living around another factory owned by the same company, were victims paid more substantial compensation.

These illustrations draw attention to how, in the manner suggested by Jänicke and by Luhmann, established institutional practices and established organizations represent a barrier to effective action in favor of environmental protection. The slowness of institutional responses can be understood if one acknowledges, after Luhmann, the problem of self-referentiality in organizations. Notwithstanding their success in bringing environmental issues onto the political agenda, environmentalists are aware of the difficulty in changing institutional practices and of the tension between these practices and new ideas. Nicholson comments on how institutions "must from their nature be rooted in the past, and thus conflict with current thoughts and aspirations" (1987: 13).

Luhmann's pessimism may, however, have led him to underrate the possibilities for communication between the political and other subsystems, a theme explored more fully in the following section.

OVERCOMING COORDINATION PROBLEMS BETWEEN ENVIRONMENTAL AND OTHER SUBSYSTEMS

The dilemmas identified by Luhmann arise in all policy areas. They can only be addressed by breaking out of the self-referential mode of operation: "All self-referential systems have to break up such internal circles—I'll do what you want if you do what I want" (Luhmann 1990b: 44). Luhmann suggests two techniques: a focus on the external environment ("externalization") and on history ("historization"). However, he is principally interested in the external environment as a means of breaking up the "circularity of political communication" (45).

Despite his pessimism, Luhmann records that self-referential systems are subject to a variety of challenges, including "public opinion" (see Papadakis 1996: chapters 15 and 16). Public opinion may play a central role in "transforming self-reference into communication." It is principally through public opinion that the political system observes the external environment (Luhmann 1990b: 215). Public opinion is used as a mirror for the political system. However, in fulfilling this role public opinion apparently reinforces the self-referential qualities of the political system (216–217).

Still, Luhmann may be unduly pessimistic. The political system can both effect and prevent or delay change. This is well illustrated by the influence of social movements, interest groups, and "new politics" parties on environmental policies over the past forty years and in efforts to achieve dialogue between different subsystems. It is possible for groups and organizations with divergent interests, different logics (or symbolic codes) at their core, and different levels of power to engage in dialogue or communication. In other words, they can communicate their concerns to each other, influence one other, set aside some of their prejudgments, and become aware of and act in response to different points of view (see the following discussion concerning the work by Miller [1994] on "intersystemic discourse").

Luhmann himself offers solutions to problems of communication and states that systems theory can improve instruments available to us for "self-observation." Teubner draws on Luhmann to develop the concept of "reflexive law," which "will neither authoritatively determine the social functions of other subsystems nor regulate their input and output performances, but will foster mechanisms that systematically *further the development of reflexion structures within other social subsystems*" (1983: 275). Above all, the legal system could serve less to decide conflicts between competing policies than "to guarantee coordination processes and to compel agreement" (277). Teubner notes that self-referentiality "does not mean that any contact between systems is excluded" (1986: 312). He suggests that one can achieve some mutual "understanding" between subsystems, despite difficulties they face in acquiring social knowledge about each other.

The concepts of dialogue and reflexivity can also be applied to environmental social movements (Papadakis 1984; 1988). Apart from the value of shifts in opinion that may play a central role in "transforming self-reference into communication," Luhmann himself notes that society cannot do without the "self-observation" fostered by social movements. Some governments and established institutions have recognized that environmental social movements may, through the process of observing society, contribute to innovation and social change. This has prompted more flexible responses by government to environmental movements and recognition that they can contribute to addressing problems of circularity of political communication. Environmental movements have evolved into green parties, influenced political agendas, and revitalized politics (Dalton and Kuechler 1990; Papadakis 1989). Social movements may also be more effective innovators than established political institutions and potentially create new social arrangements (Papadakis 1996: chapter 6).

Luhmann only hints at the possibility of responsive and effective political institutions. He underrates the potential for social communication to provide "co-ordination of modern society's different function systems" (e.g., between political and other subsystems) (Miller 1994: 104). Miller refers to this form of social communication as the possibility of "intersystemic discourse." If there were no communication at all, "modern society would not merely be split up into different function systems, it would just fall apart reiterating the tragedy of the tower of Babel" (110). According to Miller, Luhmann does not explore the following possibilities: "whether and to what extent an intersystemic discourse is empirically possible, how the logic of that discourse can be described and whether it makes sense to distinguish between forms of collective rationality and irrationality on the level of such an intersystemic discourse" (109).

Luhmann dismisses attempts by green social movements to communicate with the rest of society about their concerns. Yet, he "could probably not deny that it [the communication of new social movements] did affect society and very much determined the increasing awareness of an ecological crisis at least in some countries" (Miller 1994: 110; see also Dunlap and Scarce 1991; Papadakis 1996: chapter 16).

Despite problems of self-referentiality, the historical record also shows that social and political movements and organizations are capable of breaking out of these constraints. For instance, how did social movements for conservation and environmental protection first arise and challenge the prevailing ethos of exploitation and domination of nature throughout the world? In Australia, for instance, activists formed the Wild Life Preservation Society of Australia in 1909, the Mountain Trails Club in 1914, and the National Parks and Primitive Areas Council in the 1930s and challenged predominant approaches to land use that saw "no cultural values in preserving naturalness and wildlife" (Strom 1979: 53).

Even though environmentalism can be viewed from an evolutionary perspective, we face the paradox that this evolution was based on new discoveries, innovations, and concepts, and the "path of evolution" or "self-reference" was full of surprises. To sum up, few, if any, people anticipated that the following discoveries and breakthroughs would form the basis for environmental movements in Australia after World War II:

- the "discovery" of lifestyle differences between European settlers and indigenous people;
- the translation of this discovery through the language of romanticism;
- the creation of myths about the Australian bush by poets and artists and the connection between these ideas and ideas about nationalism, egalitarianism, and patriotism;
- the novel practice of organized lobbying by preservationists and conservationists;
- the adaptation of a U.S. model for preservation of wilderness and national parks;
- the development of innovations in ideas about tourism and environmental protection;
- the development of the craft of bushwalking;
- the early challenges to colonialist views of wildlife and of land use;
- the rediscovery of the notion of preservation for future generations.

Most of these ideas did not feature in agendas and policy speeches of major parties and leading politicians until the 1960s, when support for environmental groups was limited.[10]

Following the Great Depression and World War II, there seemed little prospect of challenging predominant views about the connection between quality of life and achieving economic development. However, there were notable international initiatives like the 1948 formation of the International Union for the Protection of Nature, the 1949 meeting of the UN Scientific Conference on the Conservation and Utilization of Resources (UNSCCUR), and the foundation of the World Wildlife Fund in 1960 (McCormick 1989).

Again, each of these initiatives represented important breakthroughs and discoveries:

- the broad-ranging agenda of the UNSCCUR, which considered the availability of resources to meet growing demands;
- the success of the UNSCCUR in placing conservation on the agenda of intergovernmental business;
- the anticipation by the International Union for the Protection of Nature of studying the effects of toxic chemicals;
- the idea of fund-raising in order to preserve wildlife promoted by Huxley and taken up by the World Wildlife Fund (McCormick 1989).

My understanding of these events leads to a focus on two developments that partially support and partially refute the pessimism by Luhmann about the capacity of political institutions to address new challenges like environmentalism. First, there is evidence of a capacity by political institutions and organizations to take up new ideas, reinforce patterns of behavior, and shape new social forces. Second, innovations tend to occur randomly and institutions are often slow to respond to fundamental challenges arising from new ideas and discoveries. These issues can be explored by identifying scientific discoveries and conceptual advances that have helped to promote environmentalism (Papadakis 1996).

The pessimism by Luhmann about possibilities for coordination and meaningful discourse between function systems can be seen as partial on several other grounds. Although different functional systems are self-referential, they also "continuously try to make joint contributions to the solution of societal problems, for example, ecological problems—or at least, they are expected by the public to do so" (Miller 1994: 111). As Miller suggests, this leads to the institutionalization of discourse between function systems, for instance, the "concerted action" involving government, business, and labor or "systems of negotiation for social policy."

A parallel example in the area of environmental policy can be found in Australia, where Labor governments created mechanisms for institutionalizing discourse. In the 1980s, one approach was to establish dialogue with leaders in the green movement and employ them as senior policy advisers. The ensuing formation of ecologically sustainable development (ESD) working groups represented one of the most thorough attempts to defuse conflicts between developers and environmentalists and integrate warring factions into a process steered by government (Papadakis 1993). This concerted action encompassed state and federal government agencies and industry and environmental groups. For organizations like Greenpeace, involvement in this kind of corporatist process was unprecedented.

The final report by ESD working groups contained around five hundred new policy proposals, many of which implied changes in behavior by individuals and in business practices. On many issues there was consensus. Some environmentalists, despite resisting market-based mechanisms for tackling environmental problems and protesting certain aspects of procedures used by the ESD groups, gained a better understanding of how a balance might be achieved between economic and environmental goals.

The government had initiated a transformation of the institutional order. Whereas interest groups and social movements had stressed differences in their perspectives, the government had persuaded them to identify common ground and gained more control of the agenda by devising new institutional mechanisms. The impact of these changes was felt during the 1993 election campaign when the Labor Party and leading environmental groups focused on both development and the environment (Papadakis 1994). These shifts in perspective could not have occurred "if collective rationality had been completely disintegrated into the specific rationalities of the different function systems" (Miller 1994: 112). One could argue that different interest groups have recently "reverted" to the rationalities of the different function systems and failed to engage in a fruitful dialogue. This does not, however, negate the evidence that it is *possible* for dialogue to emerge and some policies have been enacted that reflect the success of this process.

Miller points out that individual social actors are capable of talking in the "languages" of different subsystems and explores the following possibilities:

> If industrial managers, politicians, lawyers, scientists, theologians and any other representatives of any other relevant function system of modern society talk to each other in order to find recommendations, programmes or even concrete solutions for dealing with ecological problems—a conversational round which, for example, is quite typical for the institution of "enquête commissions" consulted by the German parliament—to what extent can they understand each other; and what do they have to accept collectively if they at least want to understand their differences; and if they understand their differences is there, in principle, any chance of finding collectively accepted answers to collectively disputed ecological questions? (1994: 115)

Whereas Luhmann, in considering environmentalism, rejects the possibility of "substantial or teleological rationality" that could "serve as a common denominator for an organizational co-ordination of different function systems" (Miller [1994: 115] refers to Luhmann [1989: 138]), Miller argues there are many examples of how to achieve, if not "basic consent," at least "co-ordinated dissent." In other words, one can achieve "collective rationality," even if it is only "formal and procedural."

The notion of coordinated dissent (and the "logic of dissent" that underlies much of the process of functional differentiation of social systems) "does not presuppose consent on all kinds of beliefs and semantic codes" or "that anything that can be understood can also be accepted." Rather, "it only presupposes the collective acceptance of at least some common basic or elementary grounds (that constitute a joint universe of discourse, for example an empirical-theoretical or normative universe of discourse) because otherwise not even differences concerning particular beliefs or systems of beliefs could be mutually understood" (Miller 1994: 116).

DIALOGUE, INNOVATION, AND INSTITUTIONAL DESIGN AS SOLUTIONS TO ENVIRONMENTAL PROBLEMS

Luhmann, as Miller mentions, offers little empirical evidence to support claims about the process of coordination between function systems. Undoubtedly, there are problems. There are also many possibilities for dialogue and effective coordination.

Support for this argument can be gleaned from various sources. At an ethical level, Bernstein (1983) explores the notion of dialogue in a community. Handler (1988) takes this preoccupation with dialogue further by focusing on questions of power, particularly between dependent people and the state. How can people or groups of people with different degrees of power and different interests engage in a meaningful dialogue?

Underlying the concept of dialogue are notions of trust and goodwill (Handler 1988). Interestingly, as mentioned earlier, by placing interpersonal trust at the center of his project Luhmann differs from Parsons in addressing the question of social order. Similarly, Putnam (1993) has drawn our attention to the importance of trust (as a component of social capital) in the performance of institutions. Trust, and dialogue that accompanies it, entails goodwill, willingness to listen, and discretion. It can alter power relationships. Handler notes that his examples of a "dialogic community" represent "tiny corners of the modern welfare state" (1988: 1091), and concludes that though the task of achieving more dialogue is far from hopeless, it does depend on "an extensive reconceptualization and re-structuring of the way we conduct our public business" (1113). A key element in this process is what Handler calls a "supporting environment" for people undertaking such an exercise since it is bound to conflict with many of "our ideologies, traditions and practices" (1113).

This brings us back to our central interests, namely, the response by political institutions and established political organizations to new challenges like environmentalism and their effectiveness in implementing new policies. Putnam has posited a strong connection between effective democratic government and civic humanism or a strong civil society. His observations, like those of Luhmann, can be read as both encouraging and discouraging. He notes that "most institutional history moves slowly" (1993: 184). If, as Putnam writes, history is slow in "erecting norms of reciprocity and networks of civic engagement," how can we address new challenges like environmental protection?

Despite the "slow movement" of history, the character of social behavior, and the significant problems in communication between function systems, there are many prospects both for coordination between subsystems and the influence of environmentalism on established institutions and of economics on environmental protection. Political institutions and organizations can become more responsive to new challenges. There is no essential conflict between the slow movement of institutional history and environmentalism. History can even play a vital role in consolidating the impact of new challenges.

Though Luhmann (1989) points out that "prescriptions" for dealing with environmental problems are often not enough, his argument can become a pretext for not doing anything, for not bothering to design solutions to pressing problems:

- How can institutions better respond to new challenges?
- How do we adapt the claims by Putnam about a strong correspondence between effective government and civic humanism, in a context where society cannot adequately be construed in terms of the boundaries of nation-states or territories?
- Are there mechanisms for political institutions to short-circuit the "virtuous circles" of history and for addressing the social character of environmentalism?
- What are the possibilities for "designing" solutions to improve the performance of established institutions (see Israel 1987; Ostrom 1990)?

A focus on institutional design and on the need for political systems to break out of self-referential modes of operation suggests several options for innovation:

1. The first is to explore more fully the mechanisms and possibilities for coordination and dialogue (suggested by Miller 1994; Bernstein 1983; Handler 1988).
2. If we have relied too much on social movements to force the state into action, we may need to focus on how the state can introduce and facilitate innovations. There are many examples of such possibilities.
3. We can explore ways of generating ideas about how to address intractable problems or to improve on current ways of doing things (Papadakis 1996: chapter 7). This may entail taking distance from traditional ways of conceiving social systems and traditional forms of logic (notably adversarial logic and rigid dichotomies and categories).
4. One can investigate the significance of discoveries and conceptual innovations (e.g., "sustainable development," "the limits to growth," and "biodiversity") that have broken the virtuous circles of history. Provided new concepts can be formulated and the opportunity arises, an issue that has smoldered in the background of political debate for long periods of time can rapidly become politically significant.
5. The previous point raises the issue of the context for change. An effective way of addressing conflicting demands on political institutions is to consider particular contexts and circumstances (rather than absolute truths and fundamental conflicts between environment and development). This approach may

direct expectations away from the state or politics as the guiding center for all
that occurs in society. It may also create opportunities for the state to address
conflicts between the values we attach to the environment and to development.

The impact of the environmental movement has been achieved not by embracing
traditional evolutionary and revolutionary models for social action but through
changing perceptions about what constitutes quality and meaning of life. This
occurred over the past forty years in several stages as new concepts were created to
articulate concerns.

In the 1960s, for instance, the notion of a *Silent Spring* (Carson 1962) referred
to the dire consequences of treating our environment in certain ways. Similarly, the
notion of *The Limits to Growth* (Meadows et al. 1974) promoted by the Club of
Rome contributed to a radical shift in perceptions of our way of life. In the 1980s
and 1990s, concerns about social justice and economic development on a global
scale combined with growing anxiety about depletion of the ozone layer and emission of greenhouse gases have led to intense efforts to define a new agenda based on
the concept of sustainable development (World Commission on Environment and
Development 1990). Many people are now conscious of possibilities either for promoting development without harming the environment or for retaining a balance
between development and environment (Papadakis 1996: chapter 16).

For those accustomed to an evolutionary model for explaining change, the survival of established organizations (e.g., political parties, interest groups, and agencies
of government) is not surprising. This is construed as another indication of the durability of norms and procedures for absorbing any challenges. Moreover, the durability of political institutions and the absence of any coup d'état executed by green
revolutionaries appear to verify the evolutionary model. For revolutionaries, there is
only disappointment. Capitalism is thriving. The old parties are still in power. The
environment remains under threat.

Adjacent to these two positions, we find that there have been, despite the appearance of normality, fundamental shifts in perceptions and behavior in business and
industry and among rulers and the population at large. The shift has occurred in fits
and starts. The environmental movement and its goals were written off on several
occasions, only to return forcefully (inspired by new concepts and ideas) onto the
political agenda. The underlying trend, with the benefit of hindsight, has been
toward greater acceptance of fundamental shifts in values and policies.

This is not to ignore the value of work by Luhmann, Putnam, and Jänicke on
structural or systemic impediments to political action. The focus on self-referential
systems and circularity of political communication (as well as path dependence and
the "virtuous circles of history") represents a great emphasis on the analysis of the
past (sometimes with a view of using it to solve problems or to predict the future).
There is, however, a need to focus on designing alternatives and developing new
concepts that assist in this process.

The approach by Luhmann, despite its "realism," can be challenged or at least extended, by exploring possibilities for dialogue (between social systems) and social communication. Although political and other systems are often self-referential, they also cooperate in solving problems. Apart from the examples in this chapter, it is useful to consider initiatives at the local (landcare groups in Australia and citizens' initiatives in Germany [Papadakis 1984]), national (ESD working groups in Australia), and international level (like the 1972 and 1992 UN conferences in Stockholm and Rio de Janeiro). Just as significant are intergovernmental agreements on greenhouse gases, oil pollution, and biodiversity as well as work by nongovernment organizations like Greenpeace, World Wide Fund for Nature, and the Business Council for Sustainable Development (see Schmidheiny 1992). Von Weizsäcker (1994) also highlights possibilities for and of actual innovations by the state in the area of environmental policy. These can be used to reinforce the argument that innovation and design may be crucial in overcoming problems of self-reference and communication. Another important finding is that a nonadversarial approach to addressing new challenges has, in the long run, shown a higher level of correspondence with effective measures to protect the environment than a conflictual one (Jänicke et al. 1989, quoted in von Weizsäcker 1994: 142). This lends further support to the emphasis on constructive dialogue to overcome problems of self-reference.

Finally, it is important to recall that identifying environmental problems has been central to the agenda of many social movements over the past four decades. Social movements present a challenge to evolutionary accounts of social change and play a valuable role in disrupting the circularity of political communication outlined by the systems theory of Luhmann. This can be ascribed to the following factors:

- Political institutions, if they are to survive as a process of conciliation and as facilitators of political communication, need to demonstrate some flexibility by taking on board ideas and issues raised by social movements.
- Social movements have frequently mobilized sufficient popular support effectively to compel established political organizations to heed public opinion.
- Social movements have regularly attracted support from and even been led by elements within established political organizations.

The impetus to social movement activities has repeatedly come from conceptual advances based on discoveries by scientists, educators, and other individuals.

We can identify elements of continuity and discontinuity in the development of the environmental movement. In dealing with new challenges to institutions, we can appreciate the importance of both. Without disruption, design, and creativity, the circular character of political communication cannot be broken. Without institutional routines and procedures, we cannot ensure that new and desirable policies will be implemented systematically and successfully. Institutions often stand, ultimately, to benefit from innovations. Innovations can only be effective if they are backed by institutional structures. Established institutions can also ensure that new ideas, particularly if they appear far-fetched or impractical, are subjected to careful scrutiny. Political institutions can also be helpful as mechanisms for "deliberate conciliation" between opposing viewpoints (Crick 1993: 19). This serves as a further reminder of the significance of political communication, the theme articulated so powerfully by Luhmann in his reconceptualization of Parsons's systems theory.

NOTES

1. They prefer to regard sociology as "the analysis of the social, which can be treated at any level (for example, dyadic interaction, social groups, large organizations or whole societies)" (Abercrombie, Hill, and Turner 1988: 231).

2. Instead, Mann investigates the complex networks of power that emerge in social relationships. Though this represents an improvement on the restrictive metaphors of functionalist sociology (as articulated by Parsons and by aspects of Marxist accounts), Mann still uses the term "society" to address the problem of studying societies in isolation from one another.

3. Again, the term "environmental" is used to refer to the system/environment distinction posited by Luhmann and not to the issue of environmental protection.

4. Luhmann sees Parsons as one of the few who can move beyond particular disciplines (1995: 11, 498n23).

5. The issue of communication arises in Habermas, from his earliest work on communication in the bourgeois public sphere (1989), to his theory of communicative action (1981). There are also significant differences between the two writers. Habermas, in a critique of Luhmann, assumes that communicative rationality is possible within social subsystems. Luhmann, on the other hand, rejects Habermas's notion of communicative rationality as inadequate for complex social systems (see Miller 1994: 110–111).

6. Luhmann describes the legal system as "normatively closed" but "cognitively open." The two conditions are seen as reciprocal: "The openness of a system bases itself upon self-referential closure, and closed 'autopoietic' reproduction refers to the environment. To paraphrase the famous definition of cybernetics by Ashby: the legal system is open to cognitive information but closed to normative control" (Luhmann 1990a: 229).

7. "Viewed sociologically, self-reference is a result of evolutionary system differentiation and political self-reference, a result of the social differentiation of specifically political systems. The development of self-referential modes of operation corresponds exactly to the requirements of this historical development. And it imposes them to the extent of its realization: self-reference makes possible system openness to changing themes with a relative constancy of the structures guiding the operations (party organization, ministerial organization, law, etc.). And it makes possible the inclusion of the entire population within the scope of politics—regardless who determines what is a political theme. Therefore one has to begin from a practically inevitable development of structures that binds us to use social functions in this way" (Luhmann 1990a: 41).

8. Luhmann refers to Bachrach and Baratz (1970) and their notion of "nondecisions" in politics and to Scharpf (1971) and his notion of "negative coordination" in administration (Luhmann 1990a).

9. The following account on oil pollution is based on Nicholson (1987: 44–46) and McCormick (1989: 57–58).

10. The main differences between the early campaigns and successes and the influence of environmentalism today lie in the number of people who have been mobilized and the influence of environmental concerns on the political agenda as whole.

REFERENCES

Abercrombie, N., S. Hill, and B. Turner. 1988. *The Penguin Dictionary of Sociology.* 2nd ed. London: Penguin.

Alexander, J. C. 1983. "Theoretical Logic in Sociology." In *The Modern Reconstruction of Classical Thought,* ed. T. Parsons. Berkeley: University of California Press.

Bachrach, P., and M. S. Baratz. 1970. *Power and Poverty: Theory and Practice.* New York: Oxford University Press.

Bernstein, R. 1983. *Beyond Objectivism and Relativism: Science, Hermeneutics and Practice.* Oxford: Basil Blackwell.

Bershady, H. J. 1973. *Ideology and Social Knowledge.* New York: Wiley.

Black, M. 1961. "Some Questions about Parsons' Theories." In *The Social Theories of Talcott Parsons,* ed. M. Black, 268–288. Carbondale: Southern Illinois University Press.

Brennan, G., and J. M. Buchanan. 1985. *The Reason of Rules: Constitutional Political Economy.* New York: Cambridge University Press.

Buchholz, R. A., A. A. Marcus, and J. E. Post. 1992. *Managing Environmental Issues: A Casebook.* Englewood Cliffs, N.J.: Prentice Hall.

Carson, R. 1962. *Silent Spring.* Boston: Houghton Mifflin.

Coser, L. 1956. *The Functions of Social Conflict.* New York: The Free Press.

Crick, B. 1993. *In Defence of Politics.* 4th ed. London: Penguin.

Dahrendorf, R. 1959. *Class and Class Conflict in an Industrial Society.* London: Routledge.

Dalton, R., and M. Kuechler, eds. 1990. *Challenging the Political Order: New Social Movements in Western Democracies.* Cambridge: Polity.

Dunlap, R. E., and R. Scarce. 1991. "The Polls—Poll Trends: Environmental Problems and Protection." *Public Opinion Quarterly* 55:651–672.

Evans, P. B., D. Rueschemeyer, and T. Skocpol, eds. 1985. *Bringing the State Back In.* New York: Cambridge University Press.

Fuchs, S. 1990. Review of *Ecological Communication* by Niklas Luhmann. *American Journal of Sociology* 96:747–748.

Gouldner, A. 1970. *The Coming Crisis of Western Sociology.* New York: Basic.

Habermas, J. 1981. *Theorie des Kommunikativen Handelns.* Vols. 1–2. Frankfurt: Suhrkamp.

———. 1989. *The Structural Transformation of the Public Sphere.* Cambridge: Polity.

Hacker, A. 1961. "Sociology and Ideology." In *The Social Theories of Talcott Parsons,* ed. M. Black, 29–301. Carbondale: Southern Illinois University Press.

Hall, P. 1986. *Governing the Economy: The Politics of State Intervention in Britain and France.* New York: Oxford University Press.

Handler, J. 1988. "Dependent People, the State, and the Modern/Postmodern Search for the Dialogic Community." *UCLA Law Review* 35:999–1113.

Israel, A. 1987. *Institutional Development: Incentive to Performance.* Baltimore, Md.: Johns Hopkins University Press.

Jänicke, M. 1990. *State Failure: The Impotence of Politics in Industrial Society.* Cambridge: Polity.

Jänicke, M., H. Mönch, T. Ranneberg, and U. E. Simonis. 1989. "Structural Change and Environmental Impact: Empirical Evidence on 31 Countries in East and West." *Intereconomics* 24:24–34.

Krippendorff, K. 1991. "Society As Self-Referential." Review of *Ecological Communication* by Niklas Luhmann. *Journal of Communication* 41:136–140.

Luhmann, N. 1975. *Macht.* Stuttgart: Enke.

————. 1980. "Talcott Parsons—Zur Zukunft eines Theorieprogramms." *Zeitschrift für Soziologie* 9:5–17.

————. 1982. *The Differentiation of Society.* New York: Columbia University Press.

————. 1989. *Ecological Communication.* Cambridge: Polity.

————. 1990a. *Essays on Self-Reference.* New York: Columbia University Press.

————. 1990b. *Political Theory and the Welfare State.* Berlin: de Gruyere.

————. 1995. *Social Systems.* Stanford, Calif.: Stanford University Press.

Mann, M. 1986. *The Sources of Social Power.* Vol. 1. Cambridge: Cambridge University Press.

March, J. G., and J. P. Olsen. 1984. "The New Institutionalism: Organizational Factors in Political Life." *American Political Science Review* 78:734–749.

————. 1989. *Rediscovering Institutions: The Organizational Basis of Politics.* New York: The Free Press.

McCormick, J. 1989. *The Global Environmental Movement.* London: Belhaven.

Meadows, D. H., J. Meadows, J. Randers, and W. W. Behrens III. 1974. *The Limits to Growth.* London: Pan.

Miller, M. 1994. "Intersystemic Discourse and Co-ordinated Dissent: A Critique of Luhmann's Concept of Ecological Communication." *Theory, Culture and Society* 11:101–121.

Mills, C. W. 1959. *The Sociological Imagination.* Harmondsworth, UK: Penguin.

Münch, R. 1981. "Talcott Parsons and the Theory of Action I: The Structure of the Kantian Core." *American Journal of Sociology* 86:709–739.

————. 1982. "Talcott Parsons and the Theory of Action II: The Continuity of the Development." *American Journal of Sociology* 87:771–826.

Murphy, J. W. 1992. "Talcott Parsons and Niklas Luhmann: Two Versions of the Social 'System' " In *Talcott Parsons: Critical Assessments*, vol. 4, ed. P. Hamilton, 286–295. London: Routledge.

Neckel, S., and J. Wolf. 1994. "The Fascination of Amorality: Luhmann's Theory of Morality and Its Resonances among German Intellectuals." *Theory, Culture and Society* 11:69–99.

Nicholson, M. 1987. *The New Environmental Age.* Cambridge: Cambridge University Press.

North, D. 1990. *Institutions, Institutional Change and Economic Performance.* New York: Cambridge University Press.

Ostrom, E. 1990. *Governing the Commons: The Evolution of Institutions for Collective Action.* New York: Cambridge University Press.

Papadakis, E. 1984. *The Green Movement in West Germany.* London: Croom Helm.

————. 1988. "Social Movements, Self-Limiting Radicalism and the Green Party in West Germany." *Sociology* 22:433–454.

————. 1989. "Green Issues and Other Parties. *Themenklau* or New Flexibility?" In *Policy Making in the West German Green Party*, ed. E. Kolinsky, 61–85. Oxford: Berg.

————. 1993. *Politics and the Environment: The Australian Experience.* Sydney: Allen and Unwin.

————. 1994. "Development and the Environment." In *The 1993 Federal Election*, ed. C. Bean. *Australian Journal of Political Science*, special issue 29:66–80.

————. 1996. *Environmental Politics and Institutional Change.* Cambridge: Cambridge University Press.

Parsons. T. 1951. *The Social System.* New York: The Free Press.

Putnam, D. 1993. *Making Democracy Work: Civic Traditions in Modern Italy.* Princeton, N.J.: Princeton University Press.

Robertson, R., and B. Turner. 1992. "Talcott Parsons and Modern Social Theory—An

Appreciation." In *Talcott Parsons: Critical Assessments*, vol. 4, ed. P. Hamilton, 314–329. London: Routledge.

Rossbach, S. 1993. "The Author's Care of Himself." In *On Friedrich Nietzsche, Michel Foucault and Niklas Luhmann*. EUI Working Papers in Political and Social Sciences, SPS No. 93/10. Florence: European University Institute.

Scharpf, F. 1971. "Planung als politischer Prozeß." *Die Verwaltung*.1–30.

Schmidheiny, S. 1992. *Changing Course: A Global Business Perspective on Development and the Environment*. Cambridge: MIT Press.

Sciulli, D. 1994. "An Interview with Niklas Luhmann." *Theory, Culture and Society* 11:37–68.

Sciulli, D., and Gerstein, D. 1992. "Social Theory and Talcott Parsons in the 1980s." In *Talcott Parsons: Critical Assessments*, vol. 4, ed. P. Hamilton, 296–313. London: Routledge.

Shepsle, K. A. 1989. "Studying Institutions: Some Lessons from the Rational Choice Approach." *Journal of Theoretical Politics* 1:131–147.

Smith, Z. A. 1992. *The Environmental Policy Paradox*. Englewood Cliffs, N.J.: Prentice Hall.

Strom, A. 1979. "Some Events in Nature Conservation over the Last Forty Years." In *Australia's 100 Years of National Parks*, ed. W. Goldstein, 65–73. Sydney: National Parks and Wildlife Service.

Teubner, G. 1983. "Substantive and Reflexive Elements in Law." *Law and Society Review* 17:239–285.

———. 1986. "After Legal Instrumentalism?" In *Dilemmas of the Welfare State*, ed. G. Teubner. Berlin: de Gruyere.

Turner, J. H. 1986. *The Structure of Sociological Theory*. 4th ed. Chicago: Dorsey.

Von Weizsäcker, E. U. 1994. *Earth Politics*. London: Zed.

World Commission on Environment and Development. 1990. *Our Common Future*. Melbourne: Oxford University Press.

Wrong, D. 1961. "The Over-socialized Conception of Man in Modern Sociology." *American Sociological Review* 26:183–193.

7

Dynamic Constellations of the Individual, Society, and Nature: Critical Theory and Environmental Sociology

Peter Wehling

ENVIRONMENTAL SOCIOLOGY "AVANT LA LETTRE"?

What distinguishes Critical Theory from the mainstream of Marxism, Western Marxism, as well as from disciplinary academic sociology in the Durkheim-Weber tradition, is the emphasis on nature as a crucial element of the historical dynamics of societies. Thus, as early as the 1950s, Critical Theory suggested a comprehensive conceptual framework of social theory that appears to be of great potential interest and relevance for any sociological attempt at combating the environmental problems of present societies:

> The relationship between the individual and society is inseparable from their relationship to nature. The constellation of all three takes a dynamic form. It is not enough to be content with insight into their perennial interplay; it is up to social theory to take a scientific approach, with a view to investigating the laws according to which this interplay develops and discovering the changing forms adopted by the individual, society and nature in their historical dynamics. (Institut für Sozialforschung 1956: 43, my translation)

The theoretical approach outlined here implies much more than that society is merely influenced by its geophysical environment or climatic factors. It also claims—as the authors emphasize with reference to Marx—"that each natural environment with which man finds himself confronted has already been socially preformed" (Institut für Sozialforschung 1956: 44). At first sight, the basic idea of this approach is not too far removed from later definitions of environmental sociology. Well known is the definition given by Catton and Dunlap (1978), according to which environmental sociology is "the study of interaction between the environment and society." But we should be careful not to neglect the differences: while Catton and Dunlap refer to the interactions between society and *environment*, Adorno, Horkheimer, and colleagues speak of society and *nature*, adding the human individual as a third factor involved in the interrelations under study. Furthermore, they emphasize that the interrelations between individuals, society, and nature are themselves permanently changing and taking different historical forms.

On the one hand, there is evidence of many points of contact between the "strong program" of critical materialist social theory outlined by the Institute of Social Research and the idea of environmental sociology. On the other hand, in a special issue of a leading German sociological journal on state-of-the-art of environmental sociology (Diekmann and Jaeger 1996), Critical Theory of the Frankfurt School is not mentioned among those theoretical perspectives that are regarded to be important and fruitful for environmental sociology.[1]

This state of affairs appears paradoxical and requires more detailed examination. It has to be determined not only how Critical Theory could be fruitfully applied to environmental issues, but also why it has scarcely been applied to date. One reason for the present situation is, of course, quite obvious, if not trivial. The basic concepts and ideas of an interdisciplinary social theory, as inaugurated by Horkheimer in the 1930s and connected with the names of Adorno, Marcuse, Löwenthal, and Benjamin, were largely formulated at a time when there was no public or scientific awareness of "environmental problems." Consequently, there has been no empirical research into environmental issues within this tradition. Therefore, one cannot seriously expect the familiar topics of environmental sociology, such as environmental consciousness, energy consumption, green social movements, and so on, to be dealt with within Critical Theory.

In addition and, theoretically speaking, of greater importance, the "second generation" of critical theorists, in particular Habermas, have performed a "linguistic turn" since the 1970s by grounding social theory on the concept of communicative action, hence moving away from the interrelations between society and nature. Thus, at the same time that industrial societies were becoming aware of the risks they were posing for their natural environments as well as for their own material reproduction, Critical Theory started to focus on the normative foundations of modernity and on crises of social integration.

This orientation, influenced by Habermas, can also be found in a new research agenda of the Institute of Social Research in Frankfurt, presented in 1997 (Institut für Sozialforschung 1997). While the environmental problems of modern societies are of course mentioned, the overriding focus of the institute's research program is seen in the "dramatic increase in crises of social integration" (Dubiel and von

Friedeburg 1996: 8). Similarly, Honneth, one of the leading scholars of contemporary Critical Theory, considers the struggle for social recognition (*soziale Anerkennung*) to be the basic issue of a renewed tradition of Critical Theory (Honneth 1996).

Nevertheless, in this chapter, I develop the thesis that Critical Theory possesses great potential for critical analysis of ecological problems in industrial capitalist societies, which has not yet been fully exploited. However, it should be said that this potential refers to a conceptual reorientation of social theory and sociology as a whole, rather than to the substantiation and refinement of a specialized subdiscipline. At present, environmental sociology to a great extent suffers from a significant lack of social theoretical foundation and reflection. Many studies are restricted to empirical measurement and analysis of single and often isolated issues, for instance, the "discrepancy between environmental consciousness and environmental behaviour." In cases where a social-theoretical foundation does exist, it tends, at least in Germany, to take its cue from modernization theory or systems theory, thus tacitly reproducing the shortcomings of these approaches (see Wehling 1992). However, there is evidence that a mere "application" of the almost classic corpus of Critical Theory to environmental problems would not be helpful at all. Instead, what is at stake is to reconstruct the theoretical approach of Critical Theory as well as to recombine its dispersed insights and findings within the context of current debates on environmental problems and politics.

Given this background, in the following section I provide a brief overview of the conceptual frameworks within which Horkheimer, Adorno, Benjamin, Marcuse, and Habermas in different stages of Critical Theory have dealt with the interrelations of society, nature, and individuals. In the second section, some conclusions are drawn concerning potential contributions of Critical Theory to a social theory of the environmental crisis. Finally, in the third section I sketch out some ideas on how to actualize both the approach and the findings of Critical Theory to form a critical theory of society's socially structured relationships to nature (*kritische Theorie gesellschaftlicher Naturverhältnisse*).

SOCIETY AND NATURE IN CRITICAL THEORY

Of course, it is impossible to give here even a brief overview of the development of Critical Theory from Horkheimer to Habermas and beyond, from its beginnings in the 1920s up to the present. In particular, we have to take into account that Critical Theory is anything but homogenous. On the contrary, in the works of different authors at different periods of time there can be found a great variety of concepts of nature and of the interrelations between society and nature (see Vogel 1996). It would therefore be most unsatisfactory to highlight one period, one author, or one concept of nature as exclusively representative for Critical Theory. Instead, I will briefly give a retrospective theoretical outline of those arguments and stages of development in Critical Theory that have most strongly influenced its concern with relations between society, individuals, and nature.

Horkheimer and Adorno: The Critique of Instrumental Reason

In its initial phase, Critical Theory was shaped mainly by the programmatic work of Horkheimer done in the early 1930s. In this period, there emerged a peculiar state of tension between the innovative project of critical, interdisciplinary, empirically oriented social research on the one hand and a more or less orthodox, Marxist-inspired philosophy of history on the other. Horkheimer sees philosophy as the unifying bond preventing the empiricist, positivist disintegration of the individual disciplines. Whereas the philosophy of history is based on the belief that the progress of societal work and development of productive forces embody an objective rationality, the empirical social sciences (with a leading role played by social psychology) should substantiate why this rationality has failed to develop into a new rational order of society.

Nature or societal relations to nature had no real role to play in this conception of Critical Theory shaped via Lukacs by Hegel: it was not the rationality of society's appropriation of nature that was in question—which is why the natural sciences were considered to be irrelevant for the interdisciplinary project of a critical theory of society—but the irrationality of a social condition blocking the rational potential inherent in the productive forces. Yet it should not be neglected that even in this period Horkheimer, influenced by Schopenhauer, laid great emphasis on the singularity and transience of the human individual's existence, thus contrasting with the Hegelian philosophy of history.

It is generally known that since the late 1930s Horkheimer's ultimately idealist philosophy of history has undergone almost complete reversal in the face of Nazism, Stalinism, and World War II. Paradigmatic for this phase, of course, is the *Dialektik der Aufklärung* (*Dialectic of Enlightenment*) drafted jointly by Horkheimer and Adorno, along with Horkheimer's *Eclipse of Reason*, both published in 1947. Reason and rational appropriation of nature now no longer seem like objective potentials of societal emancipation but as instruments of merely subjective, blind self-preservation. The basic idea behind *Dialectic of Enlightenment* is that enlightenment and reason have so far served only human self-preservation at the expense of nature. To date, enlightenment itself has remained nothing but instrumental rationality, a rational domination and suppression of nature, with nature then striking back at society and individuals: "Every attempt to break out of natural constraints by breaking nature enters all the more deeply into those constraints. Hence the course of European civilisation" (Horkheimer and Adorno 1971: 15, translation adopted from Vogel 1996: 55).

Domination of nature thus returns to society, both as social domination and as the human individual's alienation from internal and external nature.[2] "[W]orld-domination over nature turns against the thinking subject himself; nothing is left of him but that eternally same *I think* that must accompany all my ideas" (Adorno and Horkheimer 1997: 26). Horkheimer and Adorno thus create a close and causal link between mastery over nature, a state of social control and domination, and a self-repressive structure of individual identity (see also Wiggershaus 1996).

Allusions to a way out of the self-destructive dialectic of Enlightenment are made by Horkheimer and Adorno only in general and seemingly mysterious terms, with formulations such as "remembrance of nature in the subject" (*"Eingedenken der Natur im Subjekt"*) or "self-cognition of the spirit as nature in disunion with itself" (*"Selbsterkenntnis des Geistes als mit sich entzweiter Natur"*). They argue that it is not until humans recognize that they themselves are *also* nature, and that by mastering external nature they are also mastering themselves, that enlightenment can become reflexive and free itself from its entanglement in power and domination. Yet, it should be stressed that this need not imply a simplistic and harmonic view of "reconciliation with nature" as frequently ascribed to Critical Theory. For the concept of nature itself remains paradoxical in *Dialectic of Enlightenment*: on the one hand, nature is what should be released from domination, and on the other hand, nature is the driving force behind "blind" human self-preservation. As Adorno has argued later in his *Negative Dialectics*: "The suppression of nature for human ends is a mere natural relationship" (1973: 179). At the same time, this ambivalence clearly shows that "mere" nature, in its immediate form, cannot be a force or an ideal for positive reference. Thus, as Schmid Noerr (1990: 77) has put it, society cannot derive normative principles from domination of nature nor from nature itself. Horkheimer and Adorno's argument therefore does not expose a "tendency towards naturalism," as Vogel (1996: 10) suggests. Rather, it aims at a conscious and reflexive transformation of "mere natural" relationships with nature, at "a new and unprecedented form of transcendence" of nature (Soper 1999: 65).

There can be little doubt that the perspective of *Dialectic of Enlightenment* makes room for a more profound and stimulating view of the relationship between societies and their natural environment, as well as of the naturalist and idealist assumptions in traditional Marxist philosophy of history. The relationship of societies with nature appears to be structured mainly by domination, exploitation, and destruction; what is more, reason itself turns out to be almost inseparably linked to domination and repression. Hence, the critique of instrumental reason, focusing on the dialectics of reason and nature, is often, and not without good reason, seen as Critical Theory's most important contribution to an understanding of environmental problems. However, it is obvious that Horkheimer and Adorno do not primarily argue from an environmentalist perspective, at least not in its current meaning. The major threat to society posed by instrumental reason lies in the regressive naturalization of society as well as in the repression of the "internal" nature of the individual, rather than in the exploitation and destruction of the "external" environment. Accordingly, Horkheimer and Adorno draw on a concept of nature that is not based on natural sciences like physics or biology, but on philosophy and, particularly with regard to internal nature, on Freud's psychoanalytic theory.

Moreover, we should be aware that in *Dialectic of Enlightenment*, the critical argument shifts from a historical and sociological context to an anthropological or meta-historical one. It seems to be human self-preservation itself, rather than the economic rationality or the social and political structures of capitalist industrialist societies that is directing Enlightenment and civilization toward self-destruction. An important and problematic consequence is that Horkheimer and Adorno do not clearly differentiate between Weber's concept of formal purposive rationality and the concept of instrumental reason as a specific historical form turning formal rationality into social and technological domination whereby the means control and eventually replace the human ends. Hence, Horkheimer and Adorno are not able to draw a clear line between humans working on nature in general and a specific form of mastery over nature leading to nature's destruction. The critique of instrumental reason therefore tends to favor normative or aesthetic treatment of nature instead of a rational, end-oriented approach—and it is often interpreted in this way.

The hermetic, aporetical, and, at least partly, self-contradictory argument of *Dialectic of Enlightenment* has often been criticized, particularly by Habermas. Whereas many of his objections are certainly valid, his own proposal of a "switch in paradigms" leading to communicative rationality poses considerable problems, particularly regarding the understanding of the relationships between society and nature. Before dealing with this in more detail, I first devote some attention to considerations made by Benjamin and Marcuse, because these offer different possibilities for reopening the philosophical and anthropological argumentation of the *Dialectic of Enlightenment* for a sociological analysis of historical constellations of society, individuals, and nature.

Benjamin: Mastering the Relations between Society and Nature

Benjamin, who had never been a core member of the Institute of Social Research, developed a different concept of historical materialism from the 1920s onwards that was much less influenced by Hegel, Lukacs, and Weber than was Horkheimer's theory. For Benjamin, historical materialism was neither a historical philosophy of progress, nor a theory of universal societal rationalization and modernization. Modernity, therefore, is not the final stage in a process of universal rationalization, but the historical project started by the capitalist industrial societies during the nineteenth century, with all the myths, dreams, and illusions in which these societies were bound up. Domination of nature by technology, progress, and evolution were (and are) some of the most striking of these illusions. In his unfinished *Arcades Project* (*Passagen-Werk*), intended to offer an "Original History of the 19th Century" ("*Urgeschichte des 19. Jahrhunderts*"), Benjamin wanted to decipher the underlying myths, dreams, and phantasmagorias in fashion, advertising, architecture, technology, means of transportation, and so on of nineteenth-century societies (see in greater detail Buck-Morss 1991; Wehling 1992).

This point of view allowed Benjamin to conceive of the exploitation of nature as a social and cultural project of industrial capitalism, rather than a universal feature of human civilization. In his well-known "Theses on the Philosophy of History" from 1940, he demonstrates how strongly the labor movement is integrated into this project and how it has developed for itself a "vulgar Marxist" conception of work as well as of nature: The exploitation of nature "with naive complacency" is contrasted with the exploitation of the working class, as Benjamin critically remarks (1968: 261). This sentence can be said to anticipate the development of Western societies after World War II, where successful social integration of the working classes was based on environmentally harmful economic growth and the rise of a consumer society. At the moment of its decline, we can see more clearly that this link between growth, employment, and welfare is not an irreversible stage in social evolution, but a fragile historical constellation of society, individuals, and nature.

On a more theoretical level, an argument from Benjamin's essay "One Way Street" (1978a), published in 1928, turns out to be very fruitful and stimulating. Here, Benjamin argues:

> The mastery of nature, so the imperialists teach, is the purpose of all technology. But who would trust a cane wielder who proclaimed the mastery of children by adults to be the purpose of education? Is not education above all the indispensable ordering of the relationship between generations and therefore mastery, if we are to use this term, of that relationship and not of children? And likewise, technology is not the mastery of nature but of the relation between nature and man. (1978b: 93)

The issue is no longer about mastery over nature but the way in which societies structure their relationship to nature. On the one hand, this is a normative criticism of the one-dimensional idea of society's mastery over nature, favoring instead the reflexive concept that societies need to "master" their relationship to nature. Not increasing domination of nature, but "balancing out" the relations between nature and society, therefore, should be seen as the aim of societal development. On the other hand, Benjamin's argument is of analytic interest also. It poses the historical and sociological question of how and in what forms, material as well as symbolic, societies structure and express their relations to nature; and it stresses that there are strong interrelations between the way in which societies organize their relationship to nature on the one hand, and social processes, technological visions, and cultural identities on the other hand.

Marcuse: Technology As a Social Project

Another, yet in some aspects quite similar, attempt to overcome the hermetics of *Dialectic of Enlightenment* (and a forerunner of ecological argument) should be seen in Marcuse's critique of technological rationality during the 1960s. Here, the ambiguous relationship between formal purposive rationality and instrumental reason formed a main focus of Marcuse's argument. While his 1964 book *One-Dimensional Man* (London: Paladin) is well known, I prefer to illustrate his argument by concentrating on his essay "Industrialisierung und Kapitalismus im Werk Max Webers"

("Capitalism and Industrialization in the Work of Max Weber") (1965), which is based on a paper presented to the Congress of the German Sociological Association in Heidelberg in 1964.

Marcuse's intention was to demonstrate that Weber's concept of assumedly formal and universal purposive rationality turns out to be a historical and cultural project and a form of domination of both nature and society. Yet, unlike Horkheimer and Adorno, Marcuse does not trace back this project to the structure of human self-preservation as such. He argues:

> The concept of technological rationality is perhaps an ideology in itself. It is not simply the use of it but technology itself that implies mastery (over nature and man), methodological, scientific, calculated and calculating mastery. Rather than being imposed on technology "afterwards" and from the outside, certain aims and concerns of mastery are already present in the construction of the technical apparatus; in each case, technology is a historical-societal project; in it is projected what a society, and the interests governing it, intend to do with mankind and things. Such an "aim" of mastery is "material" and as such is part of the actual form of technological rationality. (1965: 127, my translation)

Two important consequences follow from this position: first, the orthodox Marxist notion of the neutrality of technology or even of technology as a vehicle of emancipation, which was still guiding Critical Theory in the 1930s, is radically called into question; and second, the idea of a formal universal rationality, going back to Weber and transported by modernization theories, is rejected. Marcuse points out that models of rationality are always based on a certain historical and cultural relationship to nature and individuals. Rationality thus appears as a cultural, societal project and technology as a social construction, although Marcuse, of course, did not analyze in detail the process of social construction of technological artifacts as current social studies of science and technology do. For this reason, he could only envisage the vague and ambiguous idea of a "new science" and "new technology," instead of analyzing how science and technology are shaped by economic interests and cultural visions and are, themselves, "constructing" nature.

Habermas: The "Linguistic Turn" to the Theory of Communicative Action

It is certainly no coincidence that within one of his most important essays from the 1960s, Habermas refers critically to Marcuse's questioning of technological rationality. He argues against Marcuse that the idea of an "alternative technology" is bound to be self-contradictory, since technology had to be seen as a project of "the human species as a whole," not as any particular social project (Habermas 1968). Drawing on Gehlen's anthropological explanation of technology as a result of human "organ deficits," Habermas finally resorts to a naturalistic foundation of technology. In his book *Erkenntnis und Interesse* (*Knowledge and Human Interests*) (1973a), he refers to an "invariant relationship of the species to ambient nature, determined by the functions of instrumental action" (49) and fixed in the long run by the "species-specific physical organisation of mankind" (57).

In this argument, technology is firstly attributed to the physical nature of humans, and secondly, it is directly connected to the structure of purposive-rational action or of work *in general*. Habermas was doubtless correct in stating that humans are inevitably bound to treat nature with technical means in the interest of self-preservation and that Marcuse's idea of an "alternative technology" remains fairly vague and questionable. But by rejecting Marcuse's criticism, he is also dismissing the important idea that technology, in its concrete historical form, is actually a socially constructed project shaped by certain conceptions of rationality, scientific models, economic interests, and so on (cf. also Whitebook 1979; Vogel 1996: 111ff.). Consequently, from Habermas's argument it would follow that the scientifically and technically mediated relations between humans and nature are not socially formed or constructed, but are anthropologically determined. This conviction leads him to neglect the dynamic relations between society and nature as a genuine and important field of Critical Theory's concern.[3]

In Habermas's aforementioned essay, we find that he had already expressed quite clearly the basic differentiation between labor (or work) and interaction that was to guide his work until the *Theory of Communicative Action* (1987).[4] Habermas argues that labor and interaction each follow different rationality types: formal purposive rationality on the one hand, and communicative rationality on the other. Hence, labor tends to be seen as a nonsocial form of action (see critically Giddens 1982) with the difference between purposive rationality and instrumental reason disappearing again as it did in Horkheimer and Adorno.

Communicative action and rationality, by contrast, are seen as the basic concepts and normative foundations of a renewed Critical Theory that claims to overcome the aporias of Horkheimer's and Adorno's critique of instrumental reason. But as a result, the material reproduction of society, the "systemic" realm of purposive-rational action, and the symbolic reproduction of the "lifeworld" based on communication are assigned by Habermas to strictly separated sectors of society. Consequently, the crises or "pathologies" of modernity do not consist of problems in the interrelations between societies and their natural environments, but in the overlapping of functional systemic imperatives onto the communicative life world. Therefore, within the conceptual framework of his theory of modernity, Habermas is neither able to adequately address environmental crises as a crucial feature of modern industrial societies, nor to find a convincing sociological approach to analyzing the societal causes and preconditions of these crises.[5]

The turn to communicative action also touches on the topic of the normative foundations of Critical Theory that Habermas has made a central focus of his criticism of Horkheimer and Adorno. He argues that for Horkheimer and Adorno the normative foundations of Critical Theory have remained ambiguous and self-contradictory due to the aporetical argument of *Dialectic of Enlightenment*, in which rationality itself is identified in terms of domination. But the "paradigm shift" to communicative rationality leads to nature, or rather the relation between society and nature, becoming overlooked in the normative foundations of modernity. This is the case if these foundations, according to Habermas, are seen merely in terms of an ideal, undistorted communication between human individuals that is free from domination. Using well-founded reasons, he therefore rejects the idea of a normative or communicative attitude toward nature. But he fails to recognize that there might be different types of purposive-rational attitudes toward nature—and an instrumental reason that tends toward the overexploitation and destruction of nature as a resource for human society turns out not to be truly "rational." Albeit in a rather abstract fashion, another normative idea of a nondestructive rational attitude toward nature has been outlined by Adorno when he envisages the aim of the "preservation of nature and its diversity within its treatment for human ends" (1972: 235).[6]

Of course, in a more political context Habermas has taken notice of ecological problems and environmental movements. And yet, under the heading of "green problems," these are introduced into the *Theory of Communicative Action* in a rather unsatisfactory way:

> The intervention of large-scale industry into ecological balances, the growing scarcity of nonrenewable natural resources, as well as demographic developments present industrially developed societies with major problems; but these challenges are abstract at first and call for technical and economic solutions, which must in turn be globally planned and implemented by administrative means. What sets off the protest is rather the tangible destruction of the urban environment; the despoliation of the countryside through housing developments, industrialization, and pollution; the impairment of health through the ravages of civilization, pharmaceutical side effects, and the like—that is, developments that noticeably affect the organic foundations of the lifeworld and make us drastically aware of standards of livability, of inflexible limits to the deprivation of sensual-aesthetic background needs. (1987: 394)

Here, environmental problems are split into a technical-administrative aspect ("abstract" problems of scale and scarcity) and a cultural and aesthetic one, whereby the latter—understood in terms of the "colonization of the lifeworld" and in conformity with the postmaterialism thesis—is seen as the major motivation and driving force for social movement and protest.[7]

Given this background, it is not too surprising that, on the one hand, Critical Theory does not play a major role at present, neither in environmental debates nor in environmental social science and that, on the other hand, environmental problems are not a focus of Critical Theory's current research interests. Only at the margins of the tradition are there some attempts to relate Critical Theory to current environmental problems and to the relationship between societies and nature (see, e.g., Schmid Noerr 1990; Wiggershaus 1996; Vogel 1996; Böhme 1999). Most of these attempts remain, however, in a philosophical rather than sociological context.

The result of historical retrospection appears to be ambiguous and somewhat paradoxical: In the course of its development toward a normative theory of modernity, Critical Theory has become ever more removed from the idea of a critical sociology addressing the dynamic constellations of individuals, society, and nature. The attempt to render Critical Theory useful for the environmental debate must therefore look back beyond the linguistic turn of Habermas, referring to the former program of the theory. But it should be remembered that the idea of a critical analysis of the changing historical constellations of individuals, nature, and society remained rather undeveloped and did not result in an original, interdisciplinary research program. I approach the task of reformulating and actualizing that idea in the third section. But first, I point out some arguments of Critical Theory that might help clarify the objectives and conceptual foundations of a social theory concerned with environmental problems and might contribute to overcoming some of the shortcomings of current environmental sociology.

CONTRIBUTIONS TO A SOCIAL THEORY
OF ENVIRONMENTAL ISSUES

The contributions of Critical Theory to a sociological analysis of environmental issues are found on a conceptual rather than empirical level. Nevertheless, Critical Theory might also be able to stimulate new approaches to empirical research. On the conceptual level, the reconsideration of Critical Theory might help to clarify the theoretical foundations of a social theory and sociology open to environmental issues. This applies primarily to the substance and subject matter of sociology. In 1952, Adorno emphasized: "Sociology is not a human science. The issues with which it deals are not essentially related with the awareness or even unawareness of the people who make up society. They relate primarily to the struggle between humans and nature and objective forms of sociation which can by no means be ascribed to the mind in the sense of a human inner disposition" (1972: 481f., my translation).

This does, of course, not make sociology as a whole into environmental sociology; inversely, it means that environmental sociology does not constitute a specific, separate area of the social sphere. Indeed, a relation with nature (both internal and external nature) is constitutive for almost all areas of the social sphere, even if the actors are unaware or not always aware of the fact. Instead of establishing a specialized and thematically demarcated subdiscipline, it is more a case of changing the conceptual basis of sociology and producing a specific research perspective. However, the Durkheim program of explaining social facts only by other social facts is not simply revoked. Social processes are seen not as determined by nonsocial ones, but as influenced by nonsocial "facts" according to the way these are socially perceived, interpreted, and transformed.

This view of social structures and processes calls for investigating to what extent and in what way those structures and processes are related to nature and form a part of society's "struggle with nature." With respect to the basic concept of society, this implies that sociology cannot afford to confine itself to an understanding of social systems as communicative systems and of social processes as exclusively communicative processes, as suggested by Luhmann. According to Critical Theory's more comprehensive concept of sociology, social processes should, instead, be interpreted in terms of both symbolic and material activities. A corresponding implication is that a rigid partition of sociology into specialized subdisciplines is not very helpful for an analysis of environmental problems. This applies not only to the separation of environmental sociology from the sociology of science and technology (cf. Buttel and Taylor 1994), but also from cultural sociology, political sociology, and other fields.

Second, Critical Theory, claiming to analyze *historical* formations of society, human individuals, and nature, formulates a counterposition to the mainstream of modernization theories with their evolutionist assumptions. The functionalist concept of modern industrial society to which many modernization theories implicitly or explicitly refer turns out to be too general and abstract to offer an appropriate framework for analyzing the emergence and consequences of environmental problems. Hence, many attempts at sketching out "ecological modernization" as a new form and stage of industrial modernization (see, e.g., Huber 1995) still remain under the influence of evolutionary thinking and technological determinism (for criticism, see Wehling 1992; 1997). Recent efforts to widen the concept of ecological modernization to a more comprehensive theory of social change (see, e.g., Mol 1997; Spaargaren 1997) provide important insights but still require further conceptual clarification. This applies particularly with regard to the underlying concept of modernity and modernization, to the role of science and technology as supposed driving forces of ecological modernization, and to the involvement of different groups of social actors.

Nevertheless, the model of "late capitalism," from which Critical Theory took its cue after World War II and which was strongly oriented toward the social democratic welfare state of the 1960s and 1970s, has itself become historically outdated and requires rethinking. Both in its Horkheimer-Adorno and in its Habermas version (Habermas 1973b), this model (referred to in a different theoretical context as "fordism") was built on the assumption of successful political regulation of capitalist economies and their contradictions. Yet, this specific constellation of social structure, forms of industrial appropriation of nature, relationships of power and political regulations, technological progress, and individual behavioral patterns has itself been subject to radical change since the 1970s. Of crucial importance here is actually that the linkage among economic growth, technological innovation, and social welfare and integration has become extremely fragile. But awareness of the limits of economic growth is also among the most important of these social changes. New arenas of political conflict and negotiations are arising, along with new institutions; the technological basis of industrial production as well as economic structures and processes are being transformed (a process commonly referred to as "globalization"); the role of the individual in society is changing; and so on. A historical actualization of Critical Theory that picks up these phenomena would certainly demonstrate a considerable degree of contiguity with the project of a theory of reflexive modernization (as a historical self-reflection of modernization theory) pursued by Beck and others (see Beck, Giddens, and Lash 1994).

Methodological "Anti-individualism"

On the empirical level, the Critical Theory thesis maintaining that the relationship to nature is inseparable from the relationship of the individual and society is
above all in a position to stimulate new social science approaches toward environmental issues. In Adorno's emphasis on "objective forms of sociation" lies a clear
counterposition to the methodological individualism that, at least in Germany, governs a large proportion of the empirical studies in the field of environmental social
science in the wake of both rational choice theories and psychological attitudinal
research. In contrast with this, the authors of the Institute of Social Research state
rather harshly: "Even the biographical single person represents a social category.
They are determined solely within a life context with others, which builds their
social character; it is only in this context that their life is given meaning under given
social conditions; it is only within this context that this person, a social character
mask, can possibly be seen as an individual" (Institut für Sozialforschung 1956, 43,
my translation).[8]

The focus is therefore not on the rationality of the individual, who is an artificially
isolated actor calculating costs and benefits, but on processes of social integration
and the construction of social meanings and symbolic structures with a fundamental
effect on individual behavior. Without denying the shortcomings of Horkheimer's
and Adorno's theory of "culture industry," we should, however, recognize that the
authors have clearly identified the vital role of mass media and communication technology for social integration and social conformism. Moreover, they have also
pointed out that media, like television, do not simply offer "right" or "wrong"
images of reality, but change modes of perceiving reality, thus creating a new understanding of what is "real." Such insights appear to be of great relevance, particularly
for understanding environmental problems. It might therefore be fruitful to separate
the analysis of culture industry from the hermetic, philosophical context given by
the *Dialectic of Enlightenment*. The focus of interest then should be on empirical
studies analyzing how symbolic structures and meanings are created and reproduced
by, or ascribed to, certain cultural and technical objects.[9]

If we consider, for instance, a complex social phenomenon with great ecological
impact such as automobile traffic, we recognize the significance of an approach that
takes into account the symbolic structures of societies. Motoring is a multifaceted
social practice in which "rational" preoccupations like getting from A to B at a minimum cost are inextricably entwined with patterns of social integration, the demonstration of social status, socially shaped and technically mediated experience of
nature and the self, and so on.[10] Thus, we find that "automobility" should be interpreted as a both material and symbolic phenomenon. Embedded in a web of symbolic meanings and distinctions, automobility is not only changing the spatial and
temporal scales of social processes, but is also installing new cultural norms and patterns of behavior. Burkart (1994), therefore, in one of the as yet rare sociologically
reflected studies on automobile traffic, speaks of "social integration by automobility" and of the car as "part of a way of life." Any scientific approach or political

proposal failing to take into account this interweaving of different levels of meaning, assuming instead that only money and time constitute the determinants of "rational travel behavior," is unlikely to prove successful.

On a more general level, the example of automobility emphasizes that (individual) environmental behavior as a main focus of environmental sociology as well as psychology is frequently no more than an artificially isolated aspect in an overlapping, socially structured practical context. Critical Theory, while insisting on the societal influences on individuals, is able to sensitize awareness of this reduction and to reintegrate such phenomena into their historical and social context. Adorno, inspired by Benjamin with phrases like "sociological micrology" ("*soziologische Mikrologie*") or "thinking in constellations" (1969), has attempted to outline a sociological methodology capable of deciphering the historical constitution of social phenomena. "Cognition of the object in its constellation is cognition of the process stored in the object" (Adorno 1973: 163).

Nature and "Nonidentity"

Critical Theory (as well as other approaches) is frequently criticized for continuing to speak of nature, but not of "environment." Nature, it is usually argued, is an outdated, "essentialist" substantial term dating from the nineteenth century, whereas environment is a functional term always referring to the relation to an organism or a social system. These arguments are certainly of the utmost significance, but before relinquishing the term "nature," I should delve a little deeper into its possible significance for social theory and environmental sociology.

It has already been shown that in Critical Theory, nature does not figure as a normative counterpart to society. Horkheimer and Adorno do not see a way out of the self-destructive dialectics of enlightenment in society's "learning" from nature (even if the concept of "mimesis" in Adorno's "Aesthetic Theory" is evaluated in a very positive light), but merely in society's self-reflexive recognition that it does not exist in complete opposition to nature and that reason and culture are *also* nature. In addition, nature is not conceived of by critical theory as the realm of that which is given and unchangeable. On the contrary, as quoted earlier, nature with which societies or individuals are confronted has always been subject to social transformation and cultural interpretation. Therefore, for human societies, nature does not exist without and outside of these socially constructed mediations.

But at the same time, the term "nature" implies to a greater extent than "environment" an awareness of difference from and "nonidentity" with human societies. While, on the one hand, nature cannot be positively determined or defined outside a socially constituted reference framework, it is, on the other hand, not entirely socially constructed. Far more, there exists a difference that society cannot remove. Against the idealistic undertone of dialectical philosophy of history from Hegel to Lukacs, this difference has been addressed by Adorno in his *Negative Dialectics*, speaking of the "primacy of the object" and of the "nonidentical." In this regard, I do not agree with Vogel's criticism that the latter notion leads back to a search or nostalgia for nature as immediacy (cf. Vogel 1996: 84ff.). This is only the case if one understands the nonidentical as some kind of positive or "really existent" object *beyond* social mediation. Instead, we should conceive of "nonidentity" as difference *within* any mediation, thus being not a substantial but a relational category. Adorno himself, although sometimes really tending to the immediacy of experience, expresses this in similar theoretical terms: The primacy of the object, he writes, "does not mean that objectivity is something immediate, that we might forget our critique of naive realism. To grant precedence to the object means to make progressive qualitative distinctions between things which in themselves are indirect, it means a moment in dialectics—not beyond dialectics, but articulated in dialectics" (1973: 184).

Here, we can find a model for conceiving nature that might overcome the shortcomings of both epistemological realism and radicalized constructionism reducing nature to nothing but a social construction. Contrary to Adorno, however, we should not speak of the "primacy of the object," but rather of the primacy of mediation or of relations between subject and object, society and nature. At the same time, the concept of nonidentity as a critical concept may help us to keep in mind that domination of nature (or environmental planning) will never be perfect and complete and that human societies must always reckon with unexpected and uncontrollable side effects.

Another important aspect of the concept of nature is that, unlike environment, it allows a connection between internal and external nature. What is usually referred to as "environment" or environmental problems concerns problems affecting "external" ecosystems or the "built" environment (see, e.g., Catton and Dunlap 1978: 44). The concept of nature broadens the perspective to include interrelations between external environmental changes and the human body. This applies not only to environmentally caused diseases, but also to changes in forms of human perception and sensitivity through to scientific-technological transformations of human body functions themselves, for instance via reproductive medicine and genetic engineering. This again does not imply normative reference to a supposedly unchangeable "human nature" as a yardstick for political action; on the contrary, it has to be recognized that human nature, too, is subject to social and technological changes. But with the theoretical approach of Critical Theory, we can at least identify changes in the human body as an important and inseparable dimension of "environmental" dangers. This might also be able to prevent the dominance of technological or even technocratic approaches that restrict environmental problems to a lack of efficiency in exploiting and using the resources of the external environment.

TOWARD A CRITICAL THEORY OF SOCIETY'S RELATIONSHIPS TO NATURE

The concept of social theory referring to historical constellations of individuals, society, and nature has not become the mainstream of Critical Theory, neither in its theoretical reflections nor in empirical research. During the 1950s and 1960s, empirical research of the Institute of Social Research focused mainly on industrial relations, studies on prejudice and authoritarianism, and on cultural issues. Only in some of his more theoretical reflections on the essence and reach of social theory did Adorno refer to the idea of incorporating society-nature relations into the field of social theory. But, as illustrated earlier, with Habermas's turn to a theory of communicative action, this line of argument was put on ice for a time. Within the framework of Habermas's theory of communicative action, Critical Theory was neither able to adequately incorporate environmental issues, nor to address science and technology as an important field of social science research.

Hence, assuming that Critical Theory provides an appropriate conceptual framework as well as a wide range of insights (albeit often implicit) that are relevant and useful for analyzing the constellations of individuals, society, and nature, we should try to reconsider and actualize the theoretical approach and reintegrate the various findings. This of course implies reformulating the original idea in line with the present political, economic, cultural, and scientific contexts. On a conceptual level, at the Institute for Social Ecological Research[11] this idea has been actualized within the framework of what we call "critical theory of society's socially structured relationships to nature" ("*kritische Theorie der gesellschaftlichen Naturverhältnisse*") (see Jahn 1990; Jahn and Wehling 1998a). In the first instance, this conception draws on Benjamin's aforementioned switch in perspective from domination of nature to mastery of society-nature relations. In fact, what societies or human individuals do is to structure, regulate, and symbolize their relationships to nature; the idea of "dominating" nature is only one historically and culturally specific form of regulating these relationships. The second basic assumption on which the theory of society's relationships to nature works lies in the fact that we are confronted with socially constructed forms of mediation between society and nature (which in the recent work of Latour [1993] are termed "hybrids"), rather then with pure "social facts" or mere "natural objects." This basic idea has been clearly expressed by Adorno: "The social process is neither solely society nor solely nature but human metabolism with the latter, permanent mediation between the two instances. The natural element present at all stages cannot be extracted from its societal form without harming the phenomena" (1972: 221, my translation).

The third important assumption claims that human action and social practice may not be seen as either material or symbolic; instead, these are only two dimensions of human action and social processes, separable only analytically. Thus, society's relationships to nature in different fields of action (like, e.g., production, nutrition, reproduction, mobility, and so on) are regulated both on a material and on a symbolic level. This can be illustrated by taking nutrition as an example: The material forms of producing, distributing, and also preparing and consuming food are evidently closely connected not only with economic and technological structures, but also with diverse symbolic practices ranging from cultural-religious eating taboos through socially shaped "nutritional styles" and "eating cultures" to scientific recommendations and legal norms. Societal relationships to nature, therefore, do not only consist of material metabolism, but also comprise the social, cultural, religious and—with ever-increasing importance—scientific projections and constructions of nature.

Given this background, the concept of society's socially structured relationships to nature can be outlined using the following four points:

1. The notion of "society's socially structured relationships to nature" implies that society and nature find themselves within a structure of interrelation and mediation that can be dissolved neither in one direction nor the other, but that can and do become modified toward either "pole." In particular, this means that an ontological or normative definition of nature, regardless of societal forms of perception and practice, has its essence swept away. Thus, natural science also represents just one of several approaches to nature; it is itself socially shaped and—as a form of highly decontextualized knowledge—finds itself in competition with, for instance, local knowledge of social actors (farmers, women, and so on).

2. Another consideration, however, is that we are faced with the mediation of a *difference*. This is to say, nature is more than and different from just a social construction. Nevertheless, this is not an essentialist statement; by contrast, the difference itself is constituted only by and within mediation. Thus, being a "nonidentical" element within mediation, nature, however, exhibits a materiality and potentiality of its own so that mediation with human needs and ends may well fail: social objectives are not attained, or else other, nonintentional, noncontrollable side effects are triggered. On the one hand, scientific knowledge provides approaches for opening up this materiality but fails, on the other hand, to provide any "objective," context-independent cognition of its themes. And in many cases, instead of producing stable bases for action, uncertainty is often created or heightened as a result of science.

3. In contrast to the (at least German) sociological mainstream, the phrase draws attention to the fact that social action requires analysis not only in its symbolic and communicative but also in its material dimensions. For a critical theory of society's socially structured relationships to nature, it is precisely the connection between these two dimensions that becomes the focus of interest. Here, it is not merely a question of social action relating to nature both symbolically and materially, but also of socially constructed and interpreted "natural facts" and "hybrid objects" (like the "greenhouse effect" or the "mad cow disease") becoming included in action networks and "acting" there with some social consequence (see Latour 1993).

4. There is little point in talking about *one* socially constructed relationship to nature that is assumed to be located on a general, normative level and to be modified only via cultural processes of moral learning. Instead, the regulation and structuring of society's relationships to nature via symbolic and material practices need to be analyzed *in different social spheres of action* such as agriculture and nutrition, leisure and tourism, mobility, and so on. Since there is no

overlapping cultural idea of the (appropriate) relationship of society to nature, the regulation of society's relationships to nature in various spheres of action will occur in very differing, even opposing and antagonistic forms: scientification can stand alongside moralization, "novel food" alongside natural foods, and, usually, we can observe social disputes about what nature actually is or the "right" approach to nature in a certain field.[12] This can (and does) lead to certain social practices becoming dominant with, above all, economic or scientific-technical regulatory forms shaping and reshaping society's relationships to nature to an ever-growing degree. But such hegemonies ultimately remain contingent and contestable: transformations of societal relations to nature must not therefore represent a homogenous and parallel process following a supposedly universal, evolutionary logic of scientific, technological, or economic rationality. This is where the idea of a theory of societal relationships to nature differs rather sharply from the idealistic and harmonistic assumptions of modernization theory.

The concept of society's relationships to nature is of course not fully developed as yet. Moreover, it is not primarily intended to provide a basic general theory, but rather a conceptual or heuristic framework for analyzing environmental problems and their dynamics in present societies. This entails guiding empirical research as well as stimulating solutions that are not restricted to technological innovations from the start, but include or even favor social innovations and structural changes. Referring again to the example of automobile traffic, we should stress that reducing the fuel consumption and toxic emissions of the single car by technical means is proving to be a very limited and presumably counterproductive "end-of-pipe" strategy. The truth of this will become particularly apparent if the technical reduction in consumption and emissions is offset by a growth in car production and utilization. Instead, critical analysis must address the social needs for mobility as well as the cultural and symbolic meanings of mobility within certain social groups and discover social and political strategies to "decouple" mobility, as a not only physical and technological but also social and cultural phenomenon, from automobility.

However, it is quite apparent that analysis of society's relationships to nature requires problem-oriented interdisciplinary cooperation, not only among social science disciplines, but also among social, natural, and technological sciences. Understood in this way, "social-ecological research" may be considered as a necessary widening of Critical Theory's interdisciplinary project. Yet, while natural scientific knowledge is indispensable even for finding and describing environmental problems as well as for outlining and assessing possible solutions, social science should not be restricted or restrict itself to some kind of "behavioral engineering" employed merely to increase social acceptance for technical solutions. Instead, critical social theory should also analyze how the problems under review are structured by politics, the economy, and, of course, science itself, thereby following Wynne's argument "that the construction of scientific knowledge is less completely determined by nature than conventional approaches assume" (1994: 184).

Beyond the Realism-Constructionism Divide?

The most controversial issue in contemporary environmental sociology should be seen in the dispute between "social constructionism" and "realism" (see, e.g., Dickens 1996: 71ff.; Burningham and Cooper 1999; Grundmann and Stehr 2000). In this regard, there are two reasons why I think that the concept of society's relationships to nature offers an initial clue on how to, if not surmount, then at least organize productively the aporias of "naturalist" and "sociocentric," or "realist" and "constructionist" approaches to environmental issues. First, this concept claims that nature or environment cannot be addressed beyond or outside of societal forms of mediation. Yet, while thus being "social constructions," environmental problems at the same time refer to the materiality of nature that both enables and constrains the process of social construction (see Redclift and Woodgate 1994). Critical analysis and reconstruction of *how* the sciences (*both* natural and social) define environmental problems, therefore, does not necessarily imply denying the existence of environmental problems and their materiality.[13]

Second, assuming that society's relationships to nature are regulated not only materially, but also symbolically, then we are not even able to understand the social causes and consequences of environmental problems once we fade out the role of science or culture in defining them and thus preforming social and political reactions. For societies or individuals do not necessarily react to the problems as they "really are," but as they are described by science, by politics, by social movements, by mass media, and so on. This applies especially in the case of many environmental problems (like global warming, depletion of the ozone layer, and so on) whose "reality" and consequences are no longer felt immediately, sensually, and physically, but solely as the result of complex scientific modeling and measurement, with a high degree of uncertainty.

Against this background, the following antagonism suggested by Dunlap and Catton appears to be rather misleading: "Limiting sociological attention to the ways in which global environmental problems have been recognised, defined and legitimated, inhibits our contributions to understanding causes, consequences and possible amelioration of such problems" (1994: 7). Here, the authors seem to imply that analyzing causes, consequences, and possible amelioration of environmental problems could strictly be separated from the ways they are recognized, defined, and so on. Instead, the focus of critical analysis should be on the complex, nonlinear and at least partly contingent *interrelations* between material and symbolic dimensions of environmental problems, and between material and symbolic regulations of society's relationships to nature.

Thus, one lesson we could and should learn from Critical Theory as an interdisciplinary project is that capitalist economy, politics, science and technology, mass media, and so on interfere and influence each other, thus driving the dynamics of society, individuals, and nature. Sociological analysis of environmental problems, therefore, has to be closely linked to a comprehensive and historically reflected social theory from which nature as the "nonidentical," on the one hand, may not be excluded. On the other hand, we have to take into account that, in Adorno's terms, the natural can never be "extracted from its societal form." Critical Theory, at least, should make us sensitive to this tension and its theoretical and political consequences.

NOTES

1. Instead, the editors list as fruitful approaches rational choice theory, systems theory, modernization theory, and human ecology.

2. This corresponds closely to Horkheimer's and Adorno's explanation of German Nazi anti-Semitism, which they conceive of as a blind "revolt of nature" (Horkheimer 1947), instrumentalized by political power.

3. Quite similar criticism of Habermas's revisions of Critical Theory comes from Eckersley (1990). Yet, unlike those of Eckersley, my objections do not attempt to replace Habermas's anthropocentric theoretical framework by an "ecocentric" one, but aim at reopening his anthropological and ultimately naturalistic conception of society-nature relations to historical and sociological reflection.

4. The further development of Habermas's theoretical project can only be sketched out here very briefly (for a more detailed argumentation, cf. Wehling 1992).

5. However, an important attempt at integrating environmental thinking into Habermas's framework has been made by Dryzek (1987). Yet, it ultimately remains ambiguous how his concept of ecological rationality could be defined in terms of the theory of communicative action: If, on the one hand, it is conceived of as a specific historical form of purposive rationality, then one would have to admit that science, technology, and (instrumental) rationality are in fact socially and historically shaped rather than anthropologically determined. If, on the other hand, ecological rationality is considered to be an application of normative or aesthetic rationality to nature, then Habermas's rigid separation among instrumental, normative, and aesthetic rationality is called into question.

6. Apparently, this is not an "ecocentric" perspective as suggested by Eckersley, but a reflexive, noninstrumentalist form of "anthropocentric" rationality.

7. Like many other approaches in environmental social theory, that of Habermas would fail to address and explain Third World environmentalism.

8. Doubtless, the constellation of society and individual has undergone dramatic change during the last two decades due, not at least, to the hegemony of neoliberalism and deregulation. Although this change certainly can be described as "individualization," it does not necessarily imply that the individuals have become more "autonomous" or "free." As Bauman has put it: "We are all individuals now; not by choice, though, but by necessity. We are individuals *de iure* regardless of whether we are individuals *de facto*; self-identification, self-management and self-assertion, and above all self-sufficiency in the performance of all these three tasks, is our duty whether or not we command the resources which the performance of the new duty demands" (1999: 127).

9. Adorno's work on television, although dating from the 1950s, could still prove stimulating for such an approach (see, e.g., Adorno 1998).

10. Within a research project into "viable forms of urban mobility," carried out at the Institute of Social-Ecological Research (ISOE), a conceptual approach has been developed that attempts to take into account this complexity on the level of empirical research. Mobility

is hereby analytically differentiated into physical-spatial, sociospatial, and sociocultural dimensions (Jahn and Wehling 1998b). In the latter context, the concept of "lifestyles" may promote understanding of the different meanings and symbolic relevance in different social groups of mobility in general and automobility in particular (cf. Götz and Jahn 1998).

11. The ISOE in Frankfurt makes reference to the tradition of Critical Theory and tries to carry it further for analysis of environmental problems in their social context and for finding societal solutions to these problems. Yet, founded in 1988, it does not directly adhere to the institutional context of Critical Theory.

12. Macnaghten and Urry, with a partly similar intention, speak of "a diversity of contested natures" instead of one singular nature, and they emphasize "that each such nature is constituted through a variety of socio-cultural processes from which such natures cannot be plausibly separated" (1998: 1).

13. The realism-constructionism dispute seems to arise largely from a confusion of ontological and epistemological statements and claims. The epistemological question of what is true or what is claimed to be true should be carefully distinguished from the ontological question of what is real. Thus, calling into question certain truth claims of (environmental) science does not automatically imply denying the reality of the problems investigated by science.

REFERENCES

Adorno, Theodor W. 1969. "Einleitung." In *Der Positivismusstreit in der deutschen Soziologie*, ed. T. W. Adorno, R. Dahrendorf, H. Pilot, H. Albert, J. Habermas, K. R. Popper, 7–79. Darmstadt, Neuwied: Luchterhand.
———. 1972. *Soziologische Schriften*. Vol. 1. Frankfurt am Main: Suhrkamp.
———. 1973. *Negative Dialectics*. London: Routledge and Kegan Paul.
———. 1998. "Prologue to Television." In *Critical Models: Interventions and Catchwords*, ed. T. W. Adorno, 49–57. New York: Columbia University Press.
Adorno, Theodor W., and Max Horkheimer. 1997. *Dialectic of Enlightenment*. London: Verso.
Bauman, Zygmunt. 1999. "Critique—Privatized and Disarmed." *Zeitschrift für kritische Theorie* 9:121–131.
Beck, Ulrich, Anthony Giddens, and Scott Lash. 1994. *Reflexive Modernization*. Cambridge: Polity.
Benjamin, Walter. 1968. *Illuminations*. New York: Harcourt, Brace.
———. 1978a. "One Way Street." In *Reflections: Essays, Aphorisms, Autobiographical Writings*, ed. W. Benjamin. New York: Harcourt, Brace, Jovanovich.
———, ed. 1978b. *Reflections: Essays, Aphorisms, Autobiographical Writings*. New York: Harcourt, Brace, Jovanovich.
———. 1982. *Passagen-Werk: Gesammelte Schriften*. Vol. 5. Frankfurt am Main: Suhrkamp.
Böhme, Gernot. 1999. "Kritische Theorie der Natur." *Zeitschrift für kritische Theorie* 9:59–71.
Buck-Morss, Susan. 1991. *The Dialectics of Seeing—Walter Benjamin and the Arcades Project*. Cambridge: MIT Press.
Burkart, Günter. 1994. "Individuelle Mobilität und soziale Integration: Zur Soziologie des Automobilismus." *Soziale Welt* 45:216–241.
Burningham, Kate, and Geoff Cooper. 1999. "Being Constructive: Social Constructionism and the Environment." *Sociology* 33:297–316.

Buttel, Fred, and Peter Taylor. 1994. "Environmental Sociology and Global Environmental Change: A Critical Assessment." In *Social Theory and the Global Environment*, ed. M. Redclift and T. Benton, 228–255. London: Routledge.

Catton, William, and Riley Dunlap. 1978. "Environmental Sociology: A New Paradigm." *The American Sociologist* 13:41–49.

Dickens, Peter. 1996. *Reconstructing Nature: Alienation, Emancipation and the Division of Labour*. London: Routledge.

Diekmann, Andreas, and Carlo Jaeger, eds. 1996. "Umweltsoziologie." *Kölner Zeitschrift für Soziologie und Sozialpsychologie*, Special Issue 36:5–584.

Dryzek, John. 1987. *Rational Ecology: Environment and Political Economy*. Oxford: Basil Blackwell.

Dubiel, Helmut, and Ludwig von Friedeburg. 1996. "Die Zukunft des Instituts für Sozialforschung." *Mitteilungen des Instituts für Sozialforschung* 7:5–12.

Dunlap, Riley, and William Catton. 1994. "Struggling with Human Exemptionalism: The Rise, Decline and Revitalization of Environmental Sociology." *The American Sociologist* 25:5–30.

Eckersley, Robyn. 1990. "Habermas and Green Political Thought: Two Roads Diverging." *Theory and Society* 19:739–776

Giddens, Anthony. 1982. "Labour and Interaction." In *Habermas: Critical Debates*, ed. J. B. Thompson and D. Held, 149–161. Cambridge: MIT Press.

Götz, Konrad, and Thomas Jahn. 1998. "Mobility Models and Traffic Behaviour: An Empirical Socio-Ecological Research Project." In *Urban Ecology*, ed. J. Breuste, H. Feldmann, and O. Uhlmann, 551–556. Berlin: Springer.

Grundmann, Reiner, and Nico Stehr. 2000. "Social Science and the Absence of Nature: Uncertainty and the Reality of Extremes." *Social Science Information* 39:155–179.

Habermas, Jürgen. 1968. *Technik und Wissenschaft als "Ideologie."* Frankfurt am Main: Suhrkamp.

———. 1973a. *Erkenntnis und Interesse*. 2nd ed. Frankfurt am Main: Suhrkamp.

———. 1973b. *Legitimationsprobleme im Spätkapitalismus*. Frankfurt am Main: Suhrkamp.

———. 1987. *The Theory of Communicative Action*. Vol. 2, *Lifeworld and System: A Critique of Functionalist Reason*. Boston: Beacon.

Honneth, Axel. 1996. "Die soziale Dynamik von Missachtung: Zur Ortsbestimmung einer kritischen Gesellschaftstheorie." *Mitteilungen des Instituts für Sozialforschung* 7:13–32.

Horkheimer, Max. 1947. *Eclipse of Reason*. New York: Oxford University Press.

Horkheimer, Max, and Theodor W. Adorno. 1971. *Dialektik der Aufklärung*. Frankfurt am Main: Fischer.

Huber, Joseph. 1995. *Nachhaltige Entwicklung: Strategien für eine ökologische und soziale Erdpolitik*. Berlin: edition sigma.

Institut für Sozialforschung. 1956. *Soziologische Exkurse*. Frankfurt am Main: Europ. Verlagsanstalt.

———. 1997. "Arbeitsprogramm des Instituts für Sozialforschung." *Mitteilungen des Instituts für Sozialforschung* 8:5–39.

Jahn, Thomas. 1990. "Das Problemverständnis sozial-ökologischer Forschung: Umrisse einer kritischen Theorie gesellschaftlicher Naturverhältnisse." In *Jahrbuch für sozial-ökologische Forschung 1*, ed. E. Becker, 15–41. Frankfurt am Main: iko-Verlag.

Jahn, Thomas, and Peter Wehling. 1998a. "Gesellschaftliche Naturverhältnisse—Konturen eines theoretischen Konzepts." In *Soziologie und Natur: Theoretische Perspektiven*, ed. K.-W. Brand, 75–93. Opladen: Leske + Budrich.

————. 1998b. "A Multidimensional Concept of Mobility—A New Approach to Urban Transportation Research and Planning." In *Urban Ecology*, ed. J. Breuste, H. Feldmann, and O. Uhlmann, 523–527. Berlin: Springer.

Latour, Bruno. 1993. *We Have Never Been Modern*. Cambridge, Mass.: Harvard University Press.

Macnaghten, Phil, and John Urry. 1998. *Contested Natures*. London: Sage.

Marcuse, Herbert. 1965. "Industrialisierung und Kapitalismus im Werk Max Webers." In *Kultur und Gesellschaft*, vol. 2, ed. H. Marcuse, 107–129. Frankfurt am Main: Suhrkamp.

Mol, Arthur. 1997. "Ecological Modernization: Industrial Transformations and Environmental Reform." In *The International Handbook of Environmental Sociology*, ed. M. Redclift and G. Woodgate, 138–149. Cheltenham, UK: Edward Elgar.

Redclift, Michael, and Graham Woodgate. 1994. "Sociology and the Environment: Discordant Discourse?" In *Social Theory and the Global Environment*, ed. M. Redclift and T. Benton, 51–66. London: Routledge.

Schmid Noerr, Gunzelin. 1990. *Das Eingedenken der Natur im Subjekt: Zur Dialektik von Vernunft und Natur in der kritischen Theorie Horkheimers, Adornos und Marcuses*. Darmstadt: Wissenschaftliche Buchgesellschaft.

Soper, Kate. 1999. "The Politics of Nature: Reflections on Hedonism, Progress and Ecology." *Capitalism, Nature, Socialism* 10:47–70.

Spaargaren, Gert. 1997. *The Ecological Modernization of Production and Consumption*. Wageningen: Landbouw Universiteit Wageningen.

Vogel, Steven. 1996. *Against Nature: The Concept of Nature in Critical Theory*. New York: SUNY Press.

Wehling, Peter. 1992. *Die Moderne als Sozialmythos: Zur Kritik sozialwissenschaftlicher Modernisierungstheorien*. Frankfurt am Main: Campus.

————. 1997. "Sustainable Development—eine Provokation für die Soziologie?" In *Nachhaltige Entwicklung—eine soziologische Herausforderung*, ed. K.-W. Brand, 35–50. Opladen: Leske + Budrich.

Whitebook, Joel. 1979. "The Problem of Nature in Habermas." *Telos* 40:41–69.

Wiggershaus, Rolf. 1996. "Antagonistische Gesellschaft und Naturverhältnis: Zur Rolle der Natur in Horkheimers und Adornos Gesellschaftskritik." *Zeitschrift für kritische Theorie* 3:5–25.

Wynne, Brian. 1994. "Scientific Knowledge and the Global Environment." In *Social Theory and the Global Environment*, ed. M. Redclift and T. Benton, 169–189. London: Routledge.

8

World-System Theory and the Environment: Toward a New Synthesis

J. Timmons Roberts and Peter E. Grimes

The U.S. National Research Council recently pointed out that "[t]o adequately address the human dimensions of global change will require analyses at the global scale. . . . Analysis of the human dimensions of global change requires a theoretical structure capable of addressing varying time scales, particularly the longer ones that correspond to the processes of physical and ecological change" (Stern, Young, and Druckman 1992: 178, 176). We believe that world-system research provides such a theoretical structure. It has the strategic advantages of combining global scope, historical perspective, theory on international political economy, and well-developed empirical techniques. A relatively recent addition to the field, world-system research has grown from its European and Latin American roots to gain a place in U.S. social science particularly by pioneering empirical transnational analyses over long time spans.

Some environmental questions seem particularly well suited for attention from World-System Theory (WST). For example, are there higher-level social structural forces that determine different nations' environmental policies and impacts? Looking backward in time, has the cyclical nature of capitalist production manifested itself as periodicities in environmental effects such as emissions added to the atmosphere? More broadly, what are the precise links between social classes, economic growth, and environmental damage?

One contribution of WST that we believe is pivotal to addressing these questions is its focus on the historical legacy of a country's "incorporation" into the global economy. This burden of history channels the avenues of development available to a nation and is especially relevant to understanding the social causes of environmental problems. These historic links to the world economy and polity shape many of the types of products a nation makes, which commodities are traded with whom and on what terms, the conditions for both capital and labor, as well as the nation's global power vis-à-vis other nations. These elements—especially the productive structure of the economy—in turn affect governmental policies toward the environment, the government's level of repressiveness over social movements, shape decisions by individual firms within those countries, and finally influence the life conditions of its peoples.

Until only very recently, however, writing in the World-System tradition has focused so closely on the social structure of accumulation (i.e., crudely, how profits are made and by whom) that it overlooked the natural environment on which it depends. Like much of social science, the theory has implicitly taken what Dunlap and Catton (1994) have called the "human exemptionalist" approach—that humans are exempt from ecological laws affecting other species. However, we believe that World-System concepts hold great and virtually untapped promise for addressing global environmental issues.

We review here the core insights of WST and explore how they might inform environmental understanding. Our approach is to first look at why WST hasn't addressed environmental issues, then in the central part of the chapter we examine in sequence the environmental utility of four World-System tenets and six questions that have received the greatest attention from its practitioners. The core tenets we examine are WST's explicit and defining globalism, its materialist perspective, its historicism, and its structuralism. We explore the environmental implications of WST's attention to secular trends and cycles in global capitalism, its attention to identifying key economic and political actors, to the causes of war, to the exploitation of peripheral (poor) nations, and finally of its concern with socialism and the transition of the former Soviet bloc nations. There are others we could have added to the list. WST is a huge field, and it is difficult to summarize its potential contribution to environmental understanding, but we will try to do so without stereotyping. In a concluding section, we assess the weaknesses and limitations of the World-System approach and propose a discussion of possibilities for future World-System analysis of pollution emissions and resource depletion. At least as narrowly defined, we do not think WST has all the answers, but it does have great potential. When integrated into a wider political economy that addresses a major shortcoming by considering culture seriously, perhaps WST can play a central role in integrating environmental sociology.

WHY HASN'T THE WST BEEN GREEN?

For a variety of reasons, the *Zeitgeist* and political agendas of the times that gave birth to WST did not place a high priority on environmental concerns. WST has intellectual roots in the works of Prebisch, Baran, Lenin, Luxembourg, and Marx

(Grimes 1988; Shannon 1996). However, its quick acceptance (in the United States) following the publication of Wallerstein's *Modern World-System I* in 1974 revealed the fertile ground created by the prior decade of radicalization among intellectuals (e.g., the civil rights movement and opposition to the Vietnam War). Emerging out of and complementing these movements in the United States was a growing concern with global inequality and the poverty of Third World nations (recall that the 1960s had been declared by the United Nations as the "Development Decade"). This concern paralleled the heightened consciousness of poverty within the United States (stimulated largely by the publication of Harrington's *The Other America* in 1962).

The popularity of WST also grew out of a questioning of the "Development Project" as formulated in Washington, D.C., after World War II in which Third World nations were placed in roles of recipients of U.S. aid and purchasers of U.S. products (McMichael 1996). WST rejected "modernization theory," the theoretical foundation of this project, which held that Third World nations were poor because they lacked modern technology, business techniques, capital, and modern cultural orientations. That is, the ills of poor nations were due to their own faults. Dependency theory developed in Latin America and Africa as a harsh rebuke to modernization views. Social scientists in the United States discovered the work of dependency theorists, especially those who were published in English (for accounts of that process, see, e.g., Cardoso [1977], Kay [1989], and Shannon [1996]). Most widely read were the works of Prebisch, Baran and Sweezy, Frank, Amin, and Cardoso and Faletto.[1]

In its contemporary form, WST's founding works were those of Braudel, who in turn profoundly influenced Wallerstein (see citations in Shannon 1996). WST applied the accumulated insights of the Latin American scholars—that unequal interactions between poorer "peripheral" nations and those of the rich "core" were founded in colonization and the bloody conquest of the former by the latter. More importantly, such inequalities continue to be reproduced today by "unequal exchange" that lead to the overall failure of development policies that attempt to bring countries worldwide out of their poverty. In so doing, they also sought a generalized, structural explanation for the expansion of global inequality across nations. This inequality was revealed in the ironic simultaneous "development" of relatively more democracy and stronger economies and states in the wealthy "core" nations, and the continued absence of self-sustaining economic growth and political freedom in the poorer "peripheral" nations.

A profound split among left academics became apparent, even in those early years. While the political struggles of the 1960s and early 1970s were generating a "New Left" and thereby laying the groundwork for the eager acceptance of WST, sections of disenchanted intellectuals sought escape by going "back" to "the land." That is, there was a perceived choice between fighting for social justice or for environmental protection and an unfortunate cultural split developed between "anti-imperialism"/Vietnam War politics and those drawn toward a more voluntaristic, lifestyle change approach (e.g., "Back to the land"). Both movements are attempting to bridge this (real or imagined) gap even today, and other nations often face the same problem (see, e.g., Bullard and Wright 1992; Christen et al. 1998). Although short lived, this phase of attempted "escape" from modern society to the land (1968–1974) accelerated the growing awareness of the elimination of wilderness and the "End of Nature" (McKibben 1989). The broad movement that culminated in the first declaration of "Earth Day" in 1970 and again found expression in the "Clean Air Act" of 1972 was directly linked to the same rebellious spirit that fueled the antiwar marches of the same era (see also Dunlap and Mertig 1992).

How, then, did WST miss the "green boat" of environmental sociology? Why did its original formulations ignore environmental concerns? Perhaps Buttel (1987) and Dunlap and Catton (1994) are correct in pointing out how environmental sociology failed in its early hopes to integrate environmental concerns into the broader discipline. On the academic front, WST reached its apex of popularity in the United States around 1983, when researchers of several stripes tried to tie their real interests to the fad by including the phrase "World System" somewhere in their paper titles. But between 1985 and 1990, WST was beginning to lose favor, retreating from the multiple attacks of volunteerists, historicists, feminists, and postmodernists, who collectively shifted the attention of social scientists away from the macrolevel and metanarratives such as theories of development toward the microlevel politics of identity. By an accident of timing, these years between 1983 and 1993 were precisely the years when popular knowledge of the ozone hole, rain forest destruction, and global warming were growing. Had it not been for the onslaught of attack and intellectual intimidation dampening the receptivity to World-System analysis at that very time, we suspect that WST would have turned to the environment ten years ago.

As it was, in the mid-1980s Bunker, working on extractive economies such as the Brazilian Amazon, was a lone voice in the proverbial wilderness—attempting to combine environment and energy issues with the central issues of WST (1985, 1994). His book *Underdeveloping the Amazon* faulted both Marxian and neoclassical economics for placing the origin of all value in human work and in production, thereby failing to understand the role of naturally occurring resources in creating value or "rent" (see also Benton [1989] and some of the works of Redclift). He proposed a reexamination of the concepts of unequal exchange to include the extraction of energy and material resources from the peripheries of the World System, and described the social and environmental consequences of the typical boom-bust resource cycle. Freudenburg (1981) and Gramling and Brabant (1990) have long examined social structures of resource boomtowns, but there was little cross-over of these insights into World-System circles. Rather, Roberts's (1992; 1994), Roberts and Dodoo's (1995), Barbosa's (1993; 1996), Cicantell's (1994), and Gellert's (1996) work seem to have most closely followed Bunker's lead.

There were some important efforts made, but little cross-over in the other direction from environmental sociology to the core of the Political Economy of the World-System (PEWS) group. Instead, environmental sociology took as needed from neo-Marxist and World-System analysis and developed on its own, while World-System theorists continued to ignore environmental thinking. For example, Schnaiberg's important 1980 contribution *The Environment*, while incorporating political economy explicitly and describing the "treadmill of production," which pushes governments and firms to always increase their environmental impact, was ignored in the World-System field. Rudel's (1989) and Rudel and Horowitz's (1993) work combining detailed analysis of deforestation in Ecuador with political economy perspectives such as Logan and Molotch's (1987) concept of the "growth machine" gained little attention within PEWS. Perelman's (1977), Burbach and Flynn's (1980), Buttel, Kenney, and Kloppenburg's (1985), and Kloppenburg's (1988) work on the international political economy of agricultural systems had explicit implications for biodiversity and other environmental issues. Likewise, the cross-national political economy of energy consumption work by Mazur and Rosa (1974), Buttel (1978), Humphrey and Buttel (1982), and Rosa, Machlis, and Keating (1988) were never widely used among World-System researchers. However, none of the environmental issues became central to the 1980s' work of World-System theorists, even those that were focused on agricultural systems, until the mid-1990s (see Mazur and Rosa 1974; Buttel 1978; Humphrey and Buttel 1982; Rosa, Machlis, and Keating 1988; McMichael 1996). The same is true of O'Connor's (1980s) essays and efforts in creating the journal *Capitalism, Nature, Socialism*. Rather, many of the questions of how the world economy and the environment were related were being taken up by human geographers and some economists (e.g., Dicken 1998; Ayres 1989; Simonis 1989). Some adopted WST concepts while adapting methodologies to their disciplinary styles (Chew 1995; 1997).

The last few years, however, have seen an explosive boom of attention to the environment within WST. It is difficult to know the durability of this wave of interest, but it is extremely promising. It can be said at the outset that explicitly environmental research in the World-System tradition has been extremely limited, and we will attempt to review that literature in the following section. The authors number less than a dozen, but that number is likely to increase, since the PEWS section of the American Sociological Association (ASA) met in the spring of 1997 with a theme of thematic focus "The Global Environment: A World-System Perspective," and sessions cosponsored between PEWS and the environment and technology sections occurred at the ASA annual conferences in 1997 and 1998.

Some examples of the new "better, greener World-System Theory" boom can be described briefly, and we will return to many of them later. Chew (1995) has recently attributed the decline of large empires throughout history to massive deforestation and land degradation. Sanderson (1995) also explicitly incorporates environmental factors to explain the succession of social forms throughout history, as do Chase-Dunn and Hall (1997) in their most recent book. Frey (1993) has presented some work on the political economy of the hazardous waste trade by building on an earlier influential piece with Covello (1990). Barnham, Bunker, and O'Hearn (1994) and Cicantell (1994) continue to work on the environmentally important sector of mining and metals, but only Bunker (1989) has explicitly made the environmental link, and then only briefly. Smith has written an exploratory essay tying environment to unequal exchange with a focus on East Asia (1994), and Gellert is working on the lumber industry in East Asia (1996), but again has apparently not clarified the larger environmental implications. To the contrary, Barbosa is publishing on how the struggle over the Amazon fits into global ecopolitics (1993; 1996).

Finally, our own work spans three areas. Roberts has summarized the Brazilian scene (1994) and drawn a wide portrait of Latin American restructuring and its environmental implications (1996a). He has also tested the ability of World-System theories and methodologies to predict which nations participate in international environmental treaties (1996b). Together, Grimes and Roberts's work has used WST and methods to explain national variations in greenhouse emissions, both presently and historically (Grimes, Roberts, and Manale 1993; Grimes and Roberts 1995; 1996; Roberts 1996a; Grimes 1997). We will return to these authors throughout the next section, but because there is quite little by way of basic theoretical foundations bridging WST and the environment, we should make clear that what follows is more an exploration than a review of previous works.

CORE TENETS AND CONCERNS OF THE WORLD-SYSTEM PERSPECTIVE, AND HOW THEY COULD INFORM ENVIRONMENTAL SOCIOLOGY

World-systems analysis evolved out of efforts over the past thirty years to explain how and why some countries in the world economy have been able to grow in power and wealth while others remain trapped in apparent stagnation (Shannon 1996). It has four central postulates. First, that the current world economy took on its defining features in Europe between 1500 and 1650. Second, that among these features are a stable three-part international stratification system of core, semiperiphery, and periphery through which individual countries may move (up or down), but which itself has not changed. Third, that the ability of countries to achieve upward mobility is constrained by their structural location within the hierarchy. Finally, this structural location—their World-System "position"—plays an important role in shaping their class structure and internal political battles. Each postulate has environmental implications.

WST asserts that the nature of a country's high-profit connections to the world economy and who has access to them are the issues shaping the avenues of development and the distribution of class power (e.g., Wallerstein 1972; Chase-Dunn 1989). Insofar as these are the same issues that affect the policies of governments to the environment and determine the life conditions of their peoples, we believe that WST provides a promising conceptual framework for understanding both global and local environmental questions.

In this section, we examine each of what we consider four of the central WST tenets, and for each the insights it could provide to our understanding of humanity's relations to its natural environment and to itself. Afterward, we examine the six questions that have received the most attention from World-System researchers.

1. We Consider the Core WST Idea: That We Must Look at Everything

Braudel once wrote: "No description can even begin to lead to a valid explanation if it does not effectively encompass the whole world." Some of us might find this requirement for any explanation impossible, but it remains an ideal for World-System researchers. Why? The reason is that WST (and dependency writings) were a strong rebuke to modernization theory, widely accepted in the 1950s and 1960s by planning and academic circles. As mentioned earlier, modernization views held that the poor nations were poor because they lacked modern machines, values, and capital, and that to resolve these problems they should import ours. The debate may seem artificial now, but despite being harshly debunked in the sociological literature in the decades that followed, modernization views continue to underlie much thinking in neoclassical economics and in the key development agencies in Washington and in many other parts of the world. To avoid what it saw as "blaming the victims," WST worked especially hard in showing the power of global forces in determining the fate of people in all parts of the global system.

This proposition implies that we cannot look at one community's or nation's relation to the environment, but that we must *also* understand how they are linked to larger social organizations and the global society and how they collectively influence and are influenced by the environment. Two examples may help illuminate the importance of this simple point. First, the ecologically damaging effects of producing monocultural crops for export have been repeatedly well documented (e.g., Perelman 1977; Wright 1990; Barkin 1995). However, to understand *why* poor and rich countries alike decide to devastate their soils and contaminate their rivers with agrotoxics, we need to understand the pressures they are under to compete in a global economy. Second, localities in the world with relatively greater environmental awareness and regulations on industry often feel pressures to lower their requirements to keep their tax base and jobs and to compete for new plant sitings (e.g., Covello and Frey 1990; Kazis and Grossman 1991; Gould 1995; Reed 1992). Furthermore, with free trade agreements such as the General Agreement on Tariffs and Trade (GATT) and the World Trade Organization (WTO), it can be considered protectionism for one nation to have unusually high environmental requirements of products produced or consumed there (Roberts 1996a). By integrating production from widely dispersed locations into one coherent, global system, the capitalist world economy likewise scatters the ecological costs of that system unequally throughout the globe.

It is easy to say that the need to raise export earnings to pay off the national debt is driving reckless resource use around the world. These are important points for policymakers to hear. However, understanding how the global capitalist system is changing and guessing the direction of likely future changes requires a sophisticated understanding of its past and emergent mechanisms. We return to secular trends and cycles in the system later, but for the present the point is that good environmental policy requires an understanding of the whole global system and how it can support or subvert local efforts at environmental protection. Elsewhere, Grimes (1997) and Roberts (1996a; 1996b) have argued that the globalizing economy holds both perils and prospects for environmental protection. While GATT/WTO-type treaties are potentially driving down the environmental sovereignty of nations, the emergence of global environmental standards hold important potential to keep firms from fleeing to so-called pollution havens (Roberts 1996a).

Ironically, while WST was built largely on Braudel's shoulders, World-System theorists who came later failed to look, as he did, at everything—including Nature. As Chew (1997) recently pointed out, the World-System approach at first included natural causative forces. Braudel, especially in his earlier works such as *The Mediterranean and the Mediterranean World in the Age of Philip II* (1972), spent much time detailing how the specifics of that society and economy grew from the nature of that land. He continued that focus in his influential three-volume work *Civilization and Capitalism* (1981; 1982; 1984), especially in volume one (*The Structures of Everyday Life*). Chew takes Wallerstein (until 1996), Amin, Frank (until his 1996 work with Gills), Chase-Dunn (until his 1997 book with Hall), and Wolf all to task for treating Nature as external and as a backdrop to the true engine of change: social relations in general and capitalism in particular. Rather, Chew points out that "the social and ecological (natural) worlds interact in a dialectical fashion whereby Nature's rhythms also impact on the dynamics of social-economic life. For example, changes in climatological trends . . . will impact on crop harvests, which in turn, will determine grain prices or the migration of people" (1997: 13). Meanwhile, human-driven "degradative effects on Nature . . . in turn loop back to impact on the dynamics of social-economic life of the World System." While this point may seem vague and obvious to anyone who has studied human-environment interactions, it represents an important step in this case. WST, being built on Marxian analysis, saw the ultimate demise of the global capitalist system coming from the contradictions in the capitalist model itself (especially accumulation crises, working-class struggles, and the inevitable socialist revolution; see Chew [1997: 22]). However, World-System theorists are finally beginning to see that the critical contradiction is more likely to be the final overtaxing of the global ecological base that has supported capitalism's rise.[2]

2. WST Is a Materialist Theory of Capitalism and Development

Its materialism is a source of strength for environmental analysis and simultaneously an important shortcoming, which we discuss later on. WST is a subfield of political economy: it is a theory of capitalism and development. WST attempts to explain how societies change, building on neo-Marxist theories of imperialism, dependency, and theories about how labor is organized in different societies (e.g., Grimes 1988; Chilcote 1984; Brewer 1980). The central conception here is that human actions based on subsistence (as socially defined and ever changing) and profit making are the core of the economy and that political and cultural structures are built around the needs of the economy (Marx 1967). As mentioned earlier, WST emerged in opposition to cultural and stage theories of development, especially modernization theory. This explains perhaps why World-System theorists have "foregrounded" economic structures as determinant while expressing a strong aversion to cultural explanations. The World-System perspective has been roundly critiqued for attempting to "read the state off the economy" (Evans, Rueschemeyer, and Skocpol 1985) and for ignoring cultural factors such as gender and culture, but the main protagonists have proven willing to incorporate many of these critiques in later work. For example, PEWS has held conferences and published volumes on the state and how households fit in the world economy.[3] Returning to WST's deep materialism, the environmental implications are clear: production and consumption directly affect the biosphere and cannot be understood without understanding the structure of the world economy. If many or even most human activities are economically motivated, or if the most damaging human actions for the environment are those based on human subsistence and economic decision making, then a materialist core for environmental theory is appropriate (see, e.g., Schnaiberg 1980; Foster 1994; O'Connor 1989; Harper 1996). Again, the uniquely World-System contribution to the discussion is that much production activity is either directly for trade or designed to facilitate trade and/or make it more profitable (e.g., military foreign policy). Production and consumption do indeed seem heavily guided by the world economy and by the needs of markets that are increasingly distant from the site of production.

3. WST Takes a Long Historical View to Understand the Development of Our Current Social/Economic System

As Shannon points out in his book *An Introduction to the World-System Perspective* (1996), WST is more historical than most of U.S. sociology and perhaps most of U.S. social science. Its most visible theoreticians—Wallerstein, Braudel, Chase-Dunn, Sanderson, Mann, and Frank—all have taken deeply historical approaches in much of their writing. Wallerstein and Braudel both began their accounts with medieval Europe. Mann, Frank, Chase-Dunn, and Sanderson went even further to describe social evolution over millennia, the latter two building their explanations of the transitions on a modified form of the Lenskis's technology-based account (Mann 1986; Frank 1978; Chase-Dunn 1989; Chase-Dunn and Hall 1997; Sanderson 1988; 1995). Incorporating archaeological information, these authors have even explored the evolution of "Pristine" states, long-distance trade, and early subsistence systems of a different world-system in the period before written history (Chase-Dunn and Hall 1996).

One central goal in these accounts has been to explain the key social transitions: from hunter-gatherer band to horticultural chiefdoms, agricultural tributary states/empires, and, finally, contemporary international industrial capitalism. A lingering disagreement exists over whether capitalism should be defined by the world trading system and market (Wallerstein 1974; Frank 1969) or by the relations of labor such as slavery or wage work to production (see Shannon [1996] for references and the summary in Chase-Dunn and Grimes [1995]). The definitional debate is tied to a heated debate over when capitalism emerged and its relation to noncapitalist societies. Frank and Gills (1996) now argue that capitalism has been around for five thousand years, not the five hundred that Wallerstein claimed (see recent pieces in the *Humboldt* journal and *Review,* and the ongoing debate on the electronic World-Systems Network list server <WSN@csf.colorado.edu>). This seemingly arcane point affects how one bounds world-system across both time and space. However, it does not change the fact that all major empires and civilizations, no matter how one labels their mode of accumulation, were brought down at least partly by land degradation. For example, many greens and environmental sociologists blame capitalism for the current ecological crisis. However, as Harper (1996), Chew (1997), and several others have pointed out, environmental crises have surfaced in societies of many types and throughout history. The policy implication is massive: Is capitalism inevitably caught on a treadmill that drives it ever forward, or can it be made sustainable? Among sociologists, World-System theorists are well positioned to answer questions about whether there have been truly stable capitalist societies and how they were successful in the face of expansionist states and markets.

Second, WST's focus on the relations between the capitalism of early Europe and other societies, and their modes of production, highlighted the pivotal importance of the colonial relations that have conditioned most nations' social and environmental situations since then. That is, we cannot understand a nation's current position and environmental behavior without understanding its colonial past.[4] Political scientist Schafer's (1994) pioneering work on commodities points out the limitations placed on nations who rely too heavily on one type of product for the majority of their exports. He relates a nation's export commodities to its available paths of development, demonstrating that the historical choices of production technologies made by former colonial powers continue to impose *political* constraints on production technology today. Barnham, Bunker, and O'Hearn (1994) have taken up this approach in an extended study of the aluminum industry (and markets around the world) and its effects on local producing nations. The environmental implication of this "dead hand of the past" is that nations heavily dependent on the export of commodities such as agricultural products, oil, or even low-priced manufactures often have weak civil societies and states dominated by the exporting sector's elite and are largely dependent on them for state revenue. This often corresponds with weak or nonexistent environmental movements and relatively little state autonomy or strong constraints on the state as it avoids making the "tough decisions" to break the resource exploitation habit and move toward higher value-added products (Bunker 1985; 1994; Ranis 1990; Roberts 1996a). The cycle of resource dependency and environmental degradation is likely to continue until all the resources have been exploited, at which time crisis and collapse will leave an even weaker state and little prospect for positive civil reform.

4. WST Holds That Nations Occupy Structural Positions in a Global Stratification System

Like class structures within nations, a few nations move up and down, but the structure remains intact over time. Also, like most national stratification systems, the majority of nations remain trapped in their current level within the global system. The relevance of attempting to characterize this global system of inequality becomes clearer if we remember Gandhi's point at the 1972 Stockholm conference that the pollution of poverty differs from the pollution of wealth. For example, much of our own previous work has shown that the relative wealth and World-System position of nations is an excellent (but not at all complete) initial predictor of the level or type of environmental degradation it is likely to be creating (Grimes, Roberts, and Manale 1993; Roberts and Grimes 1997), as well as its level of commitment to international environmental agreements (Roberts 1996b).

It was mentioned earlier that many remnants of modernization theory persist in Washington policy circles today. One derivative argument that gained favor in the 1990s was the "Environmental Kuznets's Curve." When one plots some types of pollutants such as levels of urban smog against a nation's gross national product (GNP) per capita, an upside-down U-curve is evident. This fact led economists Grossman and Krueger (1995) and the World Bank in its influential 1992 *World Development Report* and its 1995 *Monitoring Environmental Progress* to argue that countries will first get worse as they develop and after reaching some "turning point" will improve their environmental performance. The argument is based on Maslow's "hierarchy of needs" and the "postmaterialist" hypothesis (see Inglehart 1995; Roberts and Grimes 1997). On the face of it, the argument makes sense: nations will ignore pollution controls until they have dealt with basic human needs and only then will they begin to care about "quality of life" issues like clean air and water. As Salinas, the former president of Mexico, is reported to have said on the U.S. Public Broadcasting Service show *McLaughlan Group,* "We have to pollute now, to develop first and deal with pollution later." Based on the pattern for several pollutants, Grossman and Krueger put the "turning point" at about $8,000 per capita. The policy implication is that nations need economic growth *first* to reach environmental protection later.

However, based on the repeated findings of the WST school, we argue in a recent *World Development* piece (Roberts and Grimes 1997) that assuming that things will get better for the world's poor nations is extremely perilous and in fact historically counterfactual. Research presented by Sanderson (1995) demonstrates that, contra the assumptions of the modernization theory underlying the Kuznet's curve, the gap between countries has grown geometrically over the past century. Some environmental effects have Kuznet's curve-type relationships with national wealth, while others increase linearly or even more quickly as countries get richer. In our examination of the historical trend over thirty years for national carbon intensity, it becomes clear that the environmental Kuznets's curve does *not* represent a historical trend, but is merely a cross-sectional pattern that emerged in the 1980s and that is actually likely to worsen (Roberts and Grimes 1997). These findings are consistent with the expectations of WST that nations are generally trapped in the global stratification system. Certainly, there are cases of mobility, but mobility has been in both directions (up and down), and in general poverty persists. Even the World Bank in its 1995 *World Development Report* admitted that (in spite of fifty years of the "Development Project") inequality between nations has in fact worsened sharply. The clear implication is that environmental problems cannot be left to resolve themselves by economic growth alone: without massive changes in the system, there will always be poor nations being exploited and who will therefore have to exploit their natural environment. Environmental protection must be addressed at all levels of development.

Isn't the movement of factories to the poor countries, "globalization," and the "New International Division of Labor" bringing development that will help those nations move up in wealth and relative position in the global hierarchy? Again, empirical World-System research suggests this is not the case. Even as factories— once associated with development and riches—move to the semiperiphery and periphery of the World System, they are no longer bringing wealth (Dicken 1998; McMichael 1996). The reasons lie in an area well explored by a subfield of WST: the commodity chain approach. Gereffi, the Korziniewitzs, Chen, Lee, Cason, and others have pointed out (see Gereffi and Korzeniewicz 1994) that nations in the core continue to control research and marketing of most products, thereby capturing most of the profits from their sale. The commodity chain approach also moves us along the road toward understanding *which* nations are more likely to move up economically into higher standards of living. Combining some insights, those nations who soon might be able to spend more on environmental protection are those that have been selling valuable commodities on the world market and that have captured some higher-value portions of the commodity chain and especially those using flexible, small-scale technologies (Schafer 1994). Put another way, as the profits from a given method of production decline with age, such methods are exported out of the core (Dicken 1998). So industrialization outside of the core does not necessarily mean advancement, only that industries are no longer the sites of high profit that they once were a generation ago.

How strictly do types and amounts of environmental degradation vary by a nation's position in the World System? Insofar as wealth is correlated with pollution, the World-System perspective has important contributions to make. Because it is a key to empirical research utilizing the World-System approach, we discuss some details of the debate over the best way to categorize nations in the world stratification system. It is helpful to remember that while the debate seems sometimes a case of minutia, the key question is *which* nations are in a powerful enough position to have substantial control over the sources of environmental degradation in their territories and even around the world.

Some authors have argued that periphery, semiperiphery, and core play qualitatively different roles in the PEWS (following Wallerstein 1974; 1979). Furthermore, each nation is generally placed in just one of these "roles." This leads to some debate about marginal cases: Everyone agrees that the United States, Germany, and Japan are core nations, but what about wealthy but weak nations like Sweden, Spain, or Luxembourg or powerful, large but poor countries like China, Brazil, and India? Is political or economic power the most important factor? Another approach has been to conceptualize the global stratification system as a continuum and to rank nations in their total power or position in world trading networks, for example. Many researchers simply use GNP per capita, an approach they ironically share with many modernizationists (e.g., Arrighi and Drangel 1986). This approach has the distinct advantage that data is available for many nations over many years. This is not the case with more subtle classification systems. Smith and White (1992) took a more elaborate approach, classifying nations in 1970, 1980, and 1985 by network cluster analysis of the relative value of the products they imported and exported. Dutch researcher Terlouw (1992) compared several approaches to classifying nations. He first completed a factor analysis of how nations were classified in nine major WST works. These rankings were placed on a scale and compared with an index of a nation's overall presence in world trading networks—their exports as a percent of global exports. Another compromise was produced by Grimes, who combined these two indexes into one hybrid World-System position (WSP) index (Grimes, Roberts, and Manale 1993). Grimes (1996) compiled a new WSP index for every country for which adequate data was available over the past two hundred years (in five-year intervals). First, he calculated for each nation its gross domestic product (GDP) as a percent of the global GDP. Second, he weighted this GDP/global GDP measure by that nation's dependence on the most important trading partners and by the relative position of those trading partners in the World System.

How do these different classification schemes do in separating the "pollution of poverty" from that of wealth? We believe that exploring this question would be a worthwhile empirical exercise with a range of environmental outcomes. Roberts (1996b) examined the abilities of four indicators of the WSP—GDP per capita, Terlouw's consensus index, Terlouw's "presence in global trade" WSP index, and Grimes's hybrid of the two Terlouw positions—to explain whether nations had signed the major environmental treaties promulgated during the period 1963–1987. The WSP indicators were superior to GDP per capita and explained over half of the variance. This supports the idea that WSP and national wealth explain a substantial amount of nations' environmental performance, at least their political behaviors such as endorsement of international treaties. However, in all cases at all levels of income and WSP, there is tremendous variation that suggests that there is no necessary relation between a nation's wealth and its pollution and environmental degradation. At every WSP, there is a large scatter of pollution levels, demonstrating that many factors outside of either WSP or GDP per capita shape the overall pollution profile. That this relation is not cast in stone is shown also by the historical delinking of economic growth and environmental impacts in some nations (Simonis 1989).

Finally, it is important to note that the World-System approach has led its practitioners to pay special attention to nations in what are called the "rising semiperiphery." These are nations that are making industrialization drives in attempts to gain core status. These also, of course, correspond to areas of looming environmental disasters:

- Brazil's incorporation of its Amazon frontier to spur its drive to development (Bunker 1985; Barbosa 1996; Roberts 1995)

- China's rapid industrialization and its booming need for electrical power, most likely using coal and drastically increasing carbon outputs (e.g., Howard 1993)
- Malaysia's and Indonesia's logging booms that are driving rapid deforestation there (Gellert 1996)
- Eastern Europe's and Russia's reckless push for heavy industrialization (Manser 1993)

These are the emerging environmental disasters of our day, and WST can shed some much-needed light on which nations are likely to succeed in those drives to ascend in WSP, and which will fail, when, and under what conditions. What are largely lacking are any theories of which types and levels of environmental effects tend to go with WSP ascent and decline.

Having discussed the environmental implications of four of WST's central tenets, we now examine six areas that the field has discussed in depth. Again, the list is necessarily incomplete.

Research in the World-System Tradition Has Identified and Examined Key Secular Trends in Global Capitalism

These trends are surveyed in more thorough detail in Chase-Dunn and Grimes (1995), so they will be only touched on here. There are widespread trends in society such as increasing commodification, the tendency toward the greater proletarianization of the labor force (or at least its incorporation into the world economy), the expansion of the state, the growth of corporate power and its ability to escape the control of states and civil society, and "globalization" more generally.[5]

The environmental byproducts of many of these trends is enormous. Briefly, *commodification* combined with the technologies of long-distance trade and refrigeration has brought both a progressive removal of producers from consumers and the increasing specialization of production (including monocrop agriculture). Most workers are far removed from the land that sustains them and virtually everything is produced for profit, rather than for "use-value." Furthermore, the trend toward what Wallerstein calls the "commodification of everything" has also included the commodification of nature, accelerating its destruction in pursuit of increasingly rare items (e.g., black rhinoceros horns, ivory, and tropical birds).

Following Marx, *proletarianization*—the dissection of what were formerly "professions" with a high degree of job autonomy into deskilled low-autonomy routines requiring lower education and more amenable to ultimate automation—has been said to drive alienation, inequality, and fatalism (Braverman 1974). More to the point here, it enables automation, which is the substitution of inanimate energy for human labor, which drives up energy consumption and increases toxic effluents.[6] Both of these removes from workers the ability to control the effects of their labor on the environment or on their own health and safety.

On the one hand, *expanding states* require expanding militaries and bureaucracies, which in turn are extremely resource and pollution intensive (Grimes, Roberts, and

Manale 1993). On the other hand, many authors fear that *growing corporate power* and corporations' ability to flee from controlling states and civil groups such as labor and environmentalists may close one of the last means of pressure for forcing any real accountability on their part.

Finally, one example of the effects of *globalization*: rises in the stock markets in Hong Kong drive up the Dow Industrials market, which in turn spurs interest rate fears and worries about inflation "rearing its ugly head." The U.S. Federal Reserve tightens up its lending and this makes it more difficult for Third World states to gain credit to service their foreign debts. This debt crunch influences decisions about lumber leases and types of mining joint ventures they choose to enter into (Reed 1992). As times get tighter, their level of commitment to environmental protection drops (Roberts 1996b). The ongoing Mexican economic crisis is a prime example of how this system works and how debt and currency issues and the price of a key commodity (oil) can send deep shocks into an economy and drive down environmental spending (Barkin 1995). A hostile takeover of one company by another using "leveraged" buyout of stock offerings can compel the purchased target corporation to exploit its workers and resources much more harshly in order to raise the revenue to meet the new debt obligations taken on by the original author of the hostile takeover. When the affected corporate resources include extractive industries or agriculture, the environmental consequences are necessarily accelerated. Hence, the global interconnectedness of the world economy allows for the actions of traders in New York or Hong Kong to have unanticipated collateral effects on environmental degradation everywhere.

WST Identifies and Examines the Causes and Effects of Cycles of Crisis and Restructuring in Global Capitalism

The central idea is that capitalism has some internal contradictions that cause it to periodically stall, reorganize itself, and move forward once again. While many cycles have been found in historical data on prices, production, and worker militance, some are more widely accepted than others. The existence of cycles of various lengths in crucial environmental factors such as temperature and rainfall suggests that cycles in capitalism deserve our attention.

The most important cycles identified by World-System theorists include Kondratieff fifty- to sixty-year "long waves," Kuznet's cycles of fifteen to twenty years in duration, and Juglar or "regular business cycles" five to eight years in length (reviewed in Chase-Dunn and Grimes 1995). These cycles are not mutually exclusive; all continue to operate simultaneously in a "superimposed" fashion. Little work has been done relating these cycles with different types and intensities of environmental damage (see Chew 1997). However, it merits examination whether there are types of environmental damage we should expect in different parts of the different cycles. This has been the case with several other social outcomes, such as wars and strikes (e.g., Goldstein 1988; Chase-Dunn 1989; Chase-Dunn and Grimes 1995). One obvious prediction is that during cycles of economic expansion that correspond with some types of geographical expansion or colonization, certain environmental effects such as land use and energy consumption would worsen considerably. This was true in the colonization of North America (e.g., Tucker and Richards 1983) and the more contemporary expansion of the Brazilian state into the Amazon frontier since the early 1960s (Bunker 1985; Santos 1980). During these "expansionist" phases, new areas are opened up to exploitation, but many of the worst environmental effects in quantitative terms may await the more "intensifying" phase that follows.

During "down" or contractionist phases, exploitation presumably also contracts. Deforestation rates in the Brazilian Amazon, for example, slowed considerably in the 1987–1990 period, partly because of the economic crisis and wild inflation there (e.g., Barbosa 1996). However, even with continuing crisis, the rate has now been seen to be back on the rise since 1991, in keeping with the global recovery that started then. Furthermore, with highly mechanized tools of environmental destruction, even while downsizing its workforce, a lumbering or mining company can still cut or dig massive areas using fewer workers. Petroleum refineries embodying $1 billion in investments continue to produce millions of gallons of oil derivatives a year with only a few hundred permanent workers. Emissions in these cases therefore may not follow cycles as closely. Our initial findings with a two-hundred-year comparison of growth rates of the global economy and atmospheric carbon show that increases in carbon levels first became correlated with and later detached from economic cycles (Grimes and Roberts 1995).

WST Identifies a Series of Key Actors

Political economy in general and WST in particular point us to the importance of three sets of actors: states, "capital," and labor (civil society) (Grimes 1988). The three have lately been called the "regulation triangle" by French theorists in the "regulation school" (e.g., Aglietta 1979; Lipietz 1982; 1987). In its search for the most important movers in the global system, WST has isolated these actors in their manifestations as transnational corporations (TNCs), core states, export (comprador) elites in the semiperiphery and periphery, and the behavior of labor, most recently in popular organizations such as nongovernmental organizations (NGOs) and unions.

This is a powerful tool for analyzing the sources and solutions to environmental outcomes, but no simple matter. Clearly, to understand the power of environmental movements to redirect local, national, or the global economy, we need to understand who are the prime directors of that economy. Although TNCs have to be a central focus of our analysis, it is also the case that smaller national firms will be more likely to pollute recklessly and evade emerging international environmental standards (Roberts 1996a). This is because their small size allows them to escape the attention of environmental activists. Their importance is highlighted by the statistics that small- and medium-sized firms are responsible for three-quarters of the global product (Strohl 1997). Be that as it may, capital—big or small—controls the majority of the sites of production globally and thereby has a massive influence on the degree of overall pollution and resource depletion.

States seek to control the activities of capital within their borders for two reasons: to retain popular legitimacy by appearing to implement popular will in the form of operating regulations, and equally importantly, to extract tax revenue. In the sixteenth to nineteenth centuries, some states could and did expand to enclose within their boundaries the operations of the largest firms (e.g., the United States in particular, but also each of the colonial powers). Now, however, they can regulate only those corporate activities occurring inside their borders, and even then only with an eye toward the effect of those regulations on the attractiveness to capital of competing states. Indeed, nation-states may be becoming obsolete for environmental regulation because they are "too small for the big problems and too big for the small problems" (McMichael 1996). The complexity of supply chains in globalizing economies suggests that the "comprador" elite is changing and diversifying rapidly and scrambling to catch up with global diversification. Finally, both labor and environmental NGOs are themselves rapidly becoming linked globally, giving greater but highly conditional leverage to groups in the semiperiphery and periphery (Roberts 1996a; Barbosa 1993). However, the future may witness a phase of global coalition-building that may yet constrain the freedom of global capital.

Much World-System Research Has Focused on "Peripheral Exploitation" and Its Mechanisms (Coercion and the Extraction of Economic Surplus and Resources)

This topic has been touched on already, but some additional aspects need exploration. First, the question of how two countries could enter into a relationship of allegedly "free trade" and one be enriched while the other be impoverished was one of WST's first foci. This question was central to the dependency school thinkers from Latin America and Africa, and the question remains important today. As Galeano said in 1973, "The division of labor among nations is that some specialize in winning and others in losing. Our part of the world, known today as Latin America, was precocious: it has specialized in losing ever since those remote times when Renaissance Europeans ventured across the ocean and buried their teeth in the throats of the Indian civilizations. Centuries passed, and Latin America perfected its role" (11). Developed first by Emmanuel (1972), and later used and elaborated on by Amin (1974), Mandel (1975), and Cardoso and Faletto (1979), the theory of "unequal exchange" asserted that, contra Ricardo, trade between core and periphery was *not* mutually advantageous. Instead, the theory argues that higher-priced goods made by a relatively pampered workforce in the core get exchanged in the world market for many more lower-priced goods made by a coerced workforce in the periphery. The price difference between these goods results in a transfer of (labor) value from the periphery to the core. Insofar as this price difference is ultimately traceable to the vastly different political conditions surrounding core and peripheral workers (relatively protected versus relatively coerced), then to that extent the mechanisms of unequal exchange are the product of *political* conditions and are not "*economic.*"

So most of these writings traced the source of the "surplus" value from the periphery to the low rate at which labor is remunerated there (Amin 1974; Emmanuel 1972). Because of the oversupply of labor power in the periphery and the coercive political conditions, workers are paid little per unit of production. Only a few writers have considered that these differences in labor conditions might be themselves also dependent on the natural environment through some unequal "land rent" or "subsidy from nature" (personal communication with Bunker). Bunker looked to the third volume of *Capital* to examine Marx's interpretation of land rent. Meanwhile, de Janvry's influential work *The Agrarian Question and Reformism in Latin America* (1981), while not explicitly WST, did outline the importance of "disarticulated economies," and implied an impending contradiction in the long-term "mining the soil" by both plantation and *minifundia* agriculture alike.

One example is provided by Hecht, Anderson, and May (1988), who used the phrase "the Subsidy from Nature" to examine the use of naturally occurring Babassú palms in northeast Brazil to support poor seasonal laborers. This phrase deserves further exploration. We believe that several subsidies cheapen products from the World-System's noncore zones. First, urban informal (not-fully proletarianized) labor and unpaid family workers (especially women) cheapen the cost of hiring all workers and sustain them when they are not employed (Amin 1976; de Janvry 1981; Wolf 1982; Portes and Walton 1981; Roberts 1978). Second, several other irregularities push down living expenses in peripheral cities, such as squatter-invaded land, microsubsistence efforts, and so on (Roberts 1995). Finally, rural "subsistence enclaves" may be declining as a percent of the periphery's population, but have remained high in absolute numbers.

If the "subsidy from the periphery's environment" (to butcher a phrase) is truly important for the functioning of capitalism—as is implied by the theories of imperialism (see Harvey 1982)—the implications for the environment are massive. First, if the global economy requires the continuing incorporation of increasing parts of the globe into the economy, this implies that peripheral nations are indeed key elements and that a destabilizing of their environment could destabilize the larger system. Estimates of soil erosion, for example, suggest that over half of the land in Central America and Africa is in a state of serious degradation (World Resources Institute 1993). What happens when these soils run out on a sufficiently large scale? The unequal exchange made possible by a "subsidy from the periphery's nature" theory suggests that the result will not merely produce poverty, malnutrition, and refugees in those regions (as in the past), but also the dramatic price rise of products from the periphery, as capital is compelled to "internalize" more and more of the full and true cost of peripheral labor. Thus, it could be once again that the ecological contradiction is the ultimate one, a crucial point WST has missed.

WST Has Attempted to Ascertain the Structural Causes of Intra- and Interstate Conflicts

Wars have been shown to have devastating environmental consequences (e.g., Durham 1982; Homer-Dixon, Boutwell, and Rathjens 1993). While environmentalists have pointed out this truism, little work has been done to link those environmental effects with a larger theory on the causes of wars. WST has unearthed several structural causes for both the timing and motivation for war. That is, major global wars have been more common during certain phases of the "hegemonic cycle," when the central power of the declining hegemon is challenged by a rising new prospective power (Grimes 1988; Goldstein 1988; Chase-Dunn and Grimes 1995; Chase-Dunn 1989; Modelski and Thompson 1996). This occurs when one hegemonic nation (such as Holland, Spain, Great Britain, or the United States) loses its control over world trade and there is competition between would-be hegemons (e.g., Germany and Japan in the 1930s).

There has been an effort to tie these "hegemonic cycles" to the Kondratieff wave, but the results have as yet been inconclusive (Grimes 1988; Chase-Dunn and Grimes 1995; Modelski and Thompson 1996; Chase-Dunn and Pobodnik 1994; Shannon 1996). The general idea is that the Kondratieff heads into an upswing when a core country has the conditions allowing for a massive wave of investment in its productive infrastructure. Initially, this new infrastructure facilitates high-profit activities incorporating the newest technologies. But, with time, this built environment lags ever-further behind the march of innovation and simply decays with use. Hence, the rate of profit declines and capital invests elsewhere. When it does, most vigorously at the beginning of the next Kondratieff, its location will be in yet another country, catapulting that country into position to rival and threaten the first country.

The 1969 "Soccer War" between Honduras and El Salvador has been tied directly to declining land quality and its shortage (Durham 1982; Faber 1993). Homer-Dixon, Boutwell, and Rathjens (1993) have documented how resource scarcity and depletion are increasingly causing violent conflicts, especially in poorer nations. Looking ahead, as resources become depleted and the land degraded into exhaustion (both most egregiously in the politically impotent periphery), global wars over hegemonic power will doubtless continue. However, the spatial realm of production over which they will fight and preside must necessarily contract, as ever greater areas of land become unproductive waste. Meanwhile, local wars within the periphery over access to dwindling resources can be expected to increase.

Important policy implications derive from these findings. An obvious one is that the role of the United Nations should be strengthened to enable more flexible military intervention that does not require U.S. approval to minimize the number, magnitude, and duration of wars in the periphery and thereby their environmental and human effects. A current example is provided by the war in Zaire, where the environmental damage is at least on a level with human costs. To summarize, by tying such wars to predictable cycles, WST may provide a framework for understanding past environmental degradation due to wars and a theoretical early warning system for anticipating future crises.

Finally and briefly, World-System studies have paid great attention to socialism and the transition. A series of authors and pundits have pointed out that the biggest environmental disasters in the past decades have in fact occurred in eastern Europe and other state socialist countries around the world (e.g., Manser 1993; Harper 1996). What can WST add to this discussion?

WST can inform us about the nature of the transition from socialism, what state socialism was in the first place, and what the East-West competition meant to both socialism's and capitalism's unsustainability. First, WST has argued repeatedly that state socialist nations were in fact capitalist in many ways, especially since they were competing in a capitalist World System against capitalist states for political and economic power. Although labor was sometimes organized differently and economies were more influenced by state planning, state socialist societies, like Caribbean slave plantations in the past centuries, were "articulated" with global capitalism by trade in its produce, whether direct or indirect.

Concretely, WST can inform predictions of whether and how environmental conditions might change in the former socialist states: who will tend to resist and who will support whatever improvements may occur. For example, the pessimistic but likely trajectory for eastern Europe is for its role as a semiperiphery (already true in its "socialist" incarnation) to be ratified by investments from the West that would be typical of such investments in Latin America. Several east European countries are rapidly amassing foreign debts, similar to Latin American countries (World Bank 1992: 206–207). This suggests a sharpening of their subjugation to the terms of structural adjustment programs imposed by the World Bank and the International Monetary Fund. Should this prove to be the case, then we can anticipate the same situation now found in the Latin semiperiphery: continued employment of dated industrial technologies combined with coerced cheap labor generating massive air and water pollution. Alternatively, certain countries will be recipients of large amounts of concessionary-type aid such as grants in place of higher-interest loans (see, e.g., Stallings 1990).

One of the most intriguing questions is whether the logic of capitalism will be able to change now that there is no substantial antisystem with which it must compete. Can a new "Global Commonwealth" (Wager 1996) or governance structure emerge out of the need to deal with increasingly global problems, of which environmental issues are primary? To pose the negative expectation, will capitalism find a new enemy to replace the Soviets, such as Muslims, or death itself as medicine become our new Cold War spending sink? As O'Connor (1973) suggested long ago, was the *warfare* state necessary to support the welfare state? These provocative questions suggest that one of WST's greatest contributions might be to clarify the environmental implications of the post–Cold War world.

MERGING HUMAN ECOLOGY AND WST:
PROSPECTS, ISSUES, AND A
RESEARCH AGENDA

Rather than being theoretical purists, we take the omnivorous approach and remind readers that WST is one type of comparative political economy that needs the insights of other parts of that field and those of many others. On environmental issues, WST must work hard to incorporate the decades of work in human geography, international studies, and environmental sociology. That may be the easy part: more contentious will be the suggestion that the field examine work in environmental psychology and gender and cultural studies.

However, we believe that WST has certain advantages over other approaches as an integrative framework for understanding environmental damage in global capitalism. Obviously, WST brings improvements to our understanding over modernization approaches and stage theories of development and underdevelopment. We find particularly dangerous the implications of development theorists that believe poor countries will follow the paths of development taken by today's wealthy countries and their (Kuznets's curve) propositions that conditions will first get worse and then reverse themselves at some turning point. Beyond these obvious points, we believe that WST can increase our understanding of a series of environmental issues: global, transnational, those related to exports, material cycling, those that have tended to oscillate cyclically, those that are distributed unequally in the global hierarchy of poor and rich nations, and so on. That is, we believe WST has a potential contribution to make on *most* pressing environmental issues, such as global warming, deforestation, resource depletion, water struggles, ozone, food crops, the increasing frequency of major storms and human recovery from them, biodiversity, compensation of locals for management of neighboring endangered species, enactment and enforcement of international treaties, coordination of NGOs, and so on (see Grimes 1997).

It is important to acknowledge the issues that have remained underplayed or entirely unaddressed in WST and that will have to be addressed to "green" WST or applied more widely to environmental-sociological understanding. The weaknesses with WST are well summarized by Shannon (1996: 213 ff.). He points out, for example, that WST tends to overemphasize economic explanations, while remaining virtually mum on culture. This old materialism debate discussed earlier goes back to Marx and Weber, and certainly we will not resolve it here. However, despite our argument for the importance of material explanations discussed earlier, we believe that nonmaterial motivations, such as meeting culture-specific and evolving consumption expectations, and more simply the desires for status, power, love, jealousy, fun, ego-gratification, and so on, *do* have critical environmental implications, as do other social structural elements that cannot be "read off" a society's means of material production and reproduction. However, we would propose that attention to these types of causation be combined with attention to a society's material system of survival.

We agree with Shannon that WST explanations are often *overdetermined* externally to nations. WST has been weak on its analyses of culture and individual agency. Imprecision and poorly operationalized concepts (Shannon 1996: chapter 6) are major shortcomings that this young field must address. Shannon makes the important point that zones of the World System—core, semiperiphery, and periphery—do violence to the diversity of nations (213). This is an important point and in our own work we have chosen continuum measures as discussed earlier. However, the question remains of whether any one index of WSP can capture a stratification system that is multidimensional. Finally, Shannon levels tough critiques that gender still has not been adequately addressed in the field, that WST's arguments are often teleological, and that the historical accounts are often overgeneralized in the search for metanarratives (as is true of any global theory of social change or development).

Each of these weaknesses are repairable given suitable attention, and none are fatal to the central insights of the paradigm. They can be fixed. Despite these shortcomings, we believe it is clear that WST carries with it vitally important environmental implications. While we regret that these implications have yet to be more thoroughly pursued, we hope that our work along with others working on similar lines will accelerate the employment of the tools of WST to the growing environmental crisis.

NOTES

1. Frank has remarked that his own interest in the "development of underdevelopment" was sparked by the Cuban revolution, an event that reverberated throughout Latin American intellectual circles at the time, stimulating renewed questions about the "modernization" paradigm (Frank, personal communication to Grimes).

2. Should this turn out to be the case, the consignment of capitalism to the "dustbin of history" would be the result of the same ecological degradation that has likewise trashed all prior modes of accumulation (e.g., Sanderson 1995; Chew 1995).

3. Sanderson (1988) makes the excellent point that while the opportunities of ruling classes are constrained by macrostructures (the world economy in which they operate), sometimes they choose effectively and other times not. The wisdom of their decisions is determined by microissues internal to the political and historical situation in the nation itself.

4. For a fascinating approach to this question, see Crosby (1986).

5. The term "globalization"—that the network of world trade and politics is growing ever tighter—is itself an "old" WST concept that has become a buzzword for this entire decade or phase of capitalism, now used far beyond WST circles (Chase-Dunn and Grimes 1995).

6. This relationship is not necessary, since automation also depends on the price of labor and the culturally variable desire of capitalists to gain total control over the production process.

REFERENCES

Aglietta, M. 1979. *A Theory of Capitalist Regulation*. London: New Left.
Amin, Samir. 1974. *Accumulation on a World Scale*. 2 vols. New York: Monthly Review.

————. 1976. *Unequal Development*. New York: Monthly Review.

Arrighi, Giovanni, and Jessica Drangel. 1986. "The Stratification of the World-Economy: An Exploration of the Semi-peripheral Zone." *Review* 10 (Summer): 9–74.

Ayres, Robert U. 1989. "Industrial Metabolism and Global Change." *ISSJ: International Social Science Journal* 41:363–373.

Barbosa, Luis. 1993. "The World-System and the Destruction of the Brazilian Rain Forest." *Review* 16:215–240.

————. 1996. "The People of the Forest against International Capitalism: Systemic and Anti-systemic Forces in the Battle for the Preservation of the Brazilian Amazon Rainforest." *Sociological Perspectives* 39:317–331.

Barkin, David. 1995. "Wealth, Poverty, and Sustainable Development." Working Paper, Lincoln Institute, March.

Barnham, Bradford, Stephen G. Bunker, and Denis O'Hearn. 1994. *States, Firms, and Raw Materials: The World Economy and Ecology of Aluminum*. Madison: University of Wisconsin Press.

Benton, Ted. 1989. "Marxism and Natural Limits: An Ecological Critique and Reconstruction." *New Left Review* 178:51–86.

Braudel, Fernand. 1972. *The Mediterranean and the Mediterranean World in the Age of Philip II*. 2 vols. New York: Harper and Row.

————. 1981, 1982, 1984. *Civilization and Capitalism, 15th–18th Century*. 3 vols. New York: Harper and Row.

Braverman, Harry. 1974. *Labor and Monopoly Capital*. New York: Monthly Review.

Brewer, Anthony. 1980. *Marxist Theories of Imperialism: A Critical Survey*. London: Routledge and Kegan Paul.

Bullard, Robert D., and Beverly H. Wright. 1992. "The Quest for Environmental Equity: Mobilizing the African-American Community for Social Change." In *American Environmentalism: The U.S. Environmental Movement 1970–1990*, ed. Riley E. Dunlap and Angela G. Mertig, 39–49. New York: Taylor and Francis.

Bunker, Stephen G. 1985. *Underdeveloping the Amazon: Extraction, Unequal Exchange, and the Failure of the Modern State*. Urbana: University of Illinois Press.

————. 1989. "The Eternal Conquest." *NACLA Report on the Americas* 23:27–36.

————. 1994. "Flimsy Joint Ventures in Fragile Environments." In *States, Firms, and Raw Materials: The World Economy and Ecology of Aluminum*, ed. Bradford Barnham, Stephen G. Bunker, and Denis O'Hearn, 261–296. Madison: University of Wisconsin Press.

Burbach, Roger, and Patricia Flynn. 1980. *Agribusiness in the Americas*. New York: NACLA and Monthly Review.

Buttel, Frederick H. 1978. "Social Structure and Energy Efficiency: A Preliminary Cross-National Analysis." *Human Ecology* 6:145–164.

————. 1987. "New Directions in Environmental Sociology." *Annual Review of Sociology* 13:465–488.

Buttel, Frederick H., Martin Kenney, and Jack R. Kloppenburg Jr. 1985. "From Green Revolution to Biorevolution: Some Observations on the Changing Technological Bases of Economic Transformation in the Third World." *Economic Development and Cultural Change* 34 (October): 31–55.

Cardoso, Fernando Henrique. 1977. "The Consumption of Dependency Theory in the United States." *Latin American Research Review* 12:7–24.

Cardoso, Fernando Henrique, and Enzo Faletto. 1979. *Dependency and Development in Latin America*. Berkeley: University of California Press.

Chase-Dunn, Christopher. 1989. *Global Formation: Structures of the World-Economy*. Cambridge, Mass.. Basil Blackwell.

Chase-Dunn, Christopher, and Peter Grimes. 1995. "World-Systems Analysis." *Annual Review of Sociology* 21:387–417.

Chase-Dunn, Christopher, and Thomas D. Hall. 1996. "Ecological Degradation and the Evolution of World-Systems." Paper presented at the American Sociological Association's session on "The Environment and the World Economy," New York City, New York, August 17.

———. 1997. *Rise and Demise: Comparing World-Systems*. Boulder, Colo.: Westview.

Chase-Dunn, Christopher, and Bruce Pobodnik. 1994. "The World-System and World State Formation." Paper presented at the Thirteenth World Congress of Sociology of the International Sociology Association, Symposium 2, Bielefeld, Germany, July 22.

Chew, Sing C. 1995. "Environmental Transformations: Accumulation, Ecological Crisis, and Social Movements." In *A New World Order? Global Transformations in the Late Twentieth Century*, ed. David A. Smith and József Borocz, 201–215. Westport, Conn.: Praeger.

———. 1997. "For Nature: Deep Greening World-Systems Analysis for the 21st Century." *Journal of World-Systems Research* 3 (Fall): 381–402.

Chilcote, Ronald H. 1984. *Theories of Development and Underdevelopment*. Boulder, Colo.: Westview.

Christen, Catherine, Selene Herculano, Kathryn Hochstetler, Renae Prell, Marie Price, and J. Timmons Roberts. 1998. "Latin American Environmentalism: Comparative Views." *Studies in Comparative International Development* 33:58–87.

Cicantell, Paul. 1994. "The Raw Materials Route to the Semiperiphery: Raw Materials, State Development Policies and Mobility in the Capitalist World-System." Paper presented at the American Sociological Association's annual meeting, Los Angeles, California, August 5–9.

Covello, Vincent T., and R. Scott Frey. 1990. "Technology-Based Environmental Health Risks in Developing Nations." *Technological Forecasting and Social Change* 37:159–179.

Crosby, Alfred W. 1986. *Ecological Imperialism: The Biological Expansion of Europe, 900–1900*. Cambridge: Cambridge University Press.

de Janvry, Alain. 1981. *The Agrarian Question and Reformism in Latin America*. Baltimore, Md.: Johns Hopkins University Press.

Dicken, Peter. 1998. *Global Shift: Transforming the World Economy*. 3rd ed. New York: Guilford.

Dunlap, Riley E., and William R. Catton Jr. 1994. "Struggling with Human Exemptionalism: The Rise, Decline, and Revitalization of Environmental Sociology." *The American Sociologist* 25:5–30.

Dunlap, Riley E., and Angela G. Mertig, eds. 1992. *American Environmentalism: The U.S. Environmental Movement 1970–1990*. New York: Taylor and Francis.

Durham, William H. 1982. *Scarcity and Survival in Central America: Ecological Origins of the Soccer War*. Palo Alto, Calif.: Stanford University Press.

Emmanuel, Arghiri. 1972. *Unequal Exchange: A Study of the Imperialism of Trade*. New York, Monthly Review.

Evans, Peter B., Dietrich Rueschemeyer, and Taeda Skocpol, eds. 1985. *Bringing the State Back In*. New York: Cambridge University Press.

Faber, Daniel. 1993. *Environment under Fire: Imperialism and the Ecological Crisis in Central America*. New York: Monthly Review.

Foster, John Bellamy. 1994. *The Vulnerable Planet: A Short Economic History of the Environment*. New York: Cornerstone.

Frank, Andre Gunder. 1969. *Latin America: Underdevelopment or Revolution*. New York: Monthly Review.

———. 1978. *World Accumulation 1492–1789*. New York: Monthly Review.

Frank, Andre Gunder, and Barry K. Gills, eds. 1996. *The World System: Five Hundred Years or Five Thousand?* London: Routledge.

Freudenburg, William R. 1981. "Women and Men in an Energy Boomtown: Adjustment, Alienation, and Adaptation." *Rural Sociology* 46:220–244.

Frey, R. Scott. 1993. "The Capitalist World Economy, Toxic Waste Dumping, and Health Risks in the Third World." Paper presented at the American Sociological Association's annual meeting, Miami, Florida, August 13–17.

Galeano, Eduardo. 1973. *Open Veins of Latin America: Five Centuries of the Pillage of a Continent*. New York: Monthly Review.

Gellert, Paul K. 1996. "Concentrating Capital with a Spatially Diffuse Commodity: The Political Ecology and Economy of the Indonesian Timber Industry." Paper presented at the American Sociological Association's annual meeting, New York, August 16–20.

Gereffi, Gary, and Miguel Korzeniewicz, eds. 1994. *Commodity Chains and Global Capitalism*. Westport, Conn.: Praeger.

Goldstein, Joshua. 1988. *Long Cycles: Prosperity and War in the Modern Age*. New Haven, Conn.: Yale University Press.

Gould, Ken. 1995. "Transnational Trade Deregulation: A Collision Course with Sustainable Development." Paper presented at the American Sociological Association's annual meeting, Washington, D.C., August 19–23.

Gramling, Robert, and Sarah Brabant. 1990. "The Impact of a Boom/Bust Economy on Women's Employment." Paper presented at the American Sociological Association's annual meeting, Washington, D.C, August 11–13.

Grimes, Peter E. 1988. *Long Cycles, International Mobility, and Class Struggle in the World-System*. Unpublished paper, Johns Hopkins University.

———. 1996. *Economic Cycles and International Mobility in the World-System: 1790–1990*. Ph.D. diss., Johns Hopkins University.

———. 1997. "The Horsemen in the Killing Fields." Paper presented at the Twenty-second Meeting of the Political Economy of the World-System, Santa Cruz, California, April 3–5.

Grimes, Peter E., and J. Timmons Roberts. 1995. "Oscillations in Atmospheric Carbon Dioxide and Long Cycles of Production in the World Economy, 1790–1990." Paper presented at the American Sociological Association's annual meeting, Washington, D.C., August 19–23.

———. 1996. "Shifting Correlates of National Carbon Efficiency in the World System." Paper presented at the American Sociological Association's annual meeting, New York City, New York, August 16–20.

Grimes, Peter E., J. Timmons Roberts, and Jodie Manale. 1993. "Social Roots of Environmental Damage: A World-Systems Analysis of Global Warming." Paper presented at the American Sociological Association's annual meeting, Miami, Florida, August 13–17.

Grossman, Gene M., and Alan B. Krueger. 1995. "Economic Growth and the Environment." *Quarterly Journal of Economics* 110 (May): 353–377.

Harper, Charles L. 1996. *Environment and Society: Human Perspectives on Environmental Issues*. Upper Saddle River, N.J.: Prentice Hall.

Harrington, Michael. 1962. *The Other America*. New York: Penguin.

Harvey, David. 1982. *The Limits to Capital*. Chicago: University of Chicago Press.
Hecht, Susanna B., Anthony B. Anderson, and Peter May. 1988. "The Subsidy from Nature: Shifting Cultivation, Successional Palm Forests, and Rural Development." *Human Organization* 47 (Spring): 25–35.
Homer-Dixon, Thomas F., Jeffrey H. Boutwell, and George W. Rathjens. 1993. "Environmental Change and Violent Conflict." *Scientific American* (February): 38–45.
Howard, Michael C., ed. 1993. *Asia's Environmental Crisis*. Boulder, Colo.: Westview.
Humphrey, Craig R., and Frederick R. Buttel. 1982. *Environment, Energy, and Society*. Belmont, Calif.: Wadsworth.
Inglehart, Ronald. 1995. "Political Support for Environmental Protection: Objective Problems and Subjective Values in 43 Societies." *PS: Political Science and Politics* 23:57–72.
Kay, Cristobal. 1989. *Latin American Theories of Development and Underdevelopment*. New York: Routledge.
Kazis, Richard, and Richard L. Grossman. 1991. *Fear at Work: Job Blackmail, Labor and the Environment*. Philadelphia: New Society.
Kloppenburg, Jack R., Jr. 1988. *First the Seed: The Political Economy of Plant Biotechnology*. Cambridge: Cambridge University Press.
Lipietz, Alain. 1982. "Beyond Global Fordism?" *New Left Review* 132 (March–April): 33–47.
———. 1987. *Mirages and Miracles: The Crises of Global Fordism*. London: Verso.
Logan, John T., and Harvey Molotch. 1987. *Urban Fortunes: The Political Economy of Place*. Los Angeles: University of Calfornia Press.
Mandel, Ernest. 1975. *Late Capitalism*. London: New Left.
Mann, Michael. 1986. *The Sources of Social Power: A History of Power from the Beginning to A.D. 1760*. Vol. 1. New York: Cambridge University Press.
Manser, Roger. 1993. *Failed Transitions: The Eastern European Economy and Environment since the Fall of Communism*. New York: The New Press.
Marx, Karl. 1967. *Capital*. 3 vols. New York: International House.
Mazur, Allan, and Eugene Rosa. 1974. "Energy and Life-Style." *Science* 186:607–610.
McKibben, William. 1989. *The End of Nature*. New York: Anchor/Doubleday.
McMichael, Philip. 1996. "Globalization: Myths and Realities." *Rural Sociology* 61:25–55.
Modelski, George, and William R. Thompson. 1996. *Leading Sectors and World Powers: The Coevolution of Global Politics and Economics*. Columbia: University of South Carolina Press.
O'Connor, James. 1973. *The Fiscal Crisis of the State*. New York: St. Martin's.
———. 1989. "Capitalism, Nature, Socialism: A Theoretical Introduction." *Capitalism, Nature, Socialism* 1:11–38.
Perelman, Michael. 1977. *Farming for Profit in a Hungry World: Capital and the Crisis in Agriculture*. New York: Universe.
Portes, Alejandro, and John Walton. 1981. *Labor, Class, and the International System*. Orlando, Fla.: Academic.
Ranis, Gustav. 1990. "Contrasts in the Political Economy of Development Policy." In *Manufacturing Miracles: Paths of Industrialization in Latin America and East Asia*, ed. Gereffi and Wyman, 207–230. Princeton, N.J.: Princeton University Press.
Reed, David, ed. 1992. *Structural Adjustment and the Environment*. Boulder, Colo.: Westview.
Roberts, Bryan. 1978. *City of Peasants: The Political Economy of Urbanization in the Third World*. London: Edward Arnold.
Roberts, J. Timmons. 1992. *Forging Development, Fragmenting Labor: Subcontracting and Local Response in an Amazon Boomtown*. Ph.D. diss., Johns Hopkins University.

———. 1994. "Economic Crisis and Environmental Policy [Brazil]." *Hemisphere* (May): 26–30.

———. 1995. "Subcontracting and the Omitted Social Impacts of Development Projects: Household Survival at the Carajás Mines in the Brazilian Amazon." *Economic Development and Cultural Change* 43:735–758.

———. 1996a. "Global Restructuring and the Environment in Latin America." In *Latin America and the World Economy*, ed. Roberto P. Korzeniewicz and William C. Smith, 187–210. Westport, Conn.: Greenwood.

———. 1996b. "Predicting Participation in Environmental Treaties: A World-System Analysis." *Sociological Inquiry* 66:38–57.

Roberts, J. Timmons, and Peter E. Grimes. 1997. "Carbon Intensity and Economic Development 1962–1991: A Brief Exploration of the Environmental Kuznets Curve." *World Development* 25:191–198.

Roberts, J. Timmons, and F. Nai-Amoo Dodoo. 1995. "Population Growth, Sex Ratio and Women's Work on the Contemporary Amazon Frontier." In *1995 Yearbook of the Conference of Latin American Geographers*, ed. David J. Robinson, 91–105. Austin: University of Texas.

Rosa, Eugene A., Gary E. Machlis, and Kenneth M. Keating. 1988. "Energy and Society." *Annual Review of Sociology* 14:149–172.

Rudel, Thomas K. 1989. "Population, Development, and Tropical Deforestation: A Cross-National Study." *Rural Sociology* 54:327–338.

Rudel, Thomas K., and Bruce Horowitz. 1993. *Tropical Deforestation: Small Farmers and Land Clearing in the Ecuadorian Amazon*. New York: Columbia University Press.

Sanderson, Stephen K. 1988. *Macrosociology: An Introduction to Human Societies*. New York: Harper and Row.

———. 1995. *Social Transformations: A General Theory of Historical Development*. London: Basil Blackwell.

Santos, Roberto Araujo de Oliveira. 1980. *Historia Econômica da Amazônia 1800–1920*. São Paulo, Brazil: T. A. Queiroz.

Schafer, D. Michael. 1994. *Winners and Losers: How Sectors Shape the Developmental Prospects of States*. Ithaca, N.Y.: Cornell University Press.

Schnaiberg, Allan. 1980. *The Environment: From Surplus to Scarcity*. New York: Oxford University Press.

Shannon, Thomas R. 1996. *An Introduction to the World-System Perspective*. 2nd ed. Boulder, Colo.: Westview.

Simonis, Udo E. 1989. "Ecological Modernization of Industrial Society: Three Strategic Elements." *International Social Science Journal* 41:347–361.

Skocpol, Taeda. 1977. "Wallerstein's World Capitalist System: A Theoretical and Historical Critique." *American Journal of Sociology* 82:1075–1090.

Smith, David A. 1994. "Uneven Development and the Environment: Toward a World-System Perspective." *Humboldt Journal of Social Relations* 20:151–175.

Smith, David A., and Douglas R. White. 1992. "Structure and Dynamics of the Global Economy: Network Analysis of International Trade 1965–1980." *Social Forces* 70:857–893.

Stallings, Barbara. 1990. "The Role of Foreign Capital in Economic Development." In *Manufacturing Miracles: Paths of Industrialization in Latin America and East Asia*, ed. Gary Gereffi and Donald L. Wyman, 55–89. Princeton, N.J.: Princeton University Press.

194   *J. Timmons Roberts and Peter E. Grimes*

Stern, Paul C., Oran R. Young, and Daniel Druckman, eds. 1992. *Global Environmental Change: Understanding the Human Dimensions.* Washington, D.C.: National Academy.
Strohl, Derek. 1997. "Research on Multinational Corporations and Large and Small Businesses in Mexico: Hypotheses on Comparative Levels of Pollution." Unpublished mimeo.
Terlouw, Cornelis Peter. 1992. *The Regional Geography of the World-System.* Nederlandse Geografische Studies 144. Utrect: Koninklijk Nederlands Aardrijkskundig Genootschap.
Tucker, Richard P., and John F. Richards, eds. 1983. *Global Deforestation and the Nineteenth-Century World Economy.* Vol. 1. Durham, N.C.: Duke University Press.
Wager, W. Warren. 1996. "Socialism, Nationalism, and Ecocide." *Review* 19:319–233.
Wallerstein, Immanuel. 1972. "Three Paths to National Development in 16th Century Europe." *Studies in Comparative International Development* 8:95–101.
———. 1974. *The Modern World-System I: Capitalist Agriculture and the Origins of the European World Economy in the Sixteenth Century.* New York: Academic.
———. 1979. *The Capitalist World-Economy.* New York: Cambridge University Press.
Wolf, Eric. 1982. *Europe and the People without History.* Berkeley: University of California Press.
World Bank. 1992. *World Development Report 1992.* New York: Oxford University Press.
———. 1995a. *Monitoring Environmental Progress.* New York: Oxford University Press.
———. 1995b. *World Development Report 1995.* New York: Oxford University Press.
World Resources Institute. 1993. *World Resources.* New York: Oxford University Press.
Wright, Angus. 1990. *The Death of Ramón González: The Modern Agricultural Dilemma.* Austin: University of Texas Press.

Part IV

SOCIOLOGICAL THEORY
AND ENVIRONMENTAL
SOCIOLOGY IN THE LATE
1990s: MODERNITY, CULTURE,
AND THE NATURAL WORLD

9

Modernity, Politics, and the Environment: A Theoretical Perspective

Ørnulf Seippel

And the more profound the questioning, the more adventurous is the search for replacements.

—Michael Walzer

Auch Tiefe ist, . . . ein Moment der Dialektik, keine isolierte Qualität.

—Theodor W. Adorno

The process of modernization has led to a serious degradation of our natural environment and a potential for environmental destruction inconceivable a few generations ago. Modernity is also the place and time where this degradation is diagnosed. And, not the least, the remedies of modernity—voluntary social action—is what we have to rely on and hope for in coping with these problems. In short: Modernity is the cause of the environmental problems; the medium through which they are brought to light, understood, and formulated; and the prerequisite for actually coping with the degradation of and threats toward the natural environment.

If one looks at the concept of modernity, it operates with two connotations (Offe 1996), partly reflecting the role of modernity with regard to the environmental problems (Szerszynski 1996). On the one hand, there is a descriptive version of the process of modernization as leading from a traditional, mythical, uniform society toward a society consisting of social institutions set in motion and controlled by free rational individuals. This descriptive approach is, at least implicitly, coexistent with a normative stance; modernization as something worthy, and, succinctly expressed in the belief that in a not-too-distant future "the human world can become the mirror of the divine" (Alexander 1990b: 16) and that "to be modern is to believe that the masterful transformation of the world is possible, indeed that it is likely" (16). Although the environmental discourse has been rather skeptical toward these processes of modernization and its belief in progress, reminders from this school of thought are to be found within the more recent contributions of ecological modernization.

On the other hand, current contributions to the understanding of modernity do mostly question both the factual and normative premise of the process of modernization. Though the processes of modernization do set free enormous potentials within different social arenas, at the same time, the overall process does not fulfill the promises made by the enlightenment prophets: we are not really able to break free from our traditions and unsecular roots (Milbank 1990); the institutionalization of rationality does not guarantee a moral society (Bauman 1993); and the emancipation of rational forces within different areas of social interaction cannot guarantee the rationality of the overall evolution of society (Offe 1996). In general terms, Habermas is still hoping for modernity to complete itself, Bauman (1989) shows us the inherent perversions of modernity, and Eder discloses how "our growing awareness of the world-wide ecological crisis has damaged, perhaps completely, our conviction in the rationality of modern society" (1990: 67).

If one concedes that modernity is the social condition within which one has to handle environmental problems, it is important to grasp what one is into or up against. And what characterizes modernity as a societal formation is exactly the ambiguity reflected in the two modernities. On the one hand, a farewell to a tradition that opens up an enormous range of possibilities oriented toward the future; material production; cultural reproduction; health and welfare; and a democratic institutionalization of power. On the other hand, some problems remain unsolved and new problems are created. Among them are environmental problems. The environmental discourse in general and sociological approaches to environmental problems in particular reflect this ambiguity rather directly. In general: There are either no problems—all experience has hitherto shown that problems will be solved through science and new technology—or, the problems are overwhelming, with all kind of apocalypses waiting around the corner. Sociologically, one is either occupied with very abstract questions along the lines of belief in or critique of modernity, or one is absorbed in concrete policy analyses without any specific theoretical orientation.

But to approach social problems solely through one of these two approaches will, in the long run, be insufficient. Neither is it satisfactory to combine them and repeat that ambivalence is what goes to the core of modernity (as Beck [1993] does, echoing Bauman [1991]). What this situation of ambivalence implies from an analytical sociological point of view is the inadequacy of simple analytical grips. What we are up against is complexity, with regard to both natural and societal conditions, and what is needed is theories that lead beyond these general quarrels of modernity and go more into detail with regard to what is happening at a meso- and microlevel, without losing sight of the macrolink and the theoretical curiosity present in much of environmental sociology. In a comment on the theory of risk society, Kaase and Newton assert that "[a]t the moment, the arguments of Beck . . . remain a matter of intelligent speculation" (1995: 155). And if we are to pass this stage of intelligent speculations, at least two challenges are raised. The first prerequisite for producing a new and fruitful theoretical contribution to the field of environmental sociology is to limit the object for analysis; it is not possible to say everything about everything in an interesting manner. In this chapter, I concentrate on the (still broad) issue of how the environment becomes a political issue. This implies both an analysis along the lines of traditional political sociology, but also an extension of this perspective toward social movement theory.

Merton characterized the sociological work of his contemporaries as an alternation between two opposite poles; either one was obsessed with grand theory, or one was lost in the ocean of undertheorized empirical correlations (Merton 1968). The same situation dominates much of current environmental sociology. On the one hand, we have scholars working with concepts like ecological communication, reflexive modernization, ecological modernization, ecological rationality, ecocentric worldviews, ecological judgment, ecology and democracy, and questioning whether Marx, Weber, Durkheim, Mead, or Critical Theory best captures the essence of the environmental problems. On the other hand, we have others working on restricted empirical puzzles and concrete policy studies with hardly any theoretical foundations. Thus, one of the challenges for environmental sociology today is, as it was for sociology in general thirty years ago according to Merton, to generate theories that cover the space between these extremes and that mediate between macro-, meso-, and microlevels. Consequently, the second prerequisite is to supplement the macro-theoretical corpus of environmental sociology with theories that point toward meso- and microanalyses. This is also a point made in Gramling and Freudenburg's (1996: 358–359) proposal for an environmental sociological paradigm for the twenty-first century. My aim is not to argue against grand theory as such, but to contend more modestly that to be fruitful, these theories should now be challenged both by other grand theories and by theories including richer and more nuanced sets of concepts that are more appropriate for empirical analyses.

The purpose of this chapter, then, is to present a set of concepts and theories that can both contribute to more nuanced and empirical analyses of one more restricted area of social thought, and, at the same time, challenge the more abstract and theoretical contributions making up much of contemporary environmental sociology. Hence, in a theoretical context, I will proceed through four stages; from the abstract toward the middle range and back again. First, I present an approach abstract enough to encompass most of what passes as environmental sociology that, at the same time, is capable of relating to the middle-range theories to evolve from the discussions in this chapter. Next, I specify what I call the political dimensions of this perspective. Third, and this is the core of the chapter, I propose some theoretical concepts and theories to handle the political mediation of environmental problems—its sources and causes, its functioning, and its potential influence. The fourth part is devoted to an exposition of how these theories can actually contribute to what I have aimed at through a confrontation with two of the most famous "grand theory" formulations of the environmental problems: Beck's theory of risk society and the ecocentric critique of the anthropocentric culture of modern society.

MODERNITY AND POLITICS:
THE GENERAL CONDITIONS

The purpose of this section is to expose some of the most general conditions for social order and social interaction relevant for political mobilization around environmental issues within modern societies. These perspectives are, first, supposed to function as comments on the abstract theoretical contributions of environmental sociology. Second, they are supposed to relate the following mesoperspectives to the different general macroperspectives. Third, they will also function as guidelines for the discussion of the mesolevel perspectives.

Contingency and Complexity: The Unavoidable Parameters of Modernity

What the condition of modernity makes clear, and that has to be taken as a point of no return, is individual and social meaning as mediated; as something fluid, temporal, and spatial. This is reflected both in the "open human biological program" (Eisenstadt 1995: 330–331) and in the nature of social interaction as laid out by Parsons (1937). For social interaction to take place, some kind of meaning has to evolve. A fundamental question then is how meaning is structured. And, given this background, how which of the different patterns of meaning evolving will play what roles with regard to which dimensions and aspects of social interaction. Modernity is the story of how this process of creation of meaning is taking place through a process of societal differentiation, resulting in a situation where different spheres of action are constituted according to specific functions and through different forms of rationality.

Analyzing a phenomenon within the context of modernity—as contingency generating complexity and the need for social institutions—implies looking at social interaction through the lenses of constructivism. This is by now becoming a truism within environmental sociology (Lash and Urry 1994; Hannigan 1995; Eder 1996b). At the same time, without resorting to realist perspectives (Dunlap and Catton 1979; Dickens 1996), it is also obvious that the world is composed of more than social constructions. There is a difference between "brute facts" and "institutional facts" (Searle 1995), but the "institutional facts" are the "brute facts" of sociology. And, most important from a sociological point of view and what is at the core in this chapter, there are different modes of mediation with different consequences for what appear as sociopolitical issues or as problems, how they are handled, how they may function within different arenas of society, and the role different forms of mediation may play with regard to the overall development of society. What must be understood is how the environment emerges as a political issue, which sociopolitical constructions are relevant, how they are generated, and how they function.

According to Alexander, the process of "differentiation comes closer than any other contemporary conception to identifying the actual texture, the imminent dangers, and the real promises of modern life" (1990c: 11), and furthermore, it provides a "kind of nuanced self-reflection vis-à-vis theories of cultural change" (12). To introduce productive distinctions to this perspective that will contribute fruitfully to analyses of the political dimensions of environmentalism, I rely on two approaches: one emphasizing differentiation according to functionality and another occupied with the aspects of rationality within this process. And in the end, I rely on Habermas's theories where he combines these perspectives and thereby provides a theoretical framework that is capable of raising interesting theoretical questions of uttermost relevance for the understanding of how the environment becomes what kind of political issue.

Functional and Rational Differentiation

The seminal contributions to the conception of *functional* differentiation are found in the oeuvres of Durkheim and Marx. They describe how the institutionalization of material production result in "division of labor" and "modes of production" that do have social ramifications such as differences in power, anomie, and alienation. What I want to emphasize and what is implied in analyzing the process of differentiation according to the concept of functionality, is brought to light in Luhmann's assertion that "we could speak of functional-structural analysis in contrast to structural-functional analysis (Luhmann 1976: 508). While Parsons understood social systems as upheld because they contributed to the equilibrium of the society as a whole, Luhmann sees social systems as upheld because they function and do meet a problem experienced by people as requiring a solution. What is new is that fulfilling singular functions in no way guarantees the overall and final outcomes, and society is definitely not considered "an automatic equilibrating mechanism" (Alexander 1990c: 2). The current contributors to functional sociology have broken the relations to teleological and developmental beliefs and instead stress the contingency and the openness and incompleteness in the process of differentiation (Colomy 1990).

What a modern functional approach implies, and this is particularly important in Luhmann's system theory, is the lack of center in modern society; it is impossible to represent the whole of society inside a subsystem of a differentiated society (Luhmann 1986; 1987). To understand how communication and social interaction take place inside a modern society, one has to grasp how these different systems are institutionalized through communication and how they influence social interaction. What is implied in this way of thinking is that social systems are institutionalized not because someone intends to or the society requires it, but because the social system does fill some function for society as such here and now; they have a human base, fulfilling some human needs, but they are not, on the whole, intentionally settled and they do not guarantee a friendly outcome either for themselves or for the whole.

If Durkheim and Marx are posited as representatives of thinking in terms of functional differentiation, Weber could be said to personify the sociological starting point for understanding modern society as involved in a process of *rationalization*. He then stands out as the successor of Kant, the philosopher who really questions the rift between our understanding of the world and the world itself, placing the "solution" in transcendental faculties and categories. Next, Hegel placed Kant's transcendental solutions inside history, but, still for some time, rescues the classic project of modernity by giving history the direction needed to transcend the relativizing impulse inherent to rationality. Weber, with his Nietzschean leaning, operates with Kant's distinctions and Hegel's social embeddedness, but without their belief in reason or history as transcendental guarantees. In Weber's writings, Kant meets Nietzsche and gets a historical institutionalization of the rational differentiation according to the Kantian typology (objectivity, morality, and subjectivity) in art, law, and economy. And, as will become clear, these different forms of rationality are also found in the intermediation of political interests and values in our late modern society.

Compared to the perspective of functional differentiation, this approach gives a more important role to the actors involved, they are able to question the validity of the social context within which they act, and it is their way of answering these questions that in turn influence the character of different social institutions. In Habermas's perspective, some contexts for social interaction are marked by a strategic orientation, some contexts of action are normatively oriented, some are more aesthetically or subjectively based, and without making this a very important point here, Habermas introduces his concept of communicative rationality to cover an ideal typical way to combine these forms of rationality.

Anyone familiar with Habermas's writings on these topics will know that he operates with both these dimensions of differentiation (functionality and rationality) and that these distinctions are what guide his critical questions toward the process of modernization. First, it is possible to pose questions within each dimension presented earlier. How well does the economic and the political system actually function? How are they to be improved instrumentally and strategically? This perspective is easily forgotten in the context of Habermas and environmental discourse, but it is important with regard to environmental problems, and it is not contradictory to the normative perspective as such (Heath 1996).

The second straightforward way to apply these distinctions is to look at the relations between the elements, and most prominent, for what kind of rationality that dominates. A well-known issue within this theoretical tradition is the conflict between Luhmann (1990) and Habermas (1992) with regard to the possibility of normative principles (values and cultures) playing any role with regard to politics. Is politics a purely instrumental activity—"the Higher Amorality of Politics" (Luhmann 1994)—or is there a potential for values and solidarity to influence what takes place within the polity through the public sphere. A parallel topic is common in all "radical" critique where, for example, the instrumentality of the economy, science, technology, or politics is an attractive target. How these different forms of rationality actually are to be balanced is a very intricate, and so far, unsolved question (Seel 1986).

Münch is probably the sociologist who most consistently has emphasized that the process of modernization is also marked by a countertendency to Luhmann's pure differentiation, and he describes the process of modernization as a process based on interpenetration between different social systems. He makes this a general point (Münch 1984), but has also pursued it more directly with regard to environmental problems. How, for example, is the economy actually influenced by environmental values (Münch 1994)? Even though it is fruitful to understand the process of modernization as a process of differentiation, it is difficult to avoid the perspective of interpenetration, especially when it comes to the question of environmentalism as a political issue.

On a very general level, Habermas operates with the distinction between social interaction integrated through communicative rationality (lifeworld) and through instrumental rationality (systems). And, from this point of view, the general critique from Habermas is that integration through instrumental rationality gains in importance at the cost of communicatively oriented interaction. Instrumentality, in other words, expels normative orientations. As a comment on much of environmental discourse, today, the table could probably be turned around. There is an apparent lack of understanding for the necessity of instrumental reason as a factor in the production of material goods.

Politics As Social Systems

A question to be answered, then, is which social systems to include in an analysis of the political aspects of environmentalism. First, and rather obvious, an analysis of political questions should of course include the political system, which is the system coping with the problem of how to settle the problem of power with the function of reaching collectively binding decisions. Second, there has taken place a process of differentiation within the political system itself—that is, the public sphere, political parties, and the bureaucratic state administration. And, given my *Problemstellung* (political intermediation), I will concentrate on the input side of the political process: how interests and values are generated and mediated into the political system.

But important for the political movements where environmentalism has been a central feature is a widespread mistrust in the conventional political system—a lack of legitimacy—and its inefficiency with regard to environmental problems. The corollary is that environmentalists often operate with a wider concept of politics and power than usually applied in the analyses of the conventional political system. This implies that politicizing an issue does not necessarily involve working toward the political parties and the state administration, but rather toward more general changes in the public sphere, civil society, or the culture of a society. Or most basically, politicizing is to be found in the movement itself: "The medium, the movement itself as a new medium, is the message. . . . The meaning of the action has to be found in the action itself more than in the pursued goals: movements are not qualified by what they do but by what they are" (Melucci 1985: 801, 809). What comes to mind is new social movement (NSM) theory (what Beck calls subpoliticization), a more general hope for a revival of civil society (Cohen and Arato 1992), and an almost Foucauldian concept of power. In principle—and in practice—this makes it possible to politicize the environment as a political issue within any social system of modernity, say, education, religion, and consumption. To focus my analysis, I have chosen to limit my analysis of political action to conventional politics and initiatives stemming from the civil society in an organized form, that is, voluntary organizations and social movements.

However, the interests and values that occupy the political system do not stem from the political system itself. And the social institutions of most importance to the intermediation process is, in line with the classic political sociology, still the economy (structure) and the civil society (culture), although likely with a shift in mutual importance. In sum, this implies that an analysis of the politicization of the environment must focus on the political system, but at the same time operate with a general understanding of politics and also remember that the sources of values and interests are to be found outside the political system.

POLITICAL INTERMEDIATION IN A
LATE MODERN SOCIETY

The modern democratic political system is supposed to support a legitimate administration of power in the wake of the dissolution of the uniting force of myth, religion, and tradition. In this section, I take a closer look at how the process of political intermediation has been approached in political sociology. I first look at the "classic" way of understanding the process of political intermediation of interests and values and then look at some new models reflecting changes in the structures and cultures of late modern society. Having presented three phases and the corresponding understandings of political intermediation, I then discuss the cleavage concept that goes to the core of the problem of political intermediation in late modern society.

The Classic Cleavage Model, New Politics,
and Postmodernism

As a starting point, Eisenstadt takes the fact that humans lack a "biological program" and hence need social institutions to fill "the open spaces between the general propensities of human beings and the concrete specifications of these propensities" (1995: 331). This means "that the crux of concrete human activity is the 'filling in' of such spaces" (331). In line with these basic social needs of humans, there are two basic areas of social institutionalization, both of uttermost importance for the political intermediation of interests and values. The first is the structuring of social institutions helping out the material production of a society: the division of labor. The second is the cultures providing normative orientations in society. The most famous attempts to interpret political action—as voting behavior, membership in interest organizations, and participation in social movements—do take their outset in this scheme. And, as will be clear, it is changes in the structure and culture of late modern society that are at the core of the shifts in the political intermediation of late modern society. The theoretical challenge is to place the issue of the environment and environmental values into this schema or, possibly, to develop or change the scheme to give room for the environmental issue.

For a first and introductory understanding of how this process takes place, Lipset and Rokkan's (1967) seminal account of cleavages as constitutive of political mobilization will do. With their outset in Parsons's sociology, they presented what they considered a set of logically possible conflicts and values that potentially could be institutionalized in a modern society. This theoretical position was then elucidated with empirical analyses of which of these theoretically deduced possibilities that actually materialized during the era of nation-state building in the Western world. Which of these latent structural conflicts and cultural values actually manifested political institutional consequences is then explained on the basis of respectively the national and industrial revolution.

Lipset and Rokkan (1967) present four basic cleavages that they suggest are to be found in all modern nation-states. First, the national revolution brought forth a cultural (center to periphery) and a religious cleavage. Second, the industrial revolution resulted in two structural conflicts—one between employers and employees and another between primary industry and the secondary economy. This model then functions as the basis for the classical empirical approach to the process of political mediation; that is, how an issue through the structures and cultures of a society enters the political system of a nation and how political parties and interest organizations are institutionalized along these cleavage lines.

Lipset and Rokkan themselves declared their model partly outdated, because the cleavages constitutive of the political party structures they described in the late 1960s already, to a certain degree, belonged to the past. During the last decades, where changes both in the structure—from an industrial to a postindustrial society—and culture—from a modern to postmodern society—of late modern society have influenced the political intermediation fundamentally, this time lag between cleavages and party structure has become even more apparent. Structural and (traditional) cultural location of individuals has become a weaker explanatory factor with regard to political voting, and the old political issues have been challenged by new issues, among them, the environment.

The best known and most widely discussed elaboration on the cleavage model is coined in terms of "new politics," and its most famous version is Inglehart's theory of a silent revolution (1977) and a culture shift (1990)—that is, the substitution of postmaterial for material values. At the heart of Inglehart's theories are the changes taking place with regard to the upbringing and socialization of the younger generations. First, this process now takes place under less materialistic constraints than ever before. Second, the process of socialization is taking place in a more liberal climate than earlier. Taking his outset in Maslow's hierarchy of needs, Inglehart then asserts that those growing up in the postwar period are more apt to emphasize needs of an ethical and aesthetical character than earlier generations.

There will consequently emerge sets of values that correspond to this manifestation of less materialistic oriented needs, and these new value patterns will influence the politics of advanced industrial society in a way that generates a political landscape different from the one built on the structural and cultural cleavages that dominated industrial society. Among the changes taking place are the creation of new left and right parties, a more volatile electorate, and increased participation in NSMs and thereby the application of a wider repertoire of political strategies and instruments than is usual in conventional politics.

A common comment on Inglehart's theory is that what he conceptualizes as one value actually blurs two distinct values: one material/nonmaterial and one libertarian/authoritarian (Flanagan 1982). Another and maybe more promising way of conceptualizing the new value cleavages in the political landscape of late modern society is found in the concept of left-libertarian values as elaborated by Kitschelt (1989; 1994). These changes in values are also often coupled to structural changes and the emergence of a new middle class (Offe 1985; Kriesi et al. 1995).

In contrast to the classification of our society as modern or postindustrial, a postmodern approach sets forth a more radical diagnosis of the changes in the process of political intermediation, and these changes are a matter of form rather than content. An understanding of the new structural logic of modern culture is found in the works of Featherstone (1991), Lash and Urry (1994), and Bauman (1995), all emphasizing the aestheticization of everyday life, that is, an increasing relevance of an aesthetic model for understanding how the social forms of postmodern society are constituted.

All social forms are generated in an interplay between "the general" and "the particular." In the common structural and cultural explanations of the constitution of social forms, particular phenomena are given meaning in light of the general structural interests or values dominant in sectors of society: Both the industrial and postindustrial societies mobilized political action through ideological schemes subsuming the particulars under general material interests or left-libertarian values. Contrary to this, the aesthetic constitution of social forms subsumes the general under particulars, the least mediated of universals, and thereby provides a "low level of mediation" (Lash and Urry 1994: 47). This means that more local and particular social experiences, "rooted in place" (47), that is, being a member of a certain group or "tribe" (Maffesoli 1996), are what generate a more general interest in, for instance, the environment.

A fruitful way to see what characterizes a postmodern sociality in contrast to modern social forms is to compare postmodernism with postmaterialism (Gibbins and Reimer 1995). Where the postmaterialist has a teleological- and future-oriented belief in progress, the postmodernist is more keen to cultivate the present, the fragment, and the immediate; where the postmaterialist searches for authenticity, the true, and the natural, the postmodernist explores the surface and the seductive and favors simulation; the postmaterialist is a stable, steady fellow, where the postmodernist is constantly changing; and finally, where the postmaterialist is out to realize him- or herself, the postmodernist is just out to express him- or herself. In sum, the postmaterial values are homogenous where the postmodern values are heterogeneous.

What this implies for political action is still not as clear as for the new politics approach. Probably, it will, as Gibbins and Reimer (1995) suggest, imply two parallel and rather contrary developments: an individualistic postmodernism and an humanistic postmodernism. The individualistic postmodernism probably has clear negative consequences for political action because actors will prioritize their personal desires and escape the involvement politics implies. The humanistic postmodernists are probably opting for a more general political concern than the "modernists," perhaps not avoiding politics, but the result will probably become a less obligatory and stable political engagement than conventional politics theories presume.

The Three Dimensions of a Cleavage-Analytical Refinement

As a preparation for the next section, I present a discussion of the cleavage concepts that are of relevance both to the preceding and succeeding discussion. What is happening with regard to political action in the Western world in the last decades challenges the classic understanding with regard to content and form. In short, the process becomes more complex. And one way of improving on this understanding is to follow Bartolini and Mair (1990) in their discussion of the concept of cleavages.

They begin their discussion with a complaint: "The concept of 'cleavage' which tends to be adopted in the contemporary literature has remained essentially vague and ambiguous" (Bartolini and Mair 1990: 213). Consequently, what is needed is to capture more precisely what the process of political intermediation aimed at through the cleavage concept involves. Bartolini and Mair proceed by making clear the general questions the concept is intended to illuminate and answer: "[A] theoretically autonomous definition of cleavage as a concept which links social structure and political order" (215). Next, they distinguish between the different components of the process of "linking" that the concept is intended to cover:

[The] concept of cleavage can be seen to incorporate three levels: an empirical element, which identifies the empirical referent of the concept, and which we can define in social-structural terms; a normative element, that is the set of values and beliefs which provides a sense of identity and role to the empirical element, and which reflect the self-consciousness of the social group(s) involved; and an organisational/behavioral element, that is the set of individual interactions, institutions, and organisations, such as political parties, which develop as part of the cleavage. (215)

Bartolini and Mair contend that a true cleavage should comprise all three dimensions. But what actually seems to happen, concerning environmental issues in particular, is exactly that this unity breaks down and that the intermediation of political issues is ridden by differences within each component—structure, culture, and organization—as well, in the last instance probably also with consequences for their political functioning. And this is also precisely what Bartolini and Mair observe: "It is also clear that the three elements may vary quite autonomously in the cases of both existing and emerging cleavages" (219). The lesson to be learned from this development is not that a new societal formation has replaced an old one or that one logic of political mobilization has substituted another, from structure to culture, from class to values, or from industrial society to risk society. The remainder of the national and industrial revolution now coexists with the cultural products of the postindustrial and postmodern era. Looking at recent research in political science does, for example, definitely not leave the impression that left-right materialist values do not matter any more; rather, they have become, literally, a value.[1]

On this background, it is easier to grasp the complexity of the intermediation of environmental political issues. It is possible to distinguish between the three dimensions—structure, culture, and organization. One may (1) look for changes within each dimension: a new middle class (Offe 1985; Kriesi et al. 1995), a change in values, with regard to both content (Inglehart 1990) and form (Gibbins and Reimer 1995), and the proliferation of new ways to organize protest (Dalton and Kuechler 1990); but also (2) look for changes in the relation between the elements: a new class promoting new values and a more autonomous culture independent of structural interests (Alexander 1990a). But to proceed with these kinds of analyses related to our topic, we need a more elaborated set of concepts and theories.

POLITICAL INTERMEDIATION: THE SOCIAL MOVEMENT PERSPECTIVE

What emerges is a complex picture of the political intermediation process in the late modern society—a complexity probably not captured too well by fashionable phrases such as risk society, NSMs, or ecological modernization. What we need are more elaborated and complex analytical tools to get at the multidimensionality, to put the different dimensions in connection with each other, and in the last instance, to understand what this multitude of contents and forms imply with regard to the overall political situation.

The standard political science literature has contributed substantially to the understanding of these phenomena. However, I will contend that social movement theory operating in the tracks laid down in the standard political science literature, at the moment, offers a richer and more nuanced set of concepts to fill in the framework presented earlier. Social movement theory actually sets out where the cleavage perspective ends in a distinction between structure, culture, and organizational aspects. Social movement theory offers the possibility for a more accurate understanding of what causes political mobilization and also a better possibility of interpreting political action connected to the environmental question. Thus, in this section, I present what I consider the most fruitful concepts and theories to be found in recent (theoretical) works in social movement theory. I also illustrate some of these theories with relevant empirical examples.

The situation a few years ago was such that McAdam, McCarthy, and Zald (1988) could complain about the lack of theoretical approaches on the mesolevel within social movement theory. Today, the situation is rather the opposite. The two theoretical schools that dominated the field of social movement theory for a long time (NSM theory and resource mobilization theory) motivated a lot of discussants to ask for some kind of synthesis between these positions. The results are now witnessed in a synthesis emerging as a theoretical trinity comprising structure, culture, and the organizations as autonomous actors (McAdam, McCarthy, and Zald 1996a). The structural approach is mostly couched in terms of the political opportunity structure (POS), the cultural approach as cultural framing (CF), and the organizational perspective, which is not that conceptually settled, as mobilizing structure (MS). In the three sections to follow, I present, in a rather straight forward manner, the three dimensions of current social movement theory. I then indicate how these theories may do their job as middle-range theories.

Political Opportunity Structure

Basically, the POS-perspective aims at a structural explanation of political mobilization—that is, it explains how structural phenomena motivate for politics and how the structuring of the polity constrains and constructs political action. There are different applications of the POS-concept and also different attempts to sum up what it includes. Here, I rely on the presentation by Kriesi et al. (1995) in which they distinguish between four dimensions of the concept.[2]

The first dimension is the more "old-fashioned" side of the perspective, which is oriented toward how structures and cultures are constitutive of (environmental) political identities, mobilization, and action in a nation. This is a perspective identical to the classic cleavage perspective presented earlier, and here, environmentalism (and often NSMs in general) are understood in light of four theses. One version is that it is the new middle class (or some segments of it), either out of its own interests or out of universalistic values (postmaterial or left-liberal), that is mobilized politically (Eckersley 1989; Offe 1985; Cotgrove and Duff 1980; 1981; Dunlap and Mertig 1995; Skogen 1996; Kriesi et al. 1995; Inglehart 1990; Kitschelt 1989). Missing in this approach is the possibility that environmentalism in itself represents an autonomous cleavage. Both Eckersley (1989) and Lowe and Rüdig (1986) suggest that there may take place a genuine green mobilization independent of the traditional cleavages. This way of posing the problem is theoretically most succinctly put forward by Eder (1993; 1995), who actually reverses the common way to do class analysis: structure leading to culture to culture leading to class position. In this way, he proposes that concern for nature as a specific culture somehow constitutes the core of a new field of class struggle (1993: chapter 7). As a third version, one may say that since we are all environmentalists now, environmentalism is not to be taken care of by any distinct group and it will not be found in the landscape of the "good old" cleavages. This approach is implicit in the debate on ecological modernization (Hajer 1995). A fourth "materialistic" approach is to look for a direct link between the existence of environmental problems and people being affected and politically mobilized. An interesting and more indirect version of this problematique is the contention that the environmental problems one mobilizes around have repercussions on the form of the environmental movement in question.[3]

Existing empirical studies mainly confirm the first and third interpretation. On the one hand, environmentalism as such is widespread: "[I]t is clear that awareness of environmental dangers can only account in part for membership of the more activist environmental groups" (Cotgrove and Duff 1980: 334), or in a recent study, "we are compelled to return to our earlier assessment: environmental issues tend to be everybody's concern. They are equally important to men and women, young and old, blue- and white-collar workers" (Johansson 1995: 328). On the other hand, the analysis also places environmentalism into the well-known political cleavage landscape, and Johansson concludes that:

> As to individual differences in attitudes, we found that the major influences affecting people's attitudes on the environment are their position on the left-right spectrum and their outlook on a lifestyle dimension such as materialism-postmaterialism. These effects have consistently been greater that the effects of gender, social class, and the respondent's situation in the labour market. We also found that age and educational levels are influential. (339)

The most "innovative" side of the POS-perspective focuses on how each nation's polity constrains or structures political action, and Kriesi et al. (1995) divide it into three parts: institutional structures, prevailing (informal) strategies, and alliance structures. A famous and interesting example of how the political structures of a nation do influence political action is found in Kitschelt's (1986) analysis of the antinuclear movement in France, Germany, Sweden, and the United States. Here, Kitschelt makes a distinction between the openness of the political system to new demands on the input side and the capacity of political systems to implement decisions on the output side. Different combinations of these two variables are conducive to different movement strategies (assimilative or confrontational) and influence their impact (procedural, substantive, or structural) on the political process.

In their book on NSMs in Germany, France, Switzerland, and Netherlands, Kriesi et al. (1995) emphasize the importance of informal relations and strategies as explanatory factors for political mobilization: "how structural characteristics of political systems enter the hearts and minds of movement organizers and participants" (37). They make a distinction between exclusive (repressive, confrontational, and polarizing) and integrative (facilitative, cooperative, and assimilative) strategies, which they combine with the more formal state structures and apply in analyses reminiscent of those found in Kitschelt's writings.

In looking at the "alliance structures," Kriesi et al. try to get at the less stable elements of the POS-structure. This includes "the opening up of access to participation, shift in ruling alignments, the availability of influential allies, and cleavages within and among elites" (1995: 53). Operationalizing this variable, they look at the configuration of power on the left and the presence or absence of the left in government and find that these components influence the presence and activism of NSMs. For instance, the presence of strong left organizations may help bring NSMs to the fore, but this, in the next turn, depends on the configuration between the old and the new left. Diani's (1995) study of the Italian environmental movement, in which a network perspective is applied, also shows how many less formal aspects in and around the political system are of importance for the mobilization of the environmental movement.

Cultural Framing

Gamson and Meyer (1996) complain about the difficulties in distinguishing between structural and cultural factors in analyses of social movements, but nonetheless ascribe the cultural opportunities a more volatile character than most of the structural factors. And if the POS-perspective could be said to mediate between a macro- and mesolevel, the CF-perspective might be said to contribute to an understanding of the political intermediation at a meso- and microend of the spectrum. The framing concept has its origin in Goffman's sociology, but in social movement theory, the concept has first and foremost been developed by Snow and his collaborators (Snow and Benford 1988; 1992; Snow et al. 1986). A few years later, Eder (1996b), Gerhards (1996), Johnston (1995), and Zald (1996) deliver interesting contributions. Even though the theoretical discussions regarding the CF-perspective have reached a certain level of sophistication, the empirical use of the concept is, especially for environmental questions, still in its infancy. In presenting the perspective here, I rely mainly on Snow's presentation from 1986, 1988, and 1992, which covers, more or less, three distinct themes within the cultural formation and success/failure of social movements.

The CF-approach aims, basically, to grasp the meaning or significance of social movement action in itself and in the ideological context where this meaning develops and functions. Frames are the " 'schemata of interpretation' that enable individuals 'to locate, perceive, identify, and label' occurrences within their life space and the world at large" (Snow et al. 1986: 464). In their 1986 contribution to this topic, Snow et al. are occupied with what they call frame alignment—that is, "the linkage of individual and SMO [social movement organizations'] interpretative orientations, such that some set of individual interests, values and beliefs and SMO activities, goals, and ideology are congruent and complementary" (464). This process is discussed along four different dimensions. The first is frame bridging, "the linkage of two or more ideologically congruent but structurally unconnected frames regarding a particular issue or problem" (467). Second, the frame must be given life and energy: frame amplification is a prerequisite for lifting a frame from a tedious everyday life to having the status of an important issue. The third and fourth dimensions—frame extension and frame transformation—are important in cases where the frame as it originally appears is unable to cover the actual problem.

Later, Snow and Benford are more oriented toward understanding how frames "affect the mobilising potency of a movement's framing efforts and activities," and they identify "four sets of factors" (1988: 199) that influence these more outward-directed activities. One of these factors focuses on the internal structure of the "belief system" and covers three dimensions: the *centrality* of ideational elements in relation to other elements, the *range* of elements, and the degree of *interrelatedness* among the ideational elements. A second factor addresses three "core framing tasks": to *diagnose* some events or aspects of life as problematic and in need of alteration, to *propose a solution* to the diagnosed problem, and to *motivate for action*. The third and fourth factors influencing the success or failure of environmental political action are the *phenomenological resonance* provided by the different frames and how these frames cohere to the predominant *cycles of protest*.

In the third central contribution of Snow and Benford to this problematique, they illustrate how cultural mobilizing appears in relation to what they call master frames: "What we call master frames perform the same functions as movement-specific collective action frames, but they do so on a larger scale" (1992: 138). One of the important insights here is how the activity of particular movements are bound up with the general clustering of movement activity and cycles of protests.

In relation to the environmental issue, the CF-perspective has been applied by Eder (1996b), who makes it a part of what he calls a discourse analysis of ecological communication. For Eder, it involves a set of cognitive devices and a process of symbolic packages and then it must be analyzed in relation to its master frame. In the context of this chapter, this is a very interesting application, because Eder combines the perspective of frames with what I have introduced earlier as rational differentiation. The cognitive frames have to be understood along three dimensions: empirical objectivity, moral responsibility, and aesthetic judgment. This is not the place to go into detail regarding Eder's project, but it adds up to an interesting narrative on how ecological communication takes place in a modern society.

In a more minute analysis of how different ways to value nature (ecological worldviews) may influence political action, Seippel (1997) has applied the CF-perspective. The purpose of this analysis is to see how and if ecological worldviews do matter for environmental political action. It builds a model for the understanding of different ecological worldviews as "metacultures" of our society, follows them from their alleged macrolevel existence through the different national political opportunity structures, and then focuses on how the different ecological worldviews are culturally internally constructed and how they fit into the ideological-political discourses in different countries; for example, how they (do not) cohere to left-libertarian and religious worldviews, and how they (do not) influence political action in different contexts. The study indicates that there are differences between the structural and ideological climate in different Western countries that influence whether they are open or not to an ecocentric worldview as a political force.

Organizational Aspects: Mobilizing Structures

Where the POS- and CF-perspective are mostly engaged in the structural and cultural conditions for environmental political action, the MS-perspective is more directly oriented toward the tactical repertoires and organizational forms of social movements (McCarthy 1996: 141). In many situations, the POS- and CF-perspectives may function as independent variables with regard to these more organizational aspects. I want to briefly present three approaches to this subject, with two of them reflecting distinct epochs in the history of environmentalism.

The environmental movement was an important factor in the development of NSMs. According to Offe (1985), NSMs are expressions of a new political paradigm built on four pillars: new issues, a set of values different from those pertaining to the old politics, changes in the activists' social basis (new middle-class and some marginalized groups), and the internal way to organize and the way to act externally. Dalton and Kuechler (1990), in perhaps the most central book when it comes to the explicit political dimensions of NSM theory, emphasize five factors that distinguish between the old and new social movements: ideology, origins, structure, style, and goals. In short, NSMs represented a less institutionalized form of political action, new segments of the population, a group of people, new values, and new action repertoires.

Today, the most popular story on social movements seems to be very different, if not the opposite. The theme is the institutionalization, specialization, centralization, and professionalization of the environmental movement (Eder 1996a; Jamison 1996; Diani 1997). Environmental movements as literally moving political forces have had their day. What we see today are social movement organizations (SMOs). These SMOs centralize, specialize, hire professional staff, and are more eager to collect resources from their passive members and to influence (other) elites than to inspire mass protest. And they have found their place inside the political establishment: "Ecological modernization acknowledges new actors, in particular environmental organizations and to a lesser extent local residents" (Hajer 1995: 29).

Taken together, these two stories seem to validate a third kind of theory, originating from Michels's (1962) classic account of how political parties meet the oligarchical tendencies of political organizations, and thereafter (less well known from the last chapter of Michels's book) develop into a "new" and less institutionalized movement. That this actually happens, is at least partly confirmed in a stream of new and more activist environmental movements—as, for example, protests against the construction of new roads in England (Radtke 1997). In short, political and environmental movements seem to live a life according to attention cycles (Downs 1972) or movement cycles (Brand 1990; Tarrow 1994), and as they come and go, institutionalization sparks of radical action and radical action inevitably seems to turn into institutional forms. But, more specifically, how this process proceeds is probably to a large degree determined by political opportunity structures and cultural frames.

What is gained through these different contributions to environmental political sociology is a more nuanced picture of how environmentalism is, or potentially will be, put forth as an issue, mediated through structures and cultures, organized, and eventually acted on. Taken together, we have a framework that makes it possible to explain and interpret some of the political aspects of the environmental problems better than for instance Beck's rather crude theory of risk society, the theories of NSMs, or the ecological modernization perspective. In short, a theoretical apparatus is set forth that makes it possible to challenge the general theories both from a theoretical middle-range position and on the basis of empirical data. The purpose of presenting these concepts and theories are twofold. First, the aim is to make some of the themes of environmental sociology more suitable to empirical analyses. Second, the (opposite) aim is to comment on the general macroperspective of the field from this more analytically nuanced meso- and microperspective.

The theories presented in this last section have different foci and function at or between different societal levels. And even though, as I have tried to illustrate, there are well-established relations between some of the variables included in my presentation, there is much more to gain for an environmental sociology in trying to sort out relationships between these variables—an effort that will probably improve both the explanations and interpretations of the development of environmental issues as political questions. My purpose in the next section, however, is to move back toward some of the general theories dominating the field of environmental sociology and to see how some of the dimensions and concepts presented so far in this chapter could improve the understanding of the political dimensions of these general theories.

GENERAL THEORY IN LIGHT OF MIDDLE-RANGE THEORIES: RISK SOCIETY AND ECOCENTRIC VALUES

The purpose for this reordering and presentation of theories has been, first, to contribute to the understanding of how environmental issues turn into political problems in general. Second, the aim has been to contribute to a better understanding of the political dimensions of some of the most popular and abstract contributions within environmental sociology through the application of middle-range theories. To achieve this, I have presented a general framework of modern society as functionally and rationally differentiated. Next, I have looked more in detail on the political construction of issues in general and environmental issues in particular through the concepts of cleavages, political opportunity structure, cultural framing, and mobilizing structures. In this last section, I illustrate how these approaches may contribute to a more nuanced understanding of the political dimensions of two of the most famous and predominant attempts to understand the relation between society and the environment within environmental sociology and philosophy. Where possible, I also illustrate my theoretical points through empirical examples.

Risk Society and Reflexive Modernization

Beck's (1986) thesis is that two processes—the prevalence of risks and the process of individualization (detraditionalization)—together generate a genuine new social dynamics that paves the way for a new social formation: risk society. The looser grip of structures and traditional cultures and the many risks proliferating make it clear to the modern individual that the institutions of industrial society are not able to steer the development of late modern society according to the expectations raised within this society and, consequently, that these institutions are not natural or unchangeable. The result is a change in political communication and action, and, in the end, also the political institutions. The conventional political system appears as less legitimate and this leads to an increased politicization of a maze of different issues within nonpolitical social arenas, first and foremost civil society, and this new politics—or subpolitics—is qualitatively different from conventional politics, both in content and form.

In moving the political momentum outside traditional politics, Beck gains in rationality. He attacks the insufficiency of objective and instrumental criteria, suggests new objective criteria and lines of conflict to redirect political action—gender, nature, and technology (Beck 1993)—and introduces normative and aesthetic arguments to the environmental discourse. It is worth noticing, however, that Beck himself is accused of ignoring both the aesthetic and the normative dimensions of reflection confronting the risk problematique (Lash and Urry 1994; Lash 1994). What is probably more correct is to say that Beck ignores the unavoidable constitutive cultural dimensions of any form of rationality and reflection—the cultural embeddedness of social interaction—and thereby overstates the potential for rationality as such (Alexander and Smith 1996). Second, what Beck loses sight of through his maneuvers is a proper balance between these forms of rationality, in Habermas's terms, between lifeworld and systems. Third, Beck has a poor understanding of how the "new" institutions representing what Lash (1994: 120) ironically calls "nonsocial structures" may have a function (see Junge 1996). The fundamental question is how moving the political outside the conventional political system can still contribute to the function of politics—implementing collectively binding decisions—without giving in to undemocratic interests, values, or modes of action. In short, Beck's political agents gain perspective by invoking different forms of rationality but have an unrealistic trust in the social functioning of their new won rational capabilities. Blurring the boundaries between political institutions and civil society also involves, normatively, a more risky project than is discernible in Beck's writings. A last unanswered challenge is the possibility of losing both with regard to social and ecological functionality in substituting politics by subpolitics.

The first dimension in the POS-perspective tries to capture how political action is based in the basic cleavages of a nation-state. The key principle in Beck's writings is probably that the cleavages constitutive of the politics of industrial society lose in power, the fights for material gains lose in importance, and the traditional sets of values lose their legitimacy and attraction. In short, in risk society, the constitution

of politics takes place in an arena not marked by the conflicts predominant in industrial society. But instead of introducing new sets of values—as for instance Inglehart's postmaterial values—Beck contends that risk society is marked by a more
thorough drive for reflection. It wins in rationality, but again, it leaves the consequences of these possibilities rather undescribed in the shadow.

There are three more dimensions to the POS-perspective: institutional structures,
prevailing strategies, and alliance structures. Empirical analyses show that these
dimensions are important factors in explaining political action and that they differ
between countries otherwise similar (Kitschelt 1986; Rucht 1994; Kriesi et al.
1995). This point, that there are important mesofactors with regard to political
action, is mostly ignored by Beck, who seems to think that political mobilization
proceeds only according to the macrostructural changes he himself has identified.

The main point here is, nevertheless, not to argue against Beck's thesis by saying
that subpoliticization will not take place, but rather to indicate that there are more
factors that influence this political process than those occupying Beck. If Beck's
prospects come true, they will have to take place in a certain political landscape,
and there are so many and divergent factors determining the outcome of political
mobilization that it is very unlikely that what Beck calls subpoliticization will occur
in similar ways and have the same social and political functions in different (though
similar) countries.

Cultural framing is a perspective that makes it possible to grasp how the ideological elements of political action are made up, how they cohere to other ideological
elements, and how they may influence social interaction in other social systems.
And, as the structural and traditional cultural cleavages decrease in importance, the
more important will the genuine or autonomous cultural frames become. Snow et
al. (1986) emphasize how the internal construction of different frames and their
external relations to other structural and ideological factors are important prerequisites for political mobilization. Beck's reflexive modernization, none the less, seems
to remain rather empty and without concrete cultural content or surroundings. Beck
is rather exclusively occupied with how the cultural climate shifts and, in his perspective, how it tends toward being a shift in forms without a specific content.

The "modern" critique of political action in a postmodern perspective is that it
is so afraid of excluding "the other" that it forgets to include itself and to install its
own vision of a better society, and the fact that to act according to principles
includes exclusion (White 1991; Haber 1994). This critique seems to go for Beck
as well. It remains unclear what his reflexive subpoliticizing is to aim at and consist
of and how it is to line up with other existing ideologies and social systems. And also,
when it comes to these cultural dimensions of environmentalism, there are decisive
differences between otherwise similar late modern societies that will probably have
severe consequences for how risk communication will proceed.

The first wave of environmentalism brought with it a certain kind of enthusiasm
with regard to the future of environmental movements; they were new, both with
regard to their constituency, their values, their action repertoire, and their internal
organization. Two decades later or so, one seems more eager to focus on the institu-

tionalization of environmentalism than on its genuine vitality (Eder 1996a; Jamison 1996; Diani 1997). This institutionalization will (and somewhere already has) probably sparked off some more provocative and less institutionalized movements in the next round. However, Beck's understanding of the organizational aspects of the subpoliticization of risk society is reminiscent of the theories of NSMs: a never ending movement avoiding the institutionalization that seems to occur in most other settings. Again, Beck comes up against an impasse when he, contrary to most theoretical and empirical research, insists on his political mobilization to be genuinely uninstitutionalized and, at the same time as he declares his politicization to be subpolitical, also claims that it will be capable of carrying out important social functions without the negative effects stemming from conventional politics institutionalization.

To strengthen the relevance of these theoretical and critical comments on Beck's risk society and his thesis of a reflexive modernization, it is tempting to refer to some recent empirical research. Looking to the Beliefs in Government project (Kaase and Newton 1995), it seems obvious that Beck's "findings" are only partially true. First, the legitimacy of modern political systems does not seem to falter as Beck suggests.[4] Second, the influence of cleavages do change character and the constellation among structure, culture, and organization is more volatile, but we are not witnessing the disappearance of the left-right value.[5] Third, Beck is confirmed because there seems to be a steady growth in the unconventional forms of political action.[6] Finally, this new political action does seem, as time goes by, to tend toward institutionalization, professionalization, specialization, and more conventional ways to work politically.[7] New political action may still be innovative with regard to political content (issues and values), but it seems to lose its organizational newness with the passing of time.

The purpose of these comments has not been to reject Beck's insights, which I consider stimulating, important, and partly correct. But what is needed to understand (and to contribute to) this process—the politicization of the environmental problems—is to develop a more subtle set of concepts and theories. In this way, it will be possible to see more in detail how the process of modernization and the presence of environmental problems may, in interaction as Beck emphasizes, be conducive to political mobilization.

Ecocentrism As a Political Ideology

The natural environment is omnipresent, and thereby, as a problem, also invites a totalizing critique. Consequently, a great deal of attention has been devoted to the question of whether there is something fundamentally flawed with modern society. One popular answer to this question takes the form of discussions of the culture underpinning modern society: What is it like and what should it be like? A central contribution to this debate consists of a distinction between a deep and shallow ecology, and between anthropocentric and ecocentric worldviews. Naess distinguishes between "the Shallow Ecology movement" that fights "against pollution and resource depletion" with "the health and affluence of people in developed countries" as their central objective and "the Deep Ecology movement" with a much broader and deeper commitment. The latter rejects "the man-in-environment image in favor of the relational, total-field image" and endorses a "biospherical egalitarianism," "principles of diversity and of symbiosis," and so on (1973: 95–96). The more or less tacit assumptions in the ecocentric discourse is that our culture and its values will have an impact on consciousness and action,[8] including political action. And, as argued, this will have a decisive impact on the overall development of society and nature (Eckersley 1992).

In terms of differentiation, the ecocentric critique of the modernization process takes many forms. On the one hand, there is a tendency to criticize the process of functional differentiation as such and to idealize traditional, whole, and well-integrated societies. On the other hand, ecocentrism is a critique of the hegemony of instrumental reason characteristic of the process of modernization, and environmental philosophy supports "alternative rationalities" along both a normative and an aesthetic line. From a sociological point of view, such critiques are relevant even though they are often put forward in a sociologically rather unsophisticated way. The problem is that the positive consequences of societal differentiation are mostly taken for granted or neglected and the negative consequences of a return to a traditional society is not put on the agenda (Helbling 1992). This shallow understanding of deep cultures is reflected in the understanding of the function of the ecological worldviews ecocentrists promote: "[T]oday's dominant culture will inevitably decline and will eventually disintegrate. The cultural forces representing the new paradigm, on the other hand, will continue to rise and, eventually, will assume the leading role" (Capra 1995: 25). This way of understanding culture is close to the understanding within Parsons's sociology, where culture is seen as a prerequisite for social action: "Human actions system is not possible without relatively stable symbolic systems where meaning is not predominantly contingent on highly particularized situations" (1951: 11). But in addition to stressing that social interaction takes place within a more or less common social definition of situations, Parsons also observes that social interaction takes place within different social systems. To secure the basic integration of such a differentiated society, Parsons thinks there must be a basic set of values, a culture, whose function is "to control and regulate the other subsystems of the more comprehensive action system" (Schmid 1992: 93). What makes this approach appear unsatisfactory today is obvious from the critique Parsons's sociology has met with. What is necessary to comprehend the potential role of culture in late modern society is basically to pay attention to the warning given by Archer that the Parsonian perspective represents a "Myth of Cultural Integration" (1990: 116).[9] Where Parsons and environmental philosophy seems to take the existence of a common and functionally significant culture as self-evident, more recent contributions to the sociology of culture seem to stress the complexity of modern society and thus the complexity of its culture: multitudinous contents and forms functioning at and between different societal levels. What is essential for understanding the influence of particular ecological worldviews is a perspective that makes it possible to see how a culture—as it is invoked in the environmental discourse—actually operates in a late modern society: "[J]ustice cannot be understood in terms of abstract criteria and transcendental principles. It must be theorised from within the cultural practices of particular spheres of life. Social movements that ignore these structures encourage the domination and violence that has characterized the degenerate line of twentieth-century life" (Alexander 1990b: 28).

The most striking feature when it comes to the cleavage understanding of these ecological worldviews is their absence.[10] For the ecocentrists, the point is less to describe recent social changes as in risk society than to point out a cultural heritage common to all modern worldviews, since ecocentrists mostly consider themselves to move beyond structure and traditional cultures. The enemy is industrialism as such (Dobson 1990), rather than a specific part of it, and left and right are just as inadequate, as is religion, or at least some strands of Christianity (White 1967). This makes ecocentrism vulnerable to the critique that ecocentrists ignore (material) conflicts, and claiming without further ado that they represent the right and good, ecocentrists make it irresistible for sociologists to question who the "deep" actually are and what interests they actually are out to protect (Luke 1988).

As with Beck, the ecocentrists are not going into detail with regard to how the political opportunity structures of different countries will affect their influence, even though Naess (1995) on some occasions makes some optimistic remarks on the possibility of joining other ideologies. This raises the question—which is central to the POS-perspective—of the chances for making allies, and there are at least four relevant conditions for the chances of ecocentrism to succeed in this task. First, the environmental movement in most modern countries is a mixture of more traditional conservation movements and more modern political ecology movements, and there are possibilities for and problems with making allies in both directions. Second, "we are all environmentalists now" and it is difficult to find a mobilizing distinction that makes a difference. Third, there is taking place a process of differentiation within the environmental movement that both promotes and hinders political mobilization along more restricted environmental ideologies. Finally, there are differences with regard to how the general political cultures of different countries are structured. A question of relevance for the ecocentric movement (often couched in terms of animal rights) is, for example, how central the concept of rights is in the political culture of a certain nation (Tarrow 1996: 50).

The analytical sociological rejoinder to the ecocentric debate within environmental philosophy is, as with risk society, not that they are wrong in promoting a specific value, but that their understanding of the context within which their value exists and has to make its way is incomplete, and that a weak understanding may foster a political-ethical mobilization that is counterproductive to the ends at the basis of the ecocentrists' project: to ensure the self-realization of creatures through the ascription of intrinsic value to all (or most) living beings.

The message to be learned from modern cultural sociology is that there are many distinct cultures, with regard to content and form, and levels and scopes of influence. And to understand the function of an ecological worldview, it must be analyzed within this modern setting. According to Snow et al. (1986), one imperative for a culture successfully leading toward political mobilization is its ability to align different frames. That is, the ideology must in itself be able to connect different elements into a convincing whole. At present, I suggest that an ecocentric position does hold a hard and attractive core, but with less obvious ideological ramifications or practical consequences; it is not obvious what follows—and this goes for political questions as well as many other questions—from the insight that all living creatures have intrinsic value. A second cultural necessity is to interact and to relate one's ideology to the overall ideological field of modern culture. Again, a certain ambiguity is the result. There are no obvious patterns where the ecocentrists can connect, make allies or enemies, and create a difference that has an impact. A third prerequisite is that the ideology one promotes must have a certain resonance within some of the cultural master frames predominant in modern society, mass media, culture, politics, or economics.

And as in the discussions of subpoliticizing, there is a quest for radicalism within the ecocentric discourse that often points beyond normal organizations. What is needed is a consciousness of nature and a mode of being that transcends the modern hierarchical organization—that is, a change from below.

The conclusion once more seems to become that the lack of analytical understanding within the ecocentric discourse leads the discourse toward a deceptive understanding of how the values one promotes actually function and how they will have to struggle to gain an impact. And while risk society furthers reflection without a specific content, the ecocentrists may be said to promote a content without form and beyond reflection. Beck sets out to decipher trends inherent in the process of modernization and from this extract a mixture of descriptive and prescriptive principles that will lead the further modernization of risk society in a good direction. The ecocentrists, on the other hand, have detected what they see as the main problem of modern society and from this infer what they consider to be a normative necessity for an ecologically sound future world.

The point is not that the ecocentrists are wrong, that our culture is unproblematic, or that a shift in values will not lead to a better world, but that modern society is more than culture and values and that there are more values than those valuing or devaluing nature, and probably more values valuing nature than anthropocentric and ecocentric values.[11] What is important to keep in mind as analytical sociologists is that ecocentrism and the values it promotes are a phenomenon that should be described and understood in the context of modern society, and eventually, as a political phenomenon, as a movement within the context given in this chapter.

CONCLUSION

The general purpose of this chapter has been to contribute to the theoretical understanding of the political aspects of environmental problems in a modern society through the introduction of middle-range concepts and theories from political sociology and social movement theory. As a background, I chose to direct Merton's critique against the sociology of the 1960s of being either too oriented toward general theory or too involved in a theoretical empirical research, rather than toward current environmental sociology. The preoccupation with general theories and abstract concepts do generate important insights in many aspects of the social dimension of environmental problems, but, at the moment, I think that environmental sociology would profit from a change in viewpoint from a macrolevel toward theories on a meso- or microlevel. My intention was not to depreciate the value of a general and abstract environmental sociology, but to strengthen a somewhat closed discourse by confronting it with other relevant theories.

This chapter, then, represents an attempt to contribute to this endeavor in one more specific field: the theme of how environmental issues are politicized. First, I introduced some general perspectives on the process of modernization—that is, functional differentiation versus differentiation of three forms of rationality. In this way, it became possible to relate and confront the different abstract theoretical approaches with each other and to relate them to the chosen middle-range theories. Second, I presented some of the most famous contributions to my problematique from political sociology. Through a discussion of the concept of cleavages, central to most political sociology, I presented different theoretical elements, mostly from recent contributions to social movement theory, that were intended to cover the mesolevel of environmental political mobilization and action. This was the main purpose of the chapter and it proceeded along three lines.

First, I drew on the concept of political opportunity structure, which gave interesting perspectives on how the environmental issue may turn into a political issue along the traditional cleavages of modern society, and more specifically, as a political issue inside the constraints set up by the political structures of different nations: institutional structures, prevailing (informal) strategies, and alliance structures. Empirical studies have shown that these variables actually do explain many of the differences between the forms and contents of environmental political action in different countries. As an "alternative" to the many abstract theories within environmental sociology, these differences between countries otherwise considered rather similar point to the lack of explanatory and interpretative power of many of the most famous contributions to environmental sociology. The presence of environmental risks interacting with the process of detraditionalization, as in Beck's risk society, explains only to a limited degree the concrete content and form of the politicization of environmental issues. Blaming the culture of modern society as such for the environmental problems does not further fruitful sociological understandings of the social and political dimensions of the environmental problems.

Second, the concept of cultural framing was applied to get at the ideological dimensions of the political processes where environmental issues are raised. I emphasized three aspects of this perspective: how an "environmental frame" is made up by aligning different ideological elements, how the quality of the elements making up this frame are of the utmost importance for the political mobilization, and how an environmental frame is bound to make its way in the landscape of the "master frames" of a certain place and period. I referred to some attempts to apply this perspective, even though it is probably right to say that this perspective is empirically less developed than the POS-perspective. As a critique of abstract environmental sociology, it gives important insights into the question of how cultural mobilizing actually can or has to take place, and, comparing the thesis of risk society to the deep ecology perspective, it provides insight on how cultural frames vacillate between being couched exclusively in terms of form (risk society) and content (eco-centrism).

The third perspective I presented is more directly applicable to the movement organization itself, first and foremost its organizational form and repertoire of action. I showed how the understanding of social movements has shifted during two periods (from the NSM theory to the institutionalization of movements) and how this shift probably strengthens a third theoretical position: that political mobilization moves in a dialectical fashion between institutionalization and more genuine unin-stitutionalized movements. This perspective also raises skepticism with regard to the understanding of political mobilization often proffered within environmental sociol-ogy where different functional prerequisites are not very well reflected.

My presentation of middle-range theories in this chapter became a listing of con-cepts and theories. I referred to some applications of these concepts and some exam-ples of how they make up, more literally, theories. There is, nevertheless, much more to win from these concepts and theories when it comes to understanding that these environmental issues as political than I have been able to show in this chapter. This goes both for the middle-range theories at their own level, but also with regard to how they may contribute to the general approaches dominating environmental soci-ology. Another important task for those working with these concepts will be to employ them in empirical analyses, and thereafter, to provide good empirical data. Empirical data then, ideally and typically, should be lifted to the relevant theoretical level where it can contribute further to the process of establishing a more general and abstract environmental sociology.

NOTES

1. An illustration of this point is found in Knutsen and Scarbrough (1995), where they distinguish between a "true" cleavage politics comprising structure, culture, and organization and what they (somewhat equivocally) call a "value cleavage," where the cultural engagement is less firmly connected to structural position. Their conclusion as a whole, however, is that "the basis of party choice is more stable than suggested by 'new politics' accounts" (519).

2. In four points, McAdam (1996b: 27) sums up the POS-position in what he calls a "highly consensual list": (1) the relative openness or closure of the institutionalized political system, (2) the stability or instability of that broad set of elite alignments that typically under-gird a polity, (3) the presence or absence of elite allies, and (4) the state's capacity and propen-sity for repression.

3. "In environmental movements, there is a clear division between movements fighting about particular projects and facilities—nuclear installations, industrial plants, toxic waste disposal, and so on—and efforts to develop and legislate long-term environmental policies

that take into account the temporal and substantive complexity of the subject matter. While project-oriented environmentalists stay close to the direct democratic movement structures, long-term ecological policymaking is usually developed by often highly i.e. ecological interest groups, research institutions, and even parties." See Kitschelt (1993: 26–27).

4. "But the most important point is a simple one: there is no pervasive or general trend towards decreasing satisfaction with the way democracy works in the member states of the European Union between 1976 and 1991." See Kaase and Newton (1995: 61). "The citizens of West European countries have not withdrawn support from their democracies in recent decades. This holds true for both democracy as a form of constitutionally defined government and for the reality of democracy." See Fuchs and Klingemann (1995: 435). "Satisfaction with the way democracy works, trust in government, attachments to the status quo—none of these touchstones of democratic politics appear to have declined any further after the late 1960s. Thus the shifts in value orientation evident over recent decades seem to have missed one of their major targets: the national state." See van Deth and Scarbrough (1995: 528).

5. "First and foremost, we found strong evidence of left-right materialist orientations at the level of the mass public. Such orientations are manifest in all the surveys examined, and there is evidence from many countries that the items which tap left-right materialists are strongly constrained. There is no tendency for left-right materialist items to be less constrained in advanced industrial societies, although there is strong evidence for class de-alignment. In other words, left-right materialist orientations appear to be highly constrained in advanced industrial societies, although their anchoring in specific social groups seems to have declined." See Knutsen (1995: 193–194).

6. "However, rejecting the challenge hypothesis does not mean that there was no change in the relationship between citizens and the state. Citizens have become more demanding and more critical towards politicians and parties. Above all, citizens have developed the capacity and the readiness, to back up their demand by using the entire range of their potential for action." See Fuchs and Klingemann (1995: 435–436).

7. "[W]hat was once a radical, even revolutionary, system-transcendent message has now been transformed into the different and institutionally separated aspects of multinational environmentalism." See Jamison (1996: 241).

8. These discussions try to depict what Devall and Sessions call "a crisis of *character* and of *culture*" (1985: ix, emphasis added), that is, there are two ways to elaborate further on this position sociologically. One is to focus on the "character-part" of the problem, a project that leads toward the question of self-realization and a Heideggerian-inspired critique of the modern modes of being. The other focuses on culture and values and is the one I follow here.

9. Other critical points to be taken seriously are made by Parsons's own "followers"—culture is not to be understood as pregiven (Geertz 1973); culture is not necessarily a coherent whole (Smelser 1992); culture may have different functions, disintegrating as well as integrating (Eisenstadt 1995); and culture may be put to use more strategically (Swidler 1986).

10. Or, if one likes, the introduction of a new latent cleavage that actually is at the basis of all the other and more superficial cleavages.

11. Interesting discussions on this "sources of the self" and metacultures—in which metacultures are to be found within a modern society—are presented in Taylor (1989) and Tiryakian (1996). In this context, it is interesting to note that they both operate with "cultures" that are reminiscent of those found inside the environmental philosophy, but that they both also supplement these with a religious metaculture.

224   *Ørnulf Seippel*

REFERENCES

Alexander, Jeffrey C. 1990a. "Analytic debates: Understanding the Relative Autonomy of Culture." In *Culture and Society: Contemporary Debates*, ed. J. Alexander and S. Seidmans. Cambridge: Cambridge University Press.

———. 1990b. "Between Progress and Apocalypse: Social Theory and the Dream of Reason in the Twentieth Century." In *Rethinking Progress: Movements, Forces, and Ideas at the End of the 20th Century*, ed. J. Alexander and P. Sztompka. Boston: Unwin Human.

———. 1990c. "Differentiation Theory: Problems and Prospects." In *Differentiation Theory and Social Change: Comparative and Historical Perspectives*, ed. J. Alexander and P. Colomy. New York: Columbia University Press.

Alexander, Jeffrey C., and Philip Smith. 1996. "Social Science and Salvation: Risk Society As Mythical Discourse." *Zeitschrift für Soziologie* 25:251–262.

Archer, Margaret S. 1990. *Culture and Agency: The Place of Culture in Social Theory*. New York: Cambridge University Press.

Bartolini, Stefano, and Peter Mair. 1990. *Identity, Competition, and Electoral Availability*. Cambridge: Cambridge University Press.

Bauman, Zygmunt. 1989. *Modernity and the Holocaust*. Cambridge: Polity.

———. 1991. *Modernity and Ambivalence*. Cambridge: Polity.

———. 1993. *Postmodern Ethics*. Oxford: Blackwell.

———. 1995. *Life in Fragments. Essays in Postmodern Morality*. Oxford: Blackwell.

Beck, Ulrich. 1986. *Risikogesellschaft: Auf dem Weg in eine andere Moderne*. Frankfurt: Suhrkamp. (English edition: *Risk Society: Towards a New Modernity*. London: Sage, 1992).

———. 1988. *Gegengifte: Die organisierte Unverantwortlichkeit*. Frankfurt: Suhrkamp. (English edition: *Ecological Politics in an Age of Risk*. Cambridge: Polity, 1995).

———. 1993. *Die Erfindung des Politischen: Zu einer Theorie reflexiver Modernisierung*. Frankfurt: Suhrkamp. (English edition: *The Renaissance of Politics*. Oxford: Polity, 1996).

Brand, Karl-Werner. 1990. "Cyclical Aspects of New Social Movements: Waves of Cultural Criticism and Mobilization Cycles of New Middle-Class Radicalism." In *Challenging the Political Order: New Social and Political Movements in Western Democracies*, ed. R. Dalton and M. Kuechler. Cambridge: Polity.

Capra, Fritjof. 1995. "Deep Ecology: A New Paradigm." In *Deep Ecology for the Twenty-first Century*, ed. G. Sessions. Boston: Shambhala.

Cohen, Jean L., and Andrew Arato. 1992. *Civil Society and Political Theory*. Cambridge: MIT Press.

Colomy, Paul. 1990. "Revisions and Progress in Differentiation Theory." In *Differentiation Theory and Social Change: Comparative and Historical Perspectives*, ed. J. Alexander and P. Colomy. New York: Columbia University Press.

Cotgrove, Stephen, and Andrew Duff. 1980. "Environmentalism, Middle-Class Radicalism and Politics." *Sociological Review* 28:333–351.

———. 1981. "Environmentalism, Values, and Social Change." *British Journal of Sociology* 32:92–110.

Dalton, Russell J., and Manfred Kuechler, eds. 1990. *Challenging the Political Order: New Social and Political Movements in Western Democracies*. New York: Oxford University Press.

Devall, Bill, and George Sessions. 1985. *Deep Ecology*. Salt Lake City, Utah: Smith.

Diani, Mario. 1995. *Green Networks: A Structural Analysis of the Italian Environmental Movement*. Edinburgh: Edinburgh University Press.

———. 1997. "Organizational Change and Communications Styles in Western European

Environmental Organizations." Paper presented at the Twenty-fifth European Consortium for Political Research Joint Sessions of Workshops, Bern, Switzerland, February 27–March 4.

Dickens, Peter. 1996. *Reconstructing Nature: Alienation, Emancipation and the Division of Labour.* London: Routledge.

Dobson, Andrew. 1990. *Green Political Thought: An Introduction.* London: Unwin Hyman.

Downs, A. 1972. "Up and down with Ecology—the Issue Attention Cycle." *The Public Interest* 2:38–50.

Dunlap, Riley E., and William R. Catton Jr. 1979. "Environmental Sociology." *Annual Review of Sociology* 5:243–273.

Dunlap, Riley E., and Angela G. Mertig. 1995. "Global Concern for the Environment: Is Affluence a Prerequisite?" *Journal of Social Issues* 51:121–137.

Eckersley, Robyn. 1989. "Green Politics and the New Class: Selfishness or Virtue?" *Political Studies* 37:205–223.

———. 1992. *Environmentalism and Political Theory: Toward an Ecocentric Approach.* London: UCL Press.

Eder, Klaus. 1990. "The Cultural Code of Modernity and the Problem of Nature: A Critique of the Naturalistic Notion of Progress." In *Rethinking Progress: Movements, Forces, and Ideas at the End of the 20th Century.* Boston: Unwin Human.

———. 1993. *The New Politics of Class: Social Movements and Cultural Dynamics in Advanced Societies.* London: Sage.

———. 1995. "Does Social Class Matter in the Study of Social Movements? A Theory of Middle-Class Radicalism." In *Social Movements and Social Classes: The Future of Collective Action.*, ed. L. Maheu. London: Sage.

———. 1996a. "The Institutionalisation of Environmentalism: Ecological Discourse and the Second Transformation of the Public." In *Risk, Environment and Modernity: Towards a New Ecology*, ed. S. Lash, B. Szerszynski, and B. Wynne. London: Sage.

———. 1996b. *The Social Construction of Nature: A Sociology of Ecological Enlightenment.* London: Sage.

Eisenstadt, S. N. 1995. *Power, Trust, Meaning: Essays in Sociological Theory and Analysis.* Chicago: University of Chicago Press.

Featherstone, Mike. 1991. *Consumer Culture and Postmodernism.* London: Sage.

Flanagan, Scott C. 1982. "Changing Values in Advanced Industrial Societies: Inglehart's Silent Revolution from the Perspective of Japanese Findings." *Comparative Political Studies* 14:403–444.

Fuchs, Dieter, and Hans-Dieter Klingemann. 1995. "Citizens and the State: A Relationship Transformed." In *Citizens and the State*, ed. H.-D. Klingemann and D. Fuchs. Oxford: Oxford University Press.

Gamson, William A., and David S. Meyer. 1996. "Framing Political Opportunity." In *Comparative Perspectives on Social Movements: Political Opportunities, Mobilizing Structures, and Cultural Framings*, ed. D. McAdam, J. McCarthy, and M. Zald. Cambridge: Cambridge University Press.

Geertz, Clifford. 1973. *The Interpretation of Cultures: Selected Essays.* London: Fontana.

Gerhards, Jürgen. 1996. "Framing Dimensions and Framing Strategies: Contrasting Ideal- and Real-Type Frames." *Social Science Information* 34:225–248.

Gibbins, John, and Bo Reimer. 1995. "Postmodernism." In *The Impact of Values*, ed. J. W. van Deth and E. Scarbrough. Oxford: Oxford University Press.

226   *Ørnulf Seippel*

Gramling, Robert, and William R. Freudenburg. 1996. "Environmental Sociology: Toward a Paradigm for the 21st Century." *Sociological Spectrum* 16:347–371.

Haber, Honi Fern. 1994. *Beyond Postmodern Politics: Lyotard, Rorty, Foucault.* New York: Routledge.

Habermas, Jürgen. 1982. "A Reply to My Critics." In *Habermas: Critical Debates*, ed. J. B. Thompson and D. Held. London: Macmillan.

———. 1992. *Faktizität und Geltung. Beiträge zur Diskurstheorie des Rechts und des demokratischen Rechtsstaats.* Frankfurt: Suhrkamp.

Hajer, Maarten A. 1995. *The Politics of Environmental Discourse: Ecological Modernization and the Policy Process.* Oxford: Clarendon.

Hannigan, John A. 1995. *Environmental Sociology: A Social Constructivist Perspective.* London: Routledge.

Heath, Joseph. 1996. "Rational Choice As Critical Theory." *Philosophy and Social Criticism* 22:43–62.

Helbling, Jürg. 1992. "Ökologie und Politik in nicht-staatlichen Gesellschaften. Oder: Wie steht es mit der Naturverbundenheit sogenannter Naturvölker." *Kölner Zeitschrift für Soziologie und Sozialpsychologie* 44:203–225.

Heller, Agnes, and Ferenc Feher. 1988. *The Postmodern Political Condition.* Cambridge: Polity.

Inglehart, Ronald. 1977. *The Silent Revolution: Changing Values and Political Styles among Western Publics.* Princeton, N.J.: Princeton University Press.

———. 1990. *Culture Shift in Advanced Industrial Society.* Princeton, N.J.: Princeton University Press.

Jameson, Fredric. 1991. *Postmodernism: The Cultural Logic of Late-Capitalism.* London: Verso.

Jamison, Andrew. 1996. "The Shaping of the Global Environmental Agenda: The Role of Non-governmental Organisations." In *Risk, Environment and Modernity: Towards a New Ecology*, ed. S. Lash, B. Szerszynski, and B. Wynne. London: Sage.

Johansson, Olaf. 1995. "Protecting the Environment." In *The Scope of Government*, ed. O. Borre and E. Scarbrough. Oxford: Oxford University Press.

Johnston, Hank. 1995. "A Methodology for Frame Analysis: From Discourse to Cognitive Schemata." In *Social Movements and Culture*, ed. H. Johnston and B. Klandermans. London: UCL Press.

Junge, Matthias. 1996. "Individualisierungsprozesse und der Wandel von Institutionen: Ein Beitrag zur Theorie reflexiver Modernisierung." *Kölner Zeitschrift für Soziologie und Sozialpsychologie* 48:728–747.

Kaase, Mas, and Kenneth Newton. 1995. *Beliefs in Government.* Oxford: Oxford University Press.

Kitschelt, Herbert. 1986. "Political Opportunity Structures and Political Protest: Antinuclear Movements in Four Democracies." *British Journal of Political Science* 16:57–85.

———. 1989. *The Logics of Party Formation: Ecological Politics in Belgium and West Germany.* Ithaca, N.Y.: Cornell University Press.

———. 1993. "Social Movements, Political Parties, and Democratic Theory." In *Citizens, Protest and Democracy*, ed. R. Dalton. Newbury Park, Calif.: Sage.

———. 1994. *Transformation of European Social Democracy.* Cambridge: Cambridge University Press.

Knutsen, Oddbjørn. 1995. "Left-Right Materialist Value Orientation." In *The Impact of Values*, ed. J. van Deth and E. Scarbrough. Oxford: Oxford University Press.

Knutsen, Oddbjørn, and Elinor Scarbrough. 1995. "Cleavage Politics." In *The Impact of Values*, ed. J. van Deth and E. Scarbrough. Oxford: Oxford University Press.

Kriesi, Hanspeter, Ruud Koopmans, Jan Willem Duyvendak, and Marco G. Giugni. 1995. *New Social Movements in Western Europe: A Comparative Analysis*. Minneapolis: University of Minnesota Press.

Lash, Scott. 1994. "Reflexivity and Its Doubles: Structure, Aesthetics, Community." In *Reflexive Modernization: Politics, Tradition and Aesthetics in the Modern Social Order*, ed. U. Beck, A. Giddens, and S. Lash. Cambridge: Polity.

Lash, Scott, and John Urry. 1994. *Economies of Signs and Space*. London: Sage.

Lipset, Seymour M., and Stein Rokkan. 1967. "Cleavage Structures, Party Systems, and Voter Alignments: An Introduction." In *Party Systems and Voter Alignments*, ed. S. Lipset and S. Rokkan. New York: The Free Press.

Lowe, Philip D., and Wolfgang Rüdig. 1989. "Review Article: Political Ecology and the Social Sciences—the State of Art." *British Journal of Political Science* 16:513–550.

Luhmann, Niklas. 1970. *Soziologsche Aufklärung 1*. Opladen: Westdeutscher Verlag.

———. 1976. "Generalized Media and the Problem of Contingency." In *Explorations in General Theory in Social Science: Essays in Honor of Talcott Parsons*, ed. J. Loubser et al. New York: The Free Press.

———. 1986. *Ökologische Kommunikation: Kann die moderne Gesellschaft sich auf ökologische Gefährdungen einstellen?* Opladen: Westdeutscher Verlag.

———. 1987. *Soziale Systeme. Grundriß einer allgemeinen Theorie*. Frankfurt: Suhrkamp.

———. 1990. *Political Theory in the Welfare State*. Trans. John Bednarz Jr. Berlin: de Gruyere.

———. 1994. "Politicians, Honesty and the Higher Amorality of Politics." *Theory, Culture and Society* l:25–36.

Luke, Tim. 1988. "The Dreams of Deep Ecology." *Telos* 76:65–93.

Maffesoli, Michel. 1996. *The Time of the Tribes: The Decline of Individualism in Mass Society*. London: Sage.

McAdam, Doug, John D. McCarthy, and Mayer N. Zald. 1988. "Social Movements." In *Handbook of Sociology*, ed. N. Smelser. Newbury Park, Calif.: Sage.

———, eds. 1996a. *Comparative Perspectives on Social Movements: Political Opportunities, Mobilizing Structures, and Cultural Framings*. Cambridge: Cambridge University Press.

———. 1996b. "Introduction: Opportunities, Mobilizing Structures, and Framing Processes—toward a Synthetic, Comparative Perspective on Social Movements." In *Comparative Perspectives on Social Movements: Political Opportunities, Mobilizing Structures, and Cultural Framings*, ed. E. McAdam, J. McCarthy, and M. Zald. Cambridge: Cambridge University Press.

McCarthy, John D. 1996. "Constraints and Opportunities in Adopting, Adapting and Inventing." In *Comparative Perspectives on Social Movements: Political Opportunities, Mobilizing Structures, and Cultural Framings*. Cambridge: Cambridge University Press.

Melucci, Alberto. 1985. "The Symbolic Challenge of Contemporary Movements." *Social Research* l 52:789–816.

Merton, Robert K. 1968. "The Bearing of Sociological Theory on Empirical Research." In *Social Theory and Social Structure*, by R. K. Merton. New York: The Free Press.

Michels, Robert. 1962. *Political Parties: A Sociological Study of the Oligarchical Tendencies of Modern Democracies*. New York: Collier.

Milbank, John. 1990. *Theology and Social Theory: Beyond Secular Reason*. Oxford: Blackwell.

228   Ørnulf Seippel

Münch, Richard. 1984. *Die Struktur der moderne Grundmuster und differentielle Gestaltung des institutionellen Aufbaus der modernen Gesellschaften.* Frankfurt am Main: Suhrkamp.
———. 1994. "Zahlung und Achtung: Die Interpenetration von Ökonomi und Moral." *Zeitschrift für Soziologie* 23:388–410.
Naess, Arne. 1973. "The Shallow and the Deep, Long-Range Ecology Movement: A Summary." *Inquiry* 16:95–100.
———. 1995. "The Deep Ecological Movement: Some Philosophical Aspects." In *Deep Ecology for the Twenty-first Century,* ed. G. Sessions. Boston: Shambhala.
Offe, Claus. 1985. "New Social Movements: Challenging the Boundaries of Institutional Politics." *Social Research* 52:815–868.
———. 1996. *Modernity and the State.* Cambridge: Polity.
Pakulski, Jan. 1992. "Social Movements and the New Politics." In *Postmodernization: Change in Advanced Society,* ed. S. Crook, J. Pakulski, and M. Waters. London: Sage.
Parsons, Talcott. 1937. *Structure of Social Action.* New York: The Free Press.
———. 1951. *The Social System.* Glencoe, Ill.: Free Press.
Radtke, Ingrid. 1997. "Old and New Forms of Environmental Protest: The New Anti-roads Movement in Great Britain." Paper presented at the Twenty-fifth European Consortium for Political Research Joint Sessions of Workshops, Bern, Switzerland, February 27–March 4.
Reimer, Bo. 1989. "Postmodern Structures of Feeling: Values and Lifestyles in the Postmodern Age." In *Contemporary Political Culture: Politics in a Postmodern Age,* ed. J. Gibbins. London: Sage.
Rucht, Dieter. 1994. *Modernisierung und neue soziale Bewegungen: Deutschland, Frankreich und USA im Vergleich.* Frankfurt: Campus Verlag.
Schmid, Michael. 1992. "The Concept of Culture and Its Place within a Theory of Social Action: A Critique of Talcott Parsons's Theory of Culture." In *Theory of Culture,* eds. Richard Münch and Neil J. Smelser. Berkeley: University of California Press.
Searle, John R. 1995. *The Construction of Social Reality.* London: Penguin.
Seel, Martin. 1986. "Die zwei Bedeutungen 'kommunikativer' Rationalität: Bemerkungen zu Habermas' Kritik der pluralen Vernunft." In *Kommunikatives Handeln: Beiträge zu Jürgen Habermas' "Theorie des kommunikativen Handelns,"* ed. A. Honneth and H. Joas. Frankfurt: Suhrkamp.
Seippel, Ørnulf. 1997. "Consciousness of Nature and Political Action: A Comparative Study of Germany, Italy, Norway and the United States." Paper presented for the Twenty-fifth European Consortium for Political Research Joint Sessions of Workshops, Bern, Switzerland, February 27–March 4.
Skogen, Ketil. 1996. "Young Environmentalists: Post-modern Identities or Middle-Class Culture?" *Sociological Review* 44:452–473.
Smelser, Neil J. 1992. "Culture: Coherent or Incoherent." In *Theory of Culture,* ed. R. Münch and N. J. Smelser. Berkeley: University of California Press.
Snow, David A., and Robert D. Benford. 1988. "Ideology, Frame Resonance, and Participant Mobilization." In *From Structure to Action: Comparing Social Movement Research across Cultures,* ed. B. Klandermans, H. Kriesi, and S. Tarrow. Greenwich, Conn.: JAI Press.
———. 1992. "Master Frames and Cycles of Protest." In *Frontiers in Social Movement Theory,* ed. A. Morris and C. Mueller. New Haven, Conn.: Yale University Press.
Snow, David, E. Rochford, S. Worden, and R. Benford. 1986. "Frame Alignment Processes, Micromobilization, and Movement Participation." *American Sociologist Review* 51 (August): 464–481.

Szerszynski, Bronislaw. 1996. "On Knowing What to Do: Environmentalism and the Modern Problematic." In *Risk, Environment and Modernity: Towards a New Ecology*, ed. S. Lash, B. Szerszynski, and B. Wynne. London: Sage.

Swidler, Ann. 1986. "Culture in Action: Symbols and Strategies." *American Sociological Review* 51:273–286.

Tarrow, Sidney. 1994. *Power in Movement: Social Movements, Collective Action and Politics.* Cambridge: Cambridge University Press.

———. 1996. "States and Opportunites: The Political Structuring of Social Movements." In *Comparative Perspectives on Social Movements: Political Opportunities, Mobilizing Structures, and Cultural Framings*, ed. D. McAdam, J. McCarthy, and M. Zald. Cambridge: Cambridge University Press.

Taylor, Charles. 1989. *Sources of the Self: The Making of the Modern Identity*. Cambridge: Cambridge University Press.

Tiryakian, Edward A. 1996. "Three Cultures of Modernity: Christian, Gnostic, Chtonic." *Theory, Culture and Society* 13:99–118.

van Deth, Jan W., and Elinor Scarbrough. 1995. "The Concept of Values." In *The Impact of Values*, ed. J. W. van Deth and E. Scarbrough. Oxford: Oxford University Press.

White, Lynn, Jr. 1967. "The Historical Roots of Our Ecologic Crisis." *Science* 155:1203–1207.

White, Stephen K. 1991. *Political Theory and Postmodernism*. Cambridge: Cambridge University Press.

Zald, Mayer N. 1996. "Culture, Ideology, and Strategic Framing." In *Comparative Perspectives on Social Movements: Political Opportunities, Mobilizing Structures, and Cultural Framings*, ed. D. McAdam, J. McCarthy, and M. Zald. Cambridge: Cambridge University Press.

10

Inconspicuous Consumption: The Sociology of Consumption, Lifestyles, and the Environment

Elizabeth Shove and Alan Warde

The sociology of consumption has no history. Or at least the intellectual authorities of the past to whom contemporary scholars refer certainly did not think of themselves as contributing to a sociology of consumption. Hence, despite its current prominence, there is no unified line of intellectual development to which to appeal. In the traditions of sociological theory, the topic of consumption was addressed in several ways, though usually as an aside. It was examined, mostly empirically, in the context of social deprivation, through the study of poverty, its social consequences, and the policies required to alleviate distress. It was confronted as part of the study of social stratification, hence Weber's analysis of status groups and Veblen's of conspicuous consumption are concerned with processes of social classification and the demonstration of prestige. Simmel explored fashion and taste as aspects of the anatomy of modernity. The Frankfurt School made the other main contribution through its concerns with the spread of mass culture and the impact of commodification on cultural standards, social relations, and the individual psyche. Consumption remained a minor theme of sociological investigation for thirty years after World War II and was occasionally considered in the context of "the affluent society," sometimes in terms of the manipulative capacities of mass media and advertising, and, most notably by Packard, in terms of waste.

Probably three landmark intellectual developments led to the explosion of interest in recent years. First was the rediscovery of the role of consumption practices in the process of social differentiation and its refinement in sociological thought, with Bourdieu's (1984) analysis of distinction generating a wealth of critique and further empirical investigation into the relationship between social position and lifestyle. Second was exploration around the concept of collective consumption, associated particularly with Castells (1977), which drew attention to the need to understand the role of the state and its relation to capital in the process of physical, material, and social reproduction. The subsequent privatization programs of Western governments have required these matters to be explored ever more urgently, though often in different directions. Third was the emergence of cultural studies and of innovative multidisciplinary approaches to analyzing the use and meanings of goods and artifacts in everyday life. Involving historical, ethnographic, literary, and semiotic analysis, cultural studies enhanced understanding of the experiential, aesthetic, and emotional—rather than the utilitarian—aspects of consumption. From these three sources has emerged a vast and complex (and often confused and contradictory) sociological literature on consumption, the largest part of which is focused on the third theme, the operation of consumer culture and its relationship to postmodernism (for sound surveys, see Lury [1996] and Slater [1997]).

The concepts of "consumer culture" and "consumer society" are central to unlocking some of the mysteries of contemporary societies. If we now inhabit a social world where consumption has replaced work as people's central life interest (Moorhouse 1983; Offe 1985), then we might expect sustained and comprehensive analysis of the origins and consequences of such a transformation. The entrenchment of a "work and spend" orientation (Cross 1993), the ubiquity of "the consumer attitude" (Bauman 1990), the emergence of "lifestyle" as a project (Featherstone 1987), the intensification of promotional culture (Wernick 1991), and the pervasiveness in the West of "the culture of contentment" (Galbraith 1993) all offer description and diagnosis of current circumstances wherein consumption plays a major, defining role. All suggest different mechanisms that drive or motivate people to maintain or increase their levels of consumption.

Miller observes that "[m]uch, though not all, of the consumer behaviour work on consumer materialism and consumer culture has adopted a critical perspective" (1995: 67). Indeed, for at least two hundred years there has been widespread ambivalence about consumption since it is associated with notions of luxury, excess, hedonism, and other attributes antithetical to more legitimate ascetic protestant virtues. Modern consumer culture has been admonished for many reasons, because, for instance: large sections of the population of the world are excluded; material prosperity fails to bring happiness; the sacrifices entailed for producers are unacceptable; materialism compromises spiritual values; and mass culture is vulgar. But little of the critical opprobrium has been directed toward its negative environmental consequences. With a few exceptions (e.g., Gabriel and Lang 1995), sociologists of consumption have made almost no reference to the environmental impact of rapidly expanding levels of consumption.

It was initially our intention to examine some of the ways in which mechanisms driving consumer demand have direct and indirect environmental consequences. In particular, we wanted to investigate the dual role of such mechanisms, first in determining what consumers choose, and second, in prompting ever escalating demand for goods and services. It seemed appropriate, in other words, to ask why people consume as they do and as much as they do, especially when this is known to put unsustainable strains on the environment.

Prima facie, this question might be answered by reexamining mechanisms already isolated by analysts of consumer culture in their explanations of how demand for consumer goods is sustained and accelerated. Developing this approach, the first part of this chapter reviews the characteristics and environmental implications of six such mechanisms. We then take the story further, putting these mechanisms to the test with respect to a selection of key areas of environmentally significant consumption, focusing especially on those associated with increasing demand for energy, water, and other natural resources.

This exercise generates some rather surprising conclusions. In the final part of the chapter, we reflect on these insights and their implications both for the sociology of consumption and for environmental research and policy.

SIX MECHANISMS SUPPORTING ESCALATING LEVELS OF CONSUMPTION

A good deal of ink has been spilled discussing the process of emulation whereby lower classes seek to imitate the practices of their superiors, implying that there will be no cessation of demand for particular goods until the lower class has the same possessions as the higher. Once it is acknowledged that in such a system the higher class will constantly be seeking new items to mark its social status, then perpetual demand for new products appears inevitable (on positional goods, see Hirsch [1978]). Fresh desires replace previous ones, and novel items replace established ones. This is not a cycle of replacing that which is worn out, but one of inevitable obsolescence, driven by a mechanism of invidious social comparison. This crude restatement of the most prominent traditional sociological explanation of consumer behavior perhaps is sufficient to understand why it is no longer considered persuasive (for a more sustained critique of this position that is assumed to be the main sociological contribution to the field, see Fine and Leopold [1993]). The other most widely canvased explanation of these processes in the sociological heritage is probably the power and influence of capital, with its adjutant advertising and marketing agencies, which bewitch the general public by creating those false needs that the producer is, lo and behold, equipped to supply. This position has also been challenged for being one-sided, monological, and capable of recognizing neither the active discriminatory capacities of consumers, nor the complexity of the processes involved in the reproduction of consumer society. Arguably, the major progress in the sociology of consumption in the past fifteen years has arisen from identifying and dissecting a series of mechanisms, other than producers' search for profit and social processes of status competition, which maintain and expand demand for goods and services.

The emergent secondary literature seeking to synthesize speculation and research on the consumer culture offers a number of ways of classifying these mechanisms in operation. One of the most transparent is by Gabriel and Lang (1995), who list and discuss the ways that social scientists and (to a lesser degree) activists in the field of consumer advocacy have conceived of the consumer. "The Consumer" is introduced in nine different guises, as Chooser, Communicator, Explorer, Identity-Seeker, "Hedonist or Artist?", Victim, Rebel, Activist, and Citizen. The writings and arguments of key contributors to a social theory of consumerism are addressed. Each is presented as placing particular emphasis on one or the other model or feature of the process of doing consumption. So, the ideas of Simmel, Veblen, Douglas, McCracken, and Baudrillard are made to stand for the understanding of the consumer as communicator, while the work of Erikson, Giddens, Bauman, Featherstone, and Lasch, along with social psychological investigations of shopping and the meaning of objects, provides the basis for a presentation of the consumer as identity-seeker. This catalogue is oriented around the question of why people select given items. Sometimes, of course, the basis of this selection also has implications for the rate of consumption and the escalation of demand over time.

We have chosen to categorize the literature in terms of this second question, focusing more on the dynamics of escalation than on the specific processes of selecting one rather than another commodity. Our classification is not intended to be definitive or comprehensive, but we think there is some merit in grouping sociological accounts of how people are induced to consume in the escalating quantities that characterize Western societies in terms of six mechanisms: (a more sophisticated account of) social comparison, the creation of self-identity, mental stimulation and novelty, aesthetic matching, specialization of commodity production, and the requirements of sociotechnical systems.

Social Comparison

Earlier accounts of the function of consumption in social discrimination suggested that there was a fixed, legitimated, and widely known hierarchy of possessions and practices that indicated a household's position on a ladder of prestige. Recent reflections have questioned whether this remains the case. Bourdieu detects a constant struggle over the legitimacy of class cultures, with groups competing to establish their own preferences as superior because this is a way of validating cultural capital that is valuable in conflict of positions of social power. Others believe that culture is now so differentiated that pluralism has supplanted any hierarchical system of judgement. Of course, people still compare their own cultural practices with those around them, both with whom they identify with and those who are considered to belong to other cultures, but the comparison is no longer invidious. Cultural preferences continue to demarcate social group boundaries, but only in a harmless way, being no more than playful expressions of difference of taste. Which of these two accounts better describes the current condition is a matter of continuing debate. Both, however, accept that the accumulation and display of possessions is important, and both would suggest that cultural consumption is increasingly important.

As a mechanism for expanding the levels of material consumption, the processes identified have no definitive or self-evident environmental consequences. To the extent that people now consume the signs and symbols of an aestheticized everyday life as much as they devour material objects, then the environmental effect might be neutral or even positive. However, there is no real evidence that the process of social comparison is any less resource intensive than before. Moreover, there appears to be a recent trend toward engagement with as wide a variety as possible of goods, practices, and experiences.

Peterson and Kern (1996), working within a tradition of American sociology of culture, argue that there has been a tendency over the last fifteen years in the United States for persons with highbrow cultural tastes in music to also claim to like an increasing number of middle- and lowbrow genres too. This process is called "omnivorousness." Peterson and Kern interpret the trend as one whereby omnivorousness replaces snobbishness, a status system that was more hierarchical and closed, in which an elite liked only exclusive forms of culture and either did not recognize or appreciate other less exalted forms. Peterson and Kern offer a perhaps generous interpretation of omnivorousness: it is not "liking everything indiscriminately," but "an openness to appreciating everything" (904). The consequences of this trend are likely to be significant for the volume of consumption. If to experience variety means to have been everywhere, eaten everything, and heard as many types of music as possible in order to obtain the veneer of knowledge (and preferably hands-on experience) of all potentially discussible cultural items, the impact could be considerable. The omnivore will require not just recordings of opera, but also of jazz and reggae, not only a season ticket for the theatre, but also for the local professional soccer team's matches, not simply a kitchen cupboard containing native aromatics, but also the spices required for all the cuisines of the world. It will mean a preparedness to throw away items that are not pleasing, acceptable, compatible, storable, and so on. While sometimes applying the ideological injunction to variety may entail merely the substitution of one new item for another equivalent, it mostly seems like a mechanism for increasing the absolute volume of items encountered.

CREATION OF SELF-IDENTITY (IDENTITY)

Many social theorists like Beck (1992), Giddens (1991), and Bauman (1988) maintain that

> people define themselves through the messages they transmit to others through the goods and practices that they possess and display. They manipulate and manage appearances and thereby create and sustain a "self-identity." In a world where there is an increasing number of commodities available to act as props in this process, identity becomes more than ever a matter of the personal selection of self-image. Increasingly, individuals are obliged to choose their identities. (Warde 1994: 878)

Consumption then becomes more than just the pursuit of use-values or a claim to social prestige, for it is also deeply associated with the sense of self and personality. An answer to the question "what sort of person is s/he?" is now likely to be given in terms of lifestyle or form of visible attachment to a group, rather than in terms of personal virtues or characteristics. This being the case, it has been suggested (e.g., Bauman 1988) that consumer choice may become a major source of personal anxiety, since the individual is now responsible for his or her choices and mistakes. Such developments in the understanding of consumption as a form of communication are linked to a more general social process of individualization. The process is manifest in practices surrounding the "promotion of self" (Wernick 1991), the perpetual recreation of self (Featherstone 1991), and daydreaming about consumption (Campbell 1987).

This "production model of the self" implies that the acquisition of goods and services has become central to personal psychological well-being. It is no longer that just certain special objects give people a sense of security and satisfaction, which social psychologists have often observed (e.g., Dittmar 1992; Csikszentmihalyi and Rochberg-Halton 1981). Rather, it implies that attempts at personal self-development and self-growth—a major human purpose according to many contemporary guides to the art of living—increasingly entail constant consumption. To the extent that people can, relatively freely, redesign their selves by purchasing new outfits and forming new associations—a part of what Bauman and others have described as an emergent neotribalism—then a high level of demand for new, or rather different, goods is likely to pertain.

The power of this explanation of consumption has of late typically been exaggerated. As Campbell (1995) observes, consumption involves much more than social communication. Warde (1996) has argued that other sources of identity, particularly of identification with national, ethnic, occupational, and kin groups remain strong without being dependent on shared patterns of commercial consumption and that the production view of the self also overemphasizes the role of cultural products (particularly media outputs and icons of fashion) at the expense of the variety of practices that create and sustain social relations of kinship, friendship, and association. Nevertheless, there is a substantial residue of truth to the view that in a modern urban society people are known through their presentation of self and that this involves detailed attention to vigorous bouts of shopping. Again, the consequence is not necessarily the encouragement of extensive production. The symbolically significant is essentially arbitrary, since meaning can be derived from many languages. Personal identity might be expressed through a disciplined asceticism, through a rejection of glossy material culture (as in the culture of grunge or the behavior of the significant minority of the British population who are averse to shopping; see Lunt and Livingstone [1992]), or through adoption of green consciousness and commitment. But arguably, at present a majority of the citizens of Western societies are impelled to constant consumption as part of a continuous process of identity formation.

MENTAL STIMULATION (NOVELTY)

Some social-psychological accounts of consumption (e.g., Scitovsky 1976; Lane 1991; Csikszentmihalyi 1992) explain that people seek new products and new pleasures because they are stimulating; to play new games, try out new items, explore new material objects, and learn new tastes are all ways of averting boredom. The ubiquity of concepts of the new in advertising messages is a testament to the extent to which commodities are considered appealing because they are different from what went before. If coveting new products means that old ones are either retained and replaced when worn out or discarded before they wear out, then the quantity of items in production and services available might be expected to expand forever. The current cultural imperative described by Baudrillard as the obligation to experience everything is a mechanism of the former kind; the fashion system is just one powerful example of the latter. If people will neither forego interesting entertainment and equipment, nor mend and make do, nor be content to repeat already known pleasures and satisfactions, then wants become infinite. A somewhat underexplored process of this kind is the eulogization of variety discussed earlier.

While some accounts reaffirm the power of stimulation as a mechanism promoting consumption, others have seen it as potentially exhaustible. Hirschman (1982), for instance, suggests that the desire for consumer durables is terminable, precisely because people find them capable of delivering only a low level of contentment much inferior to the pleasures of social participation. Material objects inherently bear the seeds of disappointment, being useful but not pleasurable. Another countertendency is for people to ascribe particular value to older items. Antiques, the preservation of heirlooms, the retention of items perhaps given as gifts that sustain memories, and nostalgia for simple or natural implements are cases where novelty and recent vintage is not held in high regard. Furthermore, there is no particular reason to think that durability could not become a positively valued aspect; McCracken (1988: 31–43), for example, notes the kudos of "patina" in early modern times wherein something having been used well by relevant others was a sign of the quality of silverware. Certainly, some items are currently sold on the suggestion that durability guarantees quality, though no doubt many more are produced in anticipation of their imminent obsolescence.

THE DIDEROT EFFECT (MATCHING)

McCracken (1988: 118–130) recalls an essay by the Enlightenment philosopher Diderot "Regrets on Parting with My Old Dressing Gown." Diderot was given a new red dressing gown as a present. Because it made other items in his study seem shabby, Diderot gradually replaced his desk, his curtains, and other elements of the previous clutter so that they might complement his scarlet robe. In the end, the room was transformed, but Diderot reports finding the effect discomforting. The effect has a radical form, wherein a new item renders all others very quickly unacceptable, and a "rolling" form, whereby people steadily replace items as each new acquisition requires alteration to another. As McCracken observes, in both modes, "the Diderot effect has clear 'ratchet' implications for consumer expenditure. It helps to move the standard of consumption upward and prevent backward movement" (127).

Clearly, the Diderot effect, that items should match one another, would constitute a mechanism requiring constant and never ending replacement of items, for as soon as one new item is added to the collection others are likely to become disconsonant. Moreover, the mechanisms might come to apply not just to say the contents of a room, but to the entirety of a person's possessions. At least one of the many interpretations of the term "lifestyle" is that people are impelled to sustain coherence across all fields of behavior (thus, for Bourdieu this would include everything from possessions to bodily demeanor). Not only should the dressing gown match the armchair, but it should also be symbolically consistent with one's automobile, vacations, and concert-going. If shifts in any one of these requires modification to the others, then demands are likely to be exponential. Featherstone's (1991: 26–27) description of the postmodern consumer suggests a further ratcheting of the process when he argues that now people no longer seek a single identity or image, but several for different moods, and to the extent that all are equally stylish someone might acquire several matching sets of everything.

However, an alternative interpretation of postmodern aesthetic is that anything goes, that the principle of coherence, which underlies Bourdieu's model of lifestyle, is undermined by individualization and informalization. In addition, it is possible to imagine that the Diderot effect could be appropriated in support of less wasteful consumer practices, by restoring value to durability, by encouraging the matching of those items whose production and distribution is not a threat to sustainability, and so forth. In some minor way, the movement for green consumerism, with its exhortation to buy locally produced and organic foods and to use ranges of environmentally friendly domestic items like recycled paper and nontoxic detergents, might be seen to encourage Diderot unities in defense of sustainability.

SPECIALIZATION

Featherstone (1991) reflects on the tendency for the same individual to seek to present him- or herself in two or more ways, as bohemian and conventional, and as romantic and formal. He sees this as a feature of postmodernism expressed and sustained through the manipulation of imagery and style. However, there is another more material and practical level at which a mechanism encouraging specialization and pluralization operates with similar consequences for the proliferation of items that a person might acquire. This is associated with social differentiation and with the fitting of practices to a diverse range of social situations. As the number of activities in which one might participate increases, so producers widen the range of specialized products targeted at different groups of practitioners. For example, we can now buy running shoes, training shoes, squash shoes, and tennis shoes, whereas the previous generation just bought plimsolls. Once upon a time, people went rambling in their old clothes, but they now have specially designed equipment bearing the branded symbols of corporations. The paraphernalia required to be a successful social participant at Ascot, Henley, the White City, the opera, and the rock concert, as well as to be an employee, a supporter of a football team, and a dabbler in do-it-yourself is enormously varied and costly, often requiring a gallery of items that are largely or potentially alike in terms of function but that are in fact quite precisely specialized. So much so that they are no longer interchangeable. It is probably true that informalization has relaxed rules about what it is appropriate to wear on what occasions, thereby moderating the effect to some degree. But the constant invention of new activities, or more often the separation of once similar activities into demarcated and specialized fields each requiring singular gear, is a powerful social and commercial impetus to expanded consumption.

SOCIOTECHNICAL SYSTEMS

Finally, we might consider the differentiation of sociotechnical systems, to which people become attached and which themselves tend to expect, and even compel individuals to consume in particular ways. Cowan (1983) effectively demonstrates how the development of infrastructural systems has the effect of locking households, and particularly women, into particular ways of reproducing themselves on a daily basis. She considers eight technological systems, namely the systems that supply us with food, clothing, health care, transportation, water, gas, electricity, and petroleum products (71), that have, through becoming industrialized, played a part in altering the nature of domestic labor in American households. Her problem is to explain why it is still the case that women legitimately claim that their work is never done despite technological innovations that should have reduced the burden of housework. She points out that new technical systems sometimes eliminate only male tasks (as with energy, where chopping wood and fetching coal were eliminated by piped gas and electricity and gas), sometimes require more household labor (as when parents spend time driving their children to school instead of putting them on the bus), and alter expected levels of performance (as when washing machines raise expectations about how often clothes should be cleaned). These technological systems usually require consumption in their own right while also encouraging the further acquisition and use of associated products. So households consume water and electricity, but only when both are available are they likely to own washing machines, dishwashers, and showers. What is interesting is that although these technological systems structure patterns of daily life and related consumption practices, and although they represent major items of consumption in their own right, sociologists of consumption have paid them relatively little attention.

COMMENT

These six mechanisms all have the potential to increase the level and volume of consumption in society. Taken together, they probably are doing precisely that. There are, of course, countertendencies and as we have noted the extent and nature of expanding demand is often contingent, as are its associated environmental consequences. Even so, it seems reasonable to suggest that the sociology of consumption really does help us to understand processes that deplete natural resources, encourage unsustainable lifestyles, and generally have rather negative environmental impacts.

Before we end the chapter at this point, we should perhaps pause for a moment and reflect on the sorts of interests that have themselves led to the escalation of the sociology of consumption. The ideas and explanations described earlier have been developed with reference to a menu of sociological concerns about the relationship between consumption, identity and distinction, and changing systems of provision. Reasonably enough, it has made sense to focus on objects, possessions, and items— that is, on things that serve to illustrate and exemplify the processes in question.

But what if we step outside this subdisciplinary framework with its internal logic and associated examples, questions, and priorities? What happens if we appropriate ideas from the sociology of consumption, take them out of context, and apply them to forms of consumption that are important in terms of the environment? Does the sociology of consumption allow us to make sense of, say, energy or water consumption? What does it have to offer with respect to the racking up of environmentally damaging practices?

The next section works through a handful of specific examples in terms of the six mechanisms described earlier. There are two reasons for undertaking this somewhat speculative exercise. First, it allows us to explore the limits and relevance of current sociological explanation. Are the mechanisms of consumption and attendant sociological concepts up to the task and in what areas, if any, does the sociology of consumption need to develop if it is to grapple with environmentally significant practices? Second, is there anything distinctive about these practices that requires a substantially new or different set of explanations and if so, what and why should that be the case?

APPLYING THE MECHANISMS

Consider water. A first tentative thought experiment throws us into instant confusion: What could water consumption have to do with novelty or how could it relate to identity? This makes no sense. Energy consumption fares little better: Diderot and energy (what could this possibly mean?) and social comparison in terms of electrons seems daft.

Why are these examples so ridiculous? Part of the explanation lies in the fact that energy and water consumption are typically private and invisible. Water quality is more or less standardized as is the "quality" of electricity, so there are no distinctive edges to play with in that respect. Not only that, instances of energy consumption are so diverse (from boiling a kettle of water to watching the television) that it is hard to conceive. While water consumption is generally tangible (you can see that the tap is running and you can at least catch water in a bucket), the same cannot be said for electrical energy. People know they use energy but they don't know how much they consume at any one moment in time, and they don't know exactly where it goes. Although revealed in the form of a monthly bill, that bill merely represents the consequences of past actions and practices that are in any case difficult to identify (Shove 1997; Egan et al. 1996). By any standards, energy and water represent peculiar forms of consumption, so peculiar that they simply cannot be captured in the sociological language of mechanisms propelling consumer culture. But before we embark on the task of developing a whole new conceptual scheme, it is important to remember that people do not consume energy in a raw, unmediated form.

In practice, people use things that depend on energy consumption: refrigerators, fan heaters, fluorescent lights, and so on. In other words, it is the outputs that energy consumption makes possible that should be the focus of attention. Much the same applies for water for although some of it is consumed directly, much more is used in the course of cleaning clothes, dishes, and people, and in flushing toilets. So let us try the exercise again.

Do the mechanisms of consumption make more sense when we consider the practices and services that account for domestic energy or water usage, and can these mechanisms also handle issues of transport and mobility or the consumption of energy and natural resources embodied in the hardware with which we surround ourselves?

Table 10.1 includes a selection of goods and services that embody natural resources and energy or that require their direct consumption. Levels of domestic energy consumption vary widely in Western societies (Lutzenhiser 1993), but the distribution of end-uses appears to follow a fairly consistent pattern: space heating or cooling generally accounts for the largest proportion, followed by refrigerators and freezers, lighting (which is very rarely monitored), and other appliances such as washing machines, cookers, dishwashers, and televisions (Lebot et al. 1997). Though such considerations inform the sorts of consumption practices considered here, it is important to underline the sketchy nature of this enterprise. Other examples could be chosen, and other interpretations made. At this stage, the purpose is not to examine all possible dimensions of environmental consumption, but rather to see what new insights and challenges emerge.

As it happens, reviewing the relevance of the six mechanisms reveals as much about the limits of these explanations as it does about the dynamics of environmentally significant consumption.

What does this speculative exercise tell us? At first sight, the pattern of "yes," "no," "maybe," and "not now" responses seems to be pretty much of a jumble. Looking more closely, we can detect minor patterns that in turn generate further queries and questions, some focusing on the specific examples cited, and others on

Table 10.1   Mechanisms of Consumption and Environmentally Significant Practices

Environmentally Significant Consumption	Social Comparison	Identity	Novelty	Matching	Speciali-zation	Socio-technical logic
Total energy consumption	no	no	no	no	maybe	yes
Total water consumption	no	no	no	no	maybe	yes
Space heating	yes	no	not now	no	no	yes
Lighting—selecting light bulbs	no	no	not now	no	yes	yes
Lighting—creating an atmosphere	yes	yes	no	yes	yes	yes
Washing machines as objects	maybe	no	not now	no	yes	yes
Washing machines in use	no	maybe	no	no	no	no
Sending washing to a laundry	maybe	maybe	not now	no	maybe	yes
Having a shower or bath	no	maybe	no	no	yes	yes
Washing dishes by hand	no	maybe	no	no	no	yes
Cookers as objects	maybe	maybe	no	maybe	yes	yes
Cooking as a practice	yes	yes	maybe	no	yes	yes
Refrigerators and freezers as an object	no	no	not now	maybe	yes	yes
Refrigerators and freezers in use	no	no	no	no	no	maybe
Cleaning, in general	yes	yes	no	no	yes	yes
The kitchen as a whole	yes	yes	maybe	yes	yes	yes
Mobility in general	not itself	maybe	not now	no	yes	yes
Cars as objects	yes	yes	maybe	not now	maybe	yes
A specific journey	no	no	no	no	no	yes
Possessions in general	yes	yes	yes	yes	yes	maybe
Clothing	yes	yes	yes	yes	yes	maybe
Cavity wall insulation	no	no	no	no	no	maybe
Double glazing	yes	maybe	not now	not now	no	maybe

the operation (or otherwise) of the six mechanisms. Let us begin by looking down the columns.

Sociotechnical Consistency

Perhaps the most striking feature is the consistency of "yes" and "maybe" responses listed under the heading "sociotechnical logic." Of course, the exact meaning of "sociotechnical logic" varies from case to case, some systems being much more interdependent and collectively restrictive than others. For example, plumbing systems are generally as good at accommodating poor-quality washing machines as they are at providing for high-quality machines. However, a washing machine without both a plumbing system and a supply of electricity is useless. The implication is that patterns of energy or water-related consumption are strongly, and perhaps unusually, bound up with the microinfrastructure of the household and with the coevolution of sociotechnical systems. In many cases, changing practices are caught up in webs of interdependence in which other objects or services are presupposed, if not strictly required.

Specialization

The apparent significance of specialization is clearly related. Electrical energy is put to an increasingly diverse range of uses, steadily transforming what were once exclusively manual operations (like brushing teeth and carving meat). Although there are limits to what washing machines, cookers, and refrigerators are expected to do, the range of functions and facilities still increases from year to year. At times even the boundary conditions change, making it possible to develop new combinations of once separate appliances such as the refrigerator-freezer or the washer-drier. While this makes a difference to the range and scope of gadgets on the market, we need to go further if we are to consider the practical consequences of such developments for direct energy consumption. While specialization also transforms the packaging of domestic activity (new roles appear and old ones vanish with the arrival of a dishwasher), it is difficult to see how this concept relates to the frequency with which that dishwasher is actually used. As will be discussed, new questions arise when the focus is on use, rather than acquisition.

The Novel and the Normal

One of the more difficult columns to complete is that relating to novelty. As we have already observed, it is hard to imagine what the novelty of water consumption might refer to. But it is not so long ago that plumbed-in baths were a real luxury. Although installed in middle-class homes beginning in the 1880s, "they remained virtually unknown in working class houses until the 1920s" (Forty 1986: 166). The evolution of the toilet, its positioning, design, and relation to the sewerage system is even more complex and again "[c]lass differences as regards toilets were considerable" (Muthesius 1982: 60). The histories of domestic gas and electricity supply and the struggle between the two are clearly wrapped up in the parallel histories of dependent devices and systems (like electric lights or gas cookers and refrigerators), the interests and priorities of competing supply industries, and the manufacturing of demand (Cowan 1985; Forty 1986; Rybczynski 1986). So there is a sense in which we might say "yes," novelty has been crucial in all these cases. But is it now? In what sense does a household's electricity bill relate to novelty, social comparison, or self-identity? However, lack of access to a washing machine, a central heating system, or a car, when so many other people have them, may be an indication of deprivation, an important aspect of social comparison. We clearly need to take note of the collective dynamics of consumption and the points at which novelty is or is not a consideration. Taking a longer-term perspective, we should perhaps pay more attention to the process of becoming normal than to the moment of novelty: after all, it is the embedding of expectations that underpins associated energy and water consumption. Other themes appear as we read across the table.

Acquisition and Use

Compare, for instance, the combination of responses with respect to the acquisition of refrigerators, freezers, washing machines, or cars as objects in their own right and the corresponding lines that represent their use. The general pattern is one in which the six mechanisms are more appropriate for an understanding of acquisition than of use.

While use may not be such an important issue for the analysis of possessions, it is clearly crucial in terms of the continuing demands made of energy and water resources. Sociologists of consumption have taken note of the effort invested in learning to consume and in the further layers of differentiation associated with more and less "proper" use of gadgets, objects, or services, but there is rather less understanding of the conventions and habits that influence the ways in which central heating systems are used or the frequency with which washing machines whir. The notion of the "unwashed" suggests that keeping clean is, or at least can be, a point of social comparison. But once past the threshold of visible grime, it is impossible to tell how often people take a shower, for the signs of such activity are literally washed away. This, then, is a form of consumption for which there is nothing to show other than a damp towel and an emptier bottle of shampoo or shower gel. Despite the day-to-day invisibility of these practices, it is clear that standards of cleanliness have changed: "[T]he invention of the washing machine has meant more washing, of the vacuum cleaner, more cleaning" (Kyrk in Forty 1986: 211). Yet, the specific translation of social expectations regarding cleanliness (which clearly can be the subject of social comparison, identity, on so on) in the daily, but distinctly invisible, consumption of energy and water, remains both obscure and hard to describe. The lack of attention paid to consumption in the sense of routinized use is not simply due to the private nature of the activities in question. Although there is real interest in the symbolic significance of cars and in calculating average miles traveled, the day-to-day business of car driving is again difficult to explain in terms of the six mechanisms.

Which ever way we look at it, the actual use of energy-consuming items and services is relatively unexplored. Although technical researchers go to considerable lengths to record domestic energy consumption, they are generally concerned with the end result, not the process. This leaves a real gap in our understanding of environmentally significant forms of consumption.

Alternative Strategies

In theory at least, there are real environmental advantages in pooling resources and sharing facilities. The idea of equipping each household with its own washing machine clearly represents one of the more energy- and resource-intensive responses to the challenge of cleaning a nation's clothes. Comparison of the lines in the matrix relating to the acquisition and use of a washing machine or the use of a laundry suggests that each constitutes a different, and probably changing, form of consumption (Roberts 1991). On the one hand, going along to a communal laundry might variously represent the social highlight of the week (e.g., the social life of the wash house in the 1840s [Muthesius 1982]) or a mindless and essentially solitary chore (sitting on uncomfortable chairs and staring at other people's clothes spinning round). On the other hand, having clean and ironed shirts delivered to the door might well be the height of luxury. Understanding the mechanisms of consumption might also tell us something about the factors that influence the relative significance of alternative strategies, one compared with another, as well as about the distinctive qualities of each. Doing so would involve paying attention to notions of convenience as they influence different ways of doing more or less the same thing, comparing not only the different dynamics of consumption associated with each, but also the environmental consequences of one or another solution.

Categorizing Consumption

The distributions of "yes," "no," and "maybe" varies considerably depending on the precise unit of analysis. Consider, for example, the different array of responses associated with cookers as objects, cooking as a practice, or the kitchen as a whole. Issues of matching and appearance are relevant if the reference point is the kitchen in a way that is at least different if we consider the cooker alone, and largely irrelevant if cooking is the focus. This is quite significant for it influences the explanatory weight we might give to one or another of our six mechanisms. The acquisition of a new boiler is unlikely to be the subject of much social comparison and people's identities are not generally thought to be closely linked to their heating systems. However, these two mechanisms really are important when it comes to defining and creating a cozy and comfortable home, a realization that depends on the unnoticed boiler. Exactly the same division applies with respect to the selection of light bulbs, which is a nonevent in terms of purchase but whose creative deployment in the making of a distinctive ambience is, by contrast, significant and amenable to sociological explanation (Wilhite, Nakagami, and Handa 1996). In terms of energy and the environment, these points remind us to take note of the different ways in which component parts, systems (both social and technical), and combined effects are viewed and understood. Different *logics* of change may be involved at different levels. Meanwhile, the same observation reminds sociologists to consider the methodological implications of the way they categorize items of consumption.

Green Consumers

The six mechanisms are more relevant not only to the acquisition of some types of items like clothes and household fittings, but also at least to some energy saving devices. It is relatively easy to think of ways in which they actively encourage forms of green consumption. For instance, social comparison could prompt the installation of solar panels (Dard 1986), identities are readily attached to vegetarianism, people might well go out of their way to select coherently appropriate softwood furniture, and so on. Providing there are alternatives to choose from, there is no reason why the mechanisms should not favor types of consumption that embody less energy or that make less demand on natural resources. But not all types of environmentally beneficial consumption fit this pattern. Installing cavity wall insulation represents the single most effective environmental measure a householder can take (Energy Efficiency Office 1991; Shove 1991). But because no one can tell whether your walls are insulated or not, this particular consumer act slips the net, generating a miserable trail of "no's" across the matrix. Buying double glazing "works" better in consumer terms, but is of course much less effective environmentally.

Mechanisms like the Diderot effect or social comparison might also increase the rate at which these same green objects become obsolescent. The social and physical durability of objects is of real significance. It matters little how green that settee is if you throw it out and replace it after only two years. This demonstrates the dual role of the mechanisms, both in the selection between alternatives and in the "churn" rate, that is the rate at which things are replaced, demolished, and thrown away. In addition, other processes influence the actual operation of the mechanisms. That settee, green or not, is likely to have a longer life—perhaps even deserving restoration and repair—if given as a wedding present than if picked up in a bargain store or flea market on a wet Saturday afternoon. In this as in other cases, the mode of acquisition appears to modify the thing itself and thus its social durability (Appadurai 1986).

In this area, providing we retain the distinction between the selection of more and less environmentally friendly goods and the rate at which they are replaced, the language of mechanisms really does help.

Capturing Environmental Consumption

To summarize, the forms of consumption for which these six mechanisms make most sense share a number of characteristics. First, they tend to revolve around seemingly individual choice and selection. It is in this context that we can talk of the green consumer, that is, the consumer who seeks out the most environmentally friendly alternatives or who looks for less harmful ways of meeting his or her own private needs. Second, the mechanisms are especially relevant when it comes to the analysis of objects (especially visible objects or processes) or even events that are relatively discrete and that can be reviewed and considered as items or experiences in their own right.

Applying these mechanisms, we can consider the demands and dynamics that favor the consumption and production of goods and services in terms of their longevity and whether they are resource and energy intensive. Moreover, we can begin to identify and explore tendencies and countertendencies in the ratcheting up (or down) of consumption levels.

However, table 10.1 suggests that the six mechanisms do not capture some of the most important features of environmentally significant consumption. They do not fit areas of inconspicuous consumption, like the utilities, very well, and they are not especially helpful in terms of understanding the use of appliances, the role of lighting and central heating, or creeping standards of cleanliness. So what is it that is missing and what new ideas are needed?

One clue might lie in that nearly uniform column of "yes" under the sociotechnical heading and in·the realization that many of the "no" and "maybe" responses relate to issues that are boringly normal, invisible, and enmeshed in a network of related practices and habits. Despite these qualities, such features change, often rapidly, with instant and wide-ranging environmental consequences. What is needed, and what the sociology of consumption does not yet provide, is a way of analyzing the origins of change in mundane routines. The matrix exercise allows us to identify some of the missing ingredients, or at least ingredients that are only weakly represented, in the sociology of consumption.

The first is the need to take greater account of infrastructure both in the sense of urban planning and the role of utilities in the development of power lines, water mains, and so on, and in terms of the design and organization of key arenas like kitchens and bathrooms. In other words, we need to know more about the processes and decisions, often commercial, that frame the options and possibilities within which people in turn make choices. The distribution of railway networks, petrol stations, and roads makes different forms of transport more and less possible, just as the histories of past choices structure current possibilities within a household. What if there is no shower, or if the heating system runs on oil or if the toilet consumes seven, eleven, or fifteen gallons of water with every flush? In these circumstances, changing patterns of energy or water consumption are likely to involve altering an established infrastructure of taken-for-granted hardware. Tampering with taps, shower heads, boilers, and so on is rarely seen as a discrete process of "consumption," for these elements are component parts of that complicated interlocking system that people generally think of as their house.

Second, it is important to come to terms with the bunching together of expectations and choices. What is missing is a way of capturing the gradual and collective development of a sense of comfort and well being or of tracking shifting standards of cleanliness. We need to understand the evolution of the broad, ordinary sense of what is and is not normal. This is likely to require investigation of the rippling of unintended consequences, the spread of central heating, for example, leading to the decline of hot water bottles and bed socks, while also making possible new forms and styles of indoor clothing (Wilhite and Lutzenhiser 1997). While mechanisms like the Diderot effect and specialization give us some purchase on these processes, their cumulative effect remains elusive.

Third, the history of energy consumption highlights the way in which activities have been redefined and managed and shows how consumers trade time and resources (whether those be natural resources or the resources of other people's time) as they develop alternative ways of coping with different aspects of everyday life (Schipper et al. 1989). The notion of convenience is, for instance, critical. The flip of a switch takes the place of time and effort once spent on chopping logs, clearing out the ashes, or lighting a candle. And that flip also switches the location and management of energy production and consumption. More than that, it alters the balance of time available for other forms of consumption. Thinking along these lines leads toward some big questions about the relationship between resource intensity and the management of time. Whose effort and resources are redistributed in the cause of convenience and what is the net environmental effect?

Finally, and less dramatically, the ordinary examples considered in the matrix suggest the need for a complementary, but more defensive view of consumption, one focusing less on confidence and overt display and more on just-in-case scenarios. The freezer, for instance, needs to be this big just in case all the family shows up at Christmas. Similarly, the spare bedroom is needed for those rare occasions when someone comes to stay. Turned the other way around, the need to cope with all social eventualities might be seen as a variant of conspicuous consumption: those who drive enormous cars imply that they need a vehicle that big because any day now they might have to take all their friends and all their luggage somewhere important—even if that day is not today. As a protective strategy, oversizing has to be understood in terms of the management of social risk, the cost of failure, and the sheer fear of being unable to cope. Developing this idea, Wilhite and Lutzenhiser (1997) suggest that in catering for the extreme, consumers redefine what is normal: expectations of peak load become ordinary and bit by bit new peaks appear. This suggests that yet another mechanism is impelling higher levels of consumption.

This list of only weakly articulated aspects of environmental consumption revolves around three core issues: infrastructure, interdependence, and the creeping evolution of normal standards. Perhaps these missing themes need reconceptualizing. We are, after all, talking about invisible practices and shifts in sociotechnical networks that are simply not, or at least not simply, the subject of social comparison. This is the realm of inconspicuous consumption, a realm ignored by studies of consumer culture that are enthralled by the significance of immediate visual clues to social meaning.

CONCLUSION

In this chapter, we have suggested that while the sociology of consumption has developed in quite promising ways in the last decade, most of the progress has been with respect to the analysis of consumer culture in its aesthetic dimensions (i.e., issues of style and taste). One such line of progress has been an improved and more precise understanding of some of the social mechanisms that lie behind decisions about what to consume and that also impel people to consume ever increasing quantities of goods and services. We have also learned an appreciation of the complexity of the use to which goods and services are put. Consumption comprises a set of practices that permit people to express self-identity, mark attachment to social groups, accumulate resources, exhibit social distinction, ensure participation in social activities, and so on. However, these processes bear primarily on the way that individuals select among the vast array of alternative items made available in the form of commodities. It has often been suggested that there has been excessive focus on the purchase of commodities, ignoring the fact that much of what is consumed is not acquired, delivered, or enjoyed in this form because it is provided by the state, the community, and the household. It has also been suggested that too much attention has been paid to items that are often visually striking, subject to fashion, and symbolically highly significant, like vehicles, clothes, and cult objects. This chapter added weight to such critical observations by depicting the characteristics of spheres of consumption that have serious environmental implications but that seem to be rather resistant to explanation in terms that better fit the analysis of consumer culture.

Examination of the consumption of what used to be described in British industrial statistics as "the utilities" reveals a type of commodity that dances scarcely at all to the tunes of consumer culture. Only at best obliquely and indirectly does the purchase or use of water, coal, gas, or electricity confer self-identity, mark attachment to social groups, or exhibit social distinction. Yet, a sizable proportion of household income is devoted to these items and together they contribute to the most pressing of the world's environmental problems.

The analysis presented here leads to the conclusion that the most environmentally problematic aspects of consumption are almost entirely beyond the remit of current sociological approaches. It also suggests that taking analysis of these particular spheres of consumption seriously will again shift attention away from an intellectual obsession with the glamorous aspects of consumption toward its more routine, pragmatic, practical, symbolically neutral, socially determined, collectively imposed, jointly experienced, nonindividualized elements. This may be the main contribution of this chapter.

It is still the case that consideration of mechanisms isolated in the analysis of consumer culture may generate important conclusions with respect to sustainability. Yet, reflection on the characteristics of energy and water consumption implies that new and different approaches are also required, perhaps linking the sociology of consumption to the sociology of science and technology. A distinction is suggested between a world of relatively individualized consumer behavior involving the selection of discrete and visible commodities and a muddier world of embedded, interdependent practices and habits explicable in terms of background notions such as comfort, convenience, security, and normality.

Such a distinction might improve the understanding of environmentally significant consumption and provide a platform for an assessment of possibilities and strategies for promoting sustainability, making better use of resources, and racking down levels of demand. In some cases, for example, those that are comprehensible in terms of the six mechanisms, it is possible that environmentally friendly actions and practices, including the restriction of consumption, might acquire their own symbolic significance. High-status frugality is a real possibility, as is the valuing of durability and even repair and maintenance. On the face of it, there is no reason why some of these mechanisms should not promote green consumption while also slowing the escalation of social and physical obsolescence.

But for forms of consumption that are more deeply embedded in infrastructures and sociotechnical systems, the achievement of energy and resource efficiency is likely to have rather more to do with the way in which collective services are managed and handled, and with systemic shifts in routine habits and practices. Far from being visible or deliberately selected, these developments are largely unseen by those they most affect and by those whose environmental "choices" they so strongly influence. This is not to say, however, that there are no alternatives, only that they lie outside the rather narrow realm of individualized green consumerism. One way forward might be to scour the conceptual remnants of earlier analyses of collective consumption. Another could be to apply the concept of systems of provision (Fine and Leopold 1993) to the utilities and to domestic machines. Whichever, there is a profound disjuncture in our means of understanding, on the one hand, the escalating consumption of the glamorous items of an aestheticized consumer culture and, on the other, the inconspicuous mundane products associated with daily reproduction.

REFERENCES

Appadurai A. 1986. *The Social Life of Things: Commodities in Cultural Perspective.* Cambridge: Cambridge University Press.
Bauman, Z. 1988. *Freedom: Milton Keynes.* London: Open University Press.
———. 1990. *Thinking Sociologically.* Oxford: Blackwell.
Beck, U. 1992. *Risk Society: Towards a New Modernity.* London: Sage.
Bourdieu, P. 1984. *Distinction: A Social Critique of the Judgement of Taste.* London: Routledge and Kegan Paul.
Campbell, C. 1987. *The Romantic Ethic and the Spirit of Modern Consumerism.* Oxford: Blackwell.
———. 1995. "The Sociology of Consumption." In *Acknowledging Consumption: A Review of New Studies,* ed. D. Miller, 96–126. London: Routledge.
Castells, M. 1977. *The Urban Question: A Marxist Approach.* London: Edward Arnold.

Cowan, R. S. 1983. *More Work for Mother: The Ironies of Household Technology from the Open Hearth to the Microwave.* New York: Basic.

———. 1985. "How the Refrigerator Got Its Hum." In *The Social Shaping of Technology,* ed. D. Mackenzie and J. Wajcman. Buckingham: Open University Press.

Cross, G. 1993. *Time and Money: The Making of Consumer Culture.* London: Routledge.

Csikszentmihalyi, M. 1992. *Flow: The Psychology of Happiness.* London: Rider.

Csikszentmihalyi, M., and E. Rochberg-Halton. 1981. *The Meaning of Things: Domestic Symbols and the Self.* Cambridge: Cambridge University Press.

Dard, P. 1986. *Quand l'energie se Domestique.* Paris: Plan Construction et Architecture.

Department of the Environment. 1993. *Climate Change: Our National Programme for CO2 Emissions.* London: HMSO.

Dittmar, H. 1991. *The Social Psychology of Material Possessions: To Have Is to Be.* Brighton: Harvester Wheatsheaf.

———. 1992. *The Social Psychology of Material Possessions: To Have Is to Be.* Hemel Hempstead: Harvester Wheatsheaf.

Egan, C., W. Kempton, A. Eide, D. Lord, and C. Payne. 1996. "How Customers Interpret and Use Comparative Graphics of Their Energy Use." Proceedings of the American Council for an Energy Efficient Economy Summer Study on Energy Efficiency in Building, Human Dimensions of Energy Consumption. Washington, D.C.: American Council for an Energy Efficient Economy.

Energy Efficiency Office. 1991. *Insulating Your Home.* Leaflet No. Dd8240826 ENGY JO546NJ. London: HMSO.

Featherstone, M. 1987. "Lifestyle and Consumer Culture." *Theory, Culture and Society* 4, no. 1: 55–70.

———. 1991. *Consumer Culture and Postmodernism.* London: Sage.

Fine, B., and E. Leopold. 1993. *The World of Consumption.* London: Routledge.

Forty, A. 1986. *Objects of Desire: Design and Society since 1750.* London: Thames and Hudson.

Gabriel, Y., and T. Lang. 1995. *The Unmanageable Consumer: Contemporary Consumption and Its Fragmentation.* London: Sage.

Galbraith, J. K. 1993. *The Culture of Contentment.* Harmondsworth, UK: Penguin.

Giddens, A. 1991. *Modernity and Self-Identity.* Cambridge: Polity.

Hirsch, F. 1978. *Social Limits to Growth.* London: Routledge and Kegan Paul.

Hirschman, A. 1982. *Shifting Involvements: Private Interest and Public Action.* Oxford: Blackwell.

Lane, R. 1991. *The Market Experience.* Cambridge: Cambridge University Press.

Lebot, B., C. Lopes, P. Waide, and O. Sidler. 1997. "Lessons Learnt from European Metering Campaigns of Electrical End Uses in the Residential Sector." Proceedings of the European Council for an Energy Efficient Economy Summer Study. Copenhagen: Danish Energy Agency/European Council for an Energy Efficient Economy.

Lunt, P., and S. Livingstone. 1992. *Mass Consumption and Personal Identity.* Buckingham: Open University Press.

Lury, C. 1996. *Consumer Culture.* Cambridge: Polity.

Lutzenhiser, L. 1993. "Social and Behavioural Aspects of Energy Use." *Annual Review of Energy and the Environment* 18:247–289.

McCracken, G. 1988. *Culture and Consumption: New Approaches to the Symbolic Character of Consumer Goods and Activities.* Bloomington: Indiana University Press.

Miller, D. 1987. *Material Culture and Mass Consumption.* Oxford: Blackwell.

————. 1995. *Acknowledging Consumption: A Review of New Studies.* London: Routledge.

Moorhouse, H. 1983. "American Automobiles and Workers' Dreams." *Sociological Review* 31, no. 3: 403–426.

————. 1991. *Driving Ambitions: An Analysis of the American Hotrod Enthusiasm.* Manchester: Manchester University Press.

Muthesius, S. 1982. *The English Terraced House.* New Haven, Conn.: Yale University Press.

Offe, C. 1985. *Disorganized Capitalism.* Cambridge: Polity.

Peterson, R., and R. Kern. 1996. "Changing Highbrow Taste: From Snob to Omnivore." *American Sociological Review* 61:900–907.

Roberts, M. 1991. *Living in a Man-Made World.* London: Routledge.

Rybczynski, W. 1986. *Home: A Short History of an Idea.* Harmondsworth, UK: Penguin.

Schipper, L., S. Bartlett, D. Hawk, and E. Vine. 1989. "Linking Life-Styles and Energy Use: A Matter of Time." *Annual Review of Energy* 14:273–320.

Scitovsky, T. 1976. *The Joyless Economy.* New York: Oxford University Press.

Shove, E. 1991. *Filling the Gap: The Social and Economic Structure of Cavity Wall Insulation, Institute of Advanced Architectural Studies.* York: University of York.

————. 1997. "Revealing the Invisible: Sociology, Energy and the Environment." In *The International Handbook of Environmental Sociology,* ed. M. Redclift and G. Woodgate. Cheltenham: Edward Elgar.

Slater, D. 1997. *Consumer Culture and Modernity.* Cambridge: Polity.

Warde, A. 1992. "Notes on the Relationship between Production and Consumption." In *Consumption and Class: Divisions and Change,* ed. R. Burrows and C. Marsh, 15–31. London: Macmillan.

————. 1994. "Consumption, Identity-Formation and Uncertainty." *Sociology* 28:877–898.

————. 1996. "Afterword: The Future of the Sociology of Consumption." In *Consumption Matters,* Sociological Review Monograph Series A, ed. S. Edgell, K. Hetherington, and A. Warde, 302–312. Oxford: Blackwell.

Wernick, A. 1991. *Promotional Culture: Advertising, Ideology and Symbolic Expression.* London: Sage.

Wilhite, H., and L. Lutzenhiser. 1997. "Social Loading and Sustainable Consumption." Proceedings of the European Council for an Energy Efficient Economy Summer Study. Copenhagen: Danish Energy Agency/European Council for an Energy Efficient Economy.

Wilhite, H., H. Nakagami, and H. Handa. 1996. "A Cross-Cultural Analysis of Household Energy-Use Behaviour in Japan and Norway." *Energy Policy* 24:795–803.

11

Social Theory and Ecological Politics: Reflexive Modernization or Green Socialism?

Ted Benton

It is quite widely acknowledged that our contemporary experience of social movements and political parties that take environmental issues to be central to their purposes is something new. It dates from the 1960s, when writers and activists such as
Carson, Commoner, and Bookchin raised widespread public alarm about pollution
and other forms of environmental damage in the United States. The Ehrlichs's
warnings about an impending "population bomb," the United Kingdom's *Blueprint
for Survival* (Goldsmith et al. 1972), and the Club of Rome's *Limits to Growth*
(Meadows et al. 1972) sparked this growing concern into an international "moral
panic." Perhaps the most influential (and controversial) of these whistle-blowers was
the Club of Rome. Its diagnosis was that exponential growth in industrial and
agricultural production, resource use, population, and pollution must lead sooner or
later to overshooting the limits of a finite planet, with catastrophic consequences.
Urgent action was required to dramatically reduce growth rates. Conceptual and
methodological weaknesses in the *Limits* argument were soon exposed, but the issues
it addressed were now firmly on the agenda, and, indeed, were issues of truly global
proportions.

In fact, the Club of Rome's advocacy of a steady-state economy had political
implications that were even more radical than they perhaps realized. The search was
on for a strategy that could address the ecological crisis, but within the framework
of liberal democratic capitalism, and without calling into question its central cultural
dynamic of consumerism. A key strategic problem was that some crucial environmental assets were located in Third World countries and that some global ecological

"life support systems" were potentially threatened by hitherto authoritative models of economic development in Third World countries. In short, the ecological costs and requirements of continued capitalist development on the part of the rich nations could only be met or sustained on the basis of some sort of deal with the poorer countries to secure environmental protection and access. For the leaders of many Third World countries, poverty and political instability put the demand for economic growth and poverty alleviation above any concern about environmental protection.

A combination of nongovernmental organization pressure and the work of the United Nations and its various agencies yielded the concept of "sustainable development" as a bid to square this circle. Poverty was identified as a cause of ecological degradation, with the result that growth aimed at poverty alleviation would presently be beneficial to the environment. Meanwhile, it was clear that technological innovation could deliver economic growth without concomitant escalations in environmental damage. As against the *Limits*'s assumption of a contradiction between growth and environmental protection, the new discourse of sustainable development postulated a potential synergy between the two, on the basis of attention to the *kind* of growth that would be favored and its *social objectives*.

The concepts of sustainable development, and its more recent sister "ecological modernization," have been given innumerable different definitions (Weale 1992; Spaargaren and Mol 1992; Mol 1996; Dobson 1996), as they have acquired near-consensual status as the ruling environmental ideology: most of the politics of the environment is now played out within the space defined by the rival versions of these notions. However, some of the core assumptions of the strategy of sustainable development are deeply questionable. Since some of these assumptions are shared with the theorists of "reflexive modernization," I will leave detailed criticism of them for a later stage in my argument. For now, a brief indication of the problems will have to suffice. In its core definitions, sustainable development simply states a normative requirement—that growth should be such as to meet the needs of the present without undermining the opportunities for future generations to meet their needs. Leaving aside, for the sake of argument, the unresolved conceptual problems that beset the normative requirement itself, the practical question that has to be faced is what institutional forms and what substantive policies could realize it.

So far, five main "instruments" have been proposed (and, to varying extents, tried out in practice): governmental regulation, environmental taxation, green consumerism, technological innovation, and international diplomacy. Of these, green consumerism has the benefit that it engages individuals in reflection on their own contribution to the overall problem, but it is dependent on accessible, verifiable, and accurate information from producers, the ability to pay on the part of consumers, and the contingencies of environmental consciousness. However, its central failing is that it cannot address the structural conditions that shape consumer choice in the first place. At best, for example, it might lead to more people buying the least polluting cars on the market, but it can't address the features of urban design, rural isolation, and low investment in public transport that generate car dependency.

As for technological innovation, there is widespread (and justified) green skepticism about "technical fixes." However, even if we remain optimistic "in principle" about the feasibility of technical solutions such as recycling, energy efficiency, resource substitution, and the like, there are questions about how the will to invest in the necessary research, development, and deployment of new, cleaner technologies can be generated. In recent decades, there has been a marked shift in research from the public sector to research and development labs of the larger companies, and a corresponding shift in the criteria for evaluating public-sector research projects toward perceived requirements of business. Crudely put, this suggests we are likely to get cleaner technologies to the extent that it is in the interests of the larger capitalist firms to provide it. This puts the focus directly onto the first two listed "instruments": governmental regulation and environmental tax reform. Both of these are projects for public intervention to shape the boundary conditions within which markets operate. The aim is to increase the cost to businesses of ecologically damaging operations and to reward environmental responsibility. These projects have two basic assumptions. The first is that the policymakers who define the environmental targets set by regulations or the proposed levels and selected objects of taxation have adequate knowledge of the relevant environmental mechanisms and processes and of the effects on them of economic activities over appropriate time spans and spatial distributions. Uncertainties inherent in knowledges of this sort provide openings for vested interests to contest the knowledge basis of policy proposals, often successfully. This may derail environmental policy at early stages in its formulation.

The second assumption is that governments, once they have decided on a course of environmental regulation, have sovereign power over state institutions and agencies whose role it is to implement and enforce policy, and, in turn, that these institutions have power over the firms or sectors that are the targets of regulation (whether direct or, as in the case of environmental taxes, indirect). There are several reasons for thinking that this assumption is problematic. One is that state institutions are commonly highly colonized by industrial interests and pressure groups—in the United Kingdom, for instance, the agribusiness and farming interests in the Ministry of Agriculture Fisheries and Food (MAFF), the road transport industry in the Department of Transport, and the arms manufacturers in the Ministry of Defense. The second is that governments themselves in liberal democratic regimes are dependent on delivering benefits to their electorates that require high growth rates and the associated profitability and international competitiveness of their national economies. Consequently, companies, especially large employers and ones in sectors with strategic importance, have considerable bargaining power vis-à-vis both the process of policy formation and the activities of regulatory agencies themselves. This institutional power is such that regulation is most unlikely to be pressed to a point where it significantly affects profitability, while similar considerations apply to the project of environmental tax reform. These considerations are of long-standing significance in understanding the relationship between public policy and private capital, but the much-discussed processes of increased international mobility of capital and the growing significance of transnational corporations intensify the problems of would-be environmental regulators. In today's "open" economies, regulations aimed at "internalizing" ecological externalities and environmental taxes can easily be represented as imposing disadvantages in the face of foreign competition, just as have the costs of employment regulation and workers' rights. In the case of countries whose economic development depends on foreign investment, again, private capital is in a powerful position to bargain down levels of environmental regulation. More generally, extreme disparities in the economic and political location of different countries and regions in the wider global system undermine well-intentioned efforts at diplomatic agreement over environmental regulation (Grubb et al. 1993; Lang and Hines 1993; Buttel and Taylor 1994).

Against these pessimistic arguments can be set the experience of relatively high levels of environmental regulation that have already been achieved in some European countries and in North America. Advocates of ecological modernization are inclined to see these levels of regulation as the vanguard of a modernization process due to be generalized more widely: "Ecological modernisation theory puts forward a radical reform programme as regards the way modern society deals with the environment. The institutions of modern society, such as the market, the state and science and technology, will be radically transformed in coping with the environmental crisis, but not beyond recognition" (Mol 1996: 309). Against this view, the previous considerations point to these relatively regulated economies as dependent on historical contingencies, likely not to be generalizable, and probably rather temporary in duration. The contingencies that made regulation feasible in these cases are complex, but include two important conditions. The first is that some market situations are such that firms may tolerate or even actively welcome regulation. For example, if a firm is well placed to meet high environmental standards and can use those standards to protect itself from price competition from foreign imports, it is likely to support regulation. In the case of transnationals, particularly in their "headquarters" countries, benefits may be obtained from an ecologically benign public image at home by relocating ecological and social devastation to Third World countries. The case of Shell UK is a particularly dramatic recently publicized example. This sort of case also provides an illustration of the second sort of condition favoring regulation. This is that in liberal democracies conditions exist for social movements to mobilize on environmental issues, occasionally with sufficient success to threaten governments and state institutions with loss of legitimacy and firms with loss of revenue. Under such circumstances, environmentally minded governments or state agencies may acquire exceptional leverage over reluctant industrial sectors.

If we consider these two sorts of conditions further, it is clear that they depend, first, on jurisdiction over large-scale economies that are relatively insulated from external competition; second, on a correspondingly powerful position in terms of the international political-economic (dis)order; and, third, on extensive civil liberties and strong traditions of popular protest and collective action. Even in the relatively highly regulated economies, these features are threatened by several developments: powerful industrial coalitions exist, particularly in the United States, that oppose environmental regulation; the international preeminence of the regulated economies in the global political economy is now under severe threat; and traditions of popular protest have suffered marked declines, partly as a result of changed relations of power between capital and labor, and partly because of systematic erosion of civil liberties combined with aggressive policing and a dramatic increase in privatized repression of environmental activism in countries supposedly advanced along the route of "ecological modernization": "Right, lads. Sorry about yesterday. No one had a fair crack. There's going to be no pratting about today. Anything in the trees today you wack, right? Anything hanging in a tree, f*** it off. Thwack it with your helmet. Anything. And don't get caught" (Head of operations for security firm at Newbury road protest, quoted in Vidal 1996). These considerations support the hypotheses that environmental modernization is a positional good that it is unlikely to be generalizable and that, indeed, its current exemplars might be hard-put to sustain their achievements.

If this more pessimistic assessment of the prospects of environmental reformism turns out to be right, and if the ecological problems generated by contemporary capitalist forms of economic and social development continue unaddressed in any fundamental way, then we are likely to experience recurrent disasters of varying scope and scale, associated social unrest, and delegitimation of established institutions. This latter, combined with elite recognition of the urgency of the ecological threat, may well strengthen the tendency toward more authoritarian forms of rule and technocratic environmental regulation by coercive means. In such a scenario, the already apparent tendency for sustainable development to be reinterpreted in ways that focus on the maintenance of conditions for continued capital accumulation and preservation of elite lifestyles (as against the blending of ecology and poverty alleviation in earlier versions of the concept) is also likely to be intensified. Such dystopian visions of ecological reaction (or, more polemically "ecofascism") already have their advocates, and there is also a danger that some traditions of ecocentric politics ("ecocatastrophists") may provide unintended legitimation for such developments through their emphasis on the overwhelmingly urgent and threatening nature of the ecological crisis. Abrogation of civil liberties, relegation of concern with social justice, and even militaristic interventions to protect "global environmental assets" can all be legitimated by approaches that prioritize ecological survival over other moral and social values.

None of these considerations is conclusive. It remains quite possible, if unlikely, that some form of generalized and progressive regulation of the global economy adequate to the scale of ecological problems and consistent with currently prevailing institutional forms and values may be achieved. However, the grounds for skepticism about this prospect are so strong that it seems to me reasonable to take more seriously the projects and diagnoses offered by the more radical traditions of ecological politics—traditions often dismissed as "utopian" and "unrealistic." The traditions I have in mind are those characterized by Eckersley (1992) as "emancipatory ecopolitics." They include ecological feminisms, ecological anarchism ("social ecology"), and various forms of green and ecological socialism. These traditions view the ecological crisis as intrinsically connected to basic features of contemporary societies and as confirming or complementing a broader normative critique of these societies. So, resolving the ecological crisis will require fundamental social change, which is in any case desirable from the standpoint of human emancipation from exploitative, oppressive, or otherwise unjust institutional forms. There are, of course, deep differences of view among the various traditions of emancipatory ecological politics, but there is a growing consensus around the indictment of globalizing capital accumulation as the most fundamental cause of both global social injustice and socioecological destruction.

REFLEXIVE MODERNIZATION AND THE POLITICS OF RISK

The various traditions of emancipatory ecopolitics are, however, not alone in claiming the "radical" mantle. The concept of reflexive modernization is used by a group of writers, of whom Giddens and Beck are the best known, to designate what they see as a new phase of "modernity." The institutional and cultural forms, which are the major sources of social and political identity and conflict that characterized earlier phases, are in the process of being displaced in ways that take us "beyond left and right." However, the processes of radicalization of modernity itself and the "subpolitics" of new social movements hold out the prospect of a democratized and sustainable "new" modernity. Implicitly or explicitly, these writers foresee the demise of recognizably leftist and rightist politics, and they have taken from green social and political movements an awareness of the significance of ecological destruction and large-scale hazards in transforming the moral and political, as well as the physical landscape.

The theory of reflexive modernization is somewhat ambiguously placed between the notions of sustainable development and environmental/ecological modernization, on the one hand, and the more politically radical advocacies of "emancipatory ecopolitics," on the other. The reflexive modernists frame their accounts of the present in terms of a linear sequence of stages or phases of social development (in their version, from "traditional" [or "premodern"] through "simple" to "reflexive" or "high" modernity). The accounts they give of the risks and hazards associated with the present phase of "modernity" give priority to industrial and technical innovation, in abstraction from capitalist economic relations, and they are inclined to dismiss the continuing significance of class politics. In these respects, their analytical framework has much in common with the theorists of environmental/ecological modernization and with most forms of advocacy of sustainable development. However, they either foresee or advocate the emergence of new forms of political activism that they expect or hope may bring about a "new" modernity, or, alternatively, a "postmodern" society. The normative commitments of the reflexive modernizers have much in common with those of "emancipatory ecopolitics." They wish to see a society in which key decisions about scientific innovation and economic investment are opened up to democratic dialogue and participation, and they have a broadly positive (though not uncritical) valuation of the role of the progressive social movements (feminism, the greens, democratic reformers, and so on) in contributing to the new politics they favor.

There is, in my opinion, much to commend the work of the reflexive modernizers. They have been among the pioneers in exploring the significance of ecological issues and ecological social movements for sociological theory. They have attempted to integrate these new concerns within a systematically revised, general theoretical approach. In doing so, they have challenged many previously held assumptions in the discipline and have shown real insight and sharpness of perception with regard to significant changes in current social experience. Moreover, they have, unlike many other contemporary social theorists, retained links between their sociological work and a critical normative stance in relation to the status quo. However, my argument in the rest of this chapter is that there are serious empirical and conceptual weaknesses in the theory of reflexive modernization. These weaknesses lead their advocates into a defective understanding of realignments now taking place in the politics of the industrial capitalist countries, and also into a potentially catastrophic underestimation of the institutionalized power against which the "new politics" is pitched. The alternative framework of analysis that I develop in the course of my critical comments I call "green socialism." This framework draws extensively on the legacy of explanatory theory associated with the socialist traditions, as revised in the face of feminist and green criticisms. Although the approach has been developed in the context of these normative pressures, its acceptability is a matter of empirical testing and theoretical argument. If, as I think is the case, it has superior explanatory power to the theory of reflexive modernization, this should be something that can be established independently of the broader normative and political differences that separate the approaches.

The most basic differences between the two approaches concerns their rival ways of classifying societies and understanding historical change. The reflexive modernizers (notwithstanding the strong denials of some of them—e.g., Giddens 1991) have a linear-developmental or "evolutionary" view of historical change, in which the most important transition is from traditional to modern societies. The phase of social development that they call "modernity" itself has inherent tendencies whose working-through generates a twofold periodization—"simple" and "reflexive" or "high" modernity. The latter phrase designates our current historical moment. Modernity itself is defined in terms of discrete institutional dimensions, none of which is assigned any overall causal priority. The relationships between these dimensions are given no theoretical specification. The green socialist approach dispenses with the notion of long-run developmental tendencies in history and understands historical change in terms of "conjunctures" of complex social and ecological causes, in which contingency plays a significant part. This idea derives from the "antihistoricism" of Althusser. The classification of different kinds of society on this approach is therefore detached from questions of chronology and thoroughly sociological in content. The key concept here is an ecologically revised version of "mode of production," defined as the form of social organization through which nature is appropriated in the meeting of social needs. This ecological-economic form has fundamental causal importance within whole social formations in shaping both dominant forms of social conflict and patterns of relationship to nature. However, the remaining (cultural, political, legal, and so on) social structures retain their specific causal weight within the whole, so that the flow of social processes is in no way reducible to the status of "epiphenomenon" of the ecological-economic "foundation."

On this view, globalizing processes of capital accumulation, together with forms of institutional regulation and cultural penetration (consumerism) that sustain them, currently have explanatory priority in any attempt to understand the dynamics of ecological change. But these processes occur unevenly in time and space, in a way that defies any characterization of a single global "modernity." Different forms of capitalist economic organization, different forms of articulation of capitalist with noncapitalist economic forms, and different modes of combination of economic, cultural, and political institutions persist (see, e.g., Hutton 1995) in different parts of the world. If this is accepted, then the term "modernity," and its cognates such as "reflexive modernization," "ecological modernization," and so on, can be only sociologically empty ways of referring to the chronological present or, alternatively, tendentiously ethnocentric impositions of a certain normative construction of specifically Western institutions on the rest of the world (see Woodiwiss 1997).

But this normative construct or "ideal type" of Western "modernity" itself is highly questionable, as is the associated division of "modernity" into "simple" and "reflexive" phases or stages. For Giddens, simple modernity (the West since the Enlightenment) is characterized by four "institutional dimensions": a political/administrative power that is typically a liberal, representative democracy; an economic order overwhelmingly capitalist in form, with the now defunct communist regimes as a temporary variant; a relation to nature defined by modern science and industrial technology; and a state monopoly on the legitimate use of violence (1991: chapter 2). The conservative, liberal, and socialist traditions in politics are clearly, Giddens (1994) thinks, connected to this phase of modernization, but are now exhausted as a consequence of processes occurring over the last forty to fifty years. These processes are summarized by Giddens as globalization, detraditionalization, and social reflexivity. Giddens resists an economic account of globalization and focuses on the implications of new communications technologies and mass transportation. Partly because of the cultural cosmopolitanism that flows from globalization, traditions that have persisted into, or became established during simple modernization, can no longer be "legitimated in the traditional way": they have to justify themselves in the face of alternatives. This implies that individuals no longer have their lives set out for them by the contingencies of their birth, but are constantly faced with choices about how to live: whether to have children, how to dress, what to believe in, and so on. In other words, the establishment of identity increasingly becomes a life project of "reflexive" subjects.

The newly emergent conditions of reflexive modernization, according to Giddens, render the inherited political traditions obsolete. Traditional forms of class identity are dissolved; changes in the labor market and in gender relations and family forms render the institutions of the welfare state unsustainable and inappropriate; global- ization and reflexivity in lifestyle choice and consumption render centralized forms of economic control unworkable; while the established parties and political institu- tions lose their legitimacy. However, this is not the end of politics, or even of radical politics. Drawing on a schematic account of the new social movements as forms of resistance to each of the institutional dimensions of modernity, Giddens postulates the emergence of a radical "generative" or "life" politics beyond the old polarities of left and right.

In response to the political/administrative system, there are social movements aiming at the radicalization of democracy and against surveillance and authoritarian- ism. Reflexive modernization also involves democratization of personal life, in which relationships among lovers, friends, parents and children, and so on are no longer governed by traditional assumptions and expectations. In the sphere of capitalist economic relations, polarization and fragmentation continue to characterize reflex- ively modernizing societies, but the supposed demise of class politics and Giddens's acceptance of Hayek's critique of centralized economic control lead him to suggest (rather vaguely) that these problems will be corrected by a postscarcity order that owes as much to ecology and conservatism as it does to socialism. In the dimension of science and industrial technology, the project of simple modernity to control the forces of nature has generated a new order of risk—"manufactured" risk—to which the green movement has responded with a utopian desire for a return to authentic nature. In the dimension of institutional violence, the peace movement points to a growing role for dialogic forms of conflict resolution in a posttraditional, reflexive world.

Beck has a great deal in common with Giddens's way of thinking, but has a much more highly developed and original approach to the ecological dimension of reflex- ive modernization. In his view, the processes of detraditionalization, globalization, and reflexivity (which he defines rather differently from Giddens) are leading to the emergence of a new stage of modernity that deserves the title "Risk Society" (Beck 1992). Risk and uncertainty increasingly pervade all dimensions of personal and social life: increased rates of divorce and family breakdown, uncertainty and vulnera- bility in the labor market, and most centrally, for Beck, uncertainty in the face of the hazards generated by new, large-scale industrial technologies and by advances in scientific knowledge.

Beck shares with Giddens a historical periodization of risks and hazards. In pre- modern times, risks, in the shape of disease epidemics, floods, famine, and so on were experienced as having an external source in nature. Simple modernization, with the development of industrial technology displaced "external" risks in favor of self- created or "manufactured" risks—byproducts of industrialization itself. Beck's view, however, is that reflexive modernization ushers in a new order of manufactured risk with profound cultural and political implications. The "semiautonomous" develop- ment of science and technology unleashed under simple modernization has through its own dynamic yielded new large-scale technologies in the nuclear, chemical, and genetics industries that pose qualitatively new hazards and put modernity itself at risk. There are some discrepancies among Beck's various attempts to pin down exactly what is new in these hazards, but I think what he has to say can be fairly summarized under seven main features:

1. New hazards are unlimited in time and space, with global self-annihilation now a possibility.
2. New hazards are socially unlimited in scope—potentially everyone is at risk.
3. New hazards may be minimized, but not eliminated, so that risk has to be measured in terms of probabilities. An improbable event can still happen, however.
4. New hazards are irreversible.
5. New hazards have diverse sources, so that traditional methods of assigning responsibility do not work. Beck calls this "organized nonliability."
6. New hazards are on such a scale or may be literally incalculable in ways that exceed the capacities of state or private organizations to provide insurance against them or compensation.
7. New hazards may only be identified and measured by scientific means. Consequently, contested knowledge claims and growing public skepticism about science itself are important aspects of the "reflexivity" of the risk society.

The pervasiveness of risk, and especially of the new order of hazards generated by large scale technologies, leads Beck, like Giddens, to postulate a political watershed in association with reflexive modernization. In Beck's work, two clusters of themes are prominent. The first is the supposed demise of class conflict over the distribution of goods. Beck takes class conflict between capital and labor to be characteristic of simple modernization, but it is in the process of being displaced both by a new agenda of political issues and by new patterns of coalition and cleavage. Both Giddens and Beck agree that severe material inequalities continue to exist through reflexive modernization, but for them, globalization, detraditionalization, and reflexivity erode traditional forms of class consciousness and identity, so that class relations are increasingly individualized and conditions for collective class action disappear. In this respect, Giddens and Beck are in line with a welter of recent announcements of the "death of class" (see Lee and Turner 1996). Beck's particular gloss on this thesis includes the claim that the political agenda is undergoing a shift from conflict over the (class) distribution of goods to conflict over the (nonclass) distribution of "bads" (i.e., the environmental costs of continuing industrial and technical development). The new patterns of conflict characteristic of the risk society will involve conjunctural, shifting patterns of coalition and division defined by the incidence of these costs. So, we can expect workers and managements in environmentally polluting industries, for example, to be in alliance with one another against those in industries such as, say, fisheries or tourism that suffer from pollution. Finally, there is the implication that the new order of environmental hazards constitutes the basis for a potentially universal interest in environmental regulation, since the relatively wealthy and powerful can no longer avoid these hazards in the way they could escape the risks associated with earlier industrial technologies.

The second cluster of themes marking a hypothesized qualitative break with the politics of the past is also centrally connected with environmental hazards. Here, however, it is not so much a matter of differential class incidence, as of the challenge these hazards pose to the steering capacity of modern states and to political legitimacy. In essence, Beck's argument is that under simple modernization, legitimacy was achieved through the progressive development of a welfare/security state, in which either public or private institutions provided guarantees against risk in the various dimensions of life—such as public health care provisions, pensions, unemployment and sick pay, welfare benefits, and so on. Reflexive modernization, characterized by changed gender relations, family breakdown, flexible labor markets, and, above all, hazards of unprecedented scale and incalculability, exposes the growing inadequacy of the welfare/security system to deliver what it has promised. In his more recent writings, Beck (1995; 1997) has cautiously introduced the notion of a "subpolitics" that might emerge in response to this situation, pressing for more democratic participation in decisions currently taken by hierarchies of technocrats and top business executives.

It seems to me that the theorists of environmental politics in the light of reflexive modernization successfully allude to significant changes in contemporary societies. Their characterizations of these changes are often imaginative and persuasive. However, in what remains of this chapter, I show that in several key respects their claims are either empirically mistaken or theoretically defective (or both). An alternative, ecologically informed socialist analysis, I argue, is more adequate to the explanatory task at hand and points to quite different political possibilities.

ECOLOGICAL SOCIALISM VERSUS REFLEXIVE MODERNIZATION

Class, Politics, and the Environment

The weight of historical and sociological evidence suggests that the proclamations of the death of class are premature. First, it is arguable that this thesis gains what plausibility it has from an exaggeration of the role of class in the politics of earlier historical periods. Social classes have always been internally differentiated and stratified, and in all industrial capitalist societies there have always been substantial proportions of the population that could not be readily assigned to the two-class model of capital and labor. Moreover, class orientations in politics are always mediated by specific local or regional cultural resources, traditions and historical cleavages, and party structures and strategies, while ethnic, gender, religious, and other sources of social identification may either confirm or cut across class allegiance. All of this is familiar stuff and there is no reason to suppose it is any more salient now than it was, say, a century ago, at the height of the women's suffrage struggle and the nationalistic appeals of the colonial powers.

It seems likely that the death of class is being proclaimed as an overreaction to the much more geographically and historically localized demise of the "corporatist" form of class politics that characterized many of the industrial capitalist countries during the thirty years or so following World War II. There have certainly been some dramatic changes, but the evidence points against the claims of individualization and class dealignment in politics. Studies of voting behavior in the United Kingdom, for example, show reduced support for the Labour Party between 1979 and 1992, but no significant lessening of the links between class position and voting behavior in general. The decline of Labour in that period seems to have been linked to a decline in its popularity across the social classes, high levels of working-class abstention, and, possibly most important, a decline in those occupational groups that formed the main social basis of Labour's traditional support (see, e.g., Westergaard [1996] and Goldthorpe and Marshall [1996]). Comparative studies in the United States (particularly taking into account nonvoting), Italy, France, and the Netherlands show equally little support for the class dealignment thesis (Weakliem 1991). Attitude surveys and research findings in the United Kingdom also show remarkably persistent support for income redistribution in favor of the less well off, publically provided health care, and the other key items in the postwar agenda of class politics, despite nearly twenty years of Conservative rule (see Jowell et al. 1997). An influential study of class in the United Kingdom carried out in the early to mid-1980s confirmed the continuing salience of class as a source of collective identity (Marshall et al. 1988). The authors of the most recent published survey on the attitudes of UK employees concluded:

> In the eyes of employees, the working environment has clearly deteriorated since the early 1980s. Nowadays employees are more likely to feel that the gap between the high and low paid at their workplace is too large, that management and employee relations are poor, that their jobs are insecure, that their workplaces are not being managed as well as they could be, and that they do not have much say over how their work is organised. (Bryson and McKay 1997)

Finally, it is clear that contingencies of political party structure and strategy and changes in them over time may affect voting behavior in ways that do not reflect the underlying character of class-based social and political attitudes and identities.

In the case of the United Kingdom, substantial deindustrialization and public-sector reorganization during the Thatcher years reduced the size of labor's "traditional" working-class base. Two prolonged recessions, combined with both legislative and directly repressive attacks on Trade Union power further weakened organized labor as a popular social movement. These and other changes have produced a situation in which it has been demonstrated that UK government can now be conducted without the consent of organized labor. Recent class mobilizations in several European countries in response to national government policies aimed at meeting European Union "convergence criteria" still leave open the question of whether this is yet true elsewhere. However, the Trade Union movement in the United Kingdom, while considerably reduced, still has 7.2 million members, and the sociological evidence suggests the continued existence of large minorities in working-class occupations and with "traditional" working-class political orientations. Instead of class *de*alignment, recent changes are better understood in terms of a combination of class *re*alignment along with shifts in the occupational and class structure.

This is a situation that presents major strategic problems for the left, but it is certainly not new. At earlier stages in capitalist industrialization, and in the interwar period in particular, organized industrial workers have generally been in a minority, and the left has been able to exert such influence as it has through broadly based coalitions with other classes and social forces. In those industrial sectors where management regimes and individualized terms and conditions make traditional forms of collective action difficult or impossible, and among many routine nonmanual and technical employees, there is evidence of widespread stress, anxiety, insecurity, and unhappiness at work. Finally, there is a large residual population with at best a marginal position in the labor market and dependent on ever-diminishing and humiliating welfare support. The potential social basis for a broad coalition of the left clearly does exist, and we have to look for other explanations of the widespread abandonment of class politics by former parties of the left, such as the UK Labour Party.

This takes us on to the place of environmental politics as a key part of the supposed shift in content of the political agenda away from questions of distributive justice and public provision of welfare and security. Perhaps, the most influential advocacy here has been Inglehart's (1977) identification of "postmaterialist" values, such as environmental quality, as increasingly important as societies and particular groups within them become more affluent. This suggests a growing autonomy of political issues from material interests and is coherent with notions of reflexivity and detraditionalization. In the case of Beck, environmental issues are treated as concerned with distribution—but of "bads" rather than "goods." Giddens, in contrast, detaches environmental issues from questions of distribution by treating the environmental movement as a response to industrial and technological development. Against the view of environmental politics as part of a postmaterialist agenda, it may be argued that concern about the most basic conditions for survival itself, about the poisoning of food and water supplies, about the danger of industrial accidents, about the unpredictable alteration of global climates, and so on could hardly be more "materialist." Moreover, there are countless empirical studies that demonstrate the processes through which ecological disruption and degradation impact most devastatingly on the poorest and least powerful communities, both within each country and globally (Epstein 1997; Field 1997). This takes us to Beck's claim that the pattern of distribution of bads implies a qualitative break from the politics of the distribution of goods. In part, again, Beck offers a misleading picture of the past. Many thousands of socialist activists in their local communities and in their trade unions have been concerned with environmental health provision, with campaigning against air and water pollution, and with health and safety standards in the workplace. Engels's study of the *Condition of the Working Class in England* was, after all, a pioneering work of environmental socialism (see Dennehy 1996; Benton 1996). Socialist analysis has always emphasized the parallelism between a lack of "goods" and a plentiful supply of "bads" endemic to capitalism. This tradition of grassroots labor movement activism on environmental issues is very much alive in the current trade union movement and has, indeed, been highlighted by some unions as part of their response to the more hostile context for trade union activity in the post-Thatcher years: "We do not have to choose between jobs and a healthy environment—we can and we must have both. . . . As a result of a recent T&G general executive council decision, it is now the T&G's policy that all our 10,000 union safety representatives should be trained in environmental—as well as health and safety—issues" (Bill Morris, T&G General Secretary, News Release, November 13, 1996).

However, what is indeed new is the intensity and the wider resonance across society of current concerns about ecological destruction. For reasons that will be explored in the next section, these features offer potential for broadening the appeal of socialist ideas and of the left more generally, rather than grounds for abandoning them. For now, however, I should note that environmental concern is increasingly differentiated in its expressions, and clear links can be seen between different definitions and policy agenda, on the one hand, and the interests of social groups and classes, on the other. In other words, the content and direction of the contemporary phase of environmental politics can increasingly be seen as an emergent arena of class conflict—but one that transforms and extends our understanding of class as it does so. Both Beck and Giddens counterpose the politics of the environment to those of class. My argument is that class politics has always, and quite centrally at the grassroots level especially, been about environmental questions, and that the new agenda of environmental politics both extends and is intelligibly continuous with that longer history. However, there is also something that transcends class politics in the new agenda of environmental politics. Beck's identification of a new order of risk does start to capture this. Unfortunately, Beck's optimistic expectation of a recognized universal interest in addressing these hazards is hard to sustain. Knowledge communities are increasingly aligned with interest groups in ways that make the identification and measurement of hazards permanently contested, and rival interests are affected in different ways by different policy prescriptions. Arguably, the risks of "simple" modernization retain more continuing salience than Beck acknowledges, while the new large-scale risks are more contentious in ways that broadly follow class cleavages than he is prepared to allow. However, awareness of the new order of risk, including the potential jeopardization of all life on Earth has, arguably, played a part in a widespread cultural shift in recent decades. A deepening anxiety and moral horror at the scale of ecological destruction is now quite widespread (Benton 1997b). Social movements that mobilize on this basis have undergone dramatic increases in membership and mobilizing capacity since the 1960s (see table 11.1).

Table 11.1 Membership of Selected Voluntary Organizations in the United Kingdom (in thousands)

	1971	1981	1991	1995
National Trust[a]	278	1,046	2,152	2,293
Royal Society for the Protection of Birds	98	441	852	890
Greenpeace	—	30	408	380
Civic Trust[b]	214	—	222	301
Wildlife Trust[c]	64	142	233	260
National Trust for Scotland	37	105	234	230
World Wide Fund for Nature	12	60	227	219
Woodland Trust	—	20	150	150
Friends of the Earth[a]	1	18	111	110
Ramblers Association	22	37	87	109
Council for the Protection of Rural England	21	29	45	45

Source: Organization concerned, Jowell et al. (1997).
[a]Data are for England, Wales, and Northern Ireland only.
[b]Members of local amenity societies registered with the Civic Trust on November 12, 1996.
[c]Includes the Royal Society for Nature Conservation.

They and their constituency represent yet a further possible element in a new coalition of the left, one binding together both social movements organized on the basis of class interest and one deriving from moral perspectives. Again, in terms of strategy if not of cultural content, there is no qualitative break between such a project and the past history of coalitions of the left.

Capitalism or Modernity?

In their understandable anxiety to avoid economically reductionist accounts of the relationship between capitalism and other fields of social life, the reflexive modernists are reluctant to assign any causal significance to the economy beyond its own boundaries. We are left with a typology of institutional "dimensions" of "modernity," but with no attempt to characterize the relationships between them nor the processes through which they are continuously reproduced as "dimensions" of a whole society. In the absence of such theorizing, the reader is left with the impression that each dimension is to be understood as an autonomous causal order in its own right. The same applies to the social movements that, in Giddens's account, arise as forms of resistance to each institutional dimension. Though he recognizes the anomalous character of the women's movement as transcending his institutional divisions, he continues to see, for example, the environmental and labor movements as sequestered from each other in their resistance to distinct institutional dimensions.

However, from an ecological-socialist point of view it is important to make a distinction between the general theoretical question of the causal links between, say, capitalism and the institutions of the state, on the one hand, and an economically reductionist answer to that theoretical question, on the other. The outline critique of the strategy of sustainable development that I offered at the beginning of this chapter addressed such questions about the limits and conditions of state regulation of capitalist markets and the forms of economic calculation made in them. So, while Giddens and Beck rightly acknowledge that capitalist development continues to generate material inequalities (in fact, the evidence is of increasing polarization of wealth and power as a result of economic globalization and deregulation), they give accounts of their favored "life politics" and "subpolitics" in ways that seem largely innocent of the implications of these material inequalities for the conduct of private lives, for the prospects of "democratization" in the political system, or for the potential of social movements to make changes in the noneconomic institutional "dimensions."

Again, both Beck and Giddens treat the development of science and technology as autonomous processes. In the case of Giddens, this is assigned to a distinct institutional "dimension" separate from capitalist economic relations. In Beck's work, a parallel sequestration is achieved by his identification of science and technology as expressions of an abstractly defined "instrumental reason," the legacy of the European Enlightenment, and characterizing the distinctively modern relationship to nature. The upshot for both writers is a portrayal of ecological crisis and large-scale hazards as consequences of a secular process of scientific and technical development, endemic to a definite stage of modernization, and subject to resistance on the part of single-issue environmental movements. These latter are then somewhat condescendingly criticized for their utopian and retrogressive desire to return to an "authentic" nature (which, apparently, no longer exists: "Today, now that it no longer exists, nature is being rediscovered, pampered. The ecology movement has fallen prey to a naturalistic misapprehension of itself" [Beck 1995: 65]).

So what is wrong with this? The current concern over the possibility of transmission of the bovine brain disease to humans in the form of Creutzfeldt-Jakob Disease (CJD) may provide us with an example. Superficially, the case seems to conform to Beck's characterization of the new large-scale hazards. The topic is subject to heated and unresolved scientific controversy, and since the situation is unprecedented, the extent of the risk is literally incalculable. Given the pervasiveness of beef derivatives in the processing of many other foods, medicines, and other products, and the global character of contemporary food distribution, the incidence of risk transcends spatial and social boundaries. Organized nonliability is also evident in the impossibility of tracing the source of infection in any particular case of the new form of CJD. However, if we follow the actual course of the politics of Bovine Spongiform Encephalopathy (BSE)/CJD we find something rather different from the emergence of a universal interest. In the United Kingdom, the issue shifted from a problem of public health to one of protection of the interests of the UK beef industry in the space of one day (a shift with which the British media complied almost unanimously). The response of the European Union provided an occasion for large sections of the press and the Euroskeptic wing of the Conservative Party to define the issue as one in which one's patriotic duty was to eat beef in defiance of malevolent German attempts to damage the British livestock industry. The labor opposition confined itself to uttering concern about job losses in the beef industry and demanding a still tougher line with Europe.

Clearly, all of this illustrates the extent to which there can be no "reading off" of perceptions of risk and responsibility from some supposedly "objective" measure. Competing interests and discursive frames offer widely differing and conflicting "codes" for making sense of the episode. But there are other problems in such approaches as Beck's. For one thing, the hazard was not generated by a technological advance, but rather by changes in animal feed regimes that were adopted in the pursuit of profit, together with changes in standards of feed processing that were made possible by the commitment of the Conservative government to a neoliberal philosophy of deregulation. The situation was one in which a hazard already foreseen (by the 1979 Royal Commission on Environmental Pollution) was engendered by a cost-cutting nonuse of available technology, not one resulting from the implementation of a hazardous new technology. As such, this suggests that the focus on scientific and technological innovation as primary causes of environmental hazards is much too narrow. Any adequate analysis of the BSE episode would have to recognize it as an overdetermined outcome of economic, political, and cultural processes interacting with one another. It would highlight the significance of the representation of farming interests in the MAFF, the dual role of the MAFF in its responsibility for both food production and food safety, the political ideology of the Conservative government, and the relation between government regulation and technical advisory bodies.

Power relations that operate *between* and *across* the "institutional dimensions," specific institutional structures, and identifiable sources of pressure and political decision all played their part in the genesis of this particular hazard. The effect of the reflexive modernizers' abstract separation of institutional domains, together with their view of the new order of industrial hazards as endemic to a phase of development of "modernity," then, is to undermine the possibility of the sort of complex empirical analysis that would be needed to gain social scientific insight into problems like BSE. Moreover, and probably unintentionally, the notion of reflexive modernization leads us to see episodes such as this as just more examples of an impersonal process of technological development making our lives more risky—the issues are depoliticized and organized nonliability is implicitly endorsed.

More generally, where technological innovation is implicated in the genesis of ecological hazards, as in such cases as nuclear power and biotechnology, the reflexive modernizers' tendency to represent scientific and technical innovation as occurring in their own, autonomous institutional "dimension" cuts them off from important insights available from work in the sociology of science and technology. Ever since the work of the late Thomas Kuhn, in the early 1960s, sociologists have been studying the ways in which social processes within the scientific community, external interests, and wider cultural resources can all affect not just the rate of scientific innovation, but also its very content and direction. This is not to argue, as do some self-styled "constructionists," that scientifically authenticated knowledge claims are mere cultural or discursive constructs arbitrarily related to their external referents. It remains possible to acknowledge the place of evidence and scientific reasoning in the shaping of scientific research agenda and knowledge claims, while still insisting that extraneous social and cultural influences also play a significant part. Similar considerations apply to technological innovation. So, if we take the case of nuclear power, the interconnections among the development of nuclear technology, economic interests, state policy in the area of energy generation, the ideology of modernism itself, and military strategy could hardly be denied: the reflexive modernizers' segregation of the political/administrative, economic, scientific/technical, and military institutional complexes from one another rules out the kind of integrated analysis that the case requires. In the area of biotechnology, as in many other fields of scientific research, there have been two notable trends in recent decades. One is that overall investment in scientific and technical research has shifted dramatically away from the public sector and is now concentrated in the research and development departments of the big corporations. The second is that publically funded scientific research is now subjected to criteria of evaluation that give high priority to anticipated commercial use (Webster 1991; Wheale and McNally 1988). Under such circumstances, to represent scientific and technical innovation as if it were an autonomous process, a mere correlate of a certain phase of "modernity" is little short of ideological mystification. The subordination of science in key sectors to the competitive priorities of private capital is all but complete.

Two consequences follow from my interpretation of the green and environmental movements. One is that they cannot, as Giddens tends to do, be confined to the role of resistors to new industrial technologies, in abstraction from the capitalist relations under which those technologies are developed and implemented. In so far as new technologies generate environmental hazards, ecological disruption, and damage to peoples' quality of life, they do so as complex, culturally mediated outcomes of state policies, the product and marketing strategies of capitalist firms, and patterns of class power. Oppositional social movements are both diverse and fluid. Empirically, we can observe complex and changing interpretative resources evolving within the social movements and emergent patterns of differentiation and realignment. In the United Kingdom, for example, the year-long dispute between Liverpool dockers and their employer had an environmental dimension, recognized by the strikers themselves, and was subsequently supported by a coalition of road protesters and other direct action networks (*Red Pepper*, 30 November 1996, 9). Indeed, the formation of the green parties in many European countries involved coalitions among previously quite diverse groupings of socialists, anarchists, civic activists, peace movement and feminist campaigners, and so on.

The second consequence is that a sociologically informed understanding of processes of scientific and technical innovation renders imaginable a qualitatively different institutionalization of science and technology. Opposition to current directions of scientific and technical change need not take the form of a backward looking, nostalgic desire for reversion to an earlier stage along a single-line developmental process, as Giddens and Beck represent it. On the contrary, an ecologically informed socialist perspective emphasizes the extent to which the direction of change in science and technology is currently shaped by the requirements of capital accumulation and state strategies in relation to military priorities, surveillance, control over labor processes, and product innovation. Neither scientific innovation nor technological invention as such need be opposed on this perspective. The key questions become, instead, how to detach research from its current embedding within the institutional nexus of capital and the state in such a way as to open up priorities in funding to a wider public debate, and to democratize decisions about the development and deployment of new technologies (see Irwin 1995; Irwin and Wynne 1996). Of course, both Beck and Giddens also favor opening up these areas of decision making to democratic accountability. However, their treatment of science and technology as autonomous vis-à-vis capital and the political/administrative system sidesteps difficult questions about the intensity of likely resistance on the part of both capital and the state to any such project, and the immense power vested in these institutional complexes. Only powerful and broadly based coalitions of social movements could have any hope of making headway with these ideas.

Finally, there is a third respect in which trying to understand ecological problems as overdetermined outcomes of the interaction of technical, economic, political, and cultural processes has implications for how we think about environmental politics. To see what these implications are, some more has to be said about the connections between specifically capitalist forms of economic organization and ecological degradation. The inseparability of economic growth (albeit uneven in both space and time) and capitalism does not directly imply ecological destruction: in principle, changes in the composition of capital and technical innovation could allow for economic growth (measured in value terms) without concomitant growth in ecological damage. However, the dominant forms of economic calculation under capitalism are abstract and monetary, subordinating to their logic substantive and "concrete" considerations about the management of the people, places, and materials involved in actual production processes. This feature renders capital accumulation particularly liable to unforeseen and unintended consequences at this concrete level—notably taking the form of environmental dislocations of one kind or another (see Benton 1989; 1992). Considerations such as these have led O'Connor (1996), the ecological Marxist, to postulate a "second contradiction" of capitalism to complement the "first contradiction" as identified by Marx (between capital and labor). This second contradiction is between the "forces" (including technologies) of production and the "conditions" of production (including human-provided infrastructures and social institutions as well as ecological conditions). In short, capitalism tends to undermine its own ecological (and other) conditions of existence. It follows that if these conditions are to be sustained or reconstituted, noneconomic agencies (for O'Connor, the state) have to intervene. In O'Connor's view, then, the labor and the environmental movements are both forms of social movement response to basic structural contradictions of capitalism. They may constitute alternative or parallel routes to a socialist transformation.

If O'Connor's analysis is right, it suggests that there should be an affinity between radical environmentalism and the labor movement, such that they should appear natural allies. If this were the case, then the sort of coalition whose possibility I outlined earlier between the labor movement and other social movements including radical environmentalists ought to be readily attainable. However, this has proved to be far from easy in practice. Sharp polarities between elements in both movements have frequently emerged, especially over trade-offs between jobs and environmental protection. Arguably, O'Connor's analysis is limited by its insufficient attention to the cultural means and value perspectives through which greens and environmentalists experience and understand processes of environmental degradation (Benton 1997b). These cultural forms and value perspectives have elements of both convergence and disparity in relation to those pervasive in labor movements. Even where radical greens, as is often the case, perceive "greed" and "profit" as the enemies of the environment, they by no means necessarily share other elements of a socialist understanding of capitalism and generally do not see transition to a socialist society as an obvious solution (in this, they are greatly assisted by the actual environmental record of the former state centralist regimes). It remains an open question whether existing patterns of ad hoc coalition and dialogue among greens, labor movement activists, feminists, animal rights campaigners, roads protesters, and so on will generate a more organically integrated and coherent new social force on the green left.

I have so far argued that an ecologically informed socialist approach, which analyses ecological hazards and dislocations as overdetermined effects of interactions among the various economic, political, and cultural processes of modern capitalist societies, has better explanatory potential than analyses conducted in terms of the more influential alternative framework of reflexive modernization. Such a green socialist explanatory framework emphasizes the causal importance of the dynamics of capital accumulation in generating ecological degradation and shows how relationships between state institutions and capitalist interests render ecological sustainability improbable without fundamental challenges to the power of capital. Against the advocates of reflexive modernization, it is argued that class relations remain and are likely to remain an important feature of the political life of contemporary capitalist societies and that the increasing presence of environmental issues high on the political agenda poses questions of social justice and democratic accountability that have a clear affinity with earlier divisions of the left and right. In terms of its normative implications, a green socialist analysis extends the case against capitalist economic organization already established by earlier phases in the history of socialism. However, it remains to be seen whether cultural differences and remaining areas of conflicting priorities will undermine currently widespread attempts to create green left coalitions among socialists, greens, and other progressive social movements and networks. Feasible transitional strategies and proposals for institutions that secure civil and personal liberties alongside the socialization of economic relations and the decentralization of administrative functions are still in the early stages of discussion among greens, feminists, socialists, and others (as a record of one such encounter, see, e.g., Red-Green Study Group [1995]).

REFERENCES

Arthur, C. J., ed. 1996. *Engels Today: A Centenary Appreciation.* Basingstoke: Macmillan.
Beck, U. 1992. *The Risk Society.* London: Sage.
———. 1995. *Ecological Politics in an Age of Risk.* Cambridge: Polity.
———. 1997. *The Reinvention of Politics.* Cambridge: Polity.
Benton, T. 1989. "Marxism and Natural Limits." *New Left Review* 178:51–86.
———. 1992. "Ecology, Socialism and the Mastery of Nature." *New Left Review* 194:55–74.
———, ed. 1996. *The Greening of Marxism.* New York: Guilford.
———. 1997a. "Engels and the Politics of Nature." In *Engels Today: A Centenary Appreciation,* ed. C. J. Arthur. Basingstoke: Macmillan.
———. 1997b. "Imagine the Alternatives." *Red Pepper* 34:22–23.
Bryson, A., and S. McKay. 1997. "What about the Workers?" In *British Social Attitudes: The 14th Report,* ed. R. Jowell, J. Curtice, A. Park, L. Brook, K. Thomson, and C. Bryson. Aldershot: Ashgate.
Buttel, F. H., and P. J. Taylor. 1994. "Environmental Sociology and Global Environmental Change." In *Social Theory and the Global Environment,* ed. M. Redclift and T. Benton. London: Routledge.
Dennehy, A. 1996. "The Condition of the Working Class in England." In *Engels Today: A Centenary Appreciation,* ed. C. J. Arthur. Basingstoke: Macmillan.
Dobson, A. 1996. "Environmental Sustainabilities: An Analysis and a Typology." *Environmental Politics* 5:302–323.
Eckersley, R. 1992. *Environmentalism and Political Theory.* London: UCL.
Epstein, B. 1997. "The Environmental Justice/Toxics Movement: The Politics of Race and Gender." *Capitalism, Nature, Socialism* 8:63–87.
Field, R. C. 1997. "Risk and Justice: Capitalist Production and the Environment." *Capitalism, Nature, Socialism* 8:69–94.
Giddens, A. 1991. *The Consequences of Modernity.* Cambridge: Polity.
———. 1994. *Beyond Left and Right.* Cambridge: Polity.
Goldsmith, E., R. Allen, M. Allaby, J. Davoll, and S. Lawrence. 1972. *A Blueprint for Survival.* Boston: Houghton Mifflin.
Goldthorpe, J. H., and G. Marshall. 1996. "The Promising Future of Class Analysis." In *Conflicts about Class,* ed. D. J. Lee and B. S. Turner. London: Longman.
Grubb, M., M. Koch, A. Munson, E. Sullivan, and K. Thornson. 1993. *The Earth Summit Agreements.* London: Earthscan and RiIA.
Hutton, W. 1995. *The State We're In.* London: Jonathan Cape.
Inglehart, R. 1977. *The Silent Revolution.* Princeton, N.J.: Princeton University Press.
Irwin, A. 1995. *Citizen Science.* London: Routledge.
Irwin, A., and B. Wynne, eds. 1996. *Misunderstanding Science?* Cambridge: Cambridge University Press.
Jowell, R., J. Curtice, A. Park, L. Brook, K. Thomson, and C. Bryson, eds. 1997. *British Social Attitudes: The 14th Report.* Aldershot: Ashgate.
Lang, T., and C. Hines. 1993. *The New Protectionism.* London: Earthscan.
Lee, D. J., and B. S. Turner, eds. 1996. *Conflicts about Class.* London: Longman.
Marshall. G., D. Rose, A. Newby, and C. Vogler. 1988. *Social Class in Modern Britain.* London: Hutchinson.
Meadows, D. H., D. L. Meadows, J. Randers, and W. W. Behrens III. 1972. *The Limits to Growth.* New York: Universe.

Mol, A. P. J. 1996. "Ecological Modernisation and Institutional Reflexivity: Environmental Reform in the Late Modern Age." *Environmental Politics* 5:302–323.

O'Connor, James. 1996. "The Second Contradiction of Capitalism." In *The Greening of Marxism*, ed. T. Benton. New York: Guilford.

Redclift, M., and T. Benton, eds. 1994. *Social Theory and the Global Environment*. London: Routledge.

Red-Green Study Group. 1995. *What on Earth Is to Be Done?* Manchester: RGSG.

Spaargaren, G., and A. P. J. Mol. 1992. "Sociology, Environment, Modernity: Ecological Modernization As a Theory of Social Change." *Society and Natural Resources* 5:323–344.

Vidal, J. 1996. "In the Forest, In the Dark." *Guardian*, 25 January, 1–3.

Weakliem, D. 1991. "The Two Lefts? Occupation and Party Choice in France, Italy and the Netherlands." *American Journal of Sociology* 96:1327–1361.

Weale, A. 1992. *The New Politics of Pollution*. Manchester: Manchester University Press.

Webster, A. 1991. *Science, Technology and Society*. Basingstoke: Macmillan.

Westergaard, J. 1996. "Class in Britain since 1979: Facts, Theories and Ideologies." In *Conflicts about Class*, ed. D. J. Lee and B. S. Turner. London: Longman.

Wheale, P., and R. McNally. 1988. *Genetic Engineering: Catastrophe or Cornucopia?* Hemel Hempstead: Harvester Wheatsheaf.

Woodiwiss, T. 1997. "Against Modernity." *Economy and Society* 26:1–21.

12

The Social Construction of Environmental Problems: A Theoretical Review and Some Not-Very-Herculean Labors

Steven Yearley

Numerous authors in Britain, continental Europe, and North America have deployed constructionist arguments in their analyses of environmental problems (e.g., Burningham and Cooper 1999; Hannigan 1995; Irwin 1995; Jasanoff 1992; Rayner 1991; Waterton and Wynne 1996; Yearley 1992). Though these authors agree on the general utility of such an approach, their precise understanding of constructionism differs. Hannigan adopts a pluralist, "sociology of social problems" stance, while Rayner favors an approach rooted in Douglas's cultural theory, and Yearley develops analytical strategies stemming from the sociology of science. Notwithstanding their differences, all these variations on constructionism are open to similar criticisms. In essence, the counterargument is that constructionist assumptions tend to minimize the explanatory role of the actual state of environmental harm or of actual environmental problems. Not only does this tendency give rise to poor explanations, so the argument goes, it is also morally or politically insupportable because it lends succor to those who want to suggest that environmental concerns are faddish or "merely" cultural.

Rather than rehearse familiar arguments about realism and constructivism, what I want to do in this chapter is to review areas of environmental sociology where constructionists' arguments are strong in explanatory terms and rebut the counterarguments of so-called critical and other kinds of realists. I propose to consider constructionist arguments in three areas of explanation, highlighting in each case their analytical adequacy and—at least in some sense—their superiority to realist approaches. The three areas are:

- the "construction" of particular environmental problems;
- the construction of "the environment" as an arena for social action or policy interventions (this involves examining what is counted in [and what out of] environmental discourse and, consequently, amounts to a study of the construction of the very idea of "the environment," as opposed to, say, "nature"); and
- the role of construction even in the case of scientific arguments.

I then develop these arguments to show how they have implications beyond the realist/constructivist debate by applying them to ideas about ecological modernization.

THE CONSTRUCTION OF PARTICULAR ENVIRONMENTAL PROBLEMS

In many respects, this is the easiest context for making the constructionist argument. At any particular moment, there are more potential environmental problems than there is public attention and media coverage devoted to them. Accordingly, the activities of social problem "constructors" are of critical importance.

A key recent example here is the Brent Spar oil platform that came to widespread public attention in western Europe in 1995. This was a floating oil storage facility belonging to Shell that had reached the end of its usefulness. Contrary to initial plans to salvage the platform, Shell investigated the disposal options and decided that sinking it in a submarine valley in the Atlantic northwest of Scotland was the best available option. Greenpeace learned of this disposal plan and mounted a highly public and strident campaign against this sea disposal. The campaign, which focused on an occupation of the Brent Spar, was supported by consumer boycotts of Shell gas stations and by occasional extreme acts of agitation such as fire bombing their stations. Greenpeace's reasoning was that all marine dumping of industrial materials should be avoided and that, in particular, any concession in this matter was likely to set a precedent for subsequent dumping of the debris from the North Sea oil industry. In the face of such bad publicity and the rising and unpredictable cost of a continent-wide boycott of its products, Shell changed its mind, leaving the UK government isolated as the sole proponent of the sea-dumping option. The platform was subsequently towed to a Norwegian fjord, one of few sheltered locations deep enough to accommodate the floating hulk, while Shell began its consultation procedures.

My aim in relating this well-known tale is to focus attention on the elements of construction. For one thing, this issue was conducted well out of the reach of direct public perception. Members of the public in Britain and in continental Europe had no independent idea of whether the platform contained toxic and dangerous material, whether it was likely to disintegrate unless disposed of quickly, or of the effects of disposal in an Atlantic trench. The realities of the problem were not directly evident to the tens of millions of people whose attention was enrolled and who were accordingly of negligible explanatory importance in accounting for the development of the controversy. Second, this topic commanded a great deal of media attention and government interest without anyone establishing that this was, in fact, the most pressing environmental problem of the day. Elsewhere in Britain, transport policy was at a critical stage with plans for new roads and new road-financing proposals under consideration. The majority of European Union member states were shaping up to do badly in meeting their greenhouse gas abatement targets. And the loss of European habitat through the expansion of road and rail links to satisfy the demands of the travel market was continuing. Of all these problems, the one on which popular action, media attention, and—consequently—governmental attention focused was the disposal of an oil platform.

This example can be used to generate some further general points. First, it is clear that established environmental campaign organizations (such as nongovernmental organizations [NGOs]) necessarily have certain organizational rigidities. Greenpeace, Friends of the Earth, and the World Wide Fund for Nature all have campaigning priorities. Given that their success is increasingly tied to their expertise, they need to consolidate their knowledge in particular areas. Accordingly, they are reluctant to campaign in areas outside of this hard-won expertise. At any given time, campaign organizations are likely to be running between five and ten campaign priorities and each comes with staffing implications. They cannot easily enter new areas of concern. Of course, part of the strategy of Greenpeace is to engage in activities with potential for high-profile coverage.

Campaign organizations depend on the willingness of the press and broadcast media to cover them. Such coverage can be won through assiduous cultivation of key contacts. The media personnel want good stories as much as the organizations want to win good coverage for their stories. But the conventions of media coverage and the obligations of the "selling" of news in the media market impose their own dictates. As the work of the Glasgow University Media Group indicates, only stories that change are readily amenable to treatment as news (1976: 267–268). Continued bad practice—for example, a persistent road-building policy program—is not "news."

Accordingly, there are good grounds for believing that the topics that rise to the top of the public's attention are not those where the reality of the problem is most well documented or where the real impacts are the greatest, but those where the agents that propel issues into the public consciousness have worked most effectively. It seems apparent that constructionist premises are entirely appropriate for the study of cases such as the Brent Spar and that realist objections (such as those routinely provided in papers such as Murphy [1995]) are immaterial to the explanation of the course of this incident over an oil platform.

THE CONSTRUCTION OF "THE ENVIRONMENT" AND THE USE OF SOME POPULAR SURROGATES

So far, I have set myself (and constructionism) a relatively easy test. My second labor is somewhat more arduous: to consider a constructionist approach to the question of what is counted in and what is counted out of "the environment." Let me take first things that are counted "in." According to one of the few essays on this particular topic, the agenda of issues that has become known as "environmental" has been a product of sociopolitical opportunities. In other words, in "an important sense, motorways, nuclear power, agriculture and conservation—self-evidently 'environmental' as they appear to be now—all had to be invented as issues by the environmental movement in the 1970s" (Grove-White 1991: 439). And, on Grove-White's analysis, this process took place largely through the medium of small openings in the political culture. His view is that it is the nodal institutions—such as public inquiries, parliamentary select committees, European Community institutions, and the media—meeting a "combination of opportunism and invention, of moral confidence and subtle disguises, of tactical calculation and innocent surprise, of historical intuition and obsession with future trajectories, which have propelled the environmental movement itself" (437).

Though it is clear that the assembling of a variety of disparate issues into a single environmental discourse, a discourse whose talisman is the earth and the planet, is fully compatible with constructionism, it is equally instructive to consider what has been omitted from the discourse. One source here is to consider the plight of particular individual animals. In Britain in June 1993, in a case known as the "Home Alone Fish," the Royal Society for the Prevention of Cruelty to Animals pressed charges against a man who left his tropical fish at home while he was working away from home for a week (*Guardian*, 13 June 1993). Though this case attracted mostly satirical responses in the news media and from public commentators, it nicely highlights the extent to which environmental concern coexists uneasily with concern for every last animal. The more serious difficulties experienced by the Royal Society for the Protection of Birds in justifying its antipathy to escaped ornamental drakes that team up with the females of wild species, or its occasional willingness to cull one bird species to protect another, indicate how tricky and contestable are the boundaries around concern for the natural world.

Similar difficulties arise over distinctions concerning the urban environment. Some city-planning commentators have aimed to extend the notion of the environment to include the ways in which certain forms of urban development stimulate isolation and the decline of social bonds. On this reading, crime is one of our environmental problems. Such exercises in boundary drawing can also be revealed by asking exactly what the brief of an environment ministry is and how it came to be that way. Finally, related difficulties arise, perhaps even more gravely, in relation to another disputed question: population. For many in the North, particularly those in right-leaning administrations, growing population levels (especially in the South) are self-evidently an environmental problem. Development campaigners from the South dispute this notion; they argue that the North's excessive consumption is far more damaging to the planet than the South's admittedly numerous but very low-consuming citizens.

In relation to population, the notable thing is the near-silence maintained by the North's leading NGOs. Green parties that are obliged to have policies across the board have at least been forced to confront the question of what their ideal population level for, say, Germany or the United Kingdom would be; they have also had to set out their attitudes to immigration into western Europe and so on. But the North's environmental NGOs have largely avoided campaigning on this issue even though it surfaces in all major international confrontations between policymakers of North and South—as, for example, at the Earth Summit in 1992. This brought about the ironic situation in which at the time of the UN population summit in Cairo, Porritt (1994), the former director of Friends of the Earth in London and a major influence on the British Green Party for many years, wrote a newspaper article calling on UK environmental NGOs to be less timid about the population issue. To coincide with the Cairo conference, he called on them to approach the minister for Overseas Development (Baroness Chalker, a Conservative), a woman who—he suggested—was open to arguments about the need to work through the empowerment of women in the Third World. He felt NGOs should be more strident in calling for internationally agreed policies to cut the global rate of population growth. This silence is explained, I suggest, by two factors. First, NGOs' existing technical expertise has, to date, not been concentrated in this area since it has not been an issue for campaigning within the North. Thus, inertia leads them to silence on an issue of great practical importance. Silence motivated by humility is compounded by a recognition that the subject is highly contentious and that, whatever view one takes, one is likely to antagonize as many people as one attracts. Pragmatic judgments favor silence too.

Accordingly, while the realist "problematic" implies that there is one correct or best interpretation of the environment, the constructionist strategy suggests that it is more interesting to examine how issues come to be construed as environmental (or not) than to try to arrive at the right classification.

Further evidence for the difficulty in mobilizing the environment in a straightforward way comes from the use of what one might call "surrogates" in campaign strategies. While, at one level, it is assumed that we all know what "the environment" means, on reflection it is a strikingly diffuse concept. Nearly everybody has some sort of interest in one or other aspect of environmental reform, but it is difficult to instill a general concern for the environment. Unlike a lovelorn panda or an endangered rhinoceros, it is hard to identify the environment itself as a victim. Two surrogates have generally been used. One is wildlife. Even if it might be said that humans have derived benefit at the same time as they have produced masses of pollution—for example, from pharmaceuticals—so that our interest in environmental reform is tempered, the same cannot be said of wildlife. Indeed, it is rather the reverse if one looks at laboratory animals or intensively farmed creatures. It was never an attractive trade-off for them. Thus, if one can show that acid rain is bad for fish and trees, then that is an unambiguous reason for condemning our practice.

The second surrogate is health. A good deal of campaigning effort has been directed at establishing that the environmental problems on which ecological groups concentrated have serious negative implications for human health. Thus, the health dangers arising from air pollutants have been made much of by campaigners even if public health officers might see smoking as a greater health risk (and at least in the United Kingdom, campaigners are famously enthusiastic smokers—as noted by Lean [1997]). Campaigners have tried to get the public to see that sulfur dioxide can promote bronchitis and is bad for asthmatics. Particulate matter from a diesel fuel plant can promote cancers. Similarly, water pollution from factories and land-fills is presented as leading to a danger to consumers, while recent opposition to the granting of a discharge license to British Nuclear Fuels for the Sellafield site has been developed around the health risks to which local (particularly fish-eating) residents are exposed.

By putting the argument this way, I am not trying to undermine the suggestion that environmental factors can adversely affect health. What I am suggesting is that campaigners have highlighted health effects as a way of getting people to care about something as nebulous as "environmental damage"; this has been the particular forte of groups such as Greenpeace and Friends of the Earth. In turn, the use of these surrogates has left its mark on the constitution of "the environment."

Accordingly, I suggest that, once again, the practical virtues for social science research of a constructionist approach can be appreciated. A constructionist approach sensitizes the social researcher to the way in which our conception of "the environment" has been shaped. In particular, it encourages the researcher to exam-ine the role of surrogates or "stand-ins" for the environment; by becoming central to environmental campaigns, such stand-ins come—over time—to shape the very constitution of the environment (see Yearley 1993).

CONSTRUCTIONISM AND SCIENTIFIC ARGUMENTS

It is now time to examine whether my arguments about the benefits of construction-ism apply to the role of scientific arguments within environmental discourse. The example I propose to use is biodiversity. Where previously people worried in a quali-tative way about the loss of species, the language of biodiversity allows these con-cerns to be expressed in a systematic and quantitative fashion. According to Mazur and Lee:

> During the 1970s and early 1980s . . . biological scientists and wildlife ecologists articu-lated the loss of biodiversity as a new and catastrophic problem. Pleas by the World Wildlife Fund [now the World Wide Fund for Nature] and other organizations in sup-port of endangered species were no longer limited to attractive animals but now stressed

the sheer quantity of species at risk, including insects. Wilderness, especially tropical rain forest, was defended not just for its beauty, but also for its value as habitat. These problems were energetically publicized by a network of influential biologists with foundation support and good contacts to the national news organs [in the United States]. (1993: 709)

It was in the context of this rising concern that the term "biodiversity" was coined in 1986 on the occasion of a conference in Washington, D.C., to raise official consciousness of these issues (703; see also Hannigan 1995: 146–161).

As most authors now note (see UK Government 1994: 10), biodiversity is held to consist of biological diversity at three levels: diversity between and within ecosystems and habitats; the diversity of species; and genetic variation within species. Biodiversity is highest where there are many types of habitats, relatively large numbers of species (since not all habitats support many species), and a good deal of variation within each species. Following the 1992 Earth Summit at which the Biodiversity Convention was signed by over 150 nations, the protection of biodiversity has come to be accepted as one of the major objectives of environmental policy across the globe (see Rojas and Thomas 1992: 152–159; Swanson 1991).

On the face of it, the fact that the protection of biodiversity—a term first developed by biological scientists and closely related to well-established work in ecology—has come to be accepted internationally as a goal of environmental policy might lead us to expect that in this instance environmental objectives would be precisely stated and strictly agreed. However, this is not the case. For one thing, there is a difficulty caused by the threefold nature of biodiversity. One cannot produce a single measure of biodiversity that works for all situations. Generally speaking, more biological diversity is better than less but, since some habitats are naturally species-poor (e.g., bogs support fewer species than most forests), there is no single scale for measuring the wealth of biodiversity. Second, the mere fact that biodiversity is high does not mean that the area in question is particularly natural. Botanical gardens such as Kew have high levels of biological richness, so too can domestic gardens, but this does not make them valuable environments in themselves. Third, the relationship between biodiversity and the size of a nature reserve or protected area is claimed by some commentators to be based on extrapolation from few, possibly anomalous, circumstances so that recommendations for conservation policies are far from straightforward.

Lastly, in most cases the biological richness of countries' wildlife has not been comprehensively charted. One cannot make definitive calculations about the best way to boost global biodiversity in the absence of comprehensive surveys, and such surveys could cost up to $200 million according to figures from the U.S. National Science Board (1989: 14). In the light of this fourth point, without figures on current biological diversity, the scientific community cannot even hope to make the definitive policy recommendations it would wish. Accordingly, one major commitment by Northern governments has been to support biological research and the development of systematic databases in order that recommendations can be made (see, e.g., UK Government 1994: 142–150). The National Science Board envisaged a global program of information gathering and ideally this would be based on a common, worldwide methodology. At present, however, biodiversity measurements are done on the basis of "quick and dirty" surveys, using relatively few marker species and in ways that accommodate to the perceived "realities" on the ground in terms of logging interests, the difficulties of reserve management, and so on.

In summary, therefore, in this case an apparently systematic term has displaced previous more qualitative approaches. However, the term bears the signs of its own construction. Though the term has been introduced into the global discourse of environmental policy, its theoretical presuppositions are open to doubt. Moreover, it is neither susceptible of one unambiguous interpretation nor capable in practice of being applied consistently on a worldwide basis. It is not sufficiently independent of local practicalities to provide a global metric. The conclusion echoes that of Douglas's followers; there appears to be considerable scope for cultural influences on the conceptions of nature that underlie scientists' discourse about the environment (Rayner 1991: 86–89). Even on realists' "home-turf," a constructionist approach seems to have much to recommend it.

CONSTRUCTIONISM "VERSUS" ECOLOGICAL MODERNIZATION

Having sought to argue that a constructionist position has strength in three areas of environmental sociology—just where one might suspect it of weakness—I now propose to turn to the implications of constructionism for a perspective that has achieved wide recognition within environmental social science and in environmental policy studies. The theory of ecological modernization offers itself as a comprehensive theoretical perspective for environmental sociology. Of most significance to my present concerns, ecological modernization is significantly at odds with constructionism because it assumes that there can be a progressive rationalization of environmental policy in the direction of modernization. As Mol helpfully expresses this idea, "[e]cological modernization indicates the possibility of overcoming the environmental crisis while making use of the institutions of modernity and without leaving the path of modernization. The project aims at 'modernizing modernity' by repairing a structural design fault of modernity: the institutionalized destruction of nature" (1995: 37). Ecological modernization appears to offer a rationalized track along which environmental policy travels, a vision quite at odds with the contingency of constructionist views.

Though a modernization perspective can be adopted as an interpretation of how environmental policy should be, for authors such as Mol and Spaargaren it stands as an account of how social practices in fact are (see Mol 1997: 140). The assertion of authors such as Mol (1997), Spaargaren (1997), Weale (1992), and Huber (1982) is that, in specific ways, commercial development and rising environmental standards go hand in hand. In particular, such authors assert that in specific cases the theory of ecological modernization actually accounts for the way in which reforms have been instituted: "[The] theory has proved valuable in elucidating *how* the 'environment' moves into the process of chemical production and consumption and transforms it" (Mol 1995: 391, emphasis in the original). Cases such as those of low-odor (or otherwise less dependent on organic solvents) paints or less and less environmentally damaging agropesticides become paradigmatic for this analysis. There is, so to speak, a ratchet effect that drives environmental reform in a single direction and makes it cumulative. Moreover, once one country establishes demonstrable environmental improvements through the pursuit of a policy, there is enormous pressure on others to follow. If limitations on acid emissions result in improved air quality or if one country reduces demands on landfill by obligatory recycling measures, others will (in some strong sense) have to follow. Its "betterness" is indubitable. Of course, this is not to imply that ecological modernization guarantees that enough reform can be achieved to avert major ecological problems. The claim is a weaker one than that, amounting to the idea that technological development, industrial policy, and environmental improvement can pull in the same direction.

While this approach may appear persuasive, a constructionist understanding of environmental problems leads one to doubt the assumption that "social learning" takes place in the straightforward sense proposed by advocates of ecological modernization. As I argued earlier, constructionists view societal decisions about what is a leading environmental problem or about "the best" response to environmental problems as the contingent outcome of interaction and negotiation. In other words, the identity of society's primary environmental challenges at any particular time is a matter that is socially constructed. Accordingly, the constructionist cannot assume that there is a simple "directionality" in social learning about environmental policies precisely because she or he views the category of "the environmental" as a contingent construction. The constructionist tends to assert that there is no one best or correct interpretation of what is environmental and what is not.

Moreover, the social constructionist does not believe one can look to science to underwrite in any unambiguous way the directionality of the modernization process. In other words, the scientification of environmental problems does not necessarily yield the best or most correct construal of the problems facing society, as was implied in my discussion of biodiversity in the last section. In particular, a measuring system or a metric is inevitably needed for establishing whether or not environmental policy is moving in the intended direction, yet (as the biodiversity case again suggests) no measures of most environmental policy variables can be incontrovertible.

If there were only one possible explanation for the trends that the ecological modernizationists observe (the apparent developing agreement on environmental policy measures), then the thesis of ecological modernization might appear persuasive. However, we can readily think of other explanations than Platonic ones for this state of affairs. The Single European Act, for example, gives the nations of Europe a material incentive to agree about what is environmental and what is not, without giving them the obligation to provide an ultimate grounding of those definitions. Indeed, we see from the horse trading that leads to agreements (e.g., over the rate of decrease of acidic gas emissions from large combustion plants) that the agreements are largely based on conventions, not on an underlying "reality." Of course, there is administrative pressure to tidy up anomalies, but this does not amount to compelling grounds for agreement over the definition of environmental phenomena themselves (see Jasanoff 1996; Yearley 1996: 117–121).

Elsewhere in the literature, ecological modernization is presented less as a theory of contemporary social change than as a label for an emerging policy discourse or ideology. Though Weale appears to embrace the concept as an analytic theory, he also describes it as an ideology (1992: 75–79). He notes that it does not amount to a "coherent, well-formulated doctrine"; rather, there are many differences of interpretation (78). On this view, ecological modernization is attractive precisely because it "forms a category of discourse that is a flexible and powerful instrument for criticising the assumptions built into the first-wave of environmental protection. [And it] became appealing to many members of the policy elite in European countries and international organisations during the 1980s" (78).

This general interpretation of ecological modernization as a flexible interpretative construct has recently been advanced by Hajer (1995). He observes how it became a portmanteau term describing a collection of policies and outlooks. A variety of actors in various countries and supranational bodies could assent to the term without necessarily agreeing in detail about the policy proposals to which their shared commitments should allegedly lead. In his detailed tracking of the way that policies over acidification were developed in the light of avowed commitments to ecological modernization, he indicates how the two elements were mutually constructed. In so doing, Hajer also demonstrates how a constructionist approach to ecological modernization may be more empirically rewarding than an approach that treats ecological modernization at face value as a theory of social development.

CONCLUSION

In this brief chapter, I demonstrated that sociological research on the environment conducted in line with the social constructionist position is not, in fact, incapacitated by the kind of weaknesses ascribed to it by opponents such as Murphy. Far from it. I argued that in three key areas of environmental sociology, a social constructionist approach is empirically rich; it encourages the analyst to open up questions that are overlooked or regarded as nonquestions by realist authors and provides a sound basis for empirical social scientific inquiry. Moreover, the characteristic focus on the "making" of the environment as an arena for policy and political action provides a strong alternative to the presuppositions of modernist readings of the ecological modernization approach.

REFERENCES

Burningham, Kate, and Geoff Cooper. 1999. "Being Constructive: Social Construction and the Environment." *Sociology* 33:297–316.

Glasgow University Media Group. 1976. *Bad News*. London: Routledge.

Grove-White, Robin. 1991. "The Emerging Shape of Environmental Conflict in the 1990s." *Royal Society of Arts Journal* 27:437–443.

Hajer, Maarten. 1995. *The Politics of Environmental Discourse: Ecological Modernization and the Policy Process*. Oxford: Oxford University Press.

Hannigan, John. 1995. *Environmental Sociology: A Social Constructionist Perspective*. London: Routledge.

Huber, J. 1982. *Die verlorene Unschuld der Ökologie: Neue Technologien und Superindustrielle Entwicklung*. Frankfurt am Main: Fischer.

Irwin, Alan. 1995. *Citizen Science: A Study of People, Expertise and Sustainable Development*. London: Routledge.

Jasanoff, Sheila. 1992. "Science, Politics, and the Renegotiation of Expertise at EPA." *Osiris* 7:1–23.

———. 1996. "Science and Norms in Global Environmental Regimes." In *Earthly Goods: Environmental Change and Social Justice*, ed. Fen O. Hampson and Judith Reppy, 173–197. Ithaca, N.Y.: Cornell University Press.

Lean, Geoffrey. 1997. *The Independent on Sunday*, 16 March, 5.

Mazur, Allan, and Jinling Lee. 1993. "Sounding the Global Alarm: Environmental Issues in the US National News." *Social Studies of Science* 23:681–720.

Mol, Arthur. 1995. *The Refinement of Production: Ecological Modernization Theory and the Chemical Industry*. Utrecht: International.

———. 1997. "Ecological Modernization: Industrial Transformations and Environmental Reform." In *The International Handbook of Environmental Sociology*, ed. Michael Redclift and Graham Woodgate, 138–149. Cheltenham, UK: Edward Elgar.

Murphy, Raymond. 1995. "Sociology As If Nature Did Not Matter: An Ecological Critique." *British Journal of Sociology* 46:688–707.

Porritt, Jonathon. 1994. "Birth of a New World Order." *Guardian*, 2 September, 8–9.

Rayner, Steve. 1991. "A Cultural Perspective on the Structure and Implementation of Global Environmental Agreements." *Evaluation Review* 15:75–102.

Rojas, Martha, and Chris Thomas. 1992. "The Convention on Biological Diversity: Negotiating a Global Regime." In *International Environmental Treaty Making*, ed. Lawrence E. Susskind, Eric J. Dolin, and J. William Breslin, 143–162. Cambridge, Mass.: Program on Negotiation Books.

Spaargaren, Gert. 1997. *The Ecological Modernization of Production and Consumption: Essays in Environmental Sociology*. Wageningen: University of Wageningen.

Swanson, Tim. 1991. "Conserving Biological Diversity." In *Blueprint 2: Greening the World Economy*, ed. David Pearce, 181–208. London: Earthscan.

UK Government. 1994. *Biodiversity: The UK Action Plan*. London: HMSO Cm 2428.

U.S. National Science Board. 1989. *Loss of Biological Diversity: A Global Crisis Requiring International Solutions*. Washington, D.C.: National Science Foundation.

Waterton, Claire, and Brian Wynne. 1996. "Building the European Union: Science and the Cultural Dimensions of Environmental Policy." *Journal of European Public Policy* 3:421–440.

Weale, Albert. 1992. *The New Politics of Pollution*. Manchester: Manchester University Press.

Yearley, Steven. 1992. *The Green Case*. London: Routledge.

———. 1993. "Standing in for Nature: The Practicalities of Environmental Organisations' Use of Science." In *Environmentalism: The View from Anthropology*, ed. Kay Milton, 59–72. London: Routledge.

———. 1996. *Sociology, Environmentalism, Globalization*. London: Sage.

13

When the Global Meets the Local: Critical Reflections on Reflexive Modernization

Rosemary B. McKechnie and Ian Welsh

Risk and globalization were two of the most prominent categories of analysis applied to the environment during the 1990s. The concept of global environmental risk has been harnessed to a worldwide policy agenda that has sought to identify equally global solutions. It is part of our argument here that the notions of global risks and global solutions are both illusions created by the over extension of Northern science-driven perceptions. Global risk categories are byproducts of laboratory and computer modeling techniques that substitute analysis conducted in "closed" systems for analysis based on the observation of more complex lived relations (see Davis 1996). When many of the apparently strong global risks are scrutinized in this more discursive manner, they prove to be heavily mediated by local physical and social factors. For example, the impacts of acid rain and radioactive fallout depend on local soil types, while the risks of global warming depend on physical geography. Beyond these physical factors, local cultural and social practices define what becomes acknowledged as environmental risks and the appropriate responses. Without the degree of generalization achieved by the policy sciences, the apparently all-inclusive canvas of global environmental change becomes a patchwork of local differences.

The second major element of our argument is that contemporary debates about reflexive modernization and ecological modernization neglect local knowledge in the pursuit of modernist generalizable knowledge. Two consequences flow from this. First, attempts at global solutions founder on local differences, both physical and social. Second, by concentrating on the accumulation of policy-relevant "input," policy science effectively ignores and silences large areas of social space. These concerns assume a position of considerable importance in relation to recent debates about reflexivity (Beck, Giddens, and Lash 1994) that we pursue in this chapter. We argue two main points in relation to these debates that are best summarized here prior to elaboration.

The significance of the silenced social spaces we are alluding to has at least two dimensions. In terms of policy relevance, it is clear that becoming sensitive to local knowledges is desirable to produce better policy. Second, and extending far beyond this functionalist accommodation, we would argue that attention should be given to social forces prefigurative of both a revised science and a transformed society. These are the dimensions to which we devote most of our attention. It is part of our argument that among the silenced social spaces of high modernity lie multiple sources of critical reflection that are neglected, even excluded, by contemporary sociological theory. The exclusion of increasing tracts of social space from the central policy concerns of high modernity (e.g., the silencing of local voices over environmental issues and the exclusion of more and more people from welfare provision) raises the possibility of profoundly different models of social change. Sociology has approached social change as a consequence of actors pursuing some purposive goals requiring some degree of rational bargaining. We argue here that the potential for social change driven by the withdrawal of support and quiescence by citizens represents an important though neglected avenue of inquiry. Withdrawal can be selective, for example, the loss of faith in quite specific institutions, or more pervasive, for example, the loss of faith in a whole social formation such as the former Soviet Union. In what follows, we use the work of Melucci and Maffesoli to extend existing debates about reflexive modernization in an attempt to accommodate the concerns sketched earlier.

The methodological approach we advocate would lead to "theory grounded in rigorous empirical research." Knorr-Cetina makes similar calls for methodological situationalism, which demands that descriptively adequate accounts of large-scale phenomena be grounded in statements about actual social behavior in concrete situations (1988: 22). This is entirely congruent with our concern for the environment as an inescapably *social* site imbued with meaning and value created by human agency (McKechnie and Welsh 1994; Welsh 1996). We sense a growing distance among theories about risk and social change, the environment, and empirical research documenting events and issues. This distance can be dangerous in two ways.

First, the concepts relating to processes and social mapping can only be critically assessed as effective and useful insofar as empirical material can be addressed within the framework of any theoretical schema. Here, we are particularly concerned that the increasingly salient concept of "reflexivity" is becoming theoretically sophisticated even though little attempt is being made to trace the way people work reflexively with ideas about the environment, or about themselves and others, in different contexts to explore how this might be related to changing social relations and changing practice. Second, unless there is a dialogic relationship between empirical material and theory, some important areas of social change will remain undertheorized, or completely missed because they do not fit the criteria of contemporary theoretical frameworks. We contend that, at present, the actions and thoughts of large sections of the population are effectively invisible within theories of reflexive modernization. We will now address several problems with reflexive modernization before moving on to the processes of exclusion we consider so important.

First though, it is vital to recognize that the debates about reflexive modernization have been hampered by a basic difference in vocabulary that, despite attempts to produce clarity (Lash, Szerszynski, and Wynne 1996), still produces confusion and elision between social scientists of different nationalities. Accordingly, we will spend some time attempting to clarify the barriers created by language before considering the reflexive modernization theories of Beck, Giddens, and Lash.

REFLECTING ON REFLEXIVE MODERNIZATION

In this section, we focus in particular on the role played by "reflexivity" as a concept in the works of Beck, Giddens, and Lash. We argue that each of these writers has a conception of reflexivity that operates at a discrete level, both analytically and socially. Following from this, these versions of reflexivity prioritize, explicitly or implicitly, different notions of power. Part of the problem confronted in the debate around reflexive modernization, we argue, arises from slippage between these various levels of engagement and the interchangeable way in which different forms of power are implicitly evoked. This has serious consequences for the way reflexivity as a concept can be operationalized in empirical research.

To appreciate Beck's use of reflexive modernization, it is necessary to adopt the German use of reflexivity, which differs from Anglophile traditions. "Reflexivity" for Beck means "more of the same" because the root of the word "reflex" relates to a response within a limited and prescribed range. Reflexivity in this sense is completely different from the sense of "reflexive subjects" developed within ethnomethodological approaches and appropriated by Giddens via the work of Goffman (Giddens 1990; 1991). Reflexivity within Beck's discourse does not produce fundamental change; it produces more risks and more attempts to control/manage/limit risks by the same means.

For Beck, reflexivity is a necessary step on the way to reflection on modernity, where reflection means critical self-appraisal. Reflexive modernization is thus a process that produces a deepening crisis of chronic risk production. In terms of Beck's work, the key question then becomes one of how reflexivity can be transformed into critical reflection. This is an area of considerable ambiguity that underlies Beck's debate with Giddens and Lash, both of whom have models of reflexivity that are based on the potential for critical, conscious change.

A minimalist summary of Beck's position appears to be that "the concept of risk society provides a term for this relationship of reflex and reflection" (Beck 1996a: 28). In Beck's work, an important part in this relationship is performed by "subpolitics" that shapes "society from below" (Beck, Giddens, and Lash 1994: 23). For

Beck, subpolitics represents "a non-institutional renaissance of politics." Beck's argument here has several elements: the increasingly hollow nature of institutions in terms of legitimacy; the increasingly critical, that is, reflective, nature of individuals; and the capacity for collective actors' "citizens initiatives" to take initiatives that redefine political agendas (Beck 1997: 94–98). These processes blur the boundaries between institutions and subpolitics, leading to a heightened level of collective reflection. This leads Beck to characterize subpolitics as constituted by actors closely aligned to contested policy domains.

The reflective impetus of subpolitics is thus transformed into a policy-oriented, rational, strategic set of capacities (Beck 1997: 103). The actors Beck mentions—including professions, trade unions, occupations, companies, and the German nuclear industry—are revealing in this respect. For the purposes of our present argument, the point of note here is that the grassroots social movement actors gain a voice in this model of subpolitics only when their input has been translated into the language of problems recognized by more formalized actors. It is part of our argument that the process of translation in effect strips such actors of *their* voice by acknowledging only part of that which is being communicated.

This recent reformulation is consistent with Beck's earlier work. In *Risk Society* (1992), the main mechanisms of reflection included the establishment of a peoples science court through which the "critical application of science to itself" could be achieved. Beck has also endorsed the "roundtable" discussions widely used to establish social and environmental agendas in central and eastern European (CEE) countries and subsequently adopted more widely, for example, the UK government established a Roundtable on Sustainability. We have continually been skeptical about the capacity of such mechanisms *alone* to produce a state of reflection capable of producing the kind of humanist constraint implicit in Beck's arguments about a bifurcated modernity (Welsh 1996; 2000a).

The other far less well-developed route to reflection contained in Beck's work has revolved around the wider role of new social movements (NSMs). Beck recognizes the importance of the more prominent postwar social movements, particularly feminism, environmentalism, and the peace movement. At times, however, he subordinates environmental social movements to science, writing that they have to "make use of all the methods and means of scientific analysis in order to succeed with their claims" (1992: 71). In other passages, it appears that the combination of media commentary and social movement mobilizations is capable of producing reflection irrespective of the science (Beck 1996a). Here, there is a reluctance to grant NSMs any degree of autonomy. Their claims and campaigns *have* to be translated into the language of science and policy communities to have any prospect of influencing events. As Bauman wrote after reading *Risk Society*, it is almost impossible to imagine any alternative capable of being expressed in terms other than scientific and technical ones (1993: chapter 7). The influence of the deeply ingrained reliance on substantive forms of rationality within German social science and deep suspicion of affective forms of sociality, long associated with fascism, would perhaps explain this.

Beck's perspective presumes a uniformity of rational response and cognitive style over huge areas of social space. There is little engagement with the different positions from which people experience environmental risk, either in terms of the kind of reflection specific social and cultural contexts might give rise to, or to socially determined differences in actors' agency, that is, their ability to voice and act on their views. There is, then, little latitude for considering the kinds of contestation that might arise from reflection. The shifting of everyone's vision of events and institutions apparently becomes an expression of the autonomous structural dynamics of the risk society.

In our view, Beck's notion of reflexivity has to be understood as an inescapably *structural* phenomenon reproduced through institutional practices. To the extent that it produces any change, this notion of reflexivity deepens and extends the prevalence of risk in the global risk society for Beck. It is not part of a solution if it is part of the perfection of the problem that *might* enable the transition to a phase of reflection within which the constrained humanist side of modernity may reassert itself.[1]

GIDDENS AND REFLEXIVE SUBJECTS

Beck's work on reflexive modernization parallels that of Giddens and Lash and has given rise to a substantive debate within sociology and environmental sociology. It is not our intention to rehearse this debate here, as this has been done elsewhere (e.g., Beck, Giddens, and Lash 1994; Lash and Urry 1994; McKechnie and Welsh 1994; Welsh 2000a; Wynne 1996). Instead, we want to underline that the argument about silenced margins advanced here applies equally to the work of Giddens despite his apparent recognition of NSMs as a means of "riding the juggernaut of modernity."

We make this claim on two bases. First, while Giddens's model of reflexivity is based on reflexive subjects, the impetus for this reflexivity is derived from the double hermeneutic nature of knowledge spiraling in and out of social sites. Giddens's resultant schema of expert and abstract systems effectively subordinates local knowledges and cultural understandings in a manner similar to that performed by science within Beck's model (McKechnie and Welsh 1994; Welsh 2000a; Wynne 1996). Second, in arguing that NSMs can constrain or control modernity, Giddens exaggerates the capacity of such actors as bearers of reformulated knowledge and social relations. While Wynne (1996) reproaches Giddens for neglecting the sociology of science literature, we would reproach him for neglecting the NSM literature dealing with the practice and lived relations of such movements. Anyone familiar with this area as a research site is only too aware of the almost endemic conflicts and nuanced differences that permeate such activity. To argue that such unstable, conflict-ridden collectivities represent the substantive actor capable of constraining an advanced technical and social formation is barely credible.

Having said this, Giddens's preoccupation with trust in these contexts provides a useful avenue that deserves further empirical investigation capable of explicating the power dimensions embedded in his model. Power here relates to questions such as whose knowledge, knowledge constituted by what means, for what purpose, transmitted by which means, received in what ways, and, last but by no means least, knowledge based on which assumptions about the nature of the human subjects over which it is to have dominion? There is also a need to examine the ways in which the reflective margins, whether these be termed NSMs or not, become mobilized in ways that can significantly change modernity.[2]

Giddens is right to argue that there is *some* connection among institutional change, knowledge, and social movement mobilizations, but his theory sheds little substantive light on how this occurs or how knowledge is defined and contested. Giddens and Beck confront variants of the same problem here. Giddens's model of individually reflexive subjects needs to address the ways in which individual expressions coalesce into collective ones. Beck is left needing a means of explaining the transition from reflexivity to reflection.[3]

The emphasis on knowledge in general, and expert knowledge in particular, diverts attention away from specifically social and cultural aspects of reflexivity to which the term "social distance" better applies.[4] By adopting "social distance" as an analytical focus, attention is directed away from rational knowledge toward specifically social and cultural elements of reflexivity/reflection. We would suggest that social distance is a key constitutive process in the generation of reflection, *both* within institutions of modernity and the silenced margins we are centrally concerned with here. For example, we can point to various whistle-blowers from within the British nuclear industry where reflection arose through the transgression of social roles and responsibilities.[5] In a more general sense, citizens make trust judgments on social criteria as much as any other. Confronted with ambiguous or incomprehensible expert assurances, citizens' responses are mediated by the quality of interpersonal exchanges. Presentations of self that appear arrogant, condescending, or authoritarian become markers for doubt and suspicion within lay/expert interactions. Social distance is, of course, at a maximum when public expressions of dissent take forms that locate themselves outside the boundaries of conventional intervention. The growing recourse to direct action over an increasingly diverse range of environmental issues throughout the mid-1990s and early 2000s suggests that such "extreme repertoires" are becoming increasingly common.[6]

These upwellings of creative resistance require something more than a consideration of the role of knowledge and expertise to explain their purchase among an increasingly diverse range of social groups. Lash, the third contributor to the reflexive modernization debate, comes closest to developing a model of reflexivity capable of accommodating these margins.

LASH—AESTHETIC REFLEXIVITY

Lash was deeply influenced by witnessing some of the "spontaneous" mobilizations that eventually resulted in the fall of the Berlin Wall in 1989. Like Beck and others, Lash was struck by the capacity of the will of the people to exercise the last rites over an eclipsed regime. This early exposure lead Lash to argue that "reflexive action is characterised first and foremost by choice, by the recognition that alternatives exist ... in terms of (a) the ends, (b) the means, (c) the conditions, and (d) the legitimation of action" (1990: 149). Echoes of this initial formulation can be seen in Lash's subsequent formalization of reflexivity. This emphasizes the importance of structural reflexivity "in which agency, set free from the constraints of social structure, then reflects on the 'rules' and resources of such structure; reflects on agency's social conditions of existence." Second, there is "self-reflexivity in which agency reflects on itself. In self reflexivity previous heteronomous monitoring of agents is displaced by self monitoring" (Lash, Szerszynski, Wynne 1996: 115–116).

Lash is at pains to acknowledge the information/knowledge component of reflexivity, but argues for a second "aesthetic, moment of reflexivity" of a "mimetic nature" from the tradition of modernist art (Lash, Szerszynski, and Wynne 1996: 135). Lash's aesthetic thus derives from a reading of Adorno that prioritizes the importance of an iconic politics based on mimetics. In this, the cultural framing that takes place through iconic praxis mediates the role of knowledge-based cognition. Our primary reservation over this approach is that aesthetic reflexivity is presented as a "second moment," implying that the cultural processes of aestheticization operate on a range of existing categories fixed in knowledge formations. By arguing for a second moment of aesthetic reflexivity, Lash precludes the possibility that aesthetic registers can precede knowledge formation. Second, we find the notion of aesthetics sketched by Lash too restrictive in that it draws attention too firmly toward visual representations.

We would argue for a tripartite model of aesthetic reflexivity that goes some way to overcoming these limitations. First, in relation to the visual, we recognize the importance of "conscious" iconic praxis where iconic images derived from existing knowledge-based issues are deliberately produced. Greenpeace's use of focus groups to identify the most potent forms of images prior to embarking on direct actions intended to yield precisely such media footage is a clear example of this. Second, we would identify acts of "authentic" iconic praxis. In contrast to conscious forms, these involve the generation of iconic images as a byproduct of environmental engagement. British antiroads actions resulted in a plethora of such images throughout 1996 and 1997, partly as a result of innovations in direct action repertoires. These included tunneling and tree nesting to prevent site clearances.[7] Third, we want to argue for much more diverse forms of aesthetic reflexivity independent of produced images.[8]

Here, we are arguing that reflexive/reflective practices also arise from within the sphere of affect and require incorporation into existing approaches to reflexive modernization. This is an area where grounded theorizing is needed to elaborate the range of such registers, but completed work provides us with an illustrative example. Interviews with environmental activists in the 1970s and 1990s[9] suggest that one source of the intensity of feeling leading to intervention arises from the contemporary transgression of an environment of which individuals have particularly cherished and clear memories. These memories frequently date from childhood, but become significant in mobilizing individuals in adulthood. The growing linkages between environmental and social justice movements suggests to us that other likely sources include the experience and acknowledgment of inequalities. To the extent that these expressions take forms that are not recognized through the categories generated by theories of reflexive modernization, then they represent silenced social space.

THE LIMITS OF REFLEXIVE MODERNIZATION

We have taken some time to deal with each of the major contributors to the reflexive modernization debate. But it is now time to draw out the key points for the argument we develop here. The first point of importance is that to varying degrees all three authors prioritize rational components in their model of reflexivity. In Beck, this is expressed through a reliance on science to reveal the latent risks of wealth production that precipitate the risk society. In Giddens, knowledge is used in a less closely prescribed manner, but the introduction of expert systems performs a substantially similar role to that of science in Beck's account. Finally, Lash argues for a version of aesthetic reflexivity via a reading of Adorno, which emphasizes the importance of iconic praxis. We would point out that even in the hands of this accomplished and often passionate advocate, aesthetic reflexivity occurs as a "second moment" (Beck, Giddens, and Lash 1994: 140) that is prefigured by rational cognition. The prioritization of the rational cognitive process is thus still present but in a weakened, mediated form.

Our strong stance here is that there are no grounds for systematically prioritizing rational processes in configuring reflexivity or reflection. To the contrary, we would defend the primacy of social and cultural framing as sources of both reflexivity and reflection. We feel that theoretical frameworks need to be enriched by engagement with some empirical research on contemporary events. We are arguing that reflexivity be defined more widely, rather than defining it more closely; we need to open the term out so that it can encompass a variety of ways of critically working with ideas about the environment and social relations. In adopting this approach, we are decentering the role of "scientific knowledge" in the work of Beck, and "knowledge," more widely defined in the work of Giddens, in the process of reflexivity.

We argue that general shifts in the way society and the environment are lived and worked do not occur within a neat overarching definitional process, but quite the opposite. Globalization and environmental change open key concepts such as society, environment, and institutions to contestation. This very contestation is what allows risk society and reflexive modernization purchase in the first instance. Furthermore, specifically marginal social locations are particularly important sources of contestation. The first of these—the large silent areas of social space, sections of the population marginalized geographically, or by gender, race, and economic position—we have already touched on.[10] These areas continue to appear inactive in contemporary theoretical frameworks. Furthermore, the focus on individual and institutional change within reflexive modernization has led to an eclipse of interest in the boundaries and social relations that create different localities. Scratching the surface of these apparently passive and uninteresting stretches of social space could reveal how large sections of the population are participating in contemporary issues. The tendency to treat the resultant social expressions as minor, unrelated incidents rather than a large-scale, systemic phenomenon must raise questions about the wide-spread neglect of such events elsewhere. The assumption of passivity across such large tracts of social space is nothing more than an assumption. We believe that social space has far more vitality than this suggests and that, in conjunction with NSMs, apparently silent masses can become agents of change.

SILENCE AND THE GLOBAL RISK SOCIETY

This inability to address silenced social spaces further confounds social science when these social spaces inexplicably erupt in actions (for an example of such an inexplicable eruption from within the sociology of science literature, see Irwin and Wynne [1996: 42]). Wynne's work on Cumbrian sheep farmers has shown that within these apparently passive groups there is often a more developed sense of the social relations of "reflexivity." The farmers were aware of their subordinate position in the eyes of the experts with whom they had to deal and of the constraints this placed on their interactions. In contrast, the experts remained blind to this power relation, inadvertently reinforcing the silence until the dominated were forced to find voice through other means. Then, apparently acquiescent sections of the population suddenly appeared to reject expert views. It is part of our argument that we are witnessing the eruption of many such repressed pools of silence that express social forms of alienation through putatively environmental mobilizations, many of which involve "risks." For example, most media and academic commentary on the social movement actors contesting environmental and social justice issues on the streets of Seattle in 1999 reproduced the view that this movement emerged from out of the blue (Tabb 2000; Wainwright, Prudham, and Glassman 2000); Welsh (2000b), however, documented the origin of the movement in northwest Europe during the summer of 1996. Grounding theory in empirical research would overcome some of the constructed "blindness" of theoretical approaches that prioritize the concepts of the theorist. Grounding theory locates individuals' constructions of particular environmental issues within the multiplicity of wider social relations. This is important for sociological theorization, as it directs attention toward the ways in which individuals and groups have unequal abilities to articulate their views and shape their actions. The evaluation of environmental risk is accordingly either silenced or magnified by social context. This inequality is an important dynamic. As Callon points out, sociologists of science have been willing to accord equal validity to actors' views of nature and scientific/technical constructions, yet this has not been extended to actors' views about society (1986: 197). We argue that actors' social positions and identities shape not only their ideas about issues, but also the ways they voice these views, to whom, and how they are understood (or even noticed at all) by others. This has the uncomfortable consequence of dislodging science and social science from a privileged definitional position.

Material from ethnographic work on the Isle of Man carried out under the Public Understanding of Science initiative in Britain illustrates how models of reflexivity predicated on individuals and rationality appear extremely problematic from a grass-roots context. The Isle of Man is something of a constitutional oddity. The island is situated in the Irish Sea, but is not part of the United Kingdom. It is a Crown dependency, and Tynewald, the Manx parliament, has almost complete freedom to legislate in domestic matters, though the United Kingdom is responsible for international matters. The issue of post-Chernobyl contamination brought expert knowledge to bear on local practices, raising many similar issues to those described by Wynne in Cumbria (McKechnie 1996) and by Paine (1987; 1992) in relation to Lapp pastoralist populations. The livelihood of local sheep farmers, whose way of life had symbolic importance for the community, was threatened. Here, the most important issues were those of whose knowledge was communicated and expressed authoritatively and how. These questions gave rise to local framing of the issue, with the emphases on "local" rather than "individual."

Expert pronouncements were framed by institutional/political relations with the mainland and perceived to be framed by interrelated interests. In Manx eyes, institutions of radiological protection were linked with Sellafield and the UK government whose political strategies were suspect. "As for the NRBP [National Radiological Protection Board], they're seen by most as part of the government-cum-BNFL [British Nuclear Fuel Set] set, I just don't know how far that is true, but they are perceived as the same and so they just don't have credibility. Likewise MAFF [Ministry of Agriculture Fisheries and Food] are easily dismissed as just another part of the U.K. establishment" (McKechnie 1996: 145). However, the collapse of all the institutional and political boundaries concerned into a UK/Isle of Man divide meant that Manx sheep farmers were culturally less isolated than their Cumbrian counterparts. Cumbrian farmers were confronted by policies that were impracticable and alien in their formal style and planning, while their own knowledge of local habitat and farming practices were ignored. In the Manx case, common uncertainties linked local politicians, monitoring agencies, and farmers. They worked through the uncertainty together and created regimes of surveillance that recognized the practical constraints within which farmers worked. Expert knowledge crossing the Manx/UK boundary entered into a cultural field that effectively undermined the authority of scientific pronouncements. Not only was there a strong positive countervailing emphasis on "common sense" practical knowledge, but there was also the aesthetic code shaping the cultural style of communication on the island that provided a basis for dismissal of technical sophistication. Authority rested squarely on egalitarian ideas that valued "plain speech" highly and sanctioned any propensity to mobilize high culture or science in an exclusionary way. Local experts were evaluated in terms of morality, of practical competence in known fields, and style of communication. Trust preceded knowledge claims.

The Manx case is not an obvious example of risk giving rise to reflexivity, and that is exactly why it is important. From the outside, nothing much appeared to be happening; there was little visible local activity or protest, yet the Manx government took an extremely strong political stance against the British government in relation to nuclear energy policies. Furthermore, NSM activity by outsiders was unsuccessful. Outsiders perceived an incredible lack of interest and activity on the island, identifying locals as shy, backward, passive, fatalistic grumblers incapable of dealing with the problems of the modern world. Meanwhile, locals found activists' style of public pronouncement ridiculous and embarrassing. Outsiders hoping to mobilize extraneous knowledge on behalf of the Manx public were effectively excluded from local politics. In a context where the social distance between the public and its representatives was small, even negligible, apparently "ineffectual grumbling" was actually an effective continuous pressure through personal interaction and information sharing. Effective identification of the issue in local political, social, and cultural terms was carried out in a way that might well escape outsiders' notice. Those who appeared most vociferous and active—that is, those who mobilized rational arguments publicly—were not necessarily those who were listened to.

The Isle of Man may seem no more than an offshore UK oddity, but the disaffection and ambivalence toward the styles, presumptions, values, and implied hierarchy of expert knowledge are far from anomalous. Rather, it stands as an outlier indicating the presence of many other invisible pockets of resistance where culturally grounded forms of action lurk waiting to confound those who would investigate them through the spectacle frames of rationality. This ready lapse from a constructivist/hermeneutic-negotiated stance back to the dominance of expert discourses is all too evident in work on reflexive modernization.

NEW SOCIAL MOVEMENTS, RISKS, AND GLOBALIZATION

We have suggested that NSMs, and even less formally recognized collectivities, constitute a source of critical reflection that existing theories of reflexivity fail to accommodate to varying degrees. To the extent that theories of reflexive modernization incorporate NSMs, they concentrate on the capacity of such movements to produce significant policy change. NSMs thus become a key source of institutional change within high modernity. This alignment of NSMs as modernizers of modernity is part of the subordination and translation of peoples' voices into the discourse of policy science we noted in our introduction. The accommodation of NSMs within debates on reflexive modernization in this manner reflects one set of well-developed tendencies within the NSM literature itself. This accommodation is at the expense of certain basic and fundamental tenets of social movement theory that we believe must be restored if reflexive modernization is to be anything more than a functionalist accommodation to system change.

In contrast to the dominant paradigm in NSM work that increasingly embraces resource mobilization theory and seeks to appraise social movements in relation to their impact on policy processes and extension in "state space" (Flam 1994), we focus on the less coherently ordered collective expressions of "civil society." In part, this section is informed by our empirical researches, and, in part, the recent theoretical works of Melucci and Maffesoli. Through this consideration, we will argue that the term "new social movement" should be abandoned to those wishing to pursue the policy potency of various peoples' movements, and the term "civil sociation" be applied to the grass roots.

European theorists of NSMs display a remarkable degree of agreement over the basic features of their object of study, none of which are primarily concerned with the modernization of the policy sciences. It is worth summarizing these here for the sake of clarity. First and most important, Touraine and Melucci define social movements in relation to competition for *control over cultural codes/symbolic resources and meanings* (Melucci 1989; 1996; Touraine 1985; 1995). Offe joins Melucci and Touraine in regarding NSMs as *opposed to hierarchies*, engaged in *conflict*, and in pursuit of *autonomy*. Melucci and Offe share the view that NSMs also *break the limits of the existing system*.

These are not conflicts over policy options or over questions of scientific fact or interpretation; rather, these are conflicts over human direction and meaning— conflicts built around "a certain intensity of feeling." The central analytical problem for sociological theory here centers on the difficulty of maintaining some separation between the lived relations of "sociality" and the formal observable activities of NSMs.

In terms of the environment, we are suggesting that there is a significant gap between the formalized activities of environmental NSMs and contemporary grass-roots movements that, we would claim, comprehend environmental issues within the context of a sophisticated understanding of embedded power relations. A primary manifestation of these power relations lies in the granting of "voice" to specific social actors in specific social contexts. In short, we are suggesting that the environment represents a site where there is a significant reservoir of silenced social space about which we know remarkably little. Furthermore, we would suggest that this silenced social space is one from which rapid and unanticipated social change can emanate. This last point is most clearly illustrated by an example.

Work that began at the first International Sociological Association conference on the environment at Woudschoten in 1992 (Tickle and Welsh 1998) traced the development of environmentalism in the former Soviet Union (FSU) and presented the following argument. Throughout the existence of the Soviet Union, the environment constituted a site where activists, organized in a range of locations from conservation associations and university departments, continued to keep alive a series of civic associations. Far from civil society being completely repressed by state communism, the environment constituted an area where it progressively gained strength. As the Communist Party gave increasing credence to the environment as a strategic area where it was possible to have dialogue with the West at the height of the Cold War, these grassroots associations and movements gained breathing space. From this point on, the environment became increasingly discussed in the private residences of party apparatchiks and intellectuals, something reflected in the growth in environmental legislation throughout the later years of communist rule.

The important point here is that this constellation of forces within Soviet communism gave the environment legitimacy based on the support of a diverse range of groupings within the Communist Party and beyond it. These networks increasingly constituted channels of social solidarity and accreted around them wider dissent over social and political issues. Inside the FSU and throughout the CEE, environmental movements became the initial bearers of the "revolutions" of 1989. Communism did not fall simply by people "assembling on the streets," as Beck has written (1997: 100). To the extent that this was a citizen-driven event, it was the outcome of decades of submerged environmentalist networks combined with the active withdrawal of support from within the Communist Party. This is a model of social change that does not conform to those most prominent within sociology and the social sciences. Without wanting to overextend the analogy, there appear to be some striking parallels between the situation that arose in the FSU and CEE and that which confronts us around the environment and reflexive modernization (Baker and Welsh 2000).

States throughout the world have given unprecedented prominence to the environment as a policy domain and center of social and political initiatives. After twenty years of neoliberal ascendancy promising market solutions to both economic and environmental inequalities, there is a widespread public sense of failure. In the Gorbachev period, there were perestroika and glasnost. In the post–Rio de Janeiro era, we have reflexive modernization and ecological modernization. As with the rest of the FSU and CEE, these operate within a free market framework that emphasizes individualism. As good Marxists, "we" once all knew that the product of capitalism is scarcity, not plenty. It is a piece of knowledge that has lost currency at precisely the point when the insight that scarcity produces environmental degradation has gained ground. How can environmental sustainability be produced by a system that is based on the artificial creation of want and scarcity?

The question we want to pose here is: Might this contradictory quest be producing forms of social change that are not detected because they are equivalent to the withdrawal of active support of the Communist Party within the FSU? How would our existing sociological tools enable us to detect such changes? Are our existing sociological tools actually concealing rather than revealing such trends? These are centrally important questions that most social theory is *not* addressing.

It is perhaps significant that the founders of European NSM theory (Touraine and Melucci) have both returned to the fundamentals of NSMs in recent works. Their return is prompted by the changed circumstances of the 1990s within which globalization, environmental concerns, and massively transformed means of communication figure prominently. Both writers share elements of the debate around reflexive modernization we have summarized here. The common concerns include recognition of the problem of modernity as a globalizing social, economic, and political formation.

Echoing Beck's notion of bifurcation, Touraine writes that "the subject must not be crushed by rationalisation. It is essential to prevent one element of modernity from absorbing the other. To resist total oppression by rationality 'we must mobilise the total subject, the religious heritage, childhood memories, ideas and courage' " (1995: 207–211). Touraine is also drawn, like Bauman, to the notion of "life in fragments," arguing that in the face of globalization "we all belong to the same world but it is a broken and fragmented world" (217). In the face of this fragmentation, Touraine argues that individuals are becoming subjects in response to totalitarian or merely bureaucratic states that have devoured society and speak in its name. They are ventriloquist states that pretend to give society a voice when they have in fact swallowed it (218).

Part of what is expressed here is the emergence of the *will* of situated individuals to be recognized as having a voice. Touraine emphasizes the importance of autonomy precisely because he regards NSMs as centers of innovation that create new repertoires of collective action, identity, and contestation—"the flame which burns at the heart of society." These are themes that have received a powerful reformulation by Melucci, the Italian theorist of NSMs.

MELUCCI—CHALLENGING CODES

In *Challenging Codes*, Melucci provides a recapitulation of his pathbreaking 1989 text *Nomads of the Present*. The opening of this new book is on a grand scale with Melucci announcing that

> Like the prophets, the movements "speak before": they announce what is taking shape even before its direction and content become clear. . . . What they possess is not the force of the apparatuses of power but the power of the word [and one would add the power of the deed]. . . . They force the power out into the open and give it a shape and a face. They speak a language that appears to be entirely their own, but they say something that transcends their particularity and speaks to us all. (1996: 1)

It is this capacity to enunciate that is our central concern in relation to our argument about authentic aesthetic reflexivity. Melucci has long argued that the latency periods of movements rather than the mobilization phases are of central importance. He reproaches sociologists and political scientists for concentrating on visible actions to the neglect of more invisible cultural work of "declaring the stakes"—attributing meaning to issues that society has yet to recognize. In terms of global risks, this is a vitally important consideration.

Global environmental risks derived from science lay claim to vast realms of geographical and social space and inescapably colonize these domains. "The planet no longer designates just a physical location; it is also a unified social space which is culturally and symbolically perceived" (Melucci 1996: 8). For us, discourses of global risk are a key means of enclosing "a vast area of non-demand, of excluded interests repressed or kept at the margins, which do not reach the point of expression or organisation and which are deprived of access to the political system as they are not recognized as legitimate" (235).

For Melucci, globalization shapes the way these unspoken exclusions find a voice. He observes that global processes have increasingly important impacts at the individual level, bypassing existing collectivities and institutions. There is a direct link from the global to the local that effectively reconfigures sets of priorities that have dominated modernity. Perhaps the biggest casualty in this is the idea of a national interest, as it is the national that is increasingly bypassed or diminished by globalization. The reflexivity of subjects becomes focused on proximate spatial events *through nonlinear times frames*. The appeal to sacrifice a treasured local environment to a development now for the "future national interest" struggles for credibility in a global age.

Melucci likens these processes to those of youth not prepared to delay gratification or express demands in language. Youth expresses itself in silence and "fragmentary, disjointed stuttering, to the inarticulateness of spastic utterance." This is "the affirmation of a word that no longer wishes to be understood independently of emotions" (1996: 120). There is a quest for an inner wholeness and the authentic realization of this "in the now time." Lest this be misread as arguing that NSMs are primarily the preserve of the youth, he points out that youth is increasingly a matter of culture and not biology. It is possible to point to many empirical examples of environmental mobilizations where these concerns are indeed expressed by youth and a healthy contingent of "young" older people.

This notion of strategic silences and withdrawal represents a recurrent analytical theme throughout the book. The centrality of withdrawal has to be understood in terms of the need to escape from "the dominant logic of representation of the social . . . to create space in which to operate," and is presented as a "prerequisite for remaining in the world with greater awareness" (Melucci 1996: 172). This kind of withdrawal can be individual and/or collective in the creation of "temporary autonomous zones" by social movement actors (on this, see Bey 1994). Peace camps, festivals, occupied reactor projects, and road construction sites are among the most familiar examples of such sites. It is here that social movements innovate in a number of ways. These include the processes of naming already mentioned, but also extend to the active redefinition and recreation of wider movement repertoires through the intense networking that occurs within such "nodes."

In the United Kingdom, "antiroads" campaigns have produced a plethora of such sites, drawing activists from all over Europe. To Melucci, these sites become the "public space of representation" where "issues are subjected to negotiation, forwarded for decision making, and thus transformed into possibilities of change without, however, annulling the specificity and the autonomy of the conflictual actors in the process." Such sites of innovation are crucial. "As space for word, spaces for naming, they permit a new and different voice to be given to that which in society refuses to be reduced to the names that technical rationality imposes on the world"

(Melucci 1996: 221). They also represent sites that contribute to the proliferation of political actors with a particularly potent set of cultural repertoires.

The potency of these repertoires depends *not* on the contestation of scientific data about environmental hazards and risks, but on precisely the opposite. There is a withdrawal from expert testimony and counterexpertise, as this can only translate opposition into the dominant discourses, thus legitimizing dominance in the process. Instead, the conflict becomes structured around the direct intervention of actors' bodies in the simultaneous defense of a local site and celebration of the capacity to act authentically in the present. In the United Kingdom, the defense of trees has been a particularly potent symbol in such actions, which have, in Melucci's words, "spoken" to the wider public via a "symbolic multiplier." Such acts underline the capacity of what we have termed authentic iconic praxis to produce much wider impacts.[11] Such actions are part of a Europe-wide network (Welsh and McLeish 1996).

Far from being irrational ephemera, Melucci argues that these grounded expressions have symbolic logic that the more formal channels of the "political system" *must* find ways of accommodating. Despite the apparent difference between Melucci's and Beck's models, they both deny that the transformative processes they are concerned with are of the margins. Beck's notion of subpolitics is tied to the idea that the "breach is beginning" as a result of a "conflict inside modernity," and "not in its marginal zones or those which overlap with private life-worlds" (Beck, Giddens, and Lash 1994: 10). Likewise, Melucci repeatedly emphasizes that NSMs are "not of the margins" and that to survive they must "develop a relatively stable organisation and leadership" (1996: 313).

In highlighting the importance of immediate spatial and temporal concerns, Melucci has drawn attention to two important channels shaping popular responses to the environmental problematic. In arguing that movements *must* harness the insights gained to an agenda requiring the specialist language of the institutional sphere, he opens the door to the active alienation of wider publics from social movement organizations. This moves his most recent work away from the grassroots level of collective identity and mobilization we are concerned with here. Accordingly, we now turn to ways of avoiding this shortcoming. We achieve this through a consideration of the work of Ardener, which gave an earlier expression to some of the spatial and temporal issues raised by Melucci.

ARDENER, NSMS, AND THE
VOICE OF PROPHECY

Ardener defined prophecy not as prediction but as the capacity to tell what is (1989: 135). When social shifts occur, prophets are those who make change visible. In advance, prophets are not believed; afterward, they are not necessarily recognized. In advance, prophecy is incomprehensible, afterward trivial. This is as much a feature of a prophetic situation as that of prophets as people.

Ardener was concerned with the role of individuals and groups who play a key role in processes of definition involved in social change. Prophets' ability to perceive and articulate what is happening depends on their being able to escape the constraints that blind others to the novelty of the situation. For some individuals at all times, and for more sizable groups more rarely, there is a partial separation from the structure of the social space as expressed in dominant ideas, praxis, and language. It is this separation that enables them to experience and find the language to express a new vision of the social and natural world.

Here, there is a similarity with Lash's emphasis on structural reflexivity in which agency, set free from the constraints of social structure, then reflects on the " 'rules' and resources of such structure: reflects on agency's social conditions of existence" (Lash, Szerszynski, and Wynne 1996: 115–116). Ardener was particularly interested in the problem that monitoring and expressing change presents. The terms available to describe change are tied to old meanings, and any attempt to apply them to new events thus risks falling back into the old vision it is trying to escape. A new language for important shifts becomes necessary. When redefinition occurs, social space is then restructured and the new world appears self-evident, banal again. The definitions of the old world have gone, but there remain memories of curious events, the feel of the time, particular symbols that then seemed so powerful. Unless new language is successfully created and prophets identified, then "prophets" remain merely irrelevant deviants (148; see also Melucci 1996: 103).

What generates this kind of transformation? Such changes can be related to ecological and economic changes that have particularly grave impacts on particular sections of the population. However, it is not just the material impact that is important; it is the impossibility of describing the new situation in old terms that pushes those involved to create terms that can communicate their experience. This creation involves radical reflection. Ardener explores the terms "parameter collapse" and "event rich" in ways that are useful to our present purposes.

REFLEXIVE MODERNIZATION AND
PARAMETER COLLAPSE

Ardener used the term "parameter collapse" to describe situations where established definitions lose cohesion as the boundaries and the conditions defining them change fundamentally. When parameter collapse occurs, the ensuing semantic paradox helps create the conditions for prophecy.[12] As we have already alluded, the term "environment" can be seen as suffering parameter collapse. Social engagement with environmental issues is challenging preexisting definitions of the boundaries and conditions defining the environment. While powerful academic discourses, such as reflexive modernization, battle for their global visions of the environment, it is our argument that smaller, local views are also creating novel definitions that articulate different experiences of the environment. These are particularly powerful in that they often refer to and mobilize potent symbolic imagery that rational accounts try to sidestep.

Beck's writing could be seen to be prophetic itself. In the preface, *Risk Society* is described as attempting to "move the future which is just beginning to take shape into view against the still predominant past" (1992: 9). Beck points out that the control of risk, and the techniques used to monitor and contain risk, have actually created awareness of more and greater risks. The parameters of risk control threaten to collapse, and the inhabitants of "risk society" begin to experience the reversal in the previous orderly direction of progressive security. As risks multiply and become ubiquitous, expert knowledges grapple for language to describe and measure risks that permeate or colonize unimaginable areas of the social and natural environment.

As Beck argues, hitherto taken for granted values, knowledges, institutions, and social relations are suddenly visible because of heightened awareness of risks. The reconfigured world that is emerging is an uncertain place of description and redefinition. Academic prophetic visions have a lot of work to do, and the new has all sorts of dimensions. The usual problem of the prophet, finding language for expression, is set within disciplinary terminology that needs to define context, actors' capacities, and propensities and the mechanisms of change. Beck wrote that "we need ideas and theories that will allow us to conceive the new which is rolling over us in a new way" (1992: 12). It is our argument that an important source of such ideas can only come from the currently silenced margins. The relevance of margins arises both from their isolation (whether physical or social) and the symbolic significance of margins for the self definition of "centers." Put simply, there are certain messages that can only arise within reflective spheres distant from mainstream perceptions.

Reflexivity is obviously a useful concept since it provides a means of rolling perceptions of change through the whole social and cultural field. As Ardener points out—and it is one of Beck's strengths that he realizes this—the life paths of individuals must be preserved as continuous. Conceptual discontinuities can be introduced at will in academic models, but that is not a view of the world as humans live it. The lived experience of individuals is continuous even through periods of upheaval. The resources that people bring to conceptualizing the new situation, and the relationship they perceive between the old and the new, need to be examined. It may well be that individuals are forced to reflect on the social and natural world at certain critical junctures. However, the way that they do this cannot be envisaged from a distance. Their experience of the present is refracted through memories of the past, through matrixes of social and cultural knowledge. It is precisely those aspects of contemporary experience that seem most strange and that render most poignant individual and collective memories. The notion of reflexivity enables Giddens and Beck to have their imaginary populations passing from one social space to another by rational cognitive means, but this is a necessity of their modeling of society, not necessarily a reflection of how shifts are lived by people within different social and cultural contexts. The contemporary period does seem to be one of change, the kind of change that gives rise to prophecy. It is our contention that effective prophets need not necessarily be found in expected places, nor need they be speaking in scientific, policy-relevant language.

EVENT RICHNESS

One important consequence of parameter collapse suffered by the environment is that the associated processes of contested definition interact with old notions of the environment. Paradoxically, there is more and more "environment" that defines less and less. We are particularly interested in the way in which marginal social groups mobilize sets of symbolic registers that combine the old and the new. Ardener, in laying out his anthropological consideration of social space, argues that it is precisely those areas perceived as remote from civilization that tend to be "event rich." Despite such areas being perceived as backwaters where history stands still and tradition reigns less affected by modernity, while "more happenings are interpreted as events, more behaviours are interpreted as actions there" (Hastrup 1989: 226; see also Shields 1991).

Event richness stems from small-scale continuous invention of symbolic difference, a process that insiders and outsiders participate in. Ardener sees this as due to the enhanced defining powers of individuals and groups placed in such situations—a sense of vulnerability to intrusion and overdetermination of individuality go hand in hand: "[T]hose so-defined are intermittently conscious of the defining processes of others that might absorb them. That is why they are crucibles of the creation of identity and so of theoretical interest" (1989: 223).

It is part of our argument here that environmental issues give rise to the kinds of symbolic contestation that creates pockets of event richness, of heightened agency within structures. One aspect that deserves particular attention is the way each particular instance, with its idiosyncratic social, political, and cultural components, both creates and attacks social boundaries and draws on a common fund of symbolic imagery. The critical view of social relations that emerges provides insights into how the social is being reformulated in relation to environmental issues as well as the way "the environment" is symbolically framed. Many local "environmental issues," such as roads protests, create local friction, aligning local groups on opposing sides as well as attracting a variety of external activists with different views and ways of acting.[13]

The analytical focus of policymakers and social scientists often ignores much of the ensuing physical, social, and cultural activity, particularly that which concerns social boundary definition and symbolic activity, concentrating on more articulate NSM activity that mobilizes rational arguments. It is our contention that the social and political changes brought about by an accumulation of such events need to be evaluated in broader terms.

Marginal groups may also have an alternative (shared but invisible) language for description of the social world and an appreciation of the structures and relations that invalidate their own views and values. This was precisely the case with the Manx sheep farmers. Nevertheless, exceedingly inarticulate prophets could well be a source of influential visions and inarticulacy need not be a weakness. In Britain, the salience of Swampy (a British roads activist who was aesthetically and iconically valorized in media coverage) perhaps illustrates this.[14] The contestation that arises is not just about moving a protester or saving a tree. It is about saving an identity and a world-view, making it articulate in the face of superior defining forces. If Swampy were to start defining himself and his position in terms of a cost-benefit analysis of the transport system, he would cease to exist and the fascination his commentary invokes would also disappear. Dreamcatchers, trees as relatives, and hearthomes may mean little to the outside world, and diatribes against mainstream politics or waged work might not obviously chime with popular opinion. However, the passion, the humor, and the glimpses of alterity have had considerable media attention and apparently a purchase on public attention. Perhaps this is because his ideas about the relationship between human beings and the environment, about resisting the pronouncements of experts and politicians, and about self-sacrifice and bravery are more in key with popular perceptions than first appearances would suggest.

This question brings into doubt some of the key assumptions made about the way NSMs bring into existence prophetic visions that alter the world. The radical potential of less formal sociations may be undervalued. Melucci, in particular, is highly sensitive to the dangers of assuming that the social world conforms to the conceptual categories generated by theorists, and also recognizes the tortured limitation of existing language to express the forms of social and cultural practices he describes. Despite this, he retains the qualified use of the term "new social movement." In terms of our argument here, the important point is that the autonomous, innovative, transgressive, and reformative element of the movements literally move on—in Swampy's case to new threatened margins.

It strikes us that these activist cores are more akin to the neotribes of Maffesoli, which he regards as "sociations" drawing on the work of Schmallenbach (1977). These sociations are channels that give expression to the "puissance," or will to life of the people, through proxemics (situated local practices). These elements of his work reflect many of the concerns of Touraine and Melucci, but unlike these writers Maffesoli maintains the separation of his neotribes from "society." Society is too tainted by the state, control, and domination. Society is the death of puissance while community breathes the life of sociality. Rather than declaring the stakes, the neotribes' "sole reason d'etre is a preoccupation with the collective present" (Maffesoli 1996: 75), thus sharing Melucci's rejection of modernist future orientations. "No Future Now: the refrain of the younger generations has lesser but real reverberations on the whole of society" (62). Maffesoli also shares the notion of withdrawal, formulating his hypothesis that "at certain periods of history, when the masses are no longer interacting with those in government, or puissance is completely dissociated from power, the political universe dies and sociality takes over" (46). The basis of this sociality is an aesthetic capacity understood as a common ability to share an intensity of feeling. This intensity of feeling is, we would argue, an opening up to the need for new judgment.

There is a vitalism of expression and a struggle to reinvent a language of reenchantment within these forms of sociality that we have addressed under the heading of NSMs so far. Part of what we are arguing is the need for a new language of discovery, and we would now suggest that the notion of "civil sociations"[15] be applied to these innovative margins. This we believe would help focus attention on the notions of deep cultural conflict over symbolic *and* material resources that are expressed through the "inarticulate speech of the heart" (to quote singer Van Morrison [1983]) issuing from such sociations in their arenas of engagement and spaces of retreat. NSMs can then be left to refer to those areas where these symbolic and cultural contestations become aligned with more policy-related issues.

CONCLUSION

In this chapter, we reviewed some of the key theoretical formulations of reflexive modernization. We argued that this theoretical enterprise has lost sight of the fact that its concepts are only categories of engagement in the minds of their originators. Melucci's observation about the concept of an NSM being no more and no less than an intellectual construct of academic practitioners applies equally to reflexive modernization.

In arguing for the importance of a grounded theory of reflexivity and reflection, we highlighted the importance of the situated practices of "civil sociation" as specifically local/proximate/proxemic sources of reflection with a particularly strong aesthetic component. Such sites give rise to a form of authentic iconic praxis with far less predictable consequences than the conscious iconic praxis of groups like Greenpeace. We regard the reliance on science and other forms of cognate knowledge within established theories of reflexive modernization as too imperious because of their tendency to exercise closure and domination over other forms of reflexive expression. In the strong sense, the cognitive dimension attempts to enclose the planet in totalizing risk determinations.

In the face of the local and proximate, global risks dissolve in at least two senses. First, the laboratory modeling used to derive risk categories is found wanting when compared to local physical conditions and the culturally derived meanings. Second, the solutions sought by such global models are confounded by locally embedded meanings. Global risks are always read into local situations that reconfigure both the nature of the risk and the possible avenues of response. This is a crucial part of the lesson that established sciences need to relearn if they are to play a socially unalienating role in the negotiation of environmental and other risks.

The current alignment of reflexivity/reflection is too close to the long-standing institutions of modernity that permit, even promote, the domination of the rational side of the bifurcation of modernity noted by Beck. We argued that engagement with reflexivity/reflection through these institutions assumes that change occurs where the existing distribution of institutional effort and power lies. Through a consideration of the role of environmental social movements in the FSU and CEE in the fall of communism, we have argued that, in this case at least, such models proved to be of little use. Power was elsewhere—as Beck rightly argues. This social formation changed internally through increasing numbers of people withdrawing their will and turning away from established centers. They did so by masking their withdrawal and acting a charade. Through our consideration of the work of Touraine, Melucci, Ardener, and Maffesoli, we are arguing that such civil sociations represent a visible node of a more pervasive withdrawal mobilized around environmental concerns.

We reiterate our view that any approach to reflexive modernization that regards civil sociations as no more than interpreters of science is acknowledging only one, and by no means the most important, source of reflexivity/reflection from such quarters. By translating these wider sources of reflexivity/reflection into the language of science, the whole ethos of the movements/sociations is translated into the language of the dominant discourse, temporarily extending its life. It is through the avoidance of this kind of translation and absorption that the civil sociations hold out the promise of reenchantment from an "outside." Such a comment acts as prophecy in Ardener's and Melucci's sense.

Through acts of sociality, the civil sociations simultaneously name that which is nameless, revealing the existence of power and offering the prospect of new language, cultural codes, and symbolic preferences. Harvey (1996) has written of the need to revalorize the environment. It is our view that this revalorization needs the passion and vitality that flows from the civil sociations. This requires the formulation of transcendent visions. Without this, reflexive and ecological modernization offer only better rationality and more capitalism. It is hard to be excited by this.

NOTES

1. Subpolitics can be read as a global variant of the Lockean proposition that the people retain the obligation to remove unjust government. This is a preoccupation also shared in different ways by Touraine (1995) and Maffesoli (1996).

2. In the absence of such work, Giddens is left arguing, for example, that without as yet unknown technological developments "the widespread use of nuclear power is likely to be unavoidable if global processes of economic growth carry on" (1991: 222). This is characteristic of the projected demand forecasting models used by electricity utilities throughout the 1970s to legitimate further nuclear orders. There is little to suggest reflexivity here.

3. Beck frequently speaks of the impact of reflexivity on individual plant managers who then enter into reflection. His recent concern with whistle-blowers is an illustration of this, but he lacks a systematic exploration of why such reflection begins and whether, and if so how, it feeds into collective reflection.

4. The term "social distance" was first used in a British paper on the sociology of "race" to "denote the gulf of difference between alien cultures" (Patterson 1965: 20). It was adapted by Welsh (2000a) to refer to conflictual lay/expert relations observable around civil nuclear power debates in the United Kingdom from the 1950s onward.

5. Leslie, a health physicist working at Windscale during the 1950s, was the sole expert voice publicly critical of the handling of the 1957 reactor fire. His public criticism arose when his social responsibility toward his family overrode his professional affiliations. His knowledge

of regular excess discharges of radioactive particles predated the accident by at least two years (see Edwards 1983; Welsh 2000a).

6. We are grateful to Peter Jowers of the University of the West of England, Bristol, for the notion of extreme repertoires. In the United Kingdom, such direct action has been used to oppose the siting of supermarkets, roads, the live export of animals, runway extensions, Bovine Spongiform Encephalopathy incinerators, and the transport of nuclear waste. Vidal and Belos (1996) estimated that there were more than five hundred separate actions during 1995–1996. This figure was based on a survey of just twelve organizations and is almost certainly an underestimate.

7. The innovations in direct action repertoires resulted from particularly dense activist networks stretching throughout Europe. It has been claimed that activists copied the idea of tunneling from the Vietcong. Such images are of course reliant on the media and considerably facilitated by the latest broadcast technologies (see Thompson 1995).

8. Here, we follow Jowers who, via his reading of Leotard and Kant, argues that aesthetic considerations are central to the creation of a "certain intensity of feeling . . . opening onto a need for judgement" (1994: 182–183).

9. Ian Welsh interviewed antinuclear activists and Derek Wall interviewed Earth First! UK activists, respectively (Wall 1999).

10. We have two concerns here: large areas of silenced citizens who are marginalized and more culturally defined marginals closer to Marcuse's use of the term. Both are, however, united in terms of the social distance between them and science.

11. This is not to detract from the potential of intentional iconic practice to also produce unanticipated consequences, as Beck's treatment of Greenpeace's intervention over Brentspar points out (Beck 1996b).

12. Ardener used the example of altitude records to illustrate his use of parameter collapse. As he points out, with the advent of space travel, existing notions of altitude records measured in terms of physical distance above the earth were transformed. When distance becomes measured in light-years, altitude becomes enclosed in a new definitional shell, expressing a new vision of the earth, of space, and relational distance.

13. At Newbury, for example, local groups insisted on opposing a bypass through legitimate means, including a public inquiry. During this phase, outsiders mounting direct action were regarded with hostility and suspicion. Once it became clear that the road was to go ahead, sections of this once antagonistic local community embraced direct action (see Welsh and McLeish 1996).

14. Swampy rapidly became a media phenomenon, gaining sympathetic coverage in broadsheets and the tabloid press as well as becoming a regular guest on BBC Radio 4 (see Wall 1999: 91–93).

15. By avoiding the term "new," which has become the subject of intense and largely unproductive debate, we are seeking to both distance ourselves from such debate and provide a term that applies to wider less formalized spaces of social silence. In particular, we would emphasize the importance of including the less visible publics limiting their participation to withdrawal of belief and active support as well as the more visibly mobilized actors engaged in "authentic" iconic praxis.

REFERENCES

Ardener, E. 1989. "The Voice of Prophecy." In *Edwin Ardener: The Voice of Prophecy*, ed. M. Chapman. Oxford: Blackwell.

Baker, S., and I. Welsh. 2000. "Differentiating Western Influences on Transition Societies in Eastern Europe: A Preliminary Exploration." *Journal of European Area Studies* 8:79–103.

Bauman, Z. 1993. *Postmodern Ethics*. Oxford: Blackwell.

Beck, U. 1992. *Risk Society: Towards a New Modernity*. London: Sage.

———. 1996a. "Risk Society and the Provident State." In *Risk Environment and Modernity: Towards a New Ecology*, ed. S. Lash, B. Szerszynski, and B. Wynne. London: Sage.

———. 1996b. "World Risk Society As Cosmopolitan Society." *Theory Culture and Society* 13:1–32.

———. 1997. *The Reinvention of Politics*. Cambridge: Polity.

Beck, U., A. Giddens, and S. Lash. 1994. *Reflexive Modernisation*. Cambridge: Polity.

Bey, H. 1994. *Temporary Autonomous Zones*. New York: Automedia.

Callon, M. 1986. "Some Elements of a Sociology of Translation: Domestication of the Scallops and Fishermen of St Brieuc Bay." In *Power, Action and Belief: A New Sociology of Knowledge*, ed. J. Law. London: Routledge.

Davis, M. 1996. "Cosmic Dancers on History's Stage? The Permanent Revolution in the Earth Sciences." *New Left Review* 217:48–84.

Edwards, R. 1983. "A New Kind of Nuclear Victim." *New Statesman*, 22 July, 8–10.

Flam, H. 1994. *States and Anti-nuclear Movements*. Edinburgh: Edinburgh University Press.

Functowicz, S. O., and J. Ravetz. 1993. "Science for the Post-normal Age." *Futures* (September): 739–755.

Giddens, A. 1990. *The Consequences of Modernity*. Cambridge: Polity.

———. 1991. *Modernity and Self-Identity*. Cambridge: Polity.

Harvey, D. 1996. *Justice Nature and the Geography of Difference*. London: Blackwell.

Hastrup, K. 1989. "The Prophetic Condition." In *Edwin Ardener: The Voice of Prophecy*, ed. M. Chapman. Oxford: Blackwell.

Irwin, A., and B. Wynne, eds. 1996. *Misunderstanding Science? The Public Reconstruction of Science and Technology*. Cambridge: Cambridge University Press.

Jowers, P. 1994. "Towards the Politics of a 'Lesser Evil': Jean-François Lyotard's Reworking of the Kantian Sublime." In *The Lesser Evil and the Greater Good*, ed. J. Weeks. London: Rivers Oram.

Knorr-Cetina, K. 1988. "The Micro-social Order: Towards a Reconception" In *Action and Structure*, ed. N. Fielding. London: Sage.

Lash, S. 1990. "Learning from Leipzig." *Theory Culture and Society* 7:145–158.

Lash, S., and J. Urry. 1994. *Economies of Signs and Space*. London: Sage.

Lash, S., B. Szerszynski, and B. Wynne, eds. 1994. *Risk Environment and Modernity: Towards a New Ecology*. London: Sage.

Maffesoli, M. 1996. *The Times of the Tribes: The Decline of Individualism in Mass Society*. London: Sage.

McKechnie, R. 1996. "Insiders and Outsiders: Identifying Experts on Home Ground." In *Misunderstanding Science? The Public Reconstruction of Science and Technology*, ed. A. Irwin and B. Wynne. Cambridge: Cambridge University Press.

McKechnie, R., and I. Welsh. 1994. "Between the Devil and the Deep Green Sea: Defining Risk Societies and Global Threats." In *The Lesser Evil and the Greater Good: The Theory and Practice of Democracy*, ed. Jeffrey Weeks, 57–78. London: Rivers Oram.

Melucci, A. 1989. *Nomads of the Present*. London: Radius.

———. 1996. *Challenging Codes: Collective Action in the Information Age*. Cambridge: Cambridge University Press.

Morrison, Van. 1983. *Inarticulate Speech of the Heart*. Music album. Mercury Records.

Paine, R. 1987. "Accidents, Ideologies and Routines: 'Chernobyl' over Norway." *Anthropology Today* 3 (August): 7–10.

———. 1992. " 'Chernobyl' Reaches Norway: The Accident, Science and the Threat to Cultural Knowledge." *Public Understanding of Science* 1:261–280.

Patterson, S. 1965. *Dark Strangers*. Harmondsworth, UK: Penguin.

Schmalenbach, H. 1977. *Herman Schmalenbach: On Society and Experience*. Trans. G. Lushen and G. P. Stone. Chicago: University of Chicago Press.

Shields, R. 1991. *Places on the Margin: Alternative Geographies of Modernity*. London: Routledge.

Tabb, W. K. 2000. "After Seattle: Understanding the Politics of Globalisation." *Monthly Review* 51 (March): 1–18.

Thompson, J. B. 1995. *The Media and Modernity: A Social Theory of the Media*. Cambridge: Polity.

Tickle, A., and I. Welsh, eds. 1998. *Environment and Society in Eastern Europe*. Harlow: Longman.

Touraine, A. 1985. "An Introduction to the Study of Social Movements." *Social Research* 52:749–787.

———. 1995. *Critique of Modernity*. Cambridge: Cambridge University Press.

Vidal, J., and A. Belos. 1996. "Protest Lobbies Unite to Guard Rights." *Guardian*, 2 August, 5.

Wainwright, J., S. Prudham, and J. Glassman. 2000. "Global Seattle." *Environment and Planning D: Society and Space* 18:1–13.

Wall, D. 1999. *Earth First! and the Anti-roads Movement: Radical Environmentalism and Comparative Social Movements*. London: Routledge.

Welsh, I. 1996. "Risk, Global Governance and Environmental Politics." *Innovation* 9:407–420.

———. 2000a. *Mobilising Modernity: The Nuclear Moment*. London: Routledge.

———. 2000b. "New Social Movements." In *Developments in Sociology*, vol. 16, ed. M. Haralambos, 43–59. Ormskirk, UK: Causeway.

Welsh, I., and P. McLeish. 1996. "The European Road to Nowhere: Anarchism and Direct Action against the UK Roads Programme." *Anarchist Studies* 4:27–44.

Wynne, B. 1996. "May the Sheep Safely Graze." In *Risk Environment and Modernity: Towards a New Ecology*, ed. S. Lash, B. Szerszynski, and B. Wynne. London: Sage.

14

Cultural Analysis and Environmental Theory: An Agenda

John Hannigan

Over the past decade, the reemergence of culture in sociological analysis has consti-tuted a rising theoretical trend, if not a full-scale paradigmatic shift. As part of this resurgence, the traditional definition of culture as the entire way of life of a peo-ple—an implicit set of rules that underpins and governs social action—has been displaced by a more dynamic view in which culture is treated as an explicit social construction (Wuthnow and Witten 1988). In this new theorization of culture, the tendency within the discipline of sociology has been to "move from an understand-ing of social life through structures and systems to a growing appreciation of the role of contingencies and uncertainties, coupled with a growing sense of cultural diver-sity" (Featherstone and Lash 1999: 1). Thus, Swidler (1986: 277) rejects the Weber-ian metaphor of culture as a "switchman" determining the tracks along which action is propelled by interest in favor of the image of a "tool kit" from which people select differing pieces for constructing lines or strategies of action. The contents of this tool kit include a diverse array of symbols, habits, skills, styles, worldviews, dis-courses, and texts. While this "performative" view of culture applies to a wide vari-ety of social settings, it is especially salient for those who lead "unsettled" lives in which new habits of action are developing (279). In such times of crisis, mobilizing collectivities, notably social movements, reject older cultural models and articulate new ones that offer creative and novel ways of interpreting and organizing social life (Johnston and Klandermans 1995: 7–8).

Despite a long-standing concern with nature and the distribution of values and beliefs, environmental sociology has been slow to embrace culture as a guiding con-cept, opting instead to focus on ecological functions or political economy. There are several possible explanations for this. Until recently, constructionist models have been generally overlooked in favor of realist ones, largely as a result of a misplaced fear that to embrace constructionism means to deny the existence of serious ongoing environmental problems. Such apprehension was stirred up by the publication in 1982 of the still controversial book *Risk and Culture*, in which the authors Douglas and Wildavsky implied that much of what we have come to regard as the "ecological crisis" is an exaggeration, manufactured by sect-like environmental organizations such as Greenpeace and Friends of the Earth. Another possible explanation is that many of the first-generation environmental sociologists came from applied specialty areas—rural sociology, social demography, and human ecology—that were scarcely on the cusp of the developing field of cultural studies.

Recently, however, the concept of culture has begun to move into the forefront in environmental theory alongside the more established human ecology and political economy approaches. Consider, for example, the following:

- Both Lash (1994) and Wynne (1996) have taken the Beck-Giddens version of reflexive modernization to task for overlooking the cultural dimension of lay responses to expert interventions in risk debates. Lay relationships with scientific experts have, in fact, long been more skeptical and ambivalent than is commonly supposed. It is important to consider the cultural processes that lead powerless publics into suppressing and rationalizing these doubts, thereby creating the illusion of trust in expert institutions. We must, Wynne argues, "develop a more thoroughgoing culturalist conceptualisation of the character of risk than that given in the risk society thesis" (1996: 55).
- Eder (1996a; 1996b) has adopted an explicitly culturalist interpretation in pondering the future of environmentalism into the next millennium. Ecological discourse, he claims, has become a "master frame" in public discourse and a major element in the legitimating ideology of advanced modern societies. At the same time, the environmental movement has been forced to become a "cultural pressure group" competing with a range of other social actors to try to shape a discourse that it has allowed to slip from its grasp.
- According to Giner and Tabara (1999), cosmic piety, a major component of ecoreligion is becoming an essential component of modern culture in the current context of globalization. However, over time, they hypothesize, science will undermine this relationship by stripping it of its mythical contents while leaving as residues its more behavioral aspects. Until this happens, cosmic piety still "can be considered to have an invaluable cultural role in the common pursuit to adapt human societies to global environmental change" (71).
- To understand contemporary environmental disasters such as the Chernobyl nuclear accident, Adam (1999) tells us, we must go beyond the assumptions of classical science and take account of them in the context of everyday life and culture. In particular, it is important to identify and analyze the "contextual temporality" that emerges from the disaster, its implications, and cultural responses. Insomuch as the symptoms of radiation fallout from the Chernobyl

accident have permeated the globe to different degrees and at different speeds, assumptions about the linearity of time and causation must be reexamined.

While each of these authors uses the term "culture" in a somewhat different way, a common theoretical thread can be identified. In each case, the writer(s) detect a certain separation and tension between a rational, technical-scientific discourse on the one hand, and a more experiential and holistic grassroots culture of the environment on the other. Wynne looks to the latter as a necessary antidote to the tyranny of expert-dominated knowledge cultures, although he is careful to disown calls for the complete replacement of scientific or universal knowledge with lay or local knowledges and identities. In similar fashion, Adam finds the assumptions of classical science an inadequate base on which to assemble an explanation of an event that connects nuclear workers in the Ukraine, sheep farmers in north Wales, and babies in Malaysia. Eder, by contrast, expresses optimism that the "credibility gaps" that have arisen between science and lay culture will disappear within the emergent political ecology that he sees as gaining legitimacy in public discourse. Political ecology, he claims, provides a frame in which the constructed nature of science is taken for granted and scientific aims and goals become opened up to the personal wisdom and experience of people (1996a: 212). Giner and Tabara blur the lines between science and religion somewhat by identifying a type of "charismatically embedded rationality" as a constituent component of cosmic piety. Eventually, however, science is seen as getting up to its old tricks, insisting on explaining by rational means and empirical evidence those phenomena that proponents of ecoreligion have infused with charisma. As thought-provoking as theoretical meditations such as these may be, they tend to be crafted with a broad brush stroke, commenting in general terms about the relationships between science, ecology, religion, and culture. In this chapter, I aim to shift this discussion to a more mesotheoretical level by drawing on some recent scholarly work in the sociological specialty area of social movements.

Until a few years ago, social movement researchers paid scant attention to cultural factors, committed as they were to the ruling "resource mobilization" paradigm that stressed such elements as incentives, strategies, networks, opportunities, and achievements. With the exception of the concept "collective identity," culture was rarely invoked, especially by American scholars, as a force in the emergence and development of social movements (McAdam 1994: 37). Lately, however, this has begun to change with the more cultural or ideational dimensions of collective action now featured in many discussions. In part, this reflects the nature of the so-called new social movements (feminism, peace, and ecology) that are more attuned to issues of identity and life style. Additionally, however, it is related to a changing view of culture within the wider discipline of sociology that especially applies to the case of social movements and social change. In his book *The Art of Moral Protest* (1997), Jasper underlines this new prominence for culture, including it along with resources, strategies, and biography as one of four "irreducible components to protest action." Indeed, "pride of place goes to culture in this scheme" (Williams 1999: 1673) insofar as each of the other three components is to a greater or lesser extent culturally embedded. Another social movement researcher who highlights the role of culture in collective action is Polletta (1997). In Polletta's estimation, it is time that we fundamentally reconceptualize movement theorizing in order to highlight the cultural dimensions of protest life:

> Political "opportunities" should be expanded to include the contradictions and gaps in dominant ideologies which trigger opposition; . . . movement "resources" [should] be made to encompass compelling narratives and traditions of protest. . . . And movement "success" should be judged not only by the number of officials elected, legislation passed, and policies changed, but by the transformations wrought in culture and consciousness, in collective self-definitions, and in the meanings that shape everyday.
>
> "Bringing culture back in," ventures Hart has become a hot topic in social movement research with the result that "cultural sociology and social movement theory are now more engaged in dialogue than at any time since functionalist analyses of collective behavior were fashionable." (431)

TRANSFORMATION CULTURE AS PERFORMANCE AND DISCOURSE

In opting for a cultural approach, it is important to distinguish between linear and fluid movements. Linear movements follow a straight line narrative. Their career is played out in the public arena and their level of success is determined by the extent to which they are able to politically or institutionally implement a program of action. They are identifiable by their associational presence and by their participation in collective actions such as strikes, boycotts, or demonstrations. By contrast, fluid movements occur outside or in addition to organized direct action. Rather than the pursuit of a fixed agenda, they leave their societal footprint in the form of alternative meanings and cultural constructs. While they may find it necessary to engage with the political spheres, they also operate on the terrain of everyday life. Rather than a continuous mobilization, they ebb and flow in cycles of activism and abeyance (Gusfield 1981; 1994). Unlike the case of linear movements where sociological analysts tend to superimpose political over cultural meanings (Laraña 1994: 214), fluid movements constitute "communities of discourse" engaged in the enunciation of new cultural codes that very often contest dominant representations (Taylor and Whittier 1995: 180–181).

In the environmental case, a fluid conceptualization would take as the unit of analysis neither an organization nor the career of a specific issue or problem, but rather the progress of a particular discourse or set of discourses complete with their distinctive language, ideas, interpretations, and symbols. This meaning-making process is both conducted within and limited by identifiable "discursive fields" that structure the space within which cultural action occurs.

Using the case of the early development of the American conservation movement as his illustration, Hajer (1996) cautions that what we might commonly identify as a movement in fact may constitute a "discourse coalition" in which two separate parties with differing interests and goals join forces, possessing in common only "shared concepts and terms." The turn-of-the-century conservation movement was a coalition of morally charged nature preservationists with state-controlled technocrats who were interested primarily in applying new techniques of efficient resource management. In similar fashion, the ecology movement of the early 1970s fused together a core of findings from a scientific "school" within animal and plant ecology with a holistic philosophy of social living that was flourishing in the 1970s' counterculture (Macdonald 1991: 89). Key environmental discourses have rarely emerged overnight. Rather, they have tended to evolve over an extended period of time and, in some cases, represent a synthesis of several existing cultural constructions. This is very much the case with the radically new way of looking at the world represented by the concept of "wilderness."

As environmental historian Cronon (1996) has shown, wilderness constitutes a "cultural invention" developed over the course of two centuries. If you were to go back 250 years in American and European history, you would find that wilderness was equated with "wrong nature," a place that was considered barren, savage, and frightening. The wilderness where Moses wandered with his people for forty years was full of bleakness, both physically and metaphorically. Yet, by the end of the nineteenth century, the "wastelands" had been transformed in the popular imagination into a place of primeval, spiritual beauty, somewhere to be conserved rather than conquered.

Cronon characterizes the rehabilitation of the wilderness as having two broad sources, each of which could be considered as being part of a "fluid" movement. The doctrine of the sublime was transatlantic in character, finding its expression in the work of a number of nineteenth-century Romantic artists and writers such as Woodsworth, Emerson, and Thoreau. Sublime landscapes were so vast and powerful that they evoked a sense of the divine. Accordingly, protecting these sacred temples of nature became a major project for the first generation of environmentalists to the exclusion of more mundane rural ecosystems such as drylands or swamps.

A second cultural current or movement, more explicitly American but no less Romantic in its appeal was that of the frontier. We owe much of our present impression of the frontier to the celebrated historian Turner who in 1893 proclaimed that the American frontier was about to "close," taking with it the sense of vigor, independence, and creativity that had become part of the myth of American democracy. One of the foundations of this vanishing frontier, Turner claimed, was the wilderness that was said to represent the last bastion of rugged individualism. In the final decades of the nineteenth century, notions of the sublime and the frontier converged, thereby clothing the wilderness in a coat of moral values and cultural symbols that has lasted right up to the present day.

There are two important observations that can be made concerning the evolution of the concept of "wilderness." First, this alteration in the meaning of the wildlands took place over a relatively long period of time and was the synthesis of a pair of discursive elements—the sublime and the frontier. Second, rather than being situated exclusively within the boundaries of a single social movement, this synthesis occurred in the interstices between the "back to nature" movement (see Schmitt 1990) and the wider Romantic movement against industrialism. Over time, the idea of the wilderness became loaded with some of the deepest core values of American culture.

A somewhat similar development can be identified for the case of Australia where attempts to create a new sense of national identity drew on various myths and traditions about the landscape down under. In particular, the "bush" became a potent symbol of nationalism, especially near the end of the nineteenth century where a cultural movement of poets and artists reconceived the Australian landscape in distinctly nativistic terms. Whereas the English countryside was described as being fey and tired, the bush was seen as both macho and pure, an analogue for the vitality of the new world. As is the case for the wilderness in America, the preoccupation of contemporary Australian environmentalists with the preservation of the bush can be traced back to a culturally constructed ethos that arose over an extended period of time and was linked to an emerging sense of patriotic renewal (Papadakis 1993: 63).

CULTURAL RESOURCES AND RESONANCES IN THE ENVIRONMENTAL MOVEMENT

In considering the relationship between culture and collective action, three broad topics have been identified: the cultural roots of social movements, the emergence and development of distinctive movement cultures, and the cultural consequences or residues of social movements (McAdam 1994).

While social movements may often appear to orbit exclusively within their own private universe, this is rarely the case. Rather, movements that are seriously seeking or resisting change must be sensitive to the prevailing cultural currents in the community, past, present, and future. Invariably, then, the roots of a social movement reach out into the cultural soil of the host society. That is to say, elements of the dominant culture are imported, processed, and utilized within the movement's own symbol system. Williams (1995) has branded these imports as "cultural resources," distinguishing them from "structural resources" such as social movement organization (SMO) funding and membership in two significant ways: (1) they are contextual, meaning that they resonate with the host community, especially that part of it that the social movement hopes to reach and (2) they are public insofar as they depend on some measure of external consumption and interpretation in order to be fully effective. As Flynn has observed: "Social movements seeking change must engage in discourse that appears consistent with a society's sense of values and norms of behavior. Change that appears to violate these parameters is likely to be rejected as threatening social stability. Historical discourse presents a means by which social movements may transcend the parameters of present social practice by grounding their dialogue in mainstream social and political values" (1996: 136).

In order to create their vision, sociopolitical movements draw on a repertoire of rhetorical constructions. Williams (1995) has suggested that these constructions take the form of "models of public good" that represent attempts to legitimate the ideological themes of movements by situating them in broad, historical civic and religious tenets. He identifies three such models, all of which derive from the religious idiom in American society. The "covenant" model is based on the belief that the nation was created in the form of a covenant with God. One well-known example of this is the covenantal relationship that for a long time legitimated the political regime of the Boers in South Africa. In the case of the United States, a variety of social and religious movements have justified a call for reform on the basis that it is necessary in order to sustain the spirit of this covenant. According to the "contract" model, good citizenship requires the inclusion of everyone equally in the ongoing political community. Key terms here are "justice" and "fair play." The civil rights movement in the 1950s and 1960s, for example, drew in large measure on this model. Finally, the "stewardship" model maintains that we have a duty to carefully manage societal resources for the sake of both present and future generations. Thus, in order not to burden our children and grandchildren with crushing pension contributions, it is incumbent on us to raise the limits of our dues here and now.

Environmental rhetorics may tap into all three of these models, but they are particularly prone to embrace the contract and stewardship versions. The environmental justice movement, for example, extends the outlook of the civil rights movement by proclaiming three strands of "environmental equity" (see Lee 1992): procedural equity (governing rules, regulations, and evaluation criteria must be applied uniformly across all jurisdictions), geographical equity (it is unacceptable that minority communities and neighborhoods are disproportionately burdened by having petrochemical plants, hazardous waste facilities, and the like exclusively in their backyards), and social equity (race, class, and other cultural identities must be recognized in environmental decision making). The stewardship model overlays many aspects of "biocentric" ideology that were notably embraced by the Earth First organization. Similarly, it infuses the "rhetoric of entitlement" that swirls around the campaign to stop global biodiversity loss; note, for example, the fondness of environmentalists for using the slogan "we have not inherited the Earth from our parents, we have borrowed it from our children" (Hannigan 1995: 155–156). By drawing on long-established models of the public good, environmentalists are both able to mobilize new and existing followers and to smooth entry into political arenas that require a strong measure of legitimacy. Eder (1996a: 209) makes more or less the same point when he observes that ethical subframes in ecological discourse play a central role in legitimating the relationship between modern political institutions and environmental issues.

In addition to broad societal interpretations such as those cited by Williams (1995), environmental (and antienvironmental) groups look to local and regional subcultures as sources of cultural resources. This is richly illustrated in the case of a recent controversy over the future of Adirondack Park in upstate New York.

In 1990, a government-appointed body, the Commission on the Adirondacks in the Twenty-first Century, released a document containing 245 recommendations, several of which would necessarily lead to an expansion of the park area. The report split those Adirondackers residing permanently within the parameters of the park. While it had the support of several national environmental organizations, notably the Sierra Club and the National Audubon Society, as well as a small local group called the Residents Committee to Protect the Adirondacks, it also spawned a number of antienvironmental property rights groups, some of which were aligned to the "Wise Use" movement, an activist network identified with the radical right in the United States. In her analysis of this environmental conflict, Senecah (1996) demonstrates that the Wise Use/property rights message found support, expression, and legitimacy among Adirondackers because it resonated with the memories, stories, and biases of the local culture in a way in which the proenvironmental discourse did not, or perhaps could not, do.

The defining event here was a piece of legislation passed in 1892 that declared a huge tract of wild land to be part of the public domain, as indicated by a "blue line" drawn on the map to indicate the boundaries and existence of the park. Private lands within the park were never officially acknowledged, although it was implied that they would at some future point be acquired. At the same time, the State of New York sold land to a handful of exclusive private clubs who established "camps" as playgrounds for the wealthy "robber barons" of the age—the Morgans, Roosevelts, and Vanderbilts. The clubs quickly fenced in their preserves, posted "no trespassing" signs, and hired armed guards to patrol the perimeter. Local residents could no longer fish or hunt there and were forced out of economic necessity to work in service jobs for the wealthy families, making them for all intensive purposes "invisible." The property rights groups, notably the 4,300-member Citizens Council of the Adirondacks exploited these historically based feelings of powerlessness and invisibility. Blue balloons, blue-painted signs, and blue-colored ribbons were displayed at protest rallies. Some opposition groups, such as the Blue Line Council and the Blue Line Confederation (which published the newsletter *Blue Line News*), incorporated it in their names. The fact that the report recommended expanding the blue line further enhanced the power and appeal of this symbolism (needless to say, the color green did not strike a positive chord here).

Property rights groups further tapped into local history and culture by building their discourse around the memory of the Revolutionary War, which still constitutes a touchstone for many Americans. The Citizens Council of the Adirondacks incorporated pictures of the Minutemen, the Liberty Bell, and the legendary hero Paul Revere on his "Midnight Ride" on the group's letterhead and on all of their press releases. Environmentalists were equated with the wealthy elitists of the past and it was asserted that Adirondackers would be deprived of their livelihoods and culture in order that hikers and campers from the city could play. By contrast, the literature of the Sierra Club and other national environmental organizations missed the mark, casting the park in terms ("a biological treasure chest"; "a green oasis in the Northeast") that in no way resonated with local concerns and experiences.

Cantrill (1996) observed a similar pattern thousands of miles away on the threshold of Yellowstone National Park, only in this case it was the environmentalists who exploited a strong sense of local history and identity. The "Beartooth Alliance," a grassroots environmental group, had mobilized in opposition to the "New World" mine project proposed by Crowne Butte, a gold exploration firm that at that time was under Canadian ownership (it has since been sold to American owners). How the alliance packaged and communicated their opposition was very much in sync with the local traditions and cultural practices. Cantrill notes that the group's rhetorical discourse revolved around three themes. First, the Beartooth Alliance played up the extent to which the Absaroka-Beartooth Wilderness Area was a place of exceptional natural beauty that would be despoiled by the mine should it be permitted to proceed. Second, the alliance castigated "faceless bureaucrats and corporations" who were seen to be conspiring together in an effort to manipulate and take advantage of loopholes in federal regulations in order to strip the environment. The fact that Crowne Butte was a foreign-owned firm added to this sense of outsiders versus local people. Third, the alliance celebrated the efforts of a few brave "ecowarriors" who were willing to stand up against the long odds in the fight against pollution. This rhetorical package adopted by the Beartooth Alliance was in tune with U.S. western mountain state culture, which emphasizes individual rights, a distrust of both big business and big government, and empowerment through direct action. As was the case in the Adirondack controversy, local grassroots activists were able to tap into a regional rhetorical identity in a way that was closed off to national environmental organizations.

In both of these case studies, local historical experience and identity provided important additions to the toolbox of symbols and strategies employed by grassroots groups embroiled in environmental conflicts. Much the same phenomenon can be observed in other settings: inner-city communities victimized by toxic waste dumps; fishing villages facing long-term unemployment because of vastly depleted fish stocks; and native communities whose traditional lifestyle is being destroyed by nickel mines, oil and gas pipelines, or low-flying military aircraft.

CREATING AN INTERNAL ENVIRONMENTAL CULTURE

In addition to the kind of imported cultural resources that I have just discussed, social movements also actively create their own internal culture. This is important both in fashioning collective identities and in mobilizing members. In this regard, Lofland has isolated six "social locations" in social movement formation where culture is most conspicuous or prominent:

1. Expressions of general values that are distinctive enough to justify the movement's very existence;
2. material objects and associated iconic personages that are held in high esteem within the movement;
3. everyday stories told and retold with strong positive or negative emotional expression among participants in a movement;

4. characteristics of the movement's occasions (gatherings) that are regarded as positive features of the movement;
5. social roles that specialize in the creation and dissemination of ideas, artifacts, and performances endowed with positive value;
6. ways in which these specialized and other roles are expressed in the persona exhibited by participants (1995: 192).

When it reemerged in the late 1960s and early 1970s, the contemporary American version of environmentalism encompassed two quite different subcultures. On the one hand, you had an outlook associated with the New Left and the 1960s counterculture that was rooted in a general critique of the structure of power in modern society. Juxtaposed to this was the conservationist tradition that had been kept alive over the years by voluntary organizations such as the Audubon Society and the Sierra Club, which promoted hiking, bird watching, and similar recreational pursuits. Earth Day 1970, often cited as the debut of the modern environmental movement, was a curious mix of activities, events, and rhetorics representing both streams. What gave this event its definition, notes Gottlieb (1993: 113), an environmental activist and historian, was the national media that combined under a single label such varied issues as overpopulation, air and water pollution, wilderness loss, and pesticide poisoning, while emphasizing at the same time the need for remediation as opposed to wholesale structural transformation. While it is somewhat hyperbolic to label environmentalism as a "movement without a history" that had been suddenly "given a clear slate on how to proceed," as Gottlieb has done, nevertheless it was necessary for environmentalists to collectively work out an internal culture from a more or less standing position.

In order to do so, conservationist history was plumbed and reframed. The philosophical differences that had characterized the different wings of the nature protection movement at the turn of the century were magnified and sharpened. In this context, the defining event was identified as the "Hetch Hetchy" affair in which Muir, the "preservationist," was beatified as the great defender of the wilderness while Pinchot, the "resource conservationist," was vilified as the government man who sold out nature on the grounds of utilitarianism. Along with Muir, the other conservationist figure who was elevated to visionary status was Leopold. When Leopold's *A Sand County Almanac* was first published posthumously in 1949, in which he introduced his notion of a "land ethic" extending moral rights to the natural world, the book received limited notice; but when it was republished in 1968, the work zoomed to the center of environmental philosophy. Alongside these newly canonized historical figures were placed other more contemporary sources of inspiration and reverence: Abbey, Berry, Bookchin, Carson, Naess, and Schumacher.

In spite of this, some ecological observers have suggested that environmentalism has not yet developed a complete cultural repertoire, especially as compared to other movements such as the women's or civil rights movements. Delicath (1996), for example, rues the lack of utopian cultural rhetorics along ecological lines. Despite the existence of "ectopian" novels by Abbey, Callenbach, Le Guin, Robinson, and others, he maintains that the movement lacks a critical mass of literature, poetry, art, films, and documentaries that stimulate a discussion of ectopian possibilities. These all represent, he argues, potential sites of meaning, production, political theorizing, and institution building.

Part of the difficulty here, perhaps, may be that environmentalism does not spring from any ascribed sociocultural identities such as race, ethnicity, gender, or sexual preference (one notable exception here is the environmental justice movement where these categories are front and center). Consequently, environmental groups must collectively build new identities around achieved commonalities such as a distinctive lifestyle. As Gamson (1995: 100) has observed, collective identities consist of three embedded layers: organizational, movement, and solidary group. The first, organizational identity, is built around movement carriers, for example, a Greenpeace canvasser. The second, movement identity, is broader than any particular organization. In this case, one's identity as an environmentalist rests on a wider ideological affiliation than that associated with a single SMO. Finally, solidary group identity arises out of people's social location in the wider society. Environmental activists, Gamson observes, have been hobbled by the fact that their dominant social location, the professional managerial class, lacks any kind of rootedness in solidary group identities.

One way in which social movements generate a strong internal culture is through struggle, that is, by engaging in protest, suffering persecution, and overcoming adversity. The civil rights movement, for example, possesses a rich array of celebrated events and figures: Rosa Parks refusing to give up her seat and move to the back of the bus; Jackie Robinson breaking the color barrier in baseball; and Martin Luther King delivering his " I Have a Dream" speech and later falling victim to an assassin's bullet. Despite some high-profile successes such as the campaign opposing clear-cutting in the old growth forests of the Pacific Northwest, the environmental movement has fallen somewhat short in this regard, at least in First World countries. It is worth noting, for example, that two of the best known environmental martyrs, Chico Mendes (Brazil) and Ken Sara Wiwo (Nigeria), hail from Southern nations. Despite plenty of aspiring ecotroubadors, no one anthem has emerged that is capable of summing up the environmentalist experience in as powerful and memorable a way as does "We Shall Overcome" for the civil rights movement or "Solidarity Forever" for labor. While environmentalists have successfully co-opted the color green, there is thus far no universally recognized symbol such as the peace sign from the 1960s (the Greenpeace emblem is a hybrid of the ecology and peace signs).

ENVIRONMENTAL RHETORICS AND RESIDUES

Finally, it is important to look at the cultural consequences of social movements. As McAdam (1994: 49) has noted, given the degree to which opposition to such movements is firmly entrenched, it is often true that their most powerful impact is cultural in nature rather than more narrowly political and economic. We can see this especially with regard to language. Not only can social movements introduce a whole new vocabulary into our everyday lives, but they can also change existing ways of talking and writing. "Nonsexist" language, for example, is now a requirement in most books, articles, speeches, and classroom lectures, a transformation that can be traced directly to pressure from women's groups.

Myerson and Rydin (1996) have introduced the term "environet" to refer to the dynamic system of changing connections continually spread across a society with regard to environmental issues, problems, and ideas. The environet constitutes a "textual carnival," an aggregate collection of texts, words, and voices that appear in and cross over from official statistics, policy documents, and expert reports, news items, poems, political speeches, bestsellers, theories, newspaper headlines, and other communication "sites." Environmental SMOs strive to place and maintain their words and images on this environet, which constantly swirls around the arena of public discourse. To the extent that they are able to do so with some regularity, we can say that they are having a visible cultural impact on society. Myerson and Rydin further propose that this environet is influenced by three types of discourses that are invented and reinvented to shape and manage the otherwise chaotic ricocheting collection of words and notions that bounce around in a sea of environmental texts.

"New information discourses" surprise and convince us by presenting new facts. For example, Hansen's claim in 1988 that the elevated temperatures of the 1980s was not due to chance but rather constituted an indicator of a long-term global warming trend is an example of this. Over time, a new information discourse decouples from its original source. In such cases, people forget where they heard the information but swear that it must be true. Thus, the claim that the McDonald's hamburger chain is a major culprit in tropical deforestation and methane emissions because of its large cattle ranches in Central America now seems to be everywhere in popular discourse, yet few people could correctly identify the original authority. "New concept discourses" shock us with a novel way of thinking and seek to persuade the public to adopt a new set of ideas. Lovelock's "Gaia" concept, which suggests that the earth isn't merely the site of various ecosystems but is itself a living organism that follows ecological principles, is a good example of this. New concept discourses may be freshly invented or they can be reinvented for a new generation, as is the case with "acid rain," which was first identified in 1852. Finally, "new practice discourses" consider new policies, ideas for environmental management, and issues of implementation and feasibility. One recent illustration of this is the notion of "pollution taxation." Social movements are less likely to dominate the environet here, as scientific, technological, and political actors from the mainstream society are the most likely to intervene.

CONCLUSION

In this chapter, I have briefly sketched out some of the possibilities for a more culturally directed sociology of the environment. Culture here has been treated both as a context for and a product of environmental activity. We need, of course, to be careful about the way in which we utilize the concept. Otherwise, as Swidler has warned, culture "becomes a species of intellectual hand waving, creating a warm and cosy atmosphere while other factors continue to carry the real explanatory weight" (1995: 38).

Ideally, we need to look at how culture interacts with other factors in influencing environmental strategies. Gordon and Jasper (1996) have complained that much recent work on social movements has used resource mobilization models as convenient straw-men targets, assuming that either resources or cultural meanings affect protest—but not at the same time. Instead, they urge researchers to explore the manner by which resources and meanings interact. That is, it is important to be able to demonstrate how financial and other resources are utilized in order to promulgate ideologies and injustice frames, and how cultural meanings and rhetorics shape the definition and accumulation of financial resources.

In addition, we need to empirically assess some of the more theoretical assertions that have been made about culture and the environment. For example, can we take as correct Eder's (1996a; 1996b) assertion that the environmental movement has lost its monopoly on environmental discourse and that it is now reduced to one among many competing for a place in the public discourse on matters ecological. Is this equally likely to be the case outside western Europe where the environmentalist argument is less widely accepted? In unison with Polletta, environmental sociologists would be well advised to join the chorus of those calling for more empirical, comparative work of this type, especially that which helps to reveal the "circumstances in which culture inspires, impedes, and shapes collective action" (1997: 445).

One promising link between theory and research here is the threefold typology of discourses proposed by Myerson and Rydin (1996). Under what conditions do environmental groups come to dominate all or some of these discourses? What is the relationship among them? Value added? Ricocheting? At which stage of the three-part model of the social construction of environmental issues and problems proposed by Hannigan (1995) are we most likely to find activity in each of these three discourse areas?

Also helpful in guiding further inquiry is an agenda set out by Hart (1996) in his theoretical reassessment of the cultural dimension of social movements. Hart identifies five topics that are central to understanding the cultural aspects of social movements and that can help to organize future research efforts:

(i) what cultural elements—concepts, images, templates—in the cultural environment, embedded in what pre-existing traditions are drawn upon by social movements; (ii) how the structures of these pre-existing codes—for instance, the rhetorical strategies or types of narratives they make it easier or harder to formulate—condition their impact on and use by social movements; (iii) what cultural craft-work is done by movement participants as pre-existing codes are selectively appropriated, interpreted, transformed, and applied; (iv) how the cultural forms created within movements work for the movements—what kind of orientation, guidance, rituals, and legitimation they provide; and (v) how these cultural forms ultimately affect public discourse and political events. (98)

It is a case for optimism that several papers presented at the second Woudschoten conference have in various ways begun to work on Hart's research agenda with specific reference to environmentalism and environmental movements. Using a cultural framing approach borrowed from Snow and his collaborators, Seippel (1997) zeroes in on the fifth of Hart's set of questions. Specifically, he focuses on how different ecological worldviews, which he conceptualizes as "metacultures of our society," are internally constructed and how they fit into the ideological-political discourses in different countries. For example, how central is the concept of "rights" to the political culture of a certain nation and how can environmentalists tailor their discourse in order to tap into this rights frame and thereby forge important alliances both within and beyond civil society? A second paper that brings in the culture variable is Van Koppen's (1997) attempt to integrate three types of social theories that address the theme of nature conservation in environmental sociology: the sustainable use of nature as a resource, an "Arcadian" interpretation, and the social construction of nature. Combined, these three approaches can help us to address Hart's agenda by better understanding how people experience nature in their daily "lifeworld" and how movements can bridge to these meaning frames that may differ from society to society. It is scholarly work of this type that is crucial in furthering the task of situating grounded middle-range theory, rather than permitting it to drift into a wasteland of undirected linguistic and discourse analysis where little effort is made to relate cultural meanings and practices to the overlapping domains of economics and politics (see Stevenson 1996: 407).

REFERENCES

Adam, B. 1999. "Radiated Identities: In Pursuit of the Temporal Complexity of Conceptual Cultural Practices." In *Spaces of Culture: City, Nation , World*, ed. M. Featherstone and S. Lash. London: Sage.

Cantrill, J. 1996. "Gold, Yellowstone and the Search for Rhetorical Identity." In *Green Culture: Environmental Rhetoric in Contemporary America*, ed. C. G. Herndl and S. C. Brown. Madison: University of Wisconsin Press.

Cronon, W. 1996. "The Trouble with Wilderness; or Getting Back to the Wrong Nature." *Environmental History* 1:7–28.

Delicath, J. W. 1996. "In Search of Ectopia: Radical Environmentalism and the Possibilities of Utopian Rhetorics." In *Earthtalk: Communication Empowerment for Environmental Action*, ed. S. A. Muir and T. L. Veenendall. Westport, Conn.: Praeger.

Douglas, M. A., and A. Wildavsky. 1982. *Risk and Culture: An Essay on the Selection of Technological and Environmental Dangers*. Berkeley: University of California Press.

Eder, K. 1996a. "The Institutionalization of Environmentalism: Ecological Discourse and the Second Transformation of the Public Sphere." In *Risk, Environment and Modernity: Towards a New Ecology*, ed. S. Lash, B. Szerszynski, and B. Wynne. London: Sage.

———. 1996b. *The Social Construction of Nature: A Sociology of Ecological Enlightenment*. London: Sage.

Featherstone, M., and S. Lash. 1999. Introduction to *Spaces of Culture: City, Nation, World*, ed. M. Featherstone and S. Lash. London: Sage.

Flynn, T. R. 1996. "Challenging the Dominion Covenant: The Preservationist Construction of an Environmental Past." In *Earthtalk: Communication Empowerment for Environmental Action*, ed. S. A. Muir and T. I. Veenendall. Westport, Conn.: Praeger.

Gamson, W. A. 1995. "Constructing Social Protest." In *Social Movements and Culture*, ed. H. Johnston and B. Klandermans. Minneapolis: University of Minnesota Press.

Giner, S., and D. Tabara. 1999. "Cosmic Piety and Ecological Rationality." *International Sociology* 14:59–82.

Gordon, C., and J. M. Jasper. 1996. "Overcoming the 'Nimby' Label: Rhetorical and Organizational Links for Local Protesters." *Research in Social Movements, Conflict and Change* 19:159–181.

Gottlieb, R. 1993. *Forcing the Spring: The Transformation of the American Environmental Movement*. Washington, D.C.: Island.

Gusfield, J. R. 1981. "Social Movements and Social Change: Perspectives of Linearity and Fluidity." In *Research in Social Movements, Conflict and Change*, vol. 4, ed. L. Kriesberg. Greenwich, Conn.: JAI Press.

———. 1994. "The Reflexivity of Social Movements: Collective Behavior and Mass Society Revisited." In *New Social Movements: From Ideology to Identity*, ed. E. Laraña, H. Johnston, and J. R. Gusfield. Philadelphia: Temple University Press.

Hajer, M. 1996. "Ecological Modernisation As Cultural Politics." In *Risk, Environment and Modernity: Towards a New Ecology*, ed. S. Lash, B. Szerszynski, and B. Wynne. London: Sage.

Hannigan, J. A. 1995. *Environmental Sociology: A Social Constructionist Perspective*. London: Routledge.

Hart, S. 1996. "The Cultural Dimension of Social Movements: A Theoretical Reassessment and Literature Review." *Sociology of Religion* 57:87–100.

Jasper, J. 1997. *The Art of Moral Protest: Culture, Biography, and Creativity in Social Movements*. Chicago: University of Chicago Press.

Johnston, H., and B. Klandermans. 1995. "The Cultural Analysis of Social Movements." In *Social Movements and Culture*, ed. H. Johnston and B. Klandermans. Minneapolis: University of Minnesota Press.

Laraña, E. 1994. "Continuity and Unity in New Forms of Collective Action: A Comparative Analysis of Student Movements." In *New Social Movements: From Ideology to Identity*, ed. E. Laraña, H. Johnston, and J. R. Gusfield. Philadelphia: Temple University Press.

Lash, S. 1994. "Reflexivity and its Doubles: Structure, Aesthetics, Community." In *Reflexive Modernization: Politics, Tradition and Aesthetics in the Modern Social Order*, ed. U. Beck, A. Giddens, and S. Lash. Cambridge: Polity.

Lee, C., ed. 1992. Proceedings, First National People of Color Environmental Leadership Summit, United Church of Christ Commission for Racial Justice, New York City, New York, December.

Lofland, J. 1995. "Charting Degrees of Movement Culture: Discerning Discourse in Social Movements." In *Social Movements and Culture*, ed. H. Johnston and B. Klandermans. Minneapolis: University of Minnesota Press.

Macdonald, D. 1991. *The Politics of Pollution: Why Canadians Are Failing Their Environment*. Toronto: McClelland and Stewart.

McAdam. D. 1994. "Culture and Social Movements." In *New Social Movements: From Ideology to Identity*, ed. E. Laraña, H Johnston, and J. R. Gusfield. Philadelphia: Temple University Press.

Myerson, G., and Y. Rydin. 1996. *The Language of Environment: A New Rhetoric*. London: UCL Press.

Papadakis, E. 1993. *Politics and the Environment: The Australian Experience*. Sydney: Allen and Unwin.

Polletta, F. 1997. "Culture and Its Discontents: Recent Theorizing on the Cultural Dimensions of Protest." *Sociological Inquiry* 67:431–450.

Schmitt, P. J. 1990. *Back to Nature: The Arcadian Myth in Urban America*. Baltimore, Md.: Johns Hopkins University Press.

Seippel, Ø. N. 1997. *Modernity, Politics and the Environment: A Theoretical Perspective*. Paper presented at the International Sociological Association Conference on Sociological Theory and the Environment, Zeist, Netherlands, March 20–23.

Senecah, S. 1996. "Forever Wild or Forever in Battle: Metaphors of Empowerment in the Continuing Controversy over the Adirondacks." In *Earthtalk: Communication Empowerment for Environmental Action*, ed. S. A. Muir and T. L. Veenendall. Westport, Conn.: Praeger.

Stevenson, N. 1996. Review of *Cultural Studies and Beyond: Fragments of Empire* by I. Davies. *Sociology* 30:407–408.

Swidler, A. 1986. "Culture in Action: Symbols and Strategies." *American Sociological Review* 51:273–286.

———. 1995. "Cultural Power and Social Movements." In *Social Movements and Culture*, ed. Hank Johnston and Bert Klandermans. Minneapolis: University of Minnesota Press.

Taylor, V., and N. Whittier. 1995. "Analytical Approaches to Movement Culture: The Culture of the Women's Movement." In *Social Movements and Culture*, ed. H. Johnston and B. Klandermans. Minneapolis: University of Minnesota Press.

Van Koppen, C. S. A. 1997. "Resource, Arcadia, Lifeworld: Nature Valuation in Environmental Sociology." Paper presented at the International Sociological Association Conference on Sociological Theory and the Environment, Zeist, Netherlands, March 20–23.

Williams, R. H. 1995. "Constructing the Public Good: Social Movements and Cultural Resources." *Social Problems* 42:124–144.

———. 1999. Review of *The Art of Moral Protest* by J. M. Jasper. *Social Forces* 77:1673–1675.

Wuthnow, R. 1989. *Communities of Discourse*. Cambridge, Mass.: Harvard University Press.

Wuthnow, R., and M. Witten. 1988. "New Directions in the Study of Culture." *Annual Review of Sociology* 14:49–67.

Wynne, B. 1996. "May the Sheep Safely Graze? A Reflexive View of the Expert-Lay Divide." In *Risk, Environment and Modernity: Towards a New Ecology*, ed. S. Lash, B. Szerszynski, and B. Wynne. London: Sage.

Part V

SOCIOLOGICAL PARADIGMS AND ENVIRONMENTAL SOCIOLOGY

15

Paradigms, Theories, and Environmental Sociology

Riley E. Dunlap

In the late 1960s and especially the early 1970s, environmental issues were receiving a great deal of societal attention in the United States. As a result, a number of sociologists began to examine topics such as public opinion toward environmental issues, social characteristics of environmental activists, organizational characteristics and strategies of environmental organizations, and environmental politics and policy making. Such research involved applying traditional sociological perspectives on public opinion, social movements, formal organizations, and so on, and amounted to a "sociology of environmental issues." Gradually, however, a few sociologists began to analyze the relationships between modern industrial societies and their biophysical environments, ranging from local-level studies of the relationship between social class and exposure to air pollution to historical analyses of energy usage. Such analyses developed at the same time that the term "environmental sociology" began to be used, in the early and mid-1970s.

I found the term attractive and wanted to become an "environmental sociologist," but was uncertain as to what this would actually involve. It seemed to me that if there was to be a field of environmental sociology, it must involve more than simply applying perspectives from other sociological specialties to environmental issues. Consequently, working with Catton, I decided to try to make sense of the rapidly growing body of work on environmental topics being done by sociologists and to see if this work was becoming distinctive enough to warrant being considered as a new field in its own right.

Beginning our collaboration in the mid-1970s, Catton and I ended up publishing a series of articles that attempted to synthesize and codify sociological work on environmental topics and to offer a definition of the field that would highlight its distinctiveness. In the process of doing this, we realized that mainstream sociology had developed a set of traditions and taken-for-granted assumptions that led our discipline to ignore the biophysical environment. Consequently, we ended up trying to clarify these traditions and the underlying assumptions—or paradigm—that we believed were making it difficult for sociologists to recognize the importance of environmental problems. We also outlined an alternative paradigm that we hoped would facilitate the development of environmental sociology, one that highlighted the fact that even modern, industrial societies are dependent on their biophysical environments and that environmental problems therefore warranted sociological attention.

While our definition of the field proved noncontroversial, our efforts to delineate the "human exemptionalism paradigm" we saw as inhibiting mainstream sociological attention to environmental issues and to sketch out an emerging "ecological paradigm" that we felt would facilitate sociological attention to such issues did provoke controversy. The purpose of this chapter is to describe our depiction of these two paradigms and then examine the resulting controversies that they provoked. These controversies stem partly from some ambiguities in our original portrayal of the two paradigms and partly from continual misunderstandings of our intent. I will try to resolve the ambiguities in the process of reviewing three common misinterpretations of our argument, all of which involve the relationship between paradigms and theories: (1) that since we discerned an exemptionalist orientation underlying virtually all contemporary sociological theories (as of the 1970s) we were suggesting that these theoretical orientations were irrelevant in general and in the analysis of environmental issues in particular; (2) that the ecological paradigm we were proposing as an alternative to the discipline's implicit exemptionalist paradigm would replace existing *theoretical* perspectives; and (3) that our analysis of the exemptionalist orientation of mainstream sociology and contemporary sociological theory (which suggested that they stemmed in part from traditional disciplinary postures such as Durkheim's antireductionism taboo) indicated that we were suggesting that classical—as well as contemporary—sociological theory was irrelevant for environmental sociology.

This chapter will deal with each of these misunderstandings. But first let me begin with our definition of the field, since it is what stimulated our analysis of sociology's dominant paradigm and the presentation of an alternative one. Then I quickly review our analysis of the disciplinary assumptions that we felt gave rise to sociology's embrace of human exemptionalism, followed by a brief description of the human exemptionalism paradigm and our proposed alternative: the new ecological paradigm. Then I examine reactions to our analyses, dealing with the three misunderstandings noted earlier and showing how they stem from differing interpretations of the nature of and relations between paradigms and theories. I end by assessing the degree to which sociology has overcome its exemptionalist orientation and has begun to embrace a more ecological perspective in recent years, noting that the answer depends heavily on one's notion of a paradigm shift.

DEFINING THE FIELD OF
ENVIRONMENTAL SOCIOLOGY

I first came across the term "environmental sociology" in Klausner's *On Man in His Environment* (1971: 4), a couple years after publication, when it was just starting to be used. While the term had a great deal of appeal, I was not sure at the time its use was justified because the bulk of research being done involved applying standard sociological perspectives to environmental topics and amounted to a sociology of environmental issues, as noted earlier (Dunlap and Catton 1979). What made most areas of sociology distinctive were the kinds of variables they examined, as political sociology involved the analysis of political phenomena as independent or dependent variables; stratification the analysis of class, status, and so on as independent or dependent variables; and the same for other areas such as formal organization, deviance, family, and so forth. Thus, in my mind, a "real" environmental sociology would involve examination of environmental variables (especially as causes or effects) in relation to social variables. A good early example was Burch's (1976) analysis of the relationship between social class and exposure to air pollution.

With this in mind, Catton and I defined environmental sociology as "the study of interaction between the environment and society" (Catton and Dunlap 1978a: 44) or societal-environmental interactions. In this vein, we tried to demonstrate that examinations of the relationship between social class and environmental degradation or the impact of energy shortages on society were qualitatively different (because they treated environmental phenomena as "variables") than studies of public opinion toward environmental issues or of environmental activists, and that the former constituted a true "environmental sociology" rather than just a sociology of environmental issues (Dunlap and Catton, 1979).[1] But in the process of defining the field in this way, we realized that sociology was quite reluctant to deal with environmental phenomena, particularly to attribute causal powers to such conditions, because of the legacy of past excesses of environmental and geographical determinism. This, in turn, stimulated us to analyze the sociological traditions and assumptions that deflected disciplinary attention from environmental phenomena and made it difficult for sociology to recognize the growing significance of environmental problems.

DISCIPLINARY TRADITIONS

Sociology has been deeply influenced by the Western cultural traditions in which it developed, a culture that is strongly anthropocentric in viewing humans as separate from and above the rest of nature. The tendency to treat nature as existing primarily for human use was enhanced dramatically in recent centuries by scientific and technological advances. These advances, combined with discovery of the abundant resources of the "New World," generated an industrial revolution that profoundly changed Europe, the Americas, and gradually the rest of the world. Abundance and technological advances fueled dramatic economic growth and generated an optimistic belief in progress, particularly in the United States. It is within the context of this "Dominant Western Worldview" (DWW), outlined briefly in the first column of table 15.1, that our discipline took root (Catton and Dunlap 1980). Not surprisingly, sociology has at least implicitly adopted the assumption that technological development, economic growth, and progress are the normal state of affairs.

Changes in how and where people lived, especially the massive shift toward industrialism and urbanism and away from agriculture, reinforced the notion that modern societies were becoming increasingly independent from their biophysical environments. In fact, life in industrialized societies created the impression that not only was the environment a source of inexhaustible natural resources, but also that humans could manipulate and control that environment to suit their needs.

In addition to the inherently optimistic orientation toward progress that sociology adopted from Western culture, various factors unique to our discipline have strengthened sociologists' tendency to ignore the importance of the environment. To establish a new discipline, the founding fathers of sociology asserted the uniqueness of our subject matter and perspectives. Of special importance was Durkheim's emphasis on the "objective reality of social facts" and the irreducibility of such facts to the psychological properties of individuals. A corollary of this sui generis conception of social phenomena was the dictum that the *cause* of a social fact must always be found in other social, as opposed to psychological, facts. The resultant "antireductionism taboo" also legitimated sociological rejection of biological and physical variables as potential explanations of social phenomena (Catton and Dunlap 1980).

When sociology was being founded, efforts to explain social phenomena in terms of biological and physical factors were still common. Because they often suggested that biological conditions such as heredity or physical conditions such as climate were the *primary* determinants of human affairs, proponents of these explanations came to be criticized as biological or geographical "determinists." Encouraged by antireductionism, sociologists have been especially adamant in rejecting these views, to the point that the charge of determinism is now leveled—incorrectly in my view—at those who suggest that biological or environmental factors have *any* degree of influence on human affairs (Benton 1991).

Besides the Durkheimian antireductionism taboo, another major tradition in sociology contributed to our discipline's tendency to ignore the biophysical environment. Inherited from Weber and elaborated by Mead, Cooley, Thomas, and others, this tradition emphasized the importance of understanding the ways in which people define their situations in order to understand their actions. Assuming that "the reality of a situation is in the definition attached to it by the participating actors," this perspective implied "that the physical properties of the situation may be ignored" (Choldin 1978: 353). Physical properties became relevant *only* if they were perceived and defined as relevant by the actors—that is, transformed into "social facts" (see, e.g., Klausner 1971: 41). This "social definition" perspective therefore complemented Durkheim's antireductionism in leading sociologists to ignore the physical environment.[2]

Table 15.1 Comparison of Major Assumptions in the "Dominant Western Worldview," "Sociology's Human Exemptionalism Paradigm," and the Proposed "New Ecological Paradigm"

	Dominant Western Worldview (DWW)	Human Exemptionalism Paradigm (HEP)	New Ecological Paradigm (NEP)
Assumptions about the nature of human beings	DWW_1 People are fundamentally different from all other creatures on Earth, over which they have dominion.	HEP_1 Humans have a cultural heritage in addition to (and distinct from) their genetic inheritance, and thus are quite unlike all other animal species.	NEP_1 While humans have exceptional characteristics (culture, technology, and so on), they remain one among many species that are interdependently involved in the global ecosystem.
Assumptions about social causation	DWW_2 People are masters of their destiny; they can choose their goals and learn to do whatever is necessary to achieve them.	HEP_2 Social and cultural factors (including technology) are the major determinants of human affairs.	NEP_2 Human affairs are influenced not only by social and cultural factors, but also by intricate linkages of cause, effect, and feedback in the web of nature; thus, purposive human actions have many unintended consequences.
Assumptions about the context of human society	DWW_3 The world is vast, and thus provides unlimited opportunities for humans.	HEP_3 Social and cultural environments are the crucial context for human affairs, and the biophysical environment is largely irrelevant.	NEP_3 Humans live in and are dependent on a finite biophysical environment that imposes potent physical and biological restraints on human affairs.
Assumptions about constraints on human society	DWW_4 The history of humanity is one of progress; for every problem there is a solution, and thus progress need never cease.	HEP_4 Culture is cumulative; thus technological and social progress can continue indefinitely, making all social problems ultimately soluble.	NEP_4 Although the inventiveness of humans and the powers derived therefrom may seem for a while to extend carrying capacity limits, ecological laws cannot be repealed.

The impact of these disciplinary traditions can be summarized as follows: the Durkheimian antireductionism legacy suggested that the physical environment *should* be ignored, while the Weberian legacy suggested that it *could* be ignored, for it was deemed unimportant in social life (Catton and Dunlap 1980; Dunlap and Catton 1983). Should one violate these traditions and suggest that the physical environment *might* be relevant for understanding social behavior, one risked being labeled an "environmental determinist" (Franck 1984). While these strictures were understandable at a time when sociology was still seeking secure disciplinary status, they seemed outmoded by the 1970s. One consequence, for example, is that while for most other disciplines "the environment" refers to our physical surroundings, within sociology it typically refers to social and cultural factors external to the entity being examined.

THE HUMAN EXEMPTIONALISM PARADIGM

As a result of the historical, cultural, and social context in which it developed and the unique traditions it evolved in its quest for disciplinary autonomy, sociology developed a largely implicit set of assumptions about the presumed irrelevance of the physical world for modern industrial societies. While seldom made explicit, these background assumptions influence the way in which sociologists approach their subject matter and practice their craft. As such, they appear to represent a fundamental "paradigm" or "lens" through which most sociologists view the world. Inherited from the DWW, and essentially representing a narrow disciplinary version of the DWW, these assumptions are listed in the second column of table 15.1.

Catton and I (1978a; 1978b; 1980) argued that these assumptions are so taken for granted that they are virtually never made explicit; yet, they clearly influence the practice of sociology and, we argued, account for our discipline's slow recognition of the significance of environmental problems. Taken together, they constitute a paradigm that is anthropocentric, technologically optimistic, and profoundly unecological. This paradigm serves to blind sociologists to the significance of environmental problems, for it suggests that humans can solve whatever problems arise and implies that *Homo sapiens* is not subject to the ecological constraints facing other species. Indeed, the overall image of human societies portrayed by these assumptions is one that emphasizes the "exceptional" nature of our species stemming from our cultural heritage, including language, social organization, and technology. For that reason, we originally labeled them the "Human Exceptionalism Paradigm" (HEP) (Catton and Dunlap 1978a: 42–43). However, we did not wish to deny that *Homo sapiens* is an "exceptional species," but rather that our exceptional characteristics do *not* "exempt" us from ecological principles and constraints. For this reason, we subsequently renamed the HEP the "Human Exemptionalism Paradigm" (Dunlap and Catton 1979: 250).

In arguing that these assumptions constitute a sociological paradigm, Catton and I were following the lead of sociologists like Ritzer (1975: 7) who conceptualized a paradigm broadly as "a fundamental image of the subject matter" and "the broadest unit of consensus" within a discipline. In our view, the HEP created a largely consensual view among mid-twentieth-century sociologists that modern industrial societies could be understood without any consideration of their biophysical base, and therefore that environmental phenomena were irrelevant to our discipline. Although widely used by sociologists in this fashion, others have argued that such a broad conceptualization of paradigm is inconsistent with the intent of Kuhn, its progenitor (see, e.g., Eckberg and Hill 1979). Nonetheless, our conceptualization remains popular within sociology, as witness Warner's recent statement that, "[a] paradigm is a 'gestalt,' a way of seeing the world, a representation, picture or narrative of the fundamental properties of reality" (1997: 193). As we shall see, however, differing interpretations regarding the nature of paradigms and thus their relationship to theories has been a major source of the controversy stimulated by our depiction of the HEP.

In sum, Catton and I argued that our discipline was premised on a set of background assumptions or paradigm that led most sociologists—regardless of their particular *theoretical* orientation (functionalism, Marxism, interactionism, and so on)—to "see" modern societies as being "exempt" from ecological constraints (Catton and Dunlap 1978a: 42). As part of the emphasis on the exceptional characteristics of humans, by the mid-twentieth century most sociologists were totally ignoring the biophysical environment, reflecting the implicit disciplinary consensus that it was irrelevant for understanding societal dynamics. This perspective was nicely captured in an article published in the *American Sociological Review* offering a "sociocultural theory of scarcity" in which the author argued: "If one were to ask for an expression, in a single sentence, of the main accomplishment of the social sciences to date, a fair answer would be the progressive substitution of sociocultural explanations for those stressing the determinative influence of physical nature" (Stanley 1968: 855). In the process, of course, sociologists became "sociocultural determinists"!

Given the grounding of our discipline in such an inherently unecological worldview, one that failed to recognize the ecosystem-dependence of *all* human societies, it is not surprising that sociologists were slow in paying attention to environmental problems when many other disciplines had already begun to take such problems seriously. In fact, writing at the time of the first U.S. "Earth Day," the prominent and progressive sociologist Etzioni argued that "the newly found environmental dangers are being vastly exaggerated" and that "human problems" rather than "environmental problems" should continue to receive top priority (1970: 921).

The HEP not only blinded mainstream sociologists to the importance of environmental problems, but predisposed them to accept the optimism inherent in the DWW by assuming that endless growth and progress were not threatened by resource scarcities or other ecological constraints. For example, in a wide-ranging critique of opposition to nuclear power, the influential American sociologist Nisbet (1979) viewed such opposition as a manifestation of declining "faith in progress" and went on to note that it was loss of such faith—rather than shortages of energy sources—that was the *real* threat to continued progress.

These optimistic tendencies were reinforced by sociologists' habit of seeking the causes of social change solely in terms of social phenomena, rather than acknowledging the possibility that ecological conditions *might* influence modern societies. Thus, Bell, another prominent American sociologist, dismissed the idea of "*physical* limits to growth" by assuring us "that one does not need to worry about ever running out of resources," but did acknowledge the possibility that there might be "*social* limits to growth" (1977: 18). Bell thus issued a quintessential HEP response to the "anomaly" of resource constraints by saying that *if* there were limits to the development of human societies, then they would surely be social rather than physical!

THE NEW ECOLOGICAL PARADIGM

Despite the skepticism of sociologists like Nisbet and Bell and, more importantly, many sectors of society, the evidence of serious environmental problems continued to mount throughout the 1970s and has continued more or less unabated ever since. Evidence of the threats posed by local air and water pollution as well as more dispersed problems such as acid rain and ozone depletion, combined with continued energy shortages and fears of overpopulation, were seen by some sociologists as major anomalies for the HEP (and by many members of society as anomalies for the DWW) because such problems emphasized that the welfare of human societies was dependent on their biophysical environments. This awareness led some environmental sociologists to go beyond examining societal attention to environmental problems and begin analyzing more fundamental aspects of the relations between industrial societies and their environments—such as the crucial causes of environmental degradation and the societal impacts of pollution and resource scarcity (e.g., Schnaiberg 1975).

Studies of societal-environmental interactions involved rejection of the disciplinary tradition of focusing only on "social facts" as explanations of social phenomena and at least tacit rejection of the assumption that modern, industrialized societies are exempt from ecological constraints. Such work led Catton and me to argue that implicit in the emergence of environmental sociology was a set of assumptions that together constituted a worldview or paradigm that clearly challenged the inherently anthropocentric HEP. We originally labeled this alternative paradigm the "New Environmental Paradigm" (NEP) (Catton and Dunlap 1978a), but because it seeks to emphasize the ecological foundation of human societies we quickly relabeled it the "New Ecological Paradigm" (Dunlap and Catton 1979: 250).

It is difficult to portray a new paradigm with a few short assumptions, but we believe the four listed in the third column of table 15.1 convey the essence of the NEP by emphasizing the ecosystem-dependence of modern, industrialized societies. The NEP's recognition that the welfare of modern societies, even with their complex forms of social organization and sophisticated technologies, is intricately linked to the health of the ecosystems on which they depend for their existence represents a major departure from the HEP. At a minimum, the NEP sensitizes sociologists to the fact that environmental problems are socially and sociologically significant phenomena. More generally, it encourages recognition of the fact that the dynamics of modern industrial societies can only be understood by considering their growing ecological impacts and the resultant societal problems created by these impacts.

REACTION TO THE HEP-NEP DISTINCTION

HEP/NEP and Contemporary Sociology

Our original presentation of the HEP-NEP distinction, which accompanied our effort to define the field of environmental sociology (Catton and Dunlap 1978a), drew an immediate response. Interestingly, it came from Buttel, a fellow environmental sociologist and valued colleague, some of whose work we had counted as representative of the NEP. While acknowledging the significance of the HEP-NEP distinction, Buttel (1978) nonetheless argued that it was not as important as existing theoretical cleavages within sociology—most notably between "order" (e.g., structural-functionalist) and "conflict" (e.g., Marxist) theoretical perspectives.[3] In retrospect, his criticism should not have been surprising for two reasons: first, his prior effort to demonstrate the importance of the order-conflict cleavages in social science analyses of environmental issues (Buttel 1976) and second, because Catton's and my original exposition was somewhat ambiguous (in part due to the fact that our 1978 article appeared in a symposium with strict page limitations that necessitated brevity in our argument). Furthermore, as will shortly be made apparent, Buttel clearly had differing notions of paradigm and paradigm shift than did Catton and I—not surprising given the inherent ambiguity of these concepts—and this contributed to our differing interpretations of the two paradigms.

When introducing our description of the HEP, Catton and I stated: "The numerous competing theoretical perspectives in contemporary sociology—e.g., functionalism, symbolic interactionism, ethnomethodology, conflict theory, Marxism, and so forth—are prone to exaggerate their differences from each other. . . . We maintain that their apparent diversity is not as important as the fundamental anthropocentrism underlying *all* of them" (1978a: 42). To begin with, we should have made explicit something we thought was obvious by adding "when it comes to analyzing environmental issues" to the last sentence. We thought this was unnecessary because in the next paragraph we noted that "[w]e contend that acceptance of the HEP has made it difficult for most sociologists, regardless of their preferred orientation, to deal meaningfully with the social implications of ecological problems and constraints" (42). But clearly we were *not* saying that existing theoretical perspectives were no longer relevant in general, nor even—as I'll now explain—that they were irrelevant for analyzing environmental issues.

After subsequently describing the NEP, we should have emphasized something that we took for granted: that environmental sociological work premised on the NEP would nonetheless still exhibit differing theoretical approaches (and cited

338   *Riley E. Dunlap*

Buttel [1976] as a source of examples of such differing approaches!). We made this point explicitly in a subsequent opportunity to present the HEP-NEP distinction in detail (Catton and Dunlap 1980: 37–42), carefully showing how the HEP-NEP and conflict-order cleavages could be cross-classified and then illustrating each of the four resulting cells with recent work by prominent sociologists dealing with ecological scarcity (Lipset, Smelser, Rainwater, and Horowitz). In the process, we thus granted Buttel's point that adoption of the NEP would *not* erase the continuing significance of traditional theoretical cleavages, as illustrated by the differences in the ecologically grounded work of Burch (1971) versus Schnaiberg (1975) for example.[4]

In both our immediate reply to Buttel and our longer clarification of the HEP-NEP distinction (Catton and Dunlap 1978b; 1980), we also highlighted a source of confusion between our position and that of Buttel—namely, that Buttel tended to equate "paradigm" with "theory" whereas we saw the two as quite different. Following Ritzer (1975), we were using paradigm to refer to the "fundamental image of the subject matter" of a field that comes before more specific theoretical perspectives. In contrast, Buttel (1978) seemed to treat paradigms as synonymous with theories, and consequently continued by saying that despite its importance the NEP was not specific enough to allow for the deduction of testable propositions or hypotheses. Yet, Catton and I never suggested that testable hypotheses could be derived from a set of broad background assumptions like those constituting the NEP.[5]

Rather, our argument was that the NEP provided a new way of looking at modern, industrialized societies by calling attention to their ecosystem dependence. Unlike the HEP, which led sociologists to ignore the ecological dimension of modern societies, the NEP sensitizes scholars to the fact that such societies not only depend on their ecological base, but may also do serious damage to it because of their vast levels of resource use and pollution. In other words, by leading sociologists to "see" the world in a new way (to "view it ecologically," so to speak), the NEP suggests the need for new kinds of questions and research. Exactly how sociologists go about conducting that research and the kinds of questions they ask will, of course, inevitably be influenced by their more specific theoretical orientation—for example, whether they hold a macro- or microlevel orientation, whether they are a Marxist or a functionalist (to use 1970s' terminology), and so forth. This is readily apparent, for example, by comparing analyses of the relationship between ecological problems and global capitalism offered by proponents of ecological modernization theory (e.g., Mol and Sonnenfeld 2000) and World-System Theory (Goldfrank, Goodman, and Szasz 1999).

Despite this clarification, and Buttel's own subsequent illustration of the utility of the HEP-NEP distinction in conjunction with standard theoretical cleavages in making sense of differing orientations to sociological work on environmental issues (e.g., Humphrey and Buttel 1982: 102), one still encounters accusations that the NEP is not specific enough to serve as a substitute for theoretical orientations in guiding empirical research (e.g., Buttel 1986: 346; Tindall 1995). Catton and I would not disagree, but never intended the NEP to serve this purpose. Our point was that unless sociologists shed the "blinders" imposed by adherence to the HEP, they would fail to see the significance of—and need for sociological work on—environmental issues. The NEP was and remains a broad worldview that leads one to see the world in such a way that the need for sociological research on environmental issues is obvious; precisely how one goes about that research will clearly be affected by the more specific theoretical perspective employed.[6]

In retrospect, I see that our debate with Buttel not only stemmed from differing notions of a paradigm, but also from the additional ambiguity of what constitutes a paradigm "shift" or "change" as from HEP to NEP. While a new paradigm is often seen as "incommensurable" with its predecessor in the physical sciences, Sayer (1984: 67–74) suggests that this tends to be exaggerated, and this seems especially the case in the social sciences.[7] Specifically, with regard to competing paradigms he notes, "Often an illusion of incommensurability is produced by reducing the description of the competing systems of thought to those terms which are unique to them, ignoring the wealth of usually more mundane concepts which they share and to which appeal can be made in trying to resolve disputes" (68). For example, while the 1960s saw the decline of the functionalist perspective with its consensual image of society by various forms of conflict theory highlighting the ubiquity of social conflict, the "consensus" and "conflict" paradigms were far from mutually exclusive or incommensurable despite their differing emphases. While they placed relatively more emphasis on either consensus or conflict, they both employed basic concepts such as status and power; acknowledged fundamental social processes such as integration and differentiation; and at least implicitly conceptualized societies as social systems (see, e.g., Dahrendorf 1958).

I suspect that Sayer's point is especially relevant to efforts to portray differences between a new paradigm and the one it is challenging. Indeed, since Catton and I were obviously trying to highlight differences between what we saw as an emerging ecological paradigm and the traditional exemptionalist paradigm underlying mid-twentieth-century sociology, it is not surprising that we emphasized their differences and downplayed the fact that theoretical positions built on them would not be mutually exclusive nor totally incommensurable. The very nature of trying to portray a new paradigm leads one to emphasize its differences and ignore its commonalities with the one it is challenging. I believe this contributed to our failure to note the now-obvious fact that theoretical perspectives built on the NEP would nonetheless continue to employ basic sociological concepts and processes and therefore not be totally incompatible with HEP-oriented theoretical perspectives—and also to the creation of what I think are the unrealistic expectations of the result of a shift from HEP to NEP by critics like Buttel. It is for this reason that I regard a number of recent efforts to develop green versions of well-established sociological theories as evidence of the emergence of the NEP, despite the fact that such theories clearly have a great deal in common with their HEPish predecessors. Yet, it is also understandable that Buttel had higher expectations for the emerging NEP based on our original exposition and, failing to see them met, emphasized the continuing relevance of traditional sociological theories for environmental sociology.

HEP-NEP and Classical Sociological Theory

The original debate with Buttel dealt primarily with the relationship between the HEP-NEP distinction and *contemporary* (at the time we were writing) sociological theory, but our paradigmatic argument was eventually extended to classical sociological theory as well. Buttel's admirable efforts to show the continuing relevance of mainstream sociological theory for environmental sociology was extended back to the classical works of Durkheim, Weber, and Marx in an important 1986 article and subsequent work (e.g., Buttel 1986; 1996; 2000). Unfortunately, Buttel unintentionally distorted our argument substantially in his effort to show the relevance of the classical tradition for environmental sociology.[8]

The distortion becomes apparent in the following quote where Buttel begins his effort to "resurrect" Durkheim, Weber, and Marx by showing that each provided useful "roots" for environmental sociology:

> There has . . . been general agreement among environmental sociologists that the classical sociological tradition has been inhospitable to the nurturing of ecologically-informed sociological theory and research. . . .[9] Much of the blame has been placed on the anthropocentric legacies of the classical theorists—specifically, that each classical theorist has emphasized the necessary sociological primacy of explanations of social phenomena, to the neglect of incorporating ecological variables in such analyses. . . . Hence, there remains a prevailing view that contemporary sociological theory has developed with an implicit taboo against incorporating ecological variables in their analysis. (1986: 338)

In what follows, I will deal with each of the three sentences in this quote in some detail, noting points of agreement and disagreement with them.

First, ignoring the question of whether there was in fact "general agreement" with the first point, I want to emphasize that Catton and I did *not* address whether the "classical sociological tradition" per se was inhospitable to ecologically informed theory and research. Indeed, we simply did not deal with classical *theory* per se. Our original article did not cite *any* classical theorist, and when describing how a few environmental sociologists were beginning to examine societal-environmental interactions we merely noted that it appeared they recognized "that, in order to make sense of the world, it was necessary to rethink the traditional Durkheimian norm of sociological purity—i.e., that social facts can be explained *only* by linking them to other *social* facts" (Catton and Dunlap 1978a: 44). We were clearly referring to one particular aspect of Durkheim's work, his antireductionistic methodological posture—that we recognized was essential in the formative stages of our discipline—*and* how it had evolved into a "norm" within *contemporary* mainstream sociology. The latter, not Durkheim's total body of work and certainly not classical theory in toto, was the clear focus of our analysis as indicated by the fact that we cited scholars such as Parsons, Bell, Hawley, and Horowitz when critiquing the exemptionalist posture of mainstream sociology.

Even when we subsequently clarified and expanded our analysis of how sociological *traditions* had led the discipline to ignore environmental conditions, invoking legacies derived from both Durkheim and Weber (as noted earlier), we were limiting our attention to their methodological postures (antireductionism and *Verstehen*, respectively) and not their entire bodies of work (Catton and Dunlap 1980: 18–22). Thus, we were in fact doing what Buttel indicates in the second sentence of the quoted paragraph, as we felt that these "anthropocentric legacies" were serving to inhibit sociological attention to environmental issues. And, quite importantly, as I emphasized earlier, both our original and revised explications of the HEP-NEP distinction were clearly focused on *contemporary* sociology. Thus, I would also concur with the last sentence in Buttel's quote, emphasizing (as noted earlier) that the experience of abundance, technological advances, economic growth, and progress in general had also contributed to mid-twentieth-century sociology's tendency to ignore the ecosystem-dependence of industrial societies—thereby reinforcing the "implicit taboo against incorporating ecological variables."[10] Ironically, after subsequently describing the context in which the disciplinary fathers fashioned their work, especially how they reacted against existing tendencies toward biological reductionism, Buttel (1986: 340) drew a conclusion that is fully in agreement with Catton's and my argument (see the previous section on "Disciplinary Traditions" and especially Catton and Dunlap, 1980: 16–22): "The 'evolution' of social theory from Marx to Durkheim and Weber thus represented 'progress' in dissociating social structure and process from biological analogies. The legacy for social theory has clearly been the one which contemporary environmental sociologists lament: social theory has tended to be stripped of consideration of biological or ecological variables." Nonetheless, Buttel (1986: 340–343) then continued by noting that despite their antibiologistic postures, "it can be argued that a meaningful environmental sociology can be fashioned from the works of the three classical theorists" and proceeded to mine environmental insights from the work of each one.

I applaud Buttel's effort to demonstrate the continuing relevance of the founders of our discipline even for environmental sociology and for stimulating others to join in this effort (as will be noted shortly). However, I must take issue with a subsequent statement he makes concerning Catton's and my contributions to environmental sociology, provided after his review of Marx, Durkheim, and Weber. After pointing to discernible differences in Catton's and my individual work, Buttel says that we nonetheless share "the essential rejection of the classical tradition in sociology" (1986: 344). Given that neither Catton nor I addressed this tradition, except for noting that Durkheim and Weber's methodological postures had contributed to contemporary sociology's reluctance to deal with environmental matters, this claim is puzzling. Both Catton and I were well aware of the multifaceted nature of the work of these and other classical theorists, and were not surprised that among their voluminous works one can find ecological insights.[11] But this was not our concern, as we were trying to show why *contemporary* sociology was slow in recognizing the societal significance of environmental problems and why sociologists seemed inhibited in launching research on societal-environmental relations.

I have focused on what I believe is a serious but unintended distortion of Catton's and my position regarding the relevance of classical sociological theory to environmental sociology by Buttel not to be contentious. Indeed, I should acknowledge that I regard the misunderstandings, unintended distortions, and our failure to reach consensus with Buttel a small price to pay for the continuing visibility and prominence that he has given to Catton's and my work (e.g., Buttel 1986; 1987; 1996; 2000). However, I emphasize the erroneous view of our position on classical theory because it has been so readily and uncritically adopted by other commentators. For example, Lidskog charges that, "Environmental sociologists such as William Catton and Riley Dunlap . . . have claimed that classical sociology is incapable of dealing with environmental problems" (1996: 3). I trust that what I have written earlier indicates why I view statements like this with both dismay and surprise.

Interestingly, even though others have continued Buttel's quest to find useful insights for environmental sociology in the writings of classical theorists, to the point that such work has now become a virtual "cottage industry" (see, e.g., Foster [1999], Gross [2000], and references to other efforts to green sociological theory cited in the next section), a number of other social theorists and environmental sociologists have in fact been critical of classical sociology's utility for dealing with environmental matters. For example, after commenting on Durkheim, Weber, and Marx's approaches to modernity, Giddens notes that "[e]cological concerns do not brook large in the traditions [derived from these three founding fathers] incorporated into sociology, and it is not surprising that sociologists today find it hard to develop a systematic appraisal of them" (1990: 8). Similarly, early in his excellent overview of *contemporary* theoretical approaches to environmental matters, Goldblatt notes that "the theoretical legacy left to us by classical social theory has some substantial limitations both for examining the relationships between society and their environments, and for exploring the origins of a politics of the environment" (1996: 1). I leave it to others to assess the validity of these commentaries on classical theory and end by reiterating that such assessments were never part of Catton's and my arguments about *contemporary* sociology's prevailing exemptionalist paradigm.

ASSESSING THE NEP AND ENVIRONMENTAL SOCIOLOGY

As I noted at the outset, the original interest on my part that lead to the development of our call for a paradigm shift was more modest, as I was hoping to help define, codify, and legitimate the field of environmental sociology. The development of the HEP-NEP distinction evolved in pursuit of these goals. As I look back, I feel fairly good, both personally and professionally, about Catton's and my effort to help establish environmental sociology as a distinct field of inquiry. Buttel, for example, writes that "[t]here is scarcely a significant text in environmental sociology today that fails to cite one or more of these early works by Dunlap and Catton as having provided the template for modern environmental sociology" (2000: 19). While this is an exaggeration, our work has stimulated more interest and attention than I had ever expected. And, far more importantly, environmental sociology has indeed become a well-established area of inquiry in North America, much of Europe, and parts of Asia, most notably Japan (Dunlap and Catton 1994). Clearly real-world events (from the endless emergence of new environmental problems to highly visible ecological movements) and the efforts of a growing number of other scholars have had far more to do with this than has our work, but it is clearly gratifying to see the field flourish. Thus, my initial goal of having environmental sociology become a legitimate sociological specialization has been fulfilled.

The success of Catton's and my plea for replacing sociology's human exemptionalism paradigm with an ecological one is more difficult to assess, in part because it was inherently more ambiguous as well as ambitious. The assessment depends on one's interpretation of our call for a paradigmatic shift, and as the earlier-noted debates and disagreements with Buttel illustrate, there are clearly differing interpretations of our position (see also the various chapters in Mehta and Ouellet [1995] that discuss the NEP). Ultimately, how one interprets our plea is heavily influenced by one's view of paradigms and conception of paradigm shift, and there appear to be at least three distinct positions in the environmental sociology literature. I label them the "strong," "moderate," and "weak" interpretations of our argument—reflecting differing levels of expectation for the impact of shifting from an exemptionalist to an ecological paradigm.

The *strong* interpretation, typically used by our critics, treats paradigms as essentially synonymous with theories and thereby criticizes our formulation of the NEP as lacking sufficient specificity to lead to testable hypotheses (Buttel 1978; 1986; 1987; 1996; 2000; Tindall 1995). I believe this interpretation also at least implicitly assumes that paradigms are incommensurable and that an NEP-based theory would therefore be dramatically different than one based on the HEP. My response, as noted earlier, is that our depictions of both the traditional exemptionalist paradigm and our proposed ecological alternative represent sets of broad background assumptions (or worldviews) that influence the kinds of issues that are seen as appropriate for sociological scholarship and were never intended to be logically interrelated sets of propositions from which testable hypotheses could be deduced (Catton and Dunlap 1980). We made ourselves vulnerable to this charge by de-emphasizing the obvious diversity and continuing utility of existing sociological theories while emphasizing the hegemonic nature of their shared exemptionalism in our original (1978a) article—thus perhaps creating the impression that we felt that the NEP could supplant them.

In subsequently clarifying our argument, we indicated that we did *not* expect the NEP to replace existing theoretical perspectives (Catton and Dunlap 1980), but to stimulate development of more ecologically sensitive or greener versions of them. Clearly, then, we were implying that NEP-oriented theories would not be totally incommensurable with older theories, but simply be grounded in more realistic assumptions about the relationship between modern societies and the biophysical environment. This is precisely what has happened in the past decade or so as scholars who clearly endorse an ecological perspective have begun to fashion green versions of both classical theoretical perspectives such as those derived from Marx (Benton 1989; Foster 1999), Weber (Murphy 1994), and symbolic interactionism (Weigert 1997), as well as more contemporary perspectives such as modernization theory (Spaargaren and Mol 1992) and World-System Theory (Roberts and Grimes 1999).

The numerous efforts to apply Marxist perspectives to environmental matters are particularly interesting, because they reveal both the continuing appeal of an exemptionalist perspective to some scholars (Grundmann 1991) as well as a diversity of NEP-oriented reformulations (cf., e.g., Benton 1989; Dickens 1992; Foster 1999; O'Connor 1998). The latter is a superb illustration of lively theoretical debate not only *within* the NEP (something that Buttel felt Catton and I ruled out), but also among NEP-oriented scholars all working within the *same* classical theoretical tradition.[12] As such, it clearly indicates that adoption of an ecological paradigm does not, as I have noted earlier, determine the details of one's more specific theoretical perspective, nor does it require creating a theory that is incommensurable with prior ones in the same theoretical genre (e.g., Marxism). Yet, comparing the work of the "eco-Marxists" just cited with the HEP-grounded work of Grundmann (1991) also illustrates the continuing importance of the exemptionalist-ecological paradigmatic cleavage—in this case *within* the Marxist theoretical tradition.

Not only does a strong interpretation of the NEP lead to unrealistic expectations about its ability to substitute for more specific theoretical perspectives, but it also leads critics to complain (erroneously) that adoption of the NEP deflects attention away from both classical and contemporary theoretical perspectives in sociology (besides Buttel 1986; 1996; 2000; see, e.g., Spaargaren and Mol 1992; Lidskog 1996). Yet, as I have shown in this chapter, we never intended the NEP to replace or supplant existing sociological theories, but to encourage development of ecologically oriented theories and research. While Catton and I were certainly critical of contemporary "mainstream" sociology for its staunch exemptionalist orientation, we did not mean to suggest that it was useless or irrelevant! Similarly, I now see that neither were we suggesting that theories premised on the exemptionalist paradigm would prove to be totally incommensurable with those that might be developed from the NEP.

Indeed, the *weak* interpretation of our argument is that we were simply calling for sociology to shed the blinders we labeled the "Human Exemptionalism Paradigm" (HEP) in order to recognize the significance of environmental problems. Judged by this criterion, our argument has fared pretty well. First, in ensuing years other scholars have come to compatible conclusions regarding the degree to which sociological traditions have inhibited serious concern with environmental issues (e.g., Giddens 1990; Goldblatt 1996; Redclift and Woodgate 1994). Second, our portrayal of sociology's exemptionalist orientation seems to have resonated with a number of previously cited colleagues whose efforts to green one or more theoretical perspectives represent (in our view) superb examples of efforts to replace exemptionalism with more ecologically realistic perspectives.

Most important, however, is the growing attention to environmental issues within the larger discipline. While obviously a response to the increased salience of ecological problems and movements in societies around the world, rather than anything that environmental sociologists have written, such attention nonetheless continues to challenge our discipline's exemptionalist orientation. One need only compare current theorizing on modernization, ranging from theories of ecological modernization to reflexive modernization to risk society, with the modernization theories of two or three decades ago (see Hannigan 1995: 9–10) to see the declining credibility of exemptionalism in our discipline.

The *moderate* interpretation of our argument, and the one most consistent with my original goal of legitimating environmental sociology as a distinct area of inquiry by virtue of its focus on environmental variables, is that we were trying to justify incorporation of environmental variables or "nonsocial facts" into sociological analyses—something that our discipline's exemptionalist traditions prohibited. Like Gramling and Freudenburg (1996), I think that this has clearly been accomplished via numerous empirical investigations by environmental sociologists, such as studies of communities' experiences with toxic wastes, minorities' exposure to environmental hazards, patterns of tropical deforestation, and nations' contributions to carbon dioxide emissions (see, e.g., various chapters in Dunlap and Michelson [2002]). Indeed, it is becoming common to find articles in sociology journals that employ environmental "variables" in empirical analyses, and this is not only a good indication of the declining strength of traditional "taboos" against sociological consideration of environmental phenomena, but also that a "real" environmental sociology—in the sense that I felt was required to justify creation of a new field as noted in the introduction—has indeed arrived.

For all of these reasons, despite the ambiguity and subsequent confusions surrounding Catton's and my call for replacement of our discipline's exemptionalist orientation with a more ecological one, I am pleased that our effort to define the field of environmental sociology led us to make our argument about the need for a paradigm shift. In important ways, I believe this shift is occurring, as our discipline slowly reacts to such anomalies as growing evidence of the reality of human-induced global environmental change. Phenomena such ozone depletion and global warming, which have potentially significant consequences for the future welfare of modern, industrialized societies, clearly challenge the notion of human exemptionalism (Dunlap and Catton 1994). For this reason, I am optimistic that a more ecologically sound perspective will continue to gain strength in our discipline.

In sum, the degree to which one sees our discipline's staunch exemptionalist orientation as being challenged by the emergence of a new ecological paradigm clearly depends on one's notion of a paradigm and expectations regarding the nature of paradigm shifts. Nonetheless, it seems clear to me that sociology in general and sociological theory in particular are paying far more attention to the environment nowadays than was the case in the 1970s. The old assumptions that environmental problems are insignificant and that modern industrialized societies are not subject to ecological constraints are becoming more and more untenable, and one no longer finds prominent American sociologists defending these assumptions as was the case in the 1970s. The steady decline in defenses of exemptionalist thinking are coupled with growing theoretical and empirical attention to environmental phenomena. For a discipline that was virtually blind to the biophysical environment in the early 1970s, this is a monumental change. Whether it represents a true paradigmatic shift within sociology will no doubt continue to be the subject of debate.

NOTES

Thanks are extended to Peter Dickens and Annamari Kontinnen for helpful comments on an earlier draft of this chapter.

1. I should note that the distinction between environmental sociology and the sociology of environmental issues no longer seems essential to me for three reasons: (1) in contrast to the 1970s, nowadays it is common for environmental sociologists to treat environmental phenomena—ranging from levels of local environmental degradation to tropical deforestation to carbon dioxide emissions—as variables in empirical analyses; (2) the field of environmental sociology is now well established and no longer needs to be legitimated; and (3) many scholars, including myself, do both kinds of work. Consequently, I agree with Buttel (1987) that we should treat environmental sociology as consisting of the kinds of work that is conducted by self-identified environmental sociologists.

2. This perspective evolved into the "social constructivist" or "constructionist" perspective that developed in areas such as social problems and sociology of science in the 1970s and eventually gained prominence in the discipline as a whole, and became popular in environmental sociology in the 1990s (see, e.g., Yearley 1991; Hannigan 1995).

3. Drawing on work by Alford, Buttel quickly shifted to the tripartite distinction of Marxian, Weberian, and Durkheimian perspectives (Buttel and Flinn 1977; Humphrey and Buttel 1982) to illustrate the continuing relevance of traditional disciplinary theoretical/paradigmatic cleavages for environmental sociology.

4. Despite this attempt to clarify our argument, some confusion continued. In a subsequent article, Buttel wrote: "I have not argued against the validity of the [HEP-NEP] distinction, but rather have argued that there will inherently tend to be intense debate . . . within the NEP (as well as the HEP) that will reflect the postures (Marxism, conflict theory, functionalism) that Catton and Dunlap argue lie only within the HEP" (1986: 346). Yet, in our effort to clarify our position (Catton and Dunlap 1980: 37–42) we had acknowledged that traditional theoretical cleavages would pervade the NEP, illustrated cleavages within both HEP- and NEP-oriented analyses of ecological scarcity, and specifically stated that "one can detect Order-Conflict differences among environmental sociologists whose work reflects, in varying degrees, the NEP" (38).

5. Interestingly, Warner's recent usage of a similarly broad notion of paradigm (noted earlier) provoked a similar critique and led him to reply that "[a] paradigm is indeed not a theory" (1997: 196), just as Catton and I argued in response to Buttel.

6. In retrospect, I realize that what I have just described was my position, but I am not certain it was Catton's. I gradually realized that Catton (1980) did see the possibility and utility of applying ecological theory (drawn from bioecology) to human societies, whereas my interest in the NEP was at the broader paradigmatic level (for my efforts to develop a societal-level "social paradigm" version of the NEP, see Dunlap and Van Liere [1978] and Dunlap et al. [2000]). Indeed, my own hesitancy in applying bioecological concepts to human societies was a major reason that Catton and I never wrote a book together as we had originally

planned. Nonetheless, even though it might be accurate to say that Catton sensed that an ecological "perspective" (including both a broad paradigm like the NEP and more specific ecological concepts and theories) could replace mainstream sociological theories, this was clearly not the position we took in our joint publications—especially in the 1980 article. Interestingly, the difficulties and limitations involved in applying bioecological concepts and theories to human societies has been demonstrated by Freese (1997), our Washington State University colleague, whose interest in ecology was stimulated by Catton's *Overshoot* (1980).

7. I am indebted to Dickens for calling Sayer's observations, and their relevance to the HEP-NEP distinction, to my attention.

8. Such unintended distortions occur easily in the midst of academic debates. For example, I suspect that in reacting to Buttel's suggestion (e.g., Buttel and Taylor 1992) that a social contructivist perspective would be useful for analyzing global environmental change; I misinterpreted his purpose and assumed that he was suggesting that social constructivism should become the predominant perspective in environmental sociology—an idea that I found troubling for the reasons noted in Dunlap and Catton (1994).

9. Here, Buttel is referring to Catton and Dunlap (1978a; 1980) and Dunlap and Catton (1979).

10. An indication of the strength of this "taboo" at the time we presented our paradigm argument can be seen in debates over the appropriateness of employing environmental variables in sociological analyses of agricultural phenomena (Dunlap and Martin 1983).

11. Catton (1985), in particular, has devoted considerable attention to Durkheim's work, particularly the *Division of Labor*, which is often seen as providing the roots of modern sociological human ecology (Buttel 1986: 341; Schnore 1958). Even here, though, I cannot fail to note a point made by Schnore in his seminal explication of Durkheim's "ecological" approach: "A more serious weakness in Durkheim's theory [of the division of labor] is the inadequate attention accorded the physical environment. He apparently was reluctant to give such factors as climate and topography any major role in his analysis. In part, this probably is due to the restrictive character of his own rules, adherence to which obliged him to see the explanation of social facts in other social facts. He tended to dismiss the physical environment as a relevant variable and to regard the 'social environment' as the ultimate source of differentiation" (1958: 628). Thus, even when providing an ecologically oriented analysis Durkheim himself seems to have been inhibited by his antireductionist methodological posture.

12. It is interesting to observe that Foster (1999), the eco-Marxist most committed to demonstrating that an ecological perspective can be found within Marx's own writings rather that revising Marxist theory to make it more ecological along the lines of Benton (1989) and O'Connor (1998), nonetheless seems to have undergone a paradigm shift provoked by personal experience with environmental degradation (Foster 1994: 7–10). Perhaps, it was this new way of seeing the world that allowed Foster to find heretofore neglected ecological insights in Marx.

REFERENCES

Bell, Daniel. 1977. "Are There 'Social Limits' to Growth?" In *Prospects for Growth: Changing Expectations for the Future*, ed. K. D. Wilson, 13–26. New York: Praeger.

Benton, Ted. 1989. "Marxism and Natural Limits." *New Left Review* 178:51–86.

———. 1991. "Biology and Social Science: Why the Return of the Repressed Should Be Given a (Cautious) Welcome." *Sociology* 25:1–29.

Burch, William R., Jr. 1971. *Daydreams and Nightmares: A Sociological Essay on the American Environment.* New York: Harper and Row.

———. 1976. "The Peregrine Falcon and the Urban Poor: Some Sociological Interrelations." In *Human Ecology: An Environmental Approach*, ed. P. J. Richerson and J. McEvoy III , 308–316. North Scituate, Mass.: Duxbury.

Buttel, Frederick H. 1976. "Social Science and the Environment: Competing Theories." *Social Science Quarterly* 57:307–323.

———. 1978. "Environmental Sociology: A New Paradigm?" *The American Sociologist* 13:252–256.

———. 1986. "Sociology and the Environment: The Winding Road toward Human Ecology." *International Social Science Journal* 109:337–356.

———. 1987. "New Directions in Environmental Sociology." *Annual Review of Sociology* 13:465–488.

———. 1996. "Environmental and Resource Sociology: Theoretical Issues and Opportunities for Synthesis." *Rural Sociology* 61:56–76.

———. 2000. "Classical Theory and Contemporary Environmental Sociology." In *Environment and Global Modernity*, ed. G. Spaargaren, A. P. J. Mol, and F. H. Buttel, 17–39. London: Sage.

Buttel, Frederick H., and William L. Flinn. 1977. "The Interdependence of Rural and Urban Environmental Problems in Advanced Capitalist Societies: Models of Linkage." *Sociologica Ruralis* 17:255–279.

Buttel, Frederick H., and Peter J. Taylor. 1992. "Environmental Sociology and Global Environmental Change." *Society and Natural Resources* 5:211–230.

Catton, William R., Jr. 1980. *Overshoot: The Ecological Basis of Revolutionary Change.* Urbana: University of Illinois Press.

———. 1985. "Emile Who and the Division of What?" *Sociological Perspectives* 28:251–280.

Catton, William R., Jr., and Riley E. Dunlap. 1978a. "Environmental Sociology: A New Paradigm." *The American Sociologist* 13:41–49.

———. 1978b. "Paradigms, Theories, and the Primacy of the HEP-NEP Distinction." *The American Sociologist* 13:256–259.

———. 1980. "A New Ecological Paradigm for Post-exuberant Sociology." *American Behavioral Scientist* 24:15–47.

Choldin, Harvey M. 1978. "Social Life and the Physical Environment." In *Handbook of Contemporary Urban Life*, ed. D. Street, 352–384. San Francisco: Jossey-Bass.

Dahrendorf, Ralf. 1958. "Toward a Theory of Social Conflict." *Journal of Conflict Resolution* 2:170–179.

Dickens, Peter. 1992. *Society and Nature: Towards a Green Social Theory.* Philadelphia: Temple University Press.

Dunlap, Riley E., and William R. Catton Jr. 1979. "Environmental Sociology." *Annual Review of Sociology* 5:243–273.

———. 1983. "What Environmental Sociologists Have in Common (Whether Concerned with 'Built' or 'Natural' Environments)." *Sociological Inquiry* 53:113–135.

———. 1994. "Struggling with Human Exemptionalism: The Rise, Decline and Revitalization of Environmental Sociology." *The American Sociologist* 25:5–30.

Dunlap, Riley E., and Kenneth E. Martin. 1983. "Bringing Environment into the Study of Agriculture." *Rural Sociology* 48:201–218.

Dunlap, Riley E., and William Michelson, eds. 2002. *Handbook of Environmental Sociology.* Westport, Conn.: Greenwood.

Dunlap, Riley E., and Kent D. Van Liere. 1978. "The 'New Environmental Paradigm': A Proposed Measuring Instrument and Preliminary Results." *Journal of Environmental Education* 9:10–19.

Dunlap, Riley E., Kent D. Van Liere, Angela G. Mertig, and Robert Emmet Jones. 2000. "Measuring Endorsement of the New Ecological Paradigm: A Revised NEP Scale." *Journal of Social Issues* 56:425–442.

Eckberg, Douglas Lee, and Lester Hill Jr. 1979. "The Paradigm Concept and Sociology: A Critical Review." *American Sociological Review* 44:925–937.

Etzioni, Amitai. 1970. "The Wrong Top Priority." *Science* 168 (May): 921.

Foster, John Bellamy. 1994. *The Vulnerable Planet*. New York: Monthly Review.

———. 1999. "Marx's Theory of Metabolic Rift: Classical Foundations for Environmental Sociology." *American Journal of Sociology* 105:366–405.

Franck, Karen A. 1984. "Exorcising the Ghost of Physical Determinism." *Environment and Behavior* 16:411–435.

Freese, Lee. 1997. *Environmental Connections: Advances in Human Ecology*. Supp. 1. Pt. B. Greenwich, Conn.: JAI Press.

Giddens, Anthony. 1990. *The Consequences of Modernity*. Stanford, Calif.: Stanford University Press.

Goldblatt, David. 1996. *Social Theory and the Environment*. Boulder, Colo.: Westview.

Goldfrank, Walter L., David Goodman, and Andrew Szasz, eds. 1999. *Ecology and the World System*. Westport, Conn.: Greenwood.

Gramling, Robert, and William R. Freudenburg. 1996. "Environmental Sociology: Toward a Paradigm for the 21st Century." *Sociological Spectrum* 16:347–370.

Gross, Matthias. 2000. "Classical Sociology and the Restoration of Nature." *Organization and Environment* 13:277–291.

Grundmann, Reiner. 1991. *Marxism and Ecology*. Oxford: Oxford University Press.

Hannigan, John A. 1995. *Environmental Sociology: A Social Constructionist Perspective*. London: Routledge.

Humphrey, Craig R., and Frederick H. Buttel. 1982. *Environment, Energy, and Society*. Belmont, Calif.: Wadsworth.

Klausner, Samuel Z. 1971. *On Man in His Environment*. San Francisco: Jossey-Bass.

Lidskog, Rolf. 1996. "Introduction to this Special Issue on Sociology and the Environment." *Acta Sociologica* 39:3–4.

Mehta, Michael D., and Eric Ouellet, eds. 1995. *Environmental Sociology: Theory and Practice*. North York, Ontario: Captus.

Mol, Arthur P. J., and David A. Sonnenfeld, eds. 2000. *Ecological Modernization around the World: Perspectives and Critical Debates*. Ilford, UK: Frank Cass.

Murphy, Raymond. 1994. *Rationality and Nature*. Boulder, Colo.: Westview.

Nisbet, Robert. 1979. "The Rape of Progress." *Public Opinion* 2 (June–July): 2–6, 55.

O'Connor, James. 1998. *Natural Causes: Essays in Ecological Marxism*. New York: Guilford.

Redclift, Michael, and Graham Woodgate. 1994. "Sociology and the Environment: Discordant Discourse?" In *Social Theory and the Global Environment*, ed. M. Redclift and T. Benton, 51–66. London: Routledge.

Ritzer, George. 1975. *Sociology: A Multiple Paradigm Science*. Boston: Allyn and Bacon.

Roberts, J. Timmons, and Peter E. Grimes. 1999. "Extending the World-System to the Whole System: Toward a Political Economy of the Biosphere." In *Ecology and the World System*, ed. W. L. Goldfrank, D. Goodman, and A. Szasz, 59–83. Westport, Conn.: Greenwood.

Sayer, Andrew. 1984. *Method in Social Science.* London: Hutchinson.

Schnaiberg, Allan. 1975. "Social Syntheses of the Societal-Environmental Dialectic: The Role of Distributional Impacts." *Social Science Quarterly* 56:5–20.

Schnore, Leo F. 1958. "Social Morphology and Human Ecology." *American Journal of Sociology* 63:620–634.

Spaargaren, Gert, and Arthur P. J. Mol. 1992. "Sociology, Environment, and Modernity: Ecological Modernization As a Theory of Social Change." *Society and Natural Resources* 5:323–344.

Stanley, Manfred. 1968. "Nature, Culture and Scarcity: Forward to a Theoretical Synthesis." *American Sociological Review* 33:855–870.

Tindall, David B. 1995. "What Is Environmental Sociology?" In *Environmental Sociology: Theory and Practice,* ed. M. D. Mehta and E. Ouellet, 33–59. North York, Ontario: Captus.

Warner, R. Stephen. 1997. "A Paradigm Is Not a Theory: Reply to Lechner." *American Journal of Sociology* 103:192–198.

Weigert, Andrew J. 1997. *Self, Interaction, and the Natural Environment: Refocusing Our Eyesight.* Albany: SUNY Press.

Yearley, Steven. 1991. *The Green Case: A Sociology of Environmental Issues, Arguments and Politics.* London: HarperCollins.

Index

About the Contributors

Ted Benton is Professor of Sociology at the University of Essex, Colchester, United Kingdom. He is the author of *Philosophical Foundations of the Three Sociologies* (1977), *Rise and Fall of Structural Marxism* (1984), and *Natural Relations: Ecology, Animal Rights and Social Justice* (1993). He edited *The Greening of Marxism* (1996) and coedited with Michael Redclift *Social Theory and the Global Environment* (1994).

Frederick H. Buttel is Professor of Rural Sociology and Environmental Studies at the University of Wisconsin, Madison. He is currently president of the Research Committee on Environment and Society of the International Sociological Association. He is the coauthor of *Environment, Energy, and Society* (2002) and coeditor of *Labor and the Environment* (1984) and of *Environment and Global Modernity* (2000).

William R. Catton Jr., Professor Emeritus of Sociology at Washington State University, is a former president of the Pacific Sociological Association. His publications include *From Animistic to Naturalistic Sociology* (1966) and *Overshoot: The Ecological Basis of Revolutionary Change* (1980). His next book will assess the effects the division of labor has had a century after Durkheim.

Peter Dickens is Senior Research Fellow on the Faculty of Social and Political Sciences, University of Cambridge, United Kingdom. He is also Fellow and Director of Studies at Fitzwilliam College, Cambridge. His most recent publications include: *Social Darwinism: Linking Evolutionary Thought to Social Theory* (2000) and *Reconstructing Nature: Alienation, Emancipation and the Division of Labour* (1996). He is currently preparing a textbook entitled *Society and Nature.*

Riley E. Dunlap is the Boeing Distinguished Professor of Environmental Sociology at Washington State University and former president of the International Sociological Association's Research Committee on Environment and Society. He is a coeditor of *American Environmentalism* (1993), *Public Reactions to Nuclear Waste* (1993), and *Handbook of Environmental Sociology* (2002).

August Gijswijt retired as an environmental sociologist from the University of Amsterdam in 1998. In 1990 he and György Szell founded the Research Committee on Environment and Society within the International Sociological Association. His most recent publication (with Frederick H. Buttel) is the chapter "Emerging Trends in Environmental Sociology" in *The Blackwell Companion to Sociology* (2001).

Peter E. Grimes received his Ph.D. in sociology from Johns Hopkins University in 1996, and has been researching, teaching, and writing about social evolution and the environment for twenty years. In 1992 he was awarded a grant from the National Science Foundation to apply World-System Theory to the production of greenhouse gases and is currently working on a book on this topic.

John Hannigan is Professor and Associate Chair of Graduate Studies in the Department of Sociology at the University of Toronto. He is the author of *Environmental Sociology: A Social Constructionist Perspective* (1995) and *Fantasy City: Pleasure and Profit in the Postmodern Metropolis* (1998).

Rosemary B. McKechnie is a social anthropologist and Senior Lecturer in Sociology at Bath Spa University College, United Kingdom. She is a coeditor of *Extending the Boundaries of Care: Medical Ethics and Caring Practices* (1999). Her research focuses on the social and cultural identification of scientific and medical issues.

Raymond Murphy is Chair of the Department of Sociology at the University of Ottawa, Canada. He is the author of *Sociological Theories of Education* (1979), *Social Closure* (1988), *Rationality and Nature* (1994), and *Sociology and Nature* (1997).

Elim Papadakis is Professor of Modern European Studies at the Australian National University, Director of the National Europe Centre, and former vice president of the Australian Sociological Association. He is the author of *Politics and the Environment* (1993), *Environmental Politics and Institutional Change* (1996), and *Historical Dictionary of the Green Movement* (1998).

J. Timmons Roberts is Professor of Sociology and Director of the Mellon Environmental Studies Program at the College of William and Mary. He is the coauthor of *Chronicles from the Environmental Justice Frontline* (2001) and coeditor of *From Modernization to Globalization: Perspectives on Social Change and Development* (2000).

Ørnulf Seippel is Dr. Polit. and Senior Researcher at the Institute for Social Research, Oslo, Norway. He has recently published articles on environmental sociology in *Acta Sociologica*, *Environmental Politics*, *Journal of Environmental Policy*, and *Planning and Innovations*.

Elizabeth Shove is Senior Lecturer in the Department of Sociology at Lancaster University, United Kingdom. Her research focuses on the sociology of consumption, sustainability, and everyday life. Recent publications include *Energy Buildings and the Environment* (2001), with Simon Guy, and *Social Environmental Research in the European Union* (2000), with Michael Redclift, Barend van der Meulen, and Sujatha Raman.

Alan Warde is Professor of Sociology and Codirector of the ESRC Centre for Research on Innovation and Competition at the University of Manchester, United Kingdom. He is the author of *Consumption Food and Taste* (1997) and, with Lydia Martens, *Eating Out: Social Differentiation, Consumption and Pleasure* (2000).

Peter Wehling works with the Institute of Sociology at the University of Munich, Germany. His research focuses on environmental sociology, sociology of science, and social theory. He is the author of *Die Moderne als Sozialmythos* (1992) and coauthor of *Sustainability: A Cross-Disciplinary Concept for Social Transformations* (1997).

Ian Welsh lectures in Sociology at Cardiff University, United Kingdom. He is the author of *Mobilising Modernity: The Nuclear Moments* (2000) and coeditor of *Environment and Society in Eastern Europe* (1998).

Steven Yearley is Professor and Head of the Department of Sociology at the University of York, United Kingdom. He is the author of *The Green Case: A Sociology of Environmental Issues, Arguments and Politics* (1991) and *Sociology, Environmentalism, Globalization* (1996).